A Passion to Preserve

A Passion to Preserve

Gay Men as Keepers of Culture

Will Fellows

The University of Wisconsin Press

The University of Wisconsin Press
1930 Monroe Street
Madison, Wisconsin 53711

www.wisc.edu/wisconsinpress/

3 Henrietta Street
London WC2E 8LU, England

5   4   3   2   1

Printed in the United States of America

Library of Congress Cataloging-in-Publication Data
Fellows, Will.
    A passion to preserve : gay men as keepers of culture / Will Fellows.
    p. cm.
    ISBN 0-299-19680-1
    1. Gay men—United States—Biography. 2. Cultural property—Protection—United
States. I. Title.
HQ75.7.F45   2004
306.76′62′0922—dc22   2003020531

The excerpt from Mark Doty's *Still Life with Oysters and Lemon*,
copyright © 2001 by Mark Doty, is reprinted by permission of
Beacon Press, Boston. The excerpt from Mark Doty's *Heaven's Coast*,
copyright © 1996 by Mark Doty, is reprinted by permission of
HarperCollins Publishers Inc.

Book design: Alcorn Publication Design

Knowing the masculine
and nurturing the feminine
you become the river of all beneath heaven.

—Lao Tzu, *Tao Te Ching*

Contents

Preface   ix

Charlotte and Me: Preservation-Minded from Childhood   3
In Search of Gay Preservationists   13
What These Gay Men's Lives Reveal   25
Saving Old New England   37
      Mark Doty   44
      Don Leavitt   50
      Mark Sammons   53
Design-Minded in the Mid-Atlantic States   57
      Ken Lustbader   61
      James Nocito   65
      Dwight Young   69
      Greg Kinsman   73
To the Rescue in the Atlantic South   79
      Allan Gurganus   84
      Myrick Howard   90
      John Anders   95
      Robert Barker   99
      Cranford Sutton   103
Domophiles Out West   107
      Jay Yost   111
      Ken Miller   116
      Gilbert Millikan and David Richards   121
      Richard Jost and Charles Fuchs   125
California Conservative   131
      Richard Reutlinger   138
      Gerry Takano   147
      Jeffrey Samudio   150
      Jim Wilke   156
Generations of Gentlemen Keep Cooksville, Wisconsin   161
      William Wartmann   174
      Al Garland   182
      Larry Reed   186

Singular Preservationists in the Midwest   191
     Dana Duppler   204
     Joe Johnson and Ron Markwell   211
     Robert Seger   214
Cherishing Old New Orleans and Louisiana   217
     Curt Greska   230
     Lloyd Sensat   235
     Randy Plaisance   239
Toward a Larger View of Gay Men   243
Conclusion   259

Acknowledgments   265
Notes   267
Index   283

Preface

IT MAY SEEM UNLIKELY that a book about gay men as keepers of culture would be inspired by a book about gays growing up among cows and corn fields, but that's what happened. In creating my first book, *Farm Boys*, I immersed myself in the life stories of gay men who grew up in farm families. I had long suspected that my own rural upbringing exerted a lasting influence on how I lived my life as a gay man. It seemed that getting other gay men from similar backgrounds to tell me about their lives would serve as a lens through which I might gain some insight into my own life. So I traveled around the Midwest one year doing autobiographical interviews.

Gender-role nonconformity was prominent in many of those *Farm Boys* interviews: As boys, most of the men I spoke with had been especially drawn to doing things that lay outside the range of activities approved for males. Instead of working in the fields or repairing farm machinery, they preferred doing things in and around the house, and were often very good at them: gardening, cooking, food-canning, flower-arranging, decorating, sewing and other needlework. At first, I was bothered by this strong gender-atypical trend; I assumed it was the result of a pervasive bias in my self-selected group of interview subjects. There must be plenty of gay men out there who were regular, gender-typical farm boys, I thought: Perhaps the atypical ones are simply more inclined to talk about their lives. Maybe the regular guys just aren't sufficiently chatty or insightful or out of the closet to want to do this sort of interview.

Then, as it eventually occurred to me that what I was seeing was perhaps characteristic of gay childhood, this trend toward gender-atypicality began to intrigue me. For one thing, it mirrored my own childhood. And it was at odds with the old saw about gay males being no different from straight males except for their sexual orientation. This notion developed as a central tenet of the gay rights movement since the 1970s, the decade in which I came of age and came out, when gay men in America went macho in their self-presentation: "We're *men*, first and foremost; regular guys who just happen to prefer guys." All of this led me to wonder: If we differ from straight men only in terms of sexual orientation, not in any other essential ways, why was I discovering this preponderance of gay men who had been manifestly queer since childhood, usually years before their sex lives got going? In the years since *Farm Boys* was published, the responses I've had from readers have consistently affirmed the book's gender-atypical portrait.

The extraordinary and pioneering involvement of gay men in historic preservation is something of which I've long been at least vaguely aware. Though I paid little attention to it at the time, many of the men I interviewed for *Farm Boys* engaged in some sort of culture-keeping: they lived in restored older houses, often furnished and decorated with antiques, many of them family heirlooms; they compiled information and objects related to family heritage and local history. I didn't ask them specifically about these interests; they were simply evident in one way or another.

Only since completing *Farm Boys* have I considered gays-in-preservation a phenomenon worthy of exploration. To the limited extent that I gave it even a passing thought in earlier years, I suppose I saw the apparently disproportionate presence of gay men in historic preservation as the stuff of stereotype. And so I failed to take it seriously. If outside of our sex lives we gays are just like straights, then it must be only a stereotypical illusion that gay men are inordinately drawn to being house restorers and antiquarians— or interior designers, florists, hair stylists, fashion designers, and so forth. Now it's clear to me that gay men really are extraordinarily attracted to these kinds of work. Rather than dismissing these realities as the stuff of stereotype, I see them as the stuff of archetype, significant truths worthy of exploration. Gay men are a prominent and highly talented presence in many female-dominated fields that revolve around creating, restoring, and preserving beauty, order, and continuity. It's a phenomenon that seems to grow out of an essential gay difference.

In his book about why so many gay men love musical theater, John Clum hints at this essential differentness: "For me, being gay has as much to do with an investment in certain kinds of culture as it has with my sexual proclivities."[1] Gay rights pioneer Harry Hay goes further, saying that we gay men "must disenthrall ourselves of the idea that we differ only in our sexual directions, and that all we want or need in life is to be free to seek the expression of our sexual desires as we see fit."[2] *Gay men as keepers of culture* proves to be a powerful lens through which to examine some of the distinctive dimensions of gay male lives beyond sexuality per se.[3] With this book, I hope to add my small lamp to a fuller illumination of what it means to be gay.

A Passion to Preserve

Charlotte and Me
Preservation-Minded from Childhood

EXPLORING GAY MEN'S SENSIBILITIES through the lens of their culture-keeping tendencies became increasingly compelling the more I got into it, the more I paid attention to things that I had never made much note of, the more I began to remember. Besides discerning a common pattern in the lives of dozens of gay men past and present, I began to see how closely my own life fit that gender-atypical, preservation-minded archetype.

When I was eleven, my parents gave me a Bible with glossy centerfold pages between the Old and the New Testament for recording births, marriages, deaths, and the family tree. Those colorful pages awakened the documentarian in me. After noting the date on which the Bible was given to me, I filled in the names and birth dates of my brother and two sisters and me. I recorded two deaths during the next year, when a third sister was stillborn and my Grandpa Earl Fellows died. Through the next several years I blossomed into an adolescent family historian, archivist, and antiquarian.

My grandmothers encouraged these interests. I connected strongly with them, their lives and personalities were the focus of my earliest written reminiscences, and I read from those writings at their funerals. I was thirty when my Grandma Marion Fellows died, and it seemed that the breakup of her household following her death grieved me more than her death had. In light of how badly and irreparably her health had deteriorated, death was desirable. But I could see nothing beneficial in the dismantling of her home, the beautiful and harmonious composition that she had created and refined over a period of sixty years on the farm.

The farm where Grandma Fellows lived and where I grew up had been in my father's family since 1854, when my great-great-grandparents arrived in Wisconsin from New York State. George and Delila Fellows purchased about seventy acres, including a log house and stable, from a woman who operated a stagecoach tavern on the site. Only ten acres had been broken; George brought more of it into cultivation and gradually acquired adjoining land until he owned more than three hundred acres. When his two sons, Fred and Lewis, were ready to start farming on their own in the 1880s, George split the land between them.

In reciting these details of my ancestors' lives, I am helped by referring to *A Fellows History*, a three-page stapled booklet in a cover of faded
yellow construction paper. It was my first publication, in an edition of perhaps ten copies, when I was in my early teens. I was helped in compiling it
by Grandma Fellows, whose husband, Earl, had taken over the farm from
his father, Lewis, in the 1920s. After the death of my Grandpa Fellows, when
I was twelve, I began to spend more time with Grandma, and my desire to
know more about family history blossomed. We sat at her kitchen table in
the rambling 1850s farmhouse, and she answered my questions as I gleaned
names, places, and dates from brittle obituary clippings and from a thick,
leather-bound volume of biographies of early county settlers. Something drove
me to establish a sense of connection and continuity with those who had
founded and worked the family farm through the previous century.

Most compelling of all the documents in Grandma's house were the
early photographs. There were a few tintypes, but most were the cabinet-
card and calling-card prints of the late 1800s. Many were unlabeled, but
with Grandma's help we identified most of the subjects and wrote their names
on the back. I thought it important enough for the individual portraits of one
old couple to be kept together that I took an envelope, lettered their names
on it as elegantly as I could, and placed them both inside. Our photographic
record took us back as far as George and Delila, but we had an unidentified
tintype of a rather stiff and withered looking couple who were clearly older
than they. We decided they must be Frederick and Emily, George's parents,
though I was cautious enough about this conjecture to put a question mark
after their names on the protective envelope I made for them.

The two-story front portion of Grandma's white clapboard house con-
tained the dining room, living room, and bedrooms. The story-and-a-half
back portion was the kitchen and laundry wing. From the corner of the laundry room I climbed a narrow, circular staircase to the two low-ceilinged rooms
above. The room at the top of the stairs, with a window facing the farmyard
and barns, had been finished with wallpaper and linoleum as a bedroom for
the hired men of earlier years. The other was an attic room whose plaster
and floorboards had never seen paint, paper, or varnish. The remnants of a
souvenir lithograph from the 1876 Centennial celebration in Philadelphia
peeled from one wall. There were boxes of 78-rpm records, a wind-up Victrola,
castoff furniture, and stacks of old magazines—*Life, Vogue, Antiques, Wisconsin Tales and Trails*. Knee-high windows looked east toward the split-
level house my parents had built a decade earlier and west toward Evansville
a few miles up the highway.

On weekends and school-day evenings I spent many hours visiting
Grandma, helping her with housecleaning and cooking and laundry, polishing

her brass candlesticks and copper molds and silverware, ogling her antique glass, browsing through her overstuffed bookcases. When I wanted time to myself, I retreated to the attic and occupied myself with my own little projects: rearranging furniture, sorting through and straightening the old stuff, printing the family history. My parents had given me a toy printing press one Christmas, so I began setting the family history in its moveable rubber type. Several dozen words into it, I realized how tedious and time-consuming the task was going to be. I soon purchased an inexpensive mimeograph printer that I saw advertised in the back of a magazine. With that flimsy and messy device I duplicated the typewritten pages of *A Fellows History* in my workshop above Grandma's kitchen.

Grandma displayed her collection of nineteenth-century glass in a bay window at the front of the house. I learned a lot about antique glass from my scrutiny of these pieces, and I appreciated them for their beauty and value. There were pitchers, goblets, tumblers, finger bowls, rose bowls, spooners, celeries, salt cellars, sugar bowls, and vases in many colors and patterns, all arranged and rearranged for the right effect. One Christmas season Grandma placed candlesticks on the two lower plate-glass shelves of glassware. The candle flames looked lovely at night against the dark windows and colorful glass. In the kitchen having supper one evening, we heard a terrible crash in the front of the house. What we found on the window ledge and floor was a sickening jumble of shattered glass—cranberry swirl, aquamarine hobnail, amber thousand eye, daisy and button.

There had been another plate-glass shelf above each of the shelves on which the candles had stood, and the flames had heated the top shelves so much that one of them had broken and crashed through the shelf below it. I quickly extinguished the other candle and removed the pieces of glass from the endangered shelf above it. Then, as we began picking up the pieces and recognizing exactly what had been destroyed, I began to sob. As I discovered the remains of one prized piece after another, I threw back my head and let out another wail.

I had no interest in raising livestock or crops to show at the 4-H fair each summer. Instead, I acted in the 4-H drama club, dabbled in leather craft and nature conservation, and refinished antique furniture as woodworking projects. Restoring a forlorn Victorian table or washstand was far more satisfying than constructing new furniture, which probably explains why I was so captivated by *Hans and Peter,* a brightly illustrated children's book of my Grandma's. Hans and Peter live in unpleasant rooms with disagreeable views in a city house. When they play together they plan their dream house, which they will build when they have grown up. But that time seems discouragingly far way. Out for a walk one day, they discover a deserted shack in a wooded field, and when they go inside, they are delighted by the lovely, verdant view from its window. Excited by the idea of fixing it up and living in it, Hans and Peter go to work—cleaning, papering, and painting the interior, painting the exterior, repairing the door, and installing a doorbell. They build furniture from scrap lumber and collect old-fashioned, castoff furnishings from their parents. Peter makes window curtains, Hans braids a carpet, and together they give the landscape a total makeover.

When all is ready for their housewarming party, Hans and Peter invite their parents and several others: the man who permitted them to use the shack, and the painter and chimney sweep who helped them refurbish it. The owner of the shack compliments the boys on the job they have done and says that when they have finished school they can work in his construction company. "If you are as industrious as you are now," he tells them, "it won't be long before you have saved enough money to build a beautiful big house for yourselves." Hearing this makes Hans and Peter beam at each other, but for now they are content to sit together looking out the window of their own little house.[1]

Maybe I wanted a friend like Hans or Peter, but mostly I wanted my own little shack to fix up. I found it in an old poultry shed that had been converted in some previous era to a garden cottage for my grandmother. When I was fourteen, I decided that the low-ceilinged shed, about twelve feet square, would be perfect for the antique shop I wanted to open. My dad helped me move the small building closer to the highway that runs through our farm. This new location was ideal for me, halfway between my parents' house and Grandma's, about fifty yards from each. Dad and I added a wide roofed porch, installed new wood flooring, and gave it fresh paint inside and out. I made signs, "The Olde Time Shoppe," to place in front of the building and smaller "Antiques Ahead" signs to post about a quarter mile in each direction on the highway.

I used old barn boards to build display shelves and gathered merchandise wherever I could find it. Grandma gave me some things and sold me some, and I frequented secondhand stores, household auctions, and antique shops. My salary of seventy-five dollars a month as church janitor helped to finance my purchases. I kept my small shop stocked with small things, mostly pressed glass pieces in various Victorian patterns, dishes of porcelain and stoneware, kerosene lamps, cast-iron banks, jugs, crocks, and anything else that appealed to me. Grandma Franklin, my mother's mother, helped me diversify my old-time merchandise by supplying rustic bars of her home-made lye soap and boxes of her divinity candy. Mom helped me decorate the shop by providing colorful curtains for the windows and various linens, which I used in my displays.

On family camping trips my favorite destination was Nelson Dewey State Park in the Mississippi River country of southwest Wisconsin. The park was named for the state's first governor, who settled there in the 1830s and whose restored house was open to tour. I was especially drawn to Stonefield Village, an outdoor museum of farm history and village life that the Wisconsin Historical Society had developed on the site of Governor Dewey's farm. And just down the road from Stonefield Village was the small river town of Cassville, where Nelson Dewey arrived from New York State. The eastern speculators for whom he worked saw the budding settlement as the likely site for the capital of the Wisconsin Territory and built a four-story brick building there to house the new government. Instead, the building became the Denniston Hotel. It had known a rowdy and bedraggled life as a bar and rooming house for many decades before I saw it.

That dilapidated Federal-style building on the riverfront enchanted me. My fascination grew when I read *The Shadow in the Glass,* August Derleth's novelized portrait of Nelson Dewey. Perhaps I believed that by rehabilitating the debauched building I could somehow redress the great losses of the governor's life, including his lonely death in a rented room in the building. Or maybe I was simply stirred by the building's shabby fate. In any case, I fantasized about moving in and setting up shop: Dad would help me fix it up. I would sell antiques, Grandma Franklin's soap and candy, Mom's baked goods. It would be a family operation, with my sisters and maybe even my brother pitching in. We would make the place thrive again.

While many boys my age got into sports, hunting, cars, and girls, I rode the school bus home to chum with Grandma and my old-fashioned things. I hung out the open sign near the highway in front of my antique shop most days during my early high-school summers and on weekends in spring and fall. Wearing the key to my shop around my neck, I was always ready for business, though I might be doing farm chores, mowing the lawn, or working in the vegetable garden. When my help was needed with haying, I was able to watch for customers by unloading bales from the wagons in the farmyard instead of working in the distant fields or up in the hot, dusty haymow. My attraction to the antiques trade was not entirely undivided, though: I sometimes found it difficult to tear my eyes from the sweaty, muscular hired hands when they came down from the mow for water and air.

During my high school years I became the family photographer, documenting holiday gatherings and creating a photographic record of Grandma's house, inside and out. In the upstairs hallway I photographed each of the four massively framed portraits of both my paternal great-great-grandparent couples—as a record, in case there were a fire. I snapped photos of the burgeoning contents of Grandma's china closet and the heavily book-lined walls of her study. I photographed Grandma sitting in her bay-window chair, reading or looking pensive against a backdrop of flowering houseplants and antique glass, writing letters at the kitchen table, hanging Christmas decorations. At Thanksgiving I created an oral as well as a photographic record of the day. With Grandma, my parents and siblings, and an aunt, uncle, and cousins gathered around Grandma's long dining table, I tape-recorded my dad saying the blessing and then everyone in turn saying something for which he or she was thankful. I also wandered around before and after the meal, recording stretches of conversation here and there.

By my last year of high school, after a student-exchange summer abroad, running my antique shop lost its appeal. It seemed petty, musty, materialistic—at odds with the other pole of my compass, a Thoreauvian desire to jettison excess and live simply. Further, I was trying to distance myself from an arena that seemed queer and unwholesome. I had picked up on things that unsettled me: My father had insisted on accompanying me when I shopped at Charles Shannon's Magnolia House Antiques near Evansville. I had seen Charlie at auctions through the years, where in my naive eyes he made a vaguely disreputable, clownish impression. He was generally seen as a lecherous homosexual alcoholic, though I never heard my parents make disparaging remarks about him. Grandma was not one to hold her tongue out of kindness, but she made only infrequent and benign references to "*hahma*sexuals," perhaps because she wondered about her uncommon grandson. One day she told me about being on a garden tour in the South and her amusement in overhearing one man say to another in an excited, effeminate voice, "Oh, darling, that's a dogtooth violet!"

Too much of a young fogey to find hippiedom attractive, I nonetheless effected an unconventional look during my last year of high school: I went to school wearing my great-grandfather's long black Knights Templar coat and white gloves from the late 1800s. In my writing and photography for the *Evansville Post,* I found an outlet for my interest in historical things, researching and writing about the city's past. I spent one semester at the mammoth state university in Madison, where I did some writing for one of the campus newspapers. An assignment to report on the activities of a recently formed gay student group gave me an unnerving glimpse of gay people of my own age. When it began to dawn on me that I was one of them, I fled the big city and headed for a rural college town in southwest Wisconsin.

At eighteen my year in Platteville turned out to be a time for reclaiming my childhood passions and owning my queerness. For the first time since my grade-school 4-H days, I plunged into theater and appeared in several campus productions. I spent a summer weekend by myself in Cassville, getting reacquainted with the streets and dark brick buildings of Nelson Dewey's backwater town on the Mississippi. I fell headlong into my first homosexual adventures, embroidered flowers and birds on my jeans, dropped out of school for a while.

After a few months of hermitage back on the farm, I took a job in Madison and moved into a small apartment there. That summer I made my first visit to a gay bar. Feeling terribly nervous and out of place, I went home with the first person who chatted me up. That particular connection was ill conceived, but the summer was redeemed when a tall, slender, muscular man introduced himself to me at the campus bookstore where I worked. His reddish-blond hair was thinning, his beard and moustache were closely trimmed, and his eyes flashed with gentle warmth. He looked familiar. With a hint of shyness he told me that his name was Mike Saternus and that he recognized me from the summer day, a year earlier, when I had stopped by the old Cooksville Congregational church.

My sister and I had bicycled to Cooksville that day, just wandering around the tiny village, which was a few miles from the farm. When we paused to take a look at the restoration work that was going on at the church building, an attractive man introduced himself as Mike and showed us around, explaining the building's history and pointing out various design details. I was thrilled to know that the old structure was in the hands of someone who planned to restore it rather than use it as a barn or knock it down for its lumber. The deserted church building had been a landmark in my childhood. Perched high on a limestone foundation, it loomed close to the road at an intersection on the frequently traveled route to my maternal grandparents' place. The small, long-abandoned house across the road from the church also intrigued me. It languished behind a tangle of vegetation, its paintless clapboard siding long gray from weathering. Now both the 1879 church and the 1848 house were in Mike Saternus's restorative hands.

During our bookstore encounter Mike Saternus invited me to come out to Cooksville to get better acquainted, to take another look at the church, and to see what he was doing as he started restoring the dilapidated house. My weekends with Mike and his partner, Larry Reed, that summer and fall included visits with several of their gay neighbors, most notably Sunday morning coffee at the home of the village's gay elders, Marvin Raney and Chester Holway. In their company I learned more of Cooksville's rich history, including the leading role that queer men have long played in the preservation of that place. I have given them their own chapter.

I am but one manifestation on the spectrum of culture-keeping queer androgyny. In contrast to others profiled in this book, my own story falls toward the unexotic end of the range. I was a boy whose gender-atypicality was expressed more subtly than dramatically, more inwardly than overtly. I don't recall ever being called a sissy. By way of providing a reference point at the exotic end of the spectrum of gay male gender identity, I introduce Charlotte von Mahlsdorf, the self-chosen name of a cross-dressing gay man who was born in Mahlsdorf, Germany, in 1928. "I get into a housedress that fits me well and I get the urge to clean and to polish."[2] Von Mahlsdorf tells his life story in the book *I Am My Own Woman,* originally published in German as *Ich bin meine eigene Frau,* which may also be translated as "I am my own wife."

From an early age von Mahlsdorf understood himself to be a girl in a boy's body. He enjoyed a very close relationship with his mother and told her when he was twenty that he was really her oldest unmarried *daughter.* When von Mahlsdorf's mother informed him that he should start thinking of finding a woman and getting married, his response left her perplexed but smiling: "Ich bin meine eigene Frau."

"When I was five or six," von Mahlsdorf recalls, "I preferred to play with old junk rather than real toys. True, I would sometimes pass the time with the doll furniture my mother had given me, or the train set, which had been a present from my great-uncle. But what I really enjoyed was cleaning and admiring my great-uncle's old clocks, kerosene lamps, paintings, and candlesticks."[3]

"My passion for collecting things began on its own, without urging from anyone." That passion drew von Mahlsdorf inexorably to rummaging through the rubbish, even going door-to-door asking for castoff things. He quickly developed a sixth sense for furniture made in Germany in the late nineteenth century, a period known as the Gründerzeit, and would get a heart-pounding thrill whenever he spotted its characteristic columns, turned legs, and ball-shaped decorations among the rubbish. "When I found something beautiful, I had only to bring my mother around. 'Oh mommy, please. . . .' Then she would nod, 'Okay, take it upstairs with the rest of your junk.' And radiant with joy, I carried the former showpiece up to the attic where I had set up my treasure chamber." The child was happy among his treasures: "I continually rearranged things, polished my furniture, dusted, laid down a crocheted doily here, removed one there, and repaired little bits of damage."[4]

It is impossible to convey briefly the amazing and quirky richness of von Mahlsdorf's life. He is the girl-boy from Mahlsdorf who makes the rounds of secondhand shops after school and lugs furniture home on the streetcar. He collects and repairs clocks, gramophones with horn-shaped speakers, automated music players, ornate furniture. He reacts with horror to seeing obedient townspeople contribute beautiful old household articles and art objects to Nazi scrap-metal drives. Required to attend a Hitler Youth rally on a very hot day, he longs to be at home, dusting. His great-uncle says to him thoughtfully, "Child, you should have been a girl in 1900. Then I would have hired you as a servant. You would have been a pearl!"[5]

Von Mahlsdorf is the girl-boy who saves his aunt's houseful of furniture from destruction during the war by arranging to have it stored in a barn outside Berlin. At fifteen he murders his abusive father in an act of self-preservation. Required to help clear things from the ravaged apartment of a Jewish couple who have been "called for," he saves their bookcase and some of their Hebrew books. Crouching in the cellar of a house during a bombing raid, he frets about the fate of a beautiful cupboard he glimpses there: "I admit that it is completely absurd to regret the destruction of a scalloped edge in such a situation, but that's how I am. My desire to keep beautiful objects safe is stronger than any other."[6]

Von Mahlsdorf is the woman-man who, on a subsistence budget after the war, begins to resuscitate a ravaged seventeenth-century palace that is to be torn down. While cleaning one of the palace's rooms in kerchief and apron one Sunday morning, he suddenly finds himself showing the place to townspeople attracted by the sound of one of his automatic music machines. Despite living always near the edge of poverty, he finally realizes his dream of having his own Gründerzeit museum in an eighteenth-century mansion back in Mahlsdorf that had captivated him as a child: "This house is my fate. It called out to me in its greatest need, and I was there for it."[7]

For years von Mahlsdorf scavenged Berlin houses about to be torn down, finding many of the things he needed to restore his house: doorknobs, doors, stucco rosettes, skirting boards, historically accurate door moldings, windows, and window handles. "The only thing I am suited for is preserving things and making them whole," he wrote.[8] "My driving need has always been to preserve things, not for myself, but for posterity, to establish a continuity, not a senseless ending. I am inspired by that idea. *Whatever you can accomplish with your two hands,* I thought, *you must do. . . .* I am not concerned with dead stones or lifeless furniture. They are embodiments that mirror the history of the men who built them, who lived in them. Senseless destruction does away with a former way of life, the foundation of our spiritual and aesthetic culture, and irretrievably impoverishes our daily lives."[9]

"I am always sensitive to the aura of a clock, a house, or furnishings. Objects put together without love don't do anything for me." Pieces of old furniture looked at von Mahlsdorf and told him stories—"about the people who had made them, and about those people with whom they had spent decades as silent guests." When the future of Charlotte von Mahlsdorf's museum was threatened by the East German government in the 1970s, he felt "like a tree whose roots had been severed." Told by officials that he did not possess the appropriate credentials to be in charge of a museum, von Mahlsdorf blanched. "The gentlemen did not want to acknowledge that without my two hands it would all be a wasteland, that nothing would have been created here if I were not a woman in a man's body. Because as a child I had played with doll furniture, because I am still a neat housewife today, because Gründerzeit amuses me, and because I always want a home around me: that's why the museum stands."[10]

Charlotte von Mahlsdorf attributes his culture-keeping propensities to being a woman in a man's body. I attribute my own to being a male with a decided dose of feminine sensibilities. Despite these differences in our self-understanding, von Mahlsdorf and I have much in common. Queer and preservation minded from childhood, we have marvelous company in the pages that follow.

In Search of Gay Preservationists

The Belgians and Greeks do it,
Nice young men who sell antiques do it.
Let's do it, let's fall in love.
　　　—a Noël Coward version of a song by Cole Porter

GAY RIGHTS PIONEER HARRY HAY observed that history knows much about gay men that it doesn't know it knows.[1] There are many reasons for this. In some cases someone who was in fact gay is not known to have been gay. Or he is known or believed but not generally acknowledged to have been gay. The label *gay* may be declared unsuitable because, as the litany goes, it's a contemporary term of European origin, therefore not appropriate to use in relation to individuals of earlier times or other cultures; from what we know about the person in question, it appears that he did not self-identify as gay and would not have wanted to be so labeled; we don't know enough about his sex life to justify such a label; he was bisexual; he was married to a woman, fathered children, was a devoted family man, and so forth. All these barriers to identifying someone as gay make it difficult to do queer history because one faces the necessity of reaching conclusions that are sure to annoy or offend someone for one reason or another.

Contemporary gay identity does not translate easily across cultures or time periods. There is no transhistorical or cross-cultural uniformity in the understanding of concepts such as sex, gender, sexuality, gender identity, and self-identity, all of which go into defining gay. Some argue, then, that it's inappropriate to apply the term to an American Indian berdache who lived a century ago, or to an Italian artist who lived five centuries ago, or even to a celibate Irish priest living today. I do not agree.

One of the most harmful aspects of homophobia is its equating gay identity with sex alone: that is, *gay* tends to be understood quite narrowly as a synonym for *homosexual*. For this reason, it's not an ideal term to use when looking at a person's nature beyond the scope of his sexual orientation per se. But what's the alternative? Resisting the urge to coin a new term for my kind across time and cultures, I've decided to make do with the familiar word *gay* and explain what it means to me: a male who is gender atypical (psychologically and perhaps physically androgynous or effeminate) and decidedly homosexual in orientation if not in practice. Thus, my use of the term *gay* encompasses both gender identity and sexual orientation. It is not synonymous with *homosexual*.[2]

This definition frees me from needing "proof" of sexual activity when I identify a historical figure as gay. His sex life is not what I'm talking about. Many gay men, perhaps most of them through history, have had sexual relations with women, often marrying and rearing children. A gay male's sexual activity may be hetero, bi, auto, or non. Again, this is because gay identity does not hinge on homosexual activity but on being androgynous and predominantly same-sex oriented, though this gender variance may be invisible or greatly repressed, and the homosexual inclination may never be acted upon.

Undoubtedly some gay men will object to the gender-atypical part of this definition of *gay*. "I'm homosexual," they will protest, "but I'm *not* effeminate." In a culture that devalues females and so-called feminine traits, especially when they are expressed by males, the term *effeminate* is an epithet. It suggests a swishy, limp-wristed prissiness. Some gays manifest these traits without reserve; others stifle them, especially in public. But these protostereotypical characteristics are hardly the most important part of the effeminacy that shapes male androgyny. Here's a better definition of *effeminate:* having qualities or characteristics generally possessed by girls and women. These traits may be highly external and visible in one gay male—his styles of speaking, gesturing, walking, and so on. In another his effeminacy may be little or not at all apparent in these ways but may be manifested more internally in his interests, aptitudes, values, emotional constitution, and communication style. The fact that a gay man is able to appear straight with no special effort does not mean that he is not at all effeminate. Rather, he expresses his effeminacy differently than do his more swishy peers. Edward Carpenter, that singular nineteenth-century Englishman, understood gay men as "intermediate men"—"men with much of the psychologic character of women."[3] Carpenter's conception of the intermediate tribe, of which he was a member, included those who could pass as straight and those who never could.[4]

Given the longstanding gay tradition of camouflage, my efforts to identify preservation-minded gays from the past have required extensive reading between the lines. I scoured the antiques, architecture, and interiors sections of libraries and bookstores. I immersed myself in the archives of the deceased. And I simply stumbled onto some wonderful revelations: a book on the pioneering Chicago preservationist Richard Nickel, for example, came to my attention when I was scavenging for something to read at a gay-owned bed-and-breakfast in that city.

In examining a given man's life, I determined how well he fit the gay pattern through a process that was deliberative but inevitably subjective. As my friend John Anders reminded me, "Intimations can come from the slightest suggestions, what Walt Whitman calls 'faint clues and indirections.'" Considering a variety of sometimes nebulous questions, I paid attention to a constellation of indicators: In childhood and adolescence, was the individual unusually interested in doing things typically associated with females, such as diary and scrapbook keeping, and homemaking activities, such as cooking, food preservation, flower-arranging, sewing, needlework, interior decorating? Was he or could he have been described as androgynous, effeminate, sensitive, emotional, artistic, musical, or fastidious? Was he strongly engaged by religious practice? By family or community history? By theatrical activities? Was he generally averse to sports? Were his mother, grandmothers, and other females key influences in his growing-up? Did he ever marry? Did he stay married? Were there children? What kinds of relationships did he have with his wife and other women, and with other men? Was he or could he have been described as never married, a bachelor, a lifelong bachelor, a confirmed bachelor, eccentric, or in similar terms?[5] After digesting the answers to such questions, I had to make a decision that was not always clear-cut: Was he likely gay, or not? Thus, I may have included some individuals who don't belong and excluded some who do. But though the lives presented here have significance individually, it's the composite portrait that's most important. I am confident of its integrity.

The most richly revealing part of the research has been collecting and analyzing autobiographical profiles from preservation-minded gays of today. I recruited more than sixty men as interview subjects and received written responses from about twenty more. Several of these men I knew personally; some I identified as likely prospects in periodicals or books. For example, I combed through back issues of selected magazines: *Preservation, Old-House Journal, Old-House Interiors*. Perusing back issues of *Victorian Homes*, I found that five of the six issues in a recent year featured restorations by quite obviously gay couples or individuals. I then obtained the addresses of many of these individuals and sent them the following notice.

> I am doing research for a book on the extraordinary and pioneering involvement of gay men in historic preservation. My working definition of historic preservation includes not only the saving of buildings but also the saving of smaller objects and documents, as well as the compilation of family and community history. I expect that getting acquainted with the activities of contemporary preservationists will complement my historical research.
>
> What I invite you to do, if you are a gay man, is to think about your own involvement in historic preservation: In what ways have you engaged in preservation? When did your interest begin and how

has it been manifested? What have been your inspirations? Who have been your role models? Is preservation a major, minor, or middling part of your life? What do you consider to be its significance for you? For others? Do you have any thoughts about how your engagement in preservation might relate to your sexual orientation?

If you would be interested in responding to these kinds of questions, I hope that you will get in touch with me. If you are inclined to write, an informal letter or narrative would be fine. If you would rather talk about it, I would welcome a conversation. Should you decide that you have nothing in particular to say on the topic, perhaps you know someone to whom you can pass this letter along. Still, I hope that you will lodge these questions in your mind, carry them around for a while, and let me know if any thoughts emerge later.

If I were to end up quoting you or citing your experience, there would be no need for you to be identified. So, I hope you won't let concern about seeing your name in print, or being otherwise identifiable, prevent you from communicating with me on this. This is not an "outing" project. On the other hand, I would welcome your willingness to be identified by your real name.

The gay-preservation grapevine assisted my publicity efforts. I connected with it most significantly by attending the National Trust for Historic Preservation's 1998 national conference, where I distributed my project notice by various avenues, including a session on "gays and lesbians in preservation" (where men outnumbered women nine to one) and a nearly all-male reception for "gays, lesbians, and friends in preservation."

Using interview transcripts and autobiographical writings, I shaped personal narratives for about three dozen individuals from throughout the United States. Each of these men was involved in reviewing and revising his profile. I have organized the material by geographical region because of the primacy of place in preservation, and because each region of the United States offers distinctive cultural and historical backdrops against which these men's preservative enterprises can be more richly understood.

It has been illuminating to hear these men describe how their passion to preserve has been expressed, often beginning in childhood, and what they make of it, including how they think it relates to being gay. The point of this book is not so much *what* these culture-keeping gay men have accomplished, but *why* they have felt compelled to do these things. This book is not intended as a Who's Who of gay preservationists, nor as a chronicle of degrees received, awards won, things acquired. Neither is this book about gay men who focus on the preservation of gay history, though a number of these individuals are so engaged. That is a rich subject in itself.

The preservationists profiled in this book range from accomplished professionals to impassioned amateurs. Their focuses range widely. But they all have two things in common: each is gay, and each manifests a singular passion to preserve. In examining the connection between these two traits, I have sought a fuller understanding of what it means to be gay. Even more than culture keeping, that's what this book is about.

In the decades following World War II, the American imagination was exceptionally antipreservation. Tearing down the old and erecting the new became something of a national obsession. "Historic preservation was sissy stuff," recalled an Omaha architect and founder of that city's preservation group. "*Real men build*. They don't fix up. They start over and leave their mark."[6]

Sissy stuff, indeed. It has been enlightening to ask gay men what they think about the extraordinary involvement of their kind in the largely female arena of historic preservation and its related professions: architectural historians, restoration architects, antiquarians, art historians, museum curators, conservators, archivists, state and local historians, landscape architects, interior designers, color designers. One gay preservationist joked about there being little need for a gay professional group within the American Society of Architectural Historians, since there seem to be so few in the organization who are straight. Surely it must have been one of the architectural historian tribe who first described a Victorian house that put all its decorative goodies up front as having "a Queen Anne front and a Mary Ann behind." Philip Johnson, a gay man who was an architectural historian before he was an architect, was a 1960s pioneer in preservation activism, railing against the demolition of New York City's Pennsylvania and Grand Central Stations and helping to save the Glessner House in Chicago.

Most of my subjects acknowledged the extraordinary involvement of gays in preservation. However, many of them attributed the phenomenon to sociocultural factors rather than to gay men's essential qualities. One common view holds that gays often have more disposable income, no children to consume their time and energy, so they can more easily immerse themselves in costly and laborious restoration projects and buy expensive antiques. Further, childless gays can more easily move into derelict properties in neighborhoods where safety and school quality are marginal or poor.

Conversely, some suggest that it is the cheapness of living in run-down old houses that attracts gays to buy, furnish their rooms with cast-offs, and rehabilitate: with only modest incomes and a lot of work, they can eventually have magnificent homes. Another line holds that perhaps, lacking children, gay preservationists are attempting to create something that will live beyond them. There's also the theory that it's because gay men are socially stigmatized and marginalized that they take on the "marginal" work of preservation: by taking something degraded and making it whole and beautiful again, they are trying to prove themselves worthy of society's respect and move up the social ladder. Their redemptive work is really a quest for self-redemption, a pursuit of acceptance, legitimacy, validation.

These explanations collapse under scrutiny. What about the frequent manifestation of preservation impulses in childhood, often years before the individual has any conscious awareness of his gayness and its implications for his life path, his social stature, his chances of having children? What about the gay men whose culture-keeping impulses are undiminished by fathering children or by modest finances? And how to account for the relative absence of lesbians in historic preservation, despite their being subject to similar sociocultural forces? Further, if one is childless and looking to leave one's mark in the world, why take on the enormous task of restoring an old building when there are many ways to be remembered after death that are easier, cheaper, less messy, and longer lasting? And on what grounds is preservation deemed "marginal"? It seems that those who do the work of perpetuating cultural memory and identity are doing a job that is at the very center of their society's life, akin to religious work.

If one is disposed to read between the lines, the literature of preservation in the United States reveals that gay men have long been allied with women in this arena and that this natural partnership continues. According to a gay preservationist with the National Park Service, "the historic preservation movement in the United States traditionally dates itself from the founding of the Mount Vernon Ladies Association in the middle of the nineteenth century. Women were very much in the forefront of this sort of activity, and I'm sure there have always been gay men who have gotten involved in working with the ladies."

In the 1870s, the decade of the nation's centennial, patriotic women and bachelor gentlemen collaborated to sustain the memory of the nation's preindustrial golden age. A half-century later, these same types of civic-minded ladies and artistic men spearheaded efforts to save old neighborhoods from the destructive incursion of the automobile and its accouterments: gas stations, service garages, parking lots, and wider streets. In the 1970s new generations of these natural allies—"little old ladies in tennis shoes and sensitive young men in tight jeans," as one gay man put it—were trying to block the destruction wrought by freeway building, urban renewal, and suburban sprawl. A cartoon in a 1978 issue of the *New Yorker* shows a woman and a man holding placards that read "Save Radio City Music Hall." The man says to the woman, "Haven't we met someplace before? Penn Station? The Metropolitan Opera House? The Villard Houses?" Here they are, observed but unrecognized: the gay male preservationist and his straight female ally.[7]

Grasping the role of gays in preservation in the first half of the twentieth century requires some audacious conjecture. Ideally one could establish the gayness of, say, Leicester Holland—chairman in the 1930s of the American Institute of Architects committee on the Preservation of Historic Buildings—without having to infer it from a subjective cluster of "gaydar" indications, including a photo that shows him wearing a ring on only the little finger of his left hand.[8] Holland championed the Historic American Buildings Survey (HABS), which created jobs for many otherwise unemployed architects during the Depression, producing documentary records of all types of old buildings.[9]

In the 1920s gays appear to have been well represented among those planning the meticulous restoration of Colonial Williamsburg. The group of draftsmen who assembled there became the first school of architectural restoration in the United States. Most of those young men were from northern and western states and were eager to learn about the architecture of Tidewater Virginia. They were a happy, convivial, and dedicated bunch that tended to keep to themselves, often devoting weekends to searching the countryside for eighteenth-century structures to measure and photograph. Walter Macomber, the resident architect under whose supervision they worked, had a very good eye for architectural detail and proportion, but no knack for the nuts and bolts of engineering design.[10] In this more aesthetic orientation to architecture, Macomber no doubt resembled his students. Indeed, architectural practice has long been a refuge for artistically inclined men in search of respectable work. Within the field architectural history and restoration hold a special attraction for gays.

Preservation pioneers in many cities and small towns around the United States were inspired by the work at Williamsburg. It seems that the more picturesque a place was, historically and aesthetically, the more attractive it was to gay men and consequently the more likely it was to sprout early preservation initiatives. The French Quarter in New Orleans was one such place. The first Vieux Carré Commission was formed there in 1924, two years before the start of the Williamsburg restoration. In 1931 Charleston, South Carolina, became the first city in the nation to adopt a historic-district zoning ordinance; in 1944 it became the first to publish an inventory of its historic buildings. Whatever his own nature may have been, architect Albert

Simons exudes a strikingly gay ethos in his foreword to that inventory volume, *This Is Charleston:* "No Charlestonian can be expected to speak or write about his city objectively, for it is so much a part of the background of his mind and emotions that detachment is never possible. The lovely and the shabby are all woven into the same warp and woof of the familiar scene. The stucco façade of some old house, its chalky colors weather faded, its surface mapped with earthquake patches and crumbling at the windows, through a sort of empathy assumes a character akin to an aged face looming out of one of Rembrandt's later portraits, infinitely world-weary yet infinitely enduring and wise in human experience."[11]

Charleston benefited from being picturesque and, it would seem, from having a large naval presence. Gay naval officers may also have figured prominently in efforts to restore the old section of Annapolis. Despite the city's abundant architectural treasures, early preservation in Richmond, Virginia, did not fare as well—perhaps because there weren't enough dedicated women to make up for the lack of a critical mass of house-hugging gay men. The gays may have been drawn away to nearby Williamsburg or to the greener pastures of the Washington, D.C., area. The rehabilitation of Georgetown, once a slum, began early in the second decade of the twentieth century, and Alexandria was reborn in the rarefied orbit of Mount Vernon.

New England offers still another narrative. Through the 1920s and 1930s, descendants of old New England families drifted out of Boston's Back Bay. Property values fell, and the district attracted a new mix of residents, including antique dealers and artists. Conservative Brahmins winced as the area's bohemian flavor blossomed. "Beacon Hill is not and never can be temperamental," one tradition-upholding resident warned in 1923, "and those seeking to find or create there a second Greenwich Village will meet with obstacles in the shape of an old residence aristocracy whose ancestors have had their entries and exits through those charming old doorways for generations."[12]

In the 1930s and 1940s, "temperamental" gentlemen propelled the preservation of two charmingly defunct mining towns in Colorado. Central City and Georgetown were close enough to Denver to attract tourists and new residents from the city and to enable gay men with Denver connections to be involved in their restoration. Central City's preservation was sparked by a visit by the director of the New Orleans Little Theater, a group that had been active in French Quarter preservation since the early 1920s. Seeing the derelict Central City Opera House, the New Orleans director was impressed with the old theater and recommended its rehabilitation. Some of those who attended musical and theatrical performances at the restored opera house ended up buying houses in the town and restoring them. The rejuvenation of Georgetown, Colorado, was prompted by a group of men who acquired several buildings in the business district and restored them as restaurants and shops, gave tours of the town, brought in artists, showed movies, and promoted the restoration of the town's fine Victorian houses.

In the 1950s the activities of the recently founded National Trust for Historic Preservation began to encroach on the National Park Service's preservation turf. In the queer-baiting spirit of that era, one Park Service administrator reacted to this incursion by attacking the rivals as sexual deviants: he circulated a memo that referred to the National Trust's directors as a bunch of "tea-sipping eunuchs."[13] Perhaps he was truly unaware that the Historic Sites and Buildings branch of his own agency was also well staffed with so-called perverts, many of them wearing the de rigueur camouflage of marriage.

During the 1950s and 1960s, gays were well represented in local "hysterical societies" that were undertaking the new or renewed rehabilitation of urban neighborhoods, places like College Hill in Providence, SoHo in New York City, Beacon Hill in Boston, the Vieux Carré of New Orleans, the Battery District of Charleston, the old section of Savannah, and the Pacific Heights district of San Francisco. Gays were pioneering revitalizers in Philadelphia's Society Hill and South Street neighborhoods. "I moved there in 1967, when South Street was not a place you wanted to be," said one gay man. Asked why gays were drawn to rehabilitating these neighborhoods, another Philadelphia gay man said, "Because gays like things nicer, just have better taste. It happens everywhere. Gay boys move in, there goes the neighborhood, there goes the real-estate values." A gay man who moved into an apartment in central Philadelphia in the 1950s found that most landlords liked to rent to gays: "And the reasons of course were because they were clean and they would fix the place up . . . and they would be great neighbors," he said. Moving into a new place, he and his friends were known to say, "This apartment's going to be great. I'm really going to fag it up."[14]

Other than a few savvy landlords, most did not see gay men as a positive part of the urban mix. In her 1961 book, *The Death and Life of Great American Cities*, Jane Jacobs blamed gays and misguided city planners for turning one of Philadelphia's historic squares into a "pervert park." "Some things have changed in the past forty years," observes gay writer Herbert Muschamp. "A pervert park! How quaint! Today, it almost goes without saying that the survival of cities like Philadelphia had already come to depend on the denizens of that pervert park, and many other pervert parks, on the contributions of people who, forty years ago, were meant to see themselves as socially undesirable. Us perverts served the city and saved the city. We were nurtured by it, and we gave something back."[15]

The margin contains handwritten notes: *and the "religious" institution rigorously denying this*

The gay contribution to preservation has been largely obscured, if not obliterated from the record. Many historic sites and house museums carry on the tradition of concealing and denying the gayness of the men who have had so much to do with the preservation of those places—promulgating what a gay preservationist with the National Trust calls the "bachelor uncle" description of those men. As in the religious arena, with its extraordinary gay involvement, gays themselves have generally been inclined to cover their own tracks. Consider, for example, preservation dynamo William Sumner Appleton, founder in 1910 of the Society for the Preservation of New England Antiquities. Most of his personal papers were destroyed following his death. In light of Appleton's voluminous scrapbook-making penchant from childhood and his visionary archive building as an adult, it's hard to imagine such destruction being committed for any reason other than "straightening" his biographical record. Perhaps Appleton himself decided that his professional accomplishments should be the sole basis upon which his contributions are judged. And so, in his case as in many others, one must read between the lines.

The Antiquers presents biographical sketches of pioneering American antiquarians in the late nineteenth and early twentieth centuries. Of the nearly forty individuals profiled in the book, almost all were male, many of them fastidious dressers and artistic homemakers who never married, some sharing homes with their mothers for as long as their mothers lived. Published in 1980, the book goes no further in its exploration of these antiquarians' natures than to describe them as colorful, eccentric, "some of them slightly 'shady,' all of them unusual."[16] In their love and pursuit of old-fashioned things, many of them were no doubt members of what gay historian John Loughery calls "a silent brotherhood . . . a hidden society of kindred spirits . . . made up of men who were always able to recognize one another."[17] Traces of this brotherhood are evident in the neat inscription on the front flyleaf of a copy of *The Charm of the Antique*, a chatty collector's guide: "Harold, from Dick and Jack, 1924." Several decades later, a copy of *The Book of Antiques* was similarly inscribed: "To my friend Oscar.—Judd."

This silent brotherhood crowds the pages of *Collecting: An Unruly Passion*. Although nearly all the cases in the book are males, many quite likely gay, the author ignores the connection except in the obliquely winking way. As a very young boy one man showed a strong inclination toward certain foods, flowers, and colors. Another collected dolls and statuettes of saints as a child and, at the launch of his short-lived marriage, insisted on spending his honeymoon in antique shops. Rare books and manuscripts rather than attractive young ladies enchanted one twentieth-century collector, just as they captivated a monkish but flamboyant manuscript copyist and collector in the early fifteenth century.[18]

Until recently being gay was considered to be of such devastating relevance to one's essential fitness as a human being that it was absolutely not talked about. Unfortunately, some have now fled to the other extreme, declaring it utterly irrelevant: being gay has nothing to do with one's ability to do anything, they argue, so it should not even be acknowledged. This view informs a letter from a highly accomplished preservationist of national reputation, a gay man in his sixties, in response to an invitation to be interviewed for this book. "My generation always put a high premium on the separation of one's professional life from one's private concerns, and I have worked hard at this all my life. This posture appears to be the antithesis of current attitudes, which seem to dictate just the opposite. Although a gregarious individual by nature, I am in the final analysis a person who has always highly valued my personal privacy. It follows therefore that I am less than comfortable with your project, as worthy as it may be, and must respectfully decline your invitation. I have labored fervently in the vineyard of my professional career for whatever I have achieved. That professionalism and its results should be the sole basis upon which history judges my contribution to society."

Another prominent gay preservationist of about the same age and opinion informed me through a third party of his desire to be left out of this book. Numerous preservationists from all parts of the United States did not respond to my inquiries. Several others made an initial reply, then became unavailable. I respect the desire of these men to maintain their privacy; I understand that their reserve may be informed by negative life experiences. But unfortunately their caution serves to perpetuate the idea that whatever they have contributed to the culture has been accomplished *despite* their gayness rather than *because* of it. I'm grateful that many men have lent their names and unabashed voices to undermining that pernicious view.

What These Gay Men's Lives Reveal

AFTER SCRUTINIZING THE LIVES of scores of preservation-minded gay men, past and present, I've identified what impress me as the most prominent elements of a rather consistent pattern: gender atypicality, domophilia, romanticism, aestheticism, and connection- and continuity-mindedness. These traits are related to one another in complex ways. For one thing, gender atypicality seems to comprise the others to a large degree. I present them as a simple list, in no particular order, because in doing otherwise I would only be pretending to comprehend their intricate relationships.

Gender Atypicality

The profile of the boy who is not like other boys emerges in one after another of these men's stories: He is unusually sensitive, gentle, well-mannered, mature, attracted to reading and other quiet activities, to music and art, to homey things and homemaking activities. This uncommon boy is more inclined to seek "connection" than competition or conquest and is especially drawn to connections with his mother, grandmothers, aunts, and other females. Many of these boys spend much time with their grandmothers in particular, from whom they learn about the family's history and absorb the family stories. *Mon was my grandmother!*

When novelist Glenway Wescott wrote *The Grandmothers,* he created Alwyn Tower in his own queer image. Alwyn, the novel's central consciousness, is an unusually sensitive and inquisitive young man who shares with his beloved grandmother an extravagant love of the past. As a small boy he admires his grandmother's keepsakes and asks her to tell him about them. He wants to know about the lives of the people who appear in the family album of daguerreotypes and faded photographs, the women and men whose passions and exertions have produced his own life.[1]

Like Alwyn Tower and his grandmother, gay boys and their grandmothers often develop bonds of unusual intensity. It's probably this constitutional affinity that accounts for the longstanding alliance of "little old ladies and temperamental men" in historic preservation.[2] Dan Marriott, with the National Trust for Historic Preservation, says, "There's a joke at the Trust, that it's staffed by lots of gay men and divorced women, which, if you look closely, is not far from the truth."

Robert Hopcke and Laura Rafaty get even closer to the truth in their book, which examines the remarkable friendships that develop between straight women and gay men. They point to the marked confluence of gay men and straight women in the worlds of theater, fashion, decor, and the arts. "We know we are generalizing, and there are scads of exceptions, but what we have heard about these friendships and know from our own experience is that the (now somewhat politically incorrect) identification of homosexuality with femininity may not necessarily be a gross error. . . . Gay men and straight women are friends because, on some very fundamental level, they share a deep knowledge of each other, a connection that really can be described by no other term than 'soul mate.'"[3]

During his 1950s childhood, an architectural historian enjoyed a soul-mate bond with his mother: "I was the daughter she always wanted. I could never pound a nail straight or fix a car or whatever else was considered the ultimate masculine thing, but I enjoyed learning to sew and making doll clothes and all of those kinds of things. And I inherited my mother's passion for antiques and interiors and historic buildings. I really believe that I've done as well as I have in preservation *because* of my being gay: It takes a fairy to make an old building 'pretty' again. There's a sensitivity and a value system that a lot of us have, to move into a neighborhood and work to revive and preserve it. So many of us gravitate to preservation; it's about one step above (or maybe below!) a hairdresser or a florist."[4]

Doing genealogical research in North Dakota, Minneapolis resident Dallas Drake found that even "out in the middle of nowhere" gay men and straight women are allied in preservation-minded endeavors. "One man I met lives on the edge of a tiny town that's practically not there anymore," Drake says. "He would hardly let me leave; he was so happy that somebody had stopped by. He has a gayish lisp, has lived there all his life—single, in his fifties, lives with his mother, takes care of her. Has a piano off in the side room that he plays from time to time. Has connections with all the little old ladies in the area. Whenever people get together for anything historical, he's in the middle of it."

Domophilia ~~Dodlocinpou~~ *wee most likely written by a "man."*

"From my earliest memories I was always fascinated with houses and what happened inside them," says Ken Miller. One after another, these gay men express their love of houses with a past, from modest cottages to grand palaces and castles. The neologism "domophilia" suggests this exceptional love of houses and things homey, this deep domesticity, which often emerges in childhood.

Studies of children's play have shown that when a girl designs an environment it is usually that of a house interior, with people and animals placed statically inside. Boys' designs are more likely to focus on things happening outside their enclosures or buildings, which tend to be taller and more elaborate than girls' structures, with people and animals moving around.[5] Considering how many gay boys are drawn to playing house, it's easy to imagine what these studies would have found had they distinguished the gay boys from the straights. Similarly, it's been said that the propensity to "enclose space" is basic to femininity, while the innate inclination to "displace space" is characteristic of masculinity.[6]

Domophilia is prominent in two gay men who have been key players in the preservation of Willa Cather's hometown of Red Cloud, Nebraska, during the past fifty years. When each of them was asked, separately, to identify passages from Cather's writings that had particular meaning for them, each cited the same scene in the novel *Shadows on the Rock:* Cécile, a twelve-year-old girl, has just made a brief visit to a family in the countryside near Quebec City. Coming back to the simple, tidy home she shares with her widowed father in the seventeenth-century colonial outpost, she is relieved to have returned from the primitive conditions of rural life.

> She put on her apron and made a survey of the supplies in the cellar and kitchen. As she began handling her own things again, it all seemed a little different,—as if she had grown at least two years older in the two nights she had been away. She did not feel like a little girl, doing what she had been taught to do. She was accustomed to think that she did all these things so carefully to please her father, and to carry out her mother's wishes. Now she realized that she did them for herself, quite as much. . . . These coppers, big and little, these brooms and clouts and brushes, were tools; and with them one made, not shoes or cabinet-work, but life itself. One made a climate within a climate; one made the days,—the complexion, the special flavour, the special happiness of each day as it passed; one made life.
>
> Suddenly her father came into the kitchen. "Cécile, why did you not call me to make the fire? And do you need a fire so early?"
>
> "I must have hot water, Papa. It is no trouble to make a fire." She wiped her hands and threw her arms about him. "Oh, Father, I think our house is so beautiful!"[7]

Neil Miller discovered the prevalence of this kind of tradition-cherishing domophilia as he traveled around the country in the 1980s, interviewing gay men for his book, *In Search of Gay America.* "By the end of my travels," he writes, "I was convinced that running a B and B is the dream of half the gay men in the United States."[8] And why wouldn't running an old-house bed-and-breakfast be alluring to many gays? It is grounded in things homey; it demands an array of talents that revolve around decorating, domesticity, hospitality, care giving. It often has elements of theater: period set design and hostly performance for an intimate and ever-changing audience of appreciative guests. Plus, in many cases it is the only thing that makes financially feasible the restoration of captivating, commodious old houses otherwise destined for "rooming-house-and-decay" syndrome and eventual destruction.

Romanticism

This is romanticism with a small *r,* by which I mean the exceptionally imaginative and emotional ways in which many gay men relate to the past, to old buildings and places, and to the lives and possessions of their previous occupants. "Preservation is really about loving particular places and the history that's connected to them," says Gerry Takano. "I'm sort of a romantic, so I love working with people who have passionate, rooted connections with historic buildings. If it doesn't affect you in your heart, there's no real connection."

Gay writer Richard McCann touches on this impassioned sensibility when he writes, "Because beauty's source was longing, it was infused with romantic sorrow; because beauty was defined as 'feminine' and therefore as 'other,' it became hopelessly confused with my mother: . . . Mother, who lifted cut-glass vases and antique clocks from her obsessively dusted curio shelves to ask, 'If this could talk, what story would it tell?'"[9]

His quintessentially queer romanticism shaped August Derleth's description of his hometown's "atmosphere of time past" in *Atmosphere of Houses:* "There are many houses, and their combined atmospheres make up the atmosphere of my town. There are so many tranquil, peaceful houses, and their quiet helps subdue the atmosphere of houses that cry aloud in tragedy." Derleth recalled the house of his grandmother, "whose gentle eyes regarded me in much the same manner as I imagine the house itself looked upon me. There was suffering in her eyes, and there was suffering in the walls of the house, but there was peace in both, the tranquil peace that follows in the wake of suffering. They brooded together, the house and my grandmother, and had silent communication with each other."[10]

As in Derleth's musings this romanticism encourages the inclination to see old houses as persons or at least as having personalities. Jim Williams described an eighteenth-century South Carolina plantation house as "more a person than a house. One I revived, loved and adored, but never knew well enough to be at home with."[11] It's been suggested that gay men's attraction to old houses may sometimes be related to finding "stage sets" on which to project their romantic fantasies of the past or in which to live them out. Indeed, the ranks of domophiles and drama queens overlap substantially, as evidenced by the many gays who are active in the preservation of historic theaters. Artists Peter MacGough and David MacDermott, partners in life and work, exemplify this bent toward historical fantasy, spurning modern amenities while "time-traveling" among three period-style homes: 1920s, 1880s, and eighteenth-century.[12]

The historic preservation movement is said to have begun with people who walked among ruins.[13] Though at first it may seem to be at odds with the impulse to preserve, a romantic fascination with decay, even destruction, is closely related to an enchantment with restoration. Indeed, without a period of neglect, decline, and perhaps the threat of destruction, the thrilling work of redemption is not possible. As a teenager Lloyd Sensat was mesmerized by *Ghosts along the Mississippi,* a book of elegant, moody photographs showing abandoned plantation houses in states of ruin.[14] Tyler Cassity was captivated—spoken to, even—by the romantic ruins of a sixty-two-acre cemetery in Hollywood, California, the resting place of Rudolph Valentino. He bought the century-old graveyard and revived it as Hollywood Forever Cemetery.[15]

Aestheticism

Artistic once served as a code word for gay and rightly so. One after another these gay men describe the emergence in childhood of their artistic eye and aptitude, their extraordinary visual understanding of the world, their design-mindedness. As children and adolescents many of them drew elevations and floor plans of houses, real and imagined; built model houses, villages, cities; designed, decorated, and furnished interiors (usually starting with their own bedrooms); designed theater sets; restored and refinished furniture. As a child Randy Plaisance sat on the floor in his suburban New Orleans bedroom, drawing floor plans for hours. "How I even knew what floor plans were," he says, "I don't know."

"I was never rich, but I've always had a good eye," says a stained-glass artist who restored and furnished his Victorian house to the look of 1889. "Even as a child growing up in a nondescript farmhouse, I had an eye for the more interesting and attractive buildings," says Allen Young. Another gay male's nascent aestheticism led him to attempt his first visit to an antique shop when he was about eight years old. Having just read an article on the difference between French and German bisque porcelain, he wanted to see some. So he went to a local antique shop, knocked on the door, and asked the owner if she had any. She shut the door in his face. "It must have seemed odd," he says, "having a child ask such a question."

"Gay men are very sensitive to beauty," says a gay old-house dweller. "It's perhaps a hackneyed stereotype, but I believe in it—I simply *know* it. It's an aesthetic capacity, an appreciation of beauty in old things, the grace of a lovely, older house with elegant details. And when gay men are interested in something, they give it their all, tremendous amounts of creative energy and physical energy. Not many straight people would do for this house what we did for it." The critic Camille Paglia concurs: "What seems irrefutable from my studies is that male homosexuality is intricately intertwined with art."[16] Like gay men in other notably gay design fields—interior, floral, landscape, fashion, stage—gay preservationists are driven by their artistic sensibilities. In restoring a degraded structure to its rightful form, the restorer's design-mindedness exalts historical correctness, valuing tradition and continuity over innovation and change. "It's quite a thrill to get a place that's really been altered and get it back to what it was, . . . the way it was meant to be," says domophile Robert Barker.

That gays have been at this game of rescue and redemption for a long time is suggested by one gentleman's description of neighborhood revitalization in New York's Greenwich Village in the second decade of the twentieth century: "After the boardinghouse period that the swell mansions of other days pass through, when at last they are utterly run down and too drear and dirty even for lodging houses, the taste of the artist converts them into something so desirable that the tide of values in the whole neighborhood is often set running in the opposite direction to that in which it has been setting for a generation or two."[17]

Houses and entire neighborhoods transformed by the artist's taste: Considering the abundance of artists who are gay, it's not surprising that places where artists have congregated have also been notable gathering places for gays. And so it's no surprise that many of these places have been sites of pioneering architectural preservation: the New Orleans French Quarter, Provincetown, Key West, San Francisco, Monterey, Carmel, Santa Fe, Greenwich Village, Beacon Hill, Georgetown, Charleston, and many more places, large and small, with less familiar names. Gay men have long been attracted to distinctive, romantic old buildings, landscapes, and neighborhoods. They have often begun by just dwelling in those places, drawing, painting, and photographing them, and they have typically taken the lead in restoring them. "We are trying to preserve the best of the past," says Richard Jost, "just because there is something beautiful about good design itself."

Preservation-minded gays have a penchant for meticulous attention to design detail. Art Deco aficionado Larry Kreisman laments the low caliber of contemporary design, craftsmanship, and materials: "As I grow older, I become more convinced that I was born out of time," he says, "that all my sensibilities set me on the stage of life a century ago and it was only a quirky accident that brought me into the world in 1947." While on a house tour in Savannah, a Georgia preservationist remarked with a hint of scorn, "It seems like new buildings that are built to look like old buildings never have *quite* the right pitch to the roof. *Those little details.*" Chicago preservationist and Louis Sullivan devotee Richard Nickel remarked, "People say rightly of me that I'm too fussy, but if you're not analytic over everything, then soon enough you're a slob and anything goes." Believing that "all existence is rehearsal for a final performance of perfection," Georgia's Jim Williams was clearly of the same fastidious breed.

Many gays are strongly attracted to restoring broken, neglected things to states of wholeness. Whether it's a mangled silver teapot in the hands of Bob Page at Replacements, Ltd., or a ramshackle house in the care of Myrick Howard at Preservation North Carolina, these men demonstrate a singular ability to envision a thing as it once was, as it could be once again. Gay men's aesthetic and redemptive sensibilities often drive them to restore that broken-down thing, even when it's such a wreck that others would never consider rehabilitation worth the trouble or even possible. Randolph Delahanty reports approvingly that "the love for old domestic architecture in San Francisco is so deeply ingrained that truly heroic and very expensive rescue operations have been conducted on many buildings it would have been more economical to tear down."[18]

"There were so many possibilities," artist Roy Little says in recalling his first look at the fleabag Victorian house that he and his lover bought and revived in San Francisco. A run-down thirteen-room Victorian in Vermont inspired similar reactions in writer Mark Doty and his partner: "Driving by on the way to show us something else, the realtor had said, 'Oh, you don't want to look at that, that needs to be torn down.'" But the two were eager to explore the place, "full of visions of possibility." An Indiana B and B host is another to whom visions of possibility come readily: "People see pictures of how the place looked before we restored it, and so many of them think I'm this great visionary," he says. "To me, there's no vision to it; it's right there in front of you. You look at the building, it's obvious what it was, and what it was it can be again. I don't know how anyone could *not* see it."

"I've always liked to take something that is ready to be destroyed, decadent almost, and prove that it can have another life by restoring it," said Liberace, the flamboyant pianist and performer.[19] "That is a very special thrill for me."[20] To keep that thrill of redemption going, many gay preservationists have devoted years to doing one restoration after another. Over a period of thirty years Jim Williams restored more than fifty houses. Robert Barker rehabilitated his first house when he was eighteen and did a dozen more over the years. Their daunting labors were inspired not by visions of financial gain (though that sometimes accrued) but by the deeply satisfying process of taking a place that had been greatly diminished and putting it back the way it was originally, the way it was meant to be. "I'd get a house done, and then I'd see another house and think, God, I'd love to do that one!" says Barker. "The only way I could afford to do it was to sell one and move into the next."

For some of these men the attraction to rehabilitating neglected things emerged in childhood. Ken Lustbader recalls being captivated by a children's book about a family that fixes up an abandoned house. Jack Richards says, "It was wonderful to listen to my grandfather as he worked over an old piece of furniture. As he rubbed it with a special kind of oil he would say, 'This wood is coming alive again because I'm putting my energy into it.'" Growing up in Bethlehem, Pennsylvania, Doug Bauder was fascinated to learn the history of his hometown's eighteenth-century Moravian buildings. When a preservation group was formed, he became a dues-paying member at age ten. "I would bike a mile or so from our house to view the buildings and dream of the time when they would be restored to their former glory."

Connection- and Continuity-Mindedness

This singular sensibility is reflected in E. M. Forster's imperative, "Only connect." As a connection to the past is central to the definition of culture, so is a concern with connection and continuity vital to culture keeping. "There are many ways to connect with the past," says John Anders, "and that connection, that continuity, is what keeps our spirit alive." In trying to account for his inscrutable childhood longing for old things, James Nocito says, "There was some kind of connection I was making when I was in the presence of something old, something with an accumulation of history or wisdom inherent in it. I'm not quite clear on what that connection was, but I really did seek it out." Like Forster these men cherish tradition, family, community, a feeling for place, a sense of flowing history. They are enchanted not by the modern but by "something older, something slightly mysterious yet powerful," as Nicols Fox describes it.[21]

"We live in a kind of cultural continuum, like a chain," said James Van Trump. "We need a constant going back and forth from the present to the past. We have to have the past from which to move on." From a young age, these uncommon males have been exceptionally concerned with matters of connection and continuity: Who are we? Where have we come from? Who has gone before us and what were their lives like? From childhood they have been unusually attracted to old things and old people, grandparents and others. "I've always been interested in older people and their ideas, in 'oldish' things and restoring them," says Jack Richards. "Growing up, I felt more at home in the company of older people than with people my own age or even my parents' age," says Russell Bush. "Traveling somewhere on a bus once, I remember how much I enjoyed sitting next to an old lady, chatting with someone that old." They are the ones to whom old family things have been passed down, especially those items considered sentimentally or historically significant but unwanted by others. Richard Jost recalls from his youth the day of his grandmother's funeral, when his grandfather gave him two family pieces of furniture from the attic, telling Richard that he was the only one who would appreciate them.

With their early interest in family and community history, these gay males have been among those most likely to do research in those areas. Drawn to old photographs, many of them have collaborated with elders in identifying and labeling those images and recording stories connected with them. They have been earnest and meticulous keepers of photo albums, scrapbooks, and journals.[22] Randy Pace tells of looking through old family pictures with his grandmother in New Mexico when he was in high school. He made sure names, places, and dates got written on the back of each photo and soon became engrossed in genealogical research. "I was so excited to find out who we were, where we came from and when, and what was going on in history then. I wanted to make sure there was some record of it."

For these men the most meaningful preservation encompasses not just old buildings, objects, and documents, but their associations—the places, people, and events connected with them. Brian Bigler developed a strong sense of place as a Wisconsin farm boy, started buying farm-related antiques at auctions by the age of eleven, and operated his own museum as an adolescent enterprise. At twenty he founded the Mount Horeb Historical Society. "There's so much being lost," Bigler says. "There's nothing I despise more than seeing history divided up, sold off, and moved across the country. I want to preserve things locally, where they belong, where they mean something."

There is an attraction to saving old objects as tangible links with past lives, even if the names and details of those lives are unknown or only vaguely known: "The thing about antiques," says Jim Raidl, "is that you buy them because you love them, and several people have loved them before you, and several people will love them beyond you." Mark Doty loves his old silver-plate pitcher for the beauty of it dents and abrasions—evidence of the vessel's years of use by unknown people in unknown places. A decorator quoted in *Old-House Interiors* favors an old mirror with its original mercury plating, now imperfect, because it brings one in touch with all the people who have gazed into it. In collecting elegantly designed ocean-liner memorabilia, Dwight Young prefers items of paper ephemera that bear the travelers' markings: "I love the pieces that passengers have scribbled notes on or passed around the dining table and had everybody sign their names to. I love having that connection with a moment when somebody picked up a pen or a pencil and wrote his or her name on this piece of paper, which I'm now holding in my hand." James Nocito, who collects wayward photos, has a similar preference: "The photographs that totally get me are the ones with the person's handwriting on the back."

For some of these men the sense of connection with those who have gone before has a decidedly supernatural dimension. "Voices from the past speak to me," said Jim Williams. "Spirits of past events cling fast to their native locale, never leaving."[23] In some cases these lingering spirits are perceived as ghosts. Contemplating the numerous spirit presences in old buildings that he has experienced or heard about, Myrick Howard sees them as fastidious kindred spirits: "Frankly, I like the notion of having ghosts. I'd like to think that I'd stick around for a while and check on things periodically."[24]

While these men are attuned to voices from the past, contemporary community connections are of much greater significance for most of them. In his work with the Sacred Sites Program at the New York Landmarks Conservancy, Ken Lustbader fostered the preservation of many old synagogues and churches. He valued the wonderful architecture, but more important to Lustbader was "the connection that these buildings have to people—the people who worship there and care for the building, the people who are running the soup kitchens and day-care centers, being community anchors." Similarly, Rick McKinniss and Gary Broulliard's rehabilitation of wasted houses in Lafayette, Indiana, has been as much a community-cultivating enterprise as a historical-aesthetic venture. "Our houses aren't big fancy Victorians," Broulliard says. "Most of them were built as working-class duplexes." Since 1977 the couple have been leaders in their neighborhood improvement coalition and have acquired and restored seven houses, all within a block of their own residence.

"I believe there is a fundamental need in the human psyche for some assurance of permanence and continuity," says Dwight Young. "Saving old buildings and neighborhoods is an enormously effective way to make that continuity manifest in the places where we live." Historical context, rootedness, stability, sense of place: these things really matter to these men. They are strongly attracted to established neighborhoods, places with richly developed identity. "There can never be a suitable replacement for a living historic city," said Jim Williams, who played a leading role in the rescue and resuscitation of old Savannah, Georgia. "It gives its inhabitants a sense of well-being and security that only an old section can create."[25]

Gender atypicality, domophilia, romanticism, aestheticism, connection- and continuity-mindedness: this litany, though not all-encompassing, is helpful in understanding the preservation-minded dynamics of gay men's lives. Among culture-keeping gays, the passion to preserve is diverse in its manifestations. Perhaps this chapter's overview can serve as a field guide to the life stories in the chapters that follow.

Saving Old New England

BECAUSE OF THE REGION'S EARLY SETTLEMENT by Europeans and because it was the first in the United States to experience the cultural upheaval of industrialization, New England is a good place to look for likely gay men as pioneering keepers of culture. It's not hard to spot them, especially among those born in the last half of the nineteenth century, when centennial fever and the continuity-obliterating ravages of industry combined to heighten popular awareness of the nation's history and to spark a romantic revival of Colonial design.

Distinct glimmers of likely gays in historic preservation appear even a century earlier. Consider the Reverend William Bentley of Salem, Massachusetts, who delighted in collecting and preserving objects related to the history of Essex County, noting in his voluminous diary the people and events connected with those things. When an elderly Salem bachelor died in 1796, Bentley regretted that he was unable to purchase all the furniture in the man's seventeenth-century house, to preserve it intact as a set of historical documents. "I grieved to see the connection between the last and the present century so entirely lost," Bentley wrote in his diary.[1]

Within the next several decades more Americans began to feel a loss of cultural continuity. Despite the warm Currier and Ives tones in which nineteenth-century American life is often envisioned, it was a decidedly unpretty and disorienting era for many in the industrializing United States. Standardization and mechanization accelerated the pace of life. As cities grew ever larger, old buildings and neighborhoods were torn down with abandon. The rise of corporations redistributed wealth and reorganized society in oppressive ways, and massive immigration created unprecedented cross-cultural tension.

In reaction to these developments in his native Massachusetts, Henry David Thoreau retreated in his late twenties to a cabin that he built at a small lake near Concord, his hometown. Thoreau's first impulse in getting a dwelling for himself was to buy an old farmstead on the Concord River. He was attracted to the Hollowell place's seclusion, its bucolic riverside location, and "the gray color and ruinous state of the house and barn."[2] When the deal fell through, Thoreau ended up building a frugal one-room cabin instead. He acquired most of the lumber from an old shed that he bought and disassembled, and he used secondhand bricks fifty years old in building his chimney.

Thoreau's conservative sense of economy underlay this recycling, but it was more than that. Old things had an inherent appeal for him, and he wanted to perpetuate their lives and use. "How much more agreeable it is," he wrote, "to sit in the midst of old furniture like Minott's clock, and secretary and looking-glass, which have come down from other generations, than amid that which was just brought from the cabinet-maker's, smelling of varnish, like a coffin! To sit under the face of an old clock that has been ticking one hundred and fifty years—there is something mortal, not to say immortal, about it; a clock that began to tick when Massachusetts was a province."[3]

Thoreau's periods of solitude fostered philosophical meditation. His early-morning bath in the pond was a religious exercise. He attempted to live by a gospel of natural simplicity in the face of the artificial complexity that was overtaking American life. In *Walden; or, Life in the Woods,* published in 1854, Thoreau voiced an early and eloquent denunciation of rampant industrialization. The book had its small audience, including Edward Carpenter, William Morris, and other like-minded comrades. But unlike many early preservationists the ultimate golden age to which Thoreau would return was rooted not in human culture but in nature untouched by civilization: "In Wildness is the preservation of the World."[4]

Henry Thoreau's contemporary and fellow villager Cummings Elsthan Davis was a preservationist of a decidedly material stripe who amassed a rich collection of the antiques of Concord, where he was born in 1816 and where his family had lived for generations. "Whatever belongs to the remote past has an unspeakable charm for me," the village eccentric told a reporter in 1870. The first of Davis's marriages lasted less than two years, and his second wife kept her distance, preferring to reside in their house in Harvard, Massachusetts, while her husband lived in Concord with his old-fashioned things. Wearing knee breeches and long white stockings of eighteenth-century style, Davis greeted visitors to his house and lovingly described the items in his jumbled displays.[5]

As the quirky Mr. Davis was on his way out of this life, the acquisitive aesthete Henry Davis Sleeper was blossoming into it. Born in Boston in 1878, his design-mindedness extraordinarily evident in childhood, Sleeper began hauling home antiques at a young age. The house he shared with his mother on Beacon Street was soon crowded with his collections. By the time he was thirty, he commissioned the construction of a house that would accommodate everything. He began Beauport in 1907 as a twenty-six-room Queen Anne cottage overlooking the harbor at Gloucester, Massachusetts. Among the materials Sleeper used to finish the interior of these first rooms was paneling rescued from an eighteenth-century house in the nearby village of Essex.

"Mightn't it be fun," Sleeper mused, "to have a house in which each room could recapture some of the spirit of a specific mood or phase or 'period' of our American life from the time of Plymouth down through the Revolution and the early Republic?"[6] He did just that, decorating every room, alcove, and hallway to express a historical or literary theme. For twenty years Sleeper continued to build and decorate more rooms, incorporating material salvaged from demolished old houses, until he had a labyrinth of more than forty rooms and no more land on which to build.

Sleeper was a romantic artist and consummate decorator rather than a scholarly collector. Working with an eclectic but highly selective accumulation of antiques—architectural fragments, furnishings, and masses of decorative objects—he composed each room as a carefully crafted work of art to be lived in. Just as Horace Walpole's contemporaries in England had flocked to Twickenham to see Strawberry Hill, his eighteenth-century "Gothick" fantasy house, Sleeper's sprawling but intimate creation at Gloucester enchanted many visitors.

Many of Sleeper's visitors were gay men whose ability to connect with one another was fostered by the founding of the Walpole Society in 1910. A groundbreaking exhibition of American antiques at New York's Metropolitan Museum of Art in 1909 had brought together collectors from New England, New York, and Pennsylvania. Many of these men wanted to stay in touch with one another, which led to the founding of the exclusive, invitation-only, and gentlemen-only club for collectors and students of early American decorative arts. They named their group after Horace Walpole, the flaming antiquarian and Gothicizer of the eighteenth century. As Walpole's appreciation of the old English arts and crafts had been pioneering, so was the Walpoleans' embrace of early American work. In more ways than one, the club's identification with Walpole was fitting and telling: its members recognized their ties to the gentleman who was, in the admiring estimation of A. L. Rowse, "a good deal of a sprightly and clever old lady."[7] This society of fastidious connoisseurs convened wherever there were interesting houses, collections, or collectors to be visited and pronounced upon.

In an eighteenth-century gilt mirror the Walpolean saw reflected the faces of its former possessors. Behind his early American chests, chairs, and tables he saw the skillful and inventive men who made them. Fascinated by pieces of old china, his imagination conjured histories and romances to go with them. "The old glazes and enamels are ofttimes more satisfying to one than meat and raiment," one Walpolean said. Another's house was described as an antiquarian's sanctuary, orderly as only a bachelor's house could be; large blue-and-white platters were safely centered, like babies, on the soft white covers of four-poster beds upstairs. In *China Collecting in America,* Alice Morse Earle captures the door-to-door antiques-acquiring practices of those with a Walpolean disposition. "I have been on the trail with a Yankee china dealer, and his unique method of management was delightful. He worked upon the most secretive, the most furtive plan. . . . He never, by any chance, told the truth about himself, and above all never gave his correct name and place of residence, nor drove away from the house in the way he really intended to go. . . . He was at one farmhouse a tender-hearted, indulgent husband, whose delicate invalid of a wife had expressed a wish for a set of old china and he was willing to spend days of search in order to satisfy her whim. It is needless to add that he was a bachelor."[8]

It appears that the Walpole Society included not only a significant roster of confirmed bachelors but also a number of married gay men. One of these gentlemen married an heiress and, with the help of her family's money, filled three houses to overflowing with antiques. His name was at the top of the list when those who began the Walpole Society started identifying men with antiquarian propensities who might be interested in joining. Another Walpolean with three antiques-filled houses, plus additional storerooms, was never married and lived with his mother.

The Essex Institute in Salem, Massachusetts, one of the oldest and largest local historical groups in the country, appears to have been another important locus for preservation-minded gays in the early 1900s. The institute conducted and published historical research, edited old diaries for its historical collections series, and collected engravings and photographs showing Essex County life in the past. Institute members were urged to give their heirlooms to a museum rather than allowing future generations to scatter their grandmothers' things. In its innovative efforts to make the past come alive, the Essex Institute created three period rooms illustrating everyday life among ordinary citizens in the late eighteenth century. The public was already familiar with the historical tableau concept, but the well-researched accuracy of these period rooms and their museum location were unprecedented in America. The rooms were a popular success. Also a first in the nation was the institute's creation of an outdoor museum staffed by docents dressed in period costume.

William Sumner Appleton's culture-keeping vision was not satisfied by museums and archives. Convinced of the need for a concerted program to protect New England's historic houses in situ, he corralled seventeen of his friends to found the Society for the Preservation of New England Antiquities (SPNEA) in 1910. (The founding group included one woman and seventeen men, with many ministers, former ministers, and seminarians among them.)[9] Within a year, the SPNEA bought its first property, a seventeenth-century Massachusetts house. Over the next thirty-six years the group acquired fifty more properties in five states, most of them houses from the seventeenth and eighteenth centuries. These early buildings were valued both for their ancestral associations and as documents in architectural history: they embodied medieval European building techniques and showed the emergence of American methods. The society's houses were scattered throughout New England; some were lived in, some housed tearooms and gift shops, others were uninhabited and left unrestored for architectural study.

William Sumner Appleton was well known for the single-minded passion, persistence, perfectionism, and occasional autocracy with which he went about preserving these antiquities. The pages of the SPNEA newsletter, *Old-Time New England,* often carried Appleton's seethings about the "crimes" being committed against the region's old buildings. Though he had been disturbed by destruction and change in his earlier years, the acceleration of change in the first decades of the twentieth century (driven mainly by the advent of the automobile) provoked a kind of cultural vertigo and dysphoria. The job of the SPNEA, Appleton wrote, "is to restrain the ceaseless law of change with reference to certain antiquities of the past considered worthy of as prolonged a life as it is humanly possible to give them."[10]

Architect and medievalist Ralph Adams Cram participated in the change-restraining work of the SPNEA but looked back further in time for his own inspiration. "Between the years 1000 and 1500," Cram wrote, "life was, in certain fundamental respects, more nearly right than at any time before or since."[11] In the face of the ugliness and desolation inflicted by industrialism since the early 1800s, Cram believed that a return to the human touch and the human scale of medieval patterns would restore vitality, harmony, and joy to life. To that end, he became his generation's foremost preacher of the Gothic Revival. "Back to medievalism we must go, and begin again."[12]

Born in rural New Hampshire in 1863, Cram believed himself to be living in an age in which, unlike any other period in human history, beauty had been lost, or at least disfigured or mutilated. His own life was wrapped up in "the desperate nineteenth century revolt against ugliness, and for the recovery and restoration of beauty."[13] To that end, he found huge inspiration in the Englishman William Morris and the Arts and Crafts movement, whose works of architecture, art, and handicraft harkened back to the artisan guilds of the Middle Ages, to the old standard of beauty in thought, faith, art, and the conduct of life.

The Victorian standards of beauty with which he grew up were just fine for the wealthy and fastidious Charles Hammond Gibson Jr. By the time he died in 1954, Gibson had been designing the future of his family home for nearly two decades: It would be a museum of the Victorian era, "a demonstration of the manner in which a typical family lived at that time, and their principles of character, good citizenship, and taste in living."[14] The five-story townhouse on Beacon Street in Boston's Back Bay was built in 1860 by Gibson's grandmother. Gibson was born there in 1874.

Young Gibson saw many wealthy Bostonians abandon their Back Bay homes in favor of suburban enclaves. The old townhouses typically ended up being subdivided into rooming houses and apartments. Gibson would permit no such fate for 137 Beacon. After his mother died in 1934, he began to freeze the house in time, preserving everything as it had always been in his memory. (To protect old brocade upholstery from wear, he barred guests at his tea and cocktail parties from sitting on it.) Believing that his beloved Back Bay had been "the essence of a refined and cultured society," Gibson opened his house to the public in the early 1950s. For the price of admission visitors got a time-capsule glimpse of High Victorian interior fashion: the profusion of decorative objects, richly patterned carpets and curtains, embossed and gilt wallpaper, overstuffed and tasseled furniture. Because Victorian style was almost universally scorned in the 1950s, Gibson acknowledged that his preservation achievement would not be truly appreciated until long after his death.[15]

Now, fifty years after Charles Gibson's death, gay men are fully engaged as keepers and appreciators of his Victorian time capsule. "My boyfriend David and I like to visit historic houses together," says Allen Young, "and it seems to me that a lot of these places were preserved by so-called bachelors. One place that has an old bachelor as part of its story is the Gibson House in Boston. The man who took David and me on our tour was very obviously a gay man who loved the house. From the little bit we heard about the last Gibson, it seems likely that he was a gay man who lived a somewhat eccentric life."

Allen Young was born in 1941 and has lived in rural Royalston, Massachusetts, since 1973, when he and a mostly gay group of friends began living at a place they named Butterworth Farm. "For all of us preservation was part of living in this area of New England, appreciating the old buildings and trying to protect them. For Bob Gravley, who died of AIDS, it was a mission. He led a successful fight to get our beautiful mansard-roofed town hall reshingled in slate rather than the cheaper asphalt that some considered adequate. Bob was the first chairman of Royalston's historic district commission. He resigned in furious protest when the board allowed a resident to install vinyl siding. The involvement of gay men in preservation has a lot to do, I think, with our greater aesthetic sense. Even as a child growing up in a nondescript farmhouse, I had an eye for the more interesting and attractive buildings in the area. Some of the old homes, churches, and hotels that had a certain look were the ones that I liked best. They just caught my eye.

"I came from a very nonartistic background. In the 1970s, as I found myself surrounded by gay men for the first time in my life, it opened my eyes to new things and I liked what I saw. My boyfriend David was also quite repressed artistically in his childhood. Coming out and getting involved socially with gay men opened up a whole new world for him and gave him permission to get involved with his aesthetic side. There's that line from *The Boys in the Band,* 'It takes a fairy to make something pretty.' I have mixed feelings about that kind of cliché, but I do believe that many gay men have a greater appreciation for beauty and painstaking craftsmanship. While many straight men seem to really enjoy working with big machines to knock things down and build skyscrapers and new roads, I think it's a more 'feminine' value to stop and smell the lilacs and appreciate the beauty of old things."

Extraordinary sensitivity to things of distinctive beauty is manifested by the three New Englanders whose stories follow. In meditating on the beauty of a battered old silver-plate pitcher, poet Mark Doty expresses the connection- and continuity-minded bent of his passionate aestheticism. Doty's account of his and his partner's relationship with a needy Victorian house in Vermont gives a rich portrait of their romanticism-suffused domophilia and aestheticism. All these quintessential traits are evident as well in Doty's description of the allure of New England household auctions. For entrepreneur innkeeper Don Leavitt the aesthetic appeal of resurrecting grand old New Hampshire buildings is wedded to the hope of making a living from finding new uses for them. Mark Sammons, historical museum curator, was drawn to the profession twenty-five years ago by his "fantasy-of-the-past" romantic and aesthetic leanings. Those aspects are now subordinate to Sammons's desire to understand and communicate social history that reflects the realities of the past and addresses the needs of the present.

Mark Doty

In his autobiographical *Heaven's Coast* and *Still Life with Oysters and Lemon*, poet Mark Doty reveals gay preservation sensibilities, his own and those of his late partner Wally Roberts. This narrative combines excerpts from those two works, describing Doty's and Roberts's immersion in New England old-house rehabilitation and auction-going in the 1980s. Doty lives in Provincetown, Massachusetts.[16]

I HAVE AN OLD SILVERPLATE PITCHER, a sturdy and serviceable thing made for use in a hotel, or a boardinghouse, or on a train. Simple, shapely. It sits now in the center of a painted blue round table, beside a white tureen holding a small shell-pink begonia from the A&P, the flowers clenched, a little reluctant to open indoors, in March, in New England. It has been a long time since the pitcher has been in service, exactly; now it radiates a sort of dignity, acquires from the company of other things a different sort of status of being. It holds the image of the room—small rectangular frames of windows, walls bending inward—upside down in the irregular sheen of its various metals. Where the body of the vessel bells out, at its midriff, the silver's worn away, revealing the brass beneath; it's here it must have been rubbed the most, as it was washed, year after year. Along the base there are dents and indentations, abrasions where it's been set down, hard, or pushed across a counter, or jostled in a sink. These marks and wearings-down mark the evidence of time, the acclimation of the object's body to human bodies. They are what make it beautiful; it may have been handsome, to begin with, but I believe that its beauty is the result of use, of being subject to time.

When my partner, Wally, and I moved to Vermont, we bought a thirteen-room Italianate Victorian house, built in Montpelier in 1884. Let me hurry to say, lest this summon visions of grandeur, that this was never a grand house—it was built, most likely, as housing for granite workers, at the foot of a granite hill where the homes of the better-off rose in the winter sunlight. We were down in the hollow, pitched into winter shade, and in January saw little of the sun. And the house in fact seemed to have been heading downhill since it was built; the floors sloped with fun-house abandon, and the floorplan had been mysteriously altered until it also bore a certain resemblance to a carnival maze. The outside was clad in mustard-yellow clapboards with brown trim, and the whole place was ringed by a particularly sorry-looking brown picket fence, half its points snapped away by neighbor kids.

But we were eager, and full of visions of possibility, and if the house was a daunting prospect, it was a palace nonetheless. We had been together for only a couple of years, living in and around Boston; I'd been a temporary typist and a part-time teacher, Wally a designer of window displays for a failing department store, and the idea of actually having our own house seemed astonishing. But I was offered a teaching job in Vermont, and I had a grant from the Massachusetts Artists Foundation, and here was a house we could actually afford. Driving by on the way to show us something else, the realtor had said, *Oh, you don't want to look at that, that needs to be torn down.*

Which was really all we needed to hear, contrary creatures, scavengers, aficionados of barn sales and other people's attics that we were. And it did turn out to be like a barn sale, really—except that we bought the barn, for twenty-nine thousand dollars. It had no insulation, an antique wood-fired furnace that consumed whole cords of timber in a wink, and period plumbing of unquestionable authenticity. Whether the flat roof was a concession to poverty or the Italianate fashion I never knew, but in the course of one Vermont winter the absolute madness of the idea became clear. Snowfall after snowfall meant shoveling the roof, and as soon as there was a bit of a thaw ice dams pushed at the spongy old roofing material until the melting water began to drip, and then to cascade, into our bedroom.

But that was all down the road. First the sellers, Clayton and Rita, taught us the intricacies of the furnace, the mysteries of a kerosene-burning stove. Rita worked in a clothespin factory and made all Clayton's meals; he gathered mushrooms and cut firewood, though I never saw him do anything but sit at the kitchen table and smoke. They sized us up in five minutes, and seemed perfectly happy to accept us as a couple, especially once they'd figured out that Rita could talk to Wally about where to shop while Clayton told me about maintenance, shoveling, plumbing—men's work. He'd even make jokes about the fussy concerns of wives, winking at me and nodding in Rita and Wally's direction.

Once Clayton and Rita vacated for their new house, we found ourselves alone in thirteen rooms of linoleum concealing wide-plank floors, cheap lumberyard paneling covering up layer upon layer of wallpaper roses. The house had long been inhabited in the manner of poor Vermonters who made do, got by, put a patch on what broke. It had been a long time since that house had gotten any serious attention; had it *ever* gotten serious attention? But it didn't matter a bit how much work confronted us, or that the renovation would turn out, eventually, to be unfinishable work—what mattered was it was ours, a great rambling dream of a house, eccentric, temperamental, rife with character, capable of being profoundly loved. And we were thrilled; the house was ours to rescue, to uncover, to inhabit, to play with, a piece of the world on which to make our mark.

For the five years we lived there—in which time my hands, or Wally's, must have touched every surface of that house, inside and out, as we painted and plastered and stripped and cursed, built and caulked and wept—every penny we could make went into the house. Mustard and chocolate gave way to a creamy colonial yellow, white trim, and blue shutters; the town paper suddenly carried an article about "the rising tide of gentrification." In a while it had a rainproof roof shielding new insulation, new chimney linings, a huge soapstone woodstove big enough to defeat—almost—the bitter Januaries of the snow queen.

The house had a narrow double front door, still sporting its figured brass hardware, patterns half-obscured now with a hundred years of paint—handsome doors, but not very practical ones, since it was impossible to effectively block their drafty cracks and seams. For a while we sealed them off with plastic, six months of the year, and then it seemed time—the rest of the house was at least *that* much ready—to use the front door as it was meant to be used. At a salvage company I found just the right thing—for the proverbial arm and leg, but it was grant money, and it was for our *house*. Oh rationalization that justified many an expense we couldn't afford, many an hour spent in the hard folding chairs of auctions, many a Saturday rooting in some collapsing barn! Just the right thing was a pair of oak doors, multipaned; they were french doors, really, but with the right varnish and framing they made the most splendid storm doors imaginable. It was the storm door raised to the level of art, and so the entryway of the house took on its proper dignity, a happy transition from the outer world to the inner one. At Christmas they were best, decked out and inviting.

It's true the invitation was mostly to ourselves, and for a few good friends at the college where I taught, since we fit into our little Vermont town none too well; we were the only out gay male couple in the whole place, and though we were thoroughly accepted by the town's liberal community (that overlayer of exiles which make Vermont culture tolerable) we were strange new creatures to the ur-layer of native Vermonters who made up the town's human bedrock. And who, significantly, made up most of our neighborhood. Our house wasn't cheap just because the floors sagged; it took us a while to learn what people meant by that insistent talk about *location*.

But we had a world for ourselves there, and one very real advantage to living with a window designer was that he could make *anything* look good—the right arrangement, a little fussing with the details: splendor! The high ceilings accommodated a huge tree at Christmas, thus making use of the ornaments Wally had been squirreling away for a lifetime, souvenirs of other people's childhoods collected at a decade of yard sales: Bohemian glass beads strung into crystalline snowflakes, great garlands of shimmering glass, an under-tree world of ancient toys. The big granite cellar was perfect for the universe of display props Wally used for store windows. For me, a realm of gardens, borders of perennials out front (against the now properly white picket fence, every new picket of it cut with my own hands) and herbs and vegetables out back.

And doors to deck. One Christmas we made boxwood wreaths from cuttings I took from the ruins of a formal rose garden at the college; one hung on each of the gleaming oak doors. They looked so classic, and lasted so long, that by early spring they were still hanging there, plain without their ribbons and trim, cheerful and promising—qualities which Vermonters need desperately, suicidally, in February and March.

There was nothing small about the interior of that house, room after slopey room, and it sent us out into the world of yard sales and sale barns and flea markets, and that is how we found our way to the realm of auctions, a time-honored system for the redistribution of the possessions of the dead.

There is a whole community built around the reassignment and redistribution of things. It pretends to be concerned with value, and of course on one level it is; there are precious objects that escalate in price, and represent concrete forms of wealth. But many things next-to-worthless, or only of ordinary value, like my scarred pitcher, are also there to be dealt with. Things must go somewhere when they are relinquished; orphaned belongings must be placed, settled, in order to keep the world aright.

I loved best the auctions that took place at people's houses, for then the narrative of a life was most available; then those cases of canning jars and boxes of ancient magazines, those collections of screws and old latches, mixing bowls and tin cookie-cutters, horse tackle and amateur paintings of birds made a kind of sense. It was like a kind of excavation, seeing things carried out, up from cellars, out of attics and back rooms, out onto a lawn where people gathered under a tent, or on folding chairs, warming themselves with bad coffee and cheap hot dogs bought on the spot. The auctioneer droned on and on, telling jokes to spike our interest whenever attention flagged, attempting to mix desirable items in with long runs of the irredeemably dull. Often there would be one thing we wanted, and if we wanted it badly enough we would wait and wait, as he slogged through numbered lots toward the one that intrigued us. I learned to bring schoolwork with me; I'd read my students' poems and essays while the gavel fell and another armoire or lawnmower or carnival glass punchbowl was carried to the block. We befriended one auctioneer and his wife, whose sales we used to go to regularly; she'd sign us up for a bidding number and always want to talk a while, taking us both in with her eyes and nodding in a way that somehow acknowledged our status as a couple without it ever being specifically named. She held some special affection for us that was conveyed in the way she'd greet us and take time to talk; she handed us our rectangular bidding number as if it were a gift. And every once in a while, when we'd venture a small opening bid on some little thing, her husband would cry "Sold!" and it would be ours before anyone else had a chance—an auctioneer's way of rewarding a regular customer.

There are specific things I remember buying, beloved things. A green stepback cupboard, with upper doors of rippled glass, and beautiful grooves where the turning of the latch had worn the milky apple-green paint away. A wooden panel painted (badly, but delightfully) with seven different wild birds, shown in impossible proximity: eagle and hawk and owl side by side on a branch. A huge oak table—which I no longer own, and its loss pains me—from an old hotel in Barre, all its drawers autographed and dated by bellhops and waiters and kitchen staff. A big mercury glass ball, of no discernible use. An astonishing yellow chest of drawers, painted with an urn of weepy-looking lilies. A simple, cream-colored chair, with a seat of woven wooden splats, on whose ladder rungs someone painted, quite delicately, three perfect red cherries. An unfinished violin, in bird's-eye maple, in two parts—the top carved out as a single piece, complete, and the violin-shaped block of uncarved wood that would have been the fiddle's bottom half, the two parts together purchased for a dollar, and feeling, in the hand, like music emerging out of silence, or sculpture coming out of stone. A perpetual wooden emblem: something forever coming into being.

These things are informed for me, permanently, by the narrative of the auction, an experience of participation. The auctioneer and his runners—an odd assortment of small-town Vermonters, from teenagers to old men, all in their heavy work-clothes, their flannels and boiled wools—made up one cast of characters, repeated from sale to sale, with variations in the crew. We buyers or potential buyers comprised the other, an odd mix of gnarly dealers and stylish couples furnishing old houses, well-heeled buyers from elsewhere, women in handknit sweaters with sheep on them, a sprinkling of gay men. We were of a tribe who understood ourselves as curators of objects, some of which would outlast us. We eyed all that was offered, imagining where it had come from, talking to other bidders or competing with them or both. Sometimes deals were made on the spot; you could own something for a few minutes and sell it again to an eager collector, or refuse to. This one wanted only junk; this one had so much money that it was useless to bid against her; these two liked precisely what we liked. Wally had wickedly comic names for them, all of which have vanished from my memory in the years I haven't seen these people we hardly knew anyway.

There was an odd feeling of adventure about it—one might be caught up in the fever of the moment and buy something entirely unanticipated; one might take some strange risk. My heart always used to start pounding, at the moment of bidding, a little adrenaline rush, as if what was taking place were deeply risky and consequential. Well, we were poor—that was certain, so there was an element of risk, but we never spent *that* much. Instead, it was about being part of a drama, an enactment of community that went on around this box of plates, this trunk of Masonic temple costumes, this ruby glass compote. And a feeling of magic, too—no matter how early we came or how carefully we looked, the auctioneer would always hold up something we'd never seen, offer something we hadn't noticed before, as if he pulled things up out of a bottomless well.

Indeed, these things could go on and on. I used to love the moment, late in auctions, when stuff began to be crammed together into "box lots." By then the crowd would be thinning, the best things gone; only the diehards remained and the auctioneer and his carriers were running out of steam. So they began to toss things together, producing boxes from who knows where and crying, Do I hear a dollar? How many times we fell for this temptation I couldn't say; we seemed to always have boxes to sort out once we got home. They'd yield perhaps one lovely old pressed wineglass, or a single volume of some beautiful leather-bound nineteenth-century encyclopedia, or one hand-some photograph. And endless Tupperware, chamber pots, rusty kitchen utensils, old tins of paint, and jam jars full of nails and screws. It wasn't long before we'd filled the rooms of the house we actually used, tableaux and still lifes of old things spilling over, one season's purchases crowding out the last's. Then we turned an unused upstairs room into a storeroom, and soon it was piled to the ceiling, with pathways weaving in between the towers of things.

What a fragile thing a house is, though it doesn't seem so. All the energy we poured into the house in Vermont couldn't complete it; it was so big, and so needy, that I used to dream, even after five years, of part of the house falling away, the sloping floors gone their way at last, tumbling in the direction they'd always pined for. Or I'd dream of whole rooms I hadn't even discovered yet—rooms which, of course, needed immediate and serious attention. By the time I was just getting to some project I'd long postponed, I'd find that something done years before needed doing *again*. There was barely time to enjoy that particularly homosexual pleasure, decor; there was too much work to be done. Paint peels, plaster cracks, and gardens, of course, are the most ephemeral constructions of all.

What disappears faster than a garden without a gardener?

Don Leavitt

In 1998 an Associated Press article titled "Showcase of the Shakers Reborn" announced the restoration of the Shakers' Great Stone Dwelling in Enfield, New Hampshire. A photograph showed the six-story granite structure, which was completed in 1841, the centerpiece of a community that existed from the 1790s to the 1920s. Another photo showed forty-year-old Don Leavitt, co-owner of an inn in the building, sitting proudly on a beautifully banistered staircase. "It's just about the most spectacular, most famous of all Shaker buildings ever constructed and was probably their greatest engineering feat," he said.

"Rick Miller and Don Leavitt have made a habit of buying down-at-heels estates in order to save them," began a piece in *Old-House Journal* in 1998. "Thirteen years ago, they turned to innkeeping to support their first major purchase, a long-vacant 1904 Colonial Revival mansion in New Hampshire's Lakes region. The Red Hill Inn was up and running in little over a year. Since then, Miller and Leavitt have restored the Shaker Inn in Enfield in partnership with the Enfield Shaker Museum. Still under restoration is Kimball's Castle in Gilford, a re-creation of a Rhine castle with a 320-degree view of Lake Winnipesaukee and the surrounding countryside."[17]

Leavitt lives with his life partner, Todd Paine, in Orange, New Hampshire.

I MET RICK, MY BUSINESS PARTNER, many years ago when I stopped to admire his classic 1939 Chris Craft runabout. We've been great friends since then and have tackled many preservation projects. We have the affliction of falling in love with derelict old buildings and then convincing ourselves that there is a money-making venture lurking somewhere in the plaster dust.

In 1982 Rick showed me an abandoned sixty-acre summer estate with seven crumbling buildings, including a mansion. He decided it would make a great inn. I thought he was nuts, but the more he pursued it the more it seemed like a great idea. In 1984 we quit our jobs, declined his parents' offer to pay for therapy to knock this silly idea out of our heads, and somehow convinced investors and a bank to finance the venture. The Red Hill Inn in Center Harbor was launched in 1985. We spent sixteen years slowly renovating room after room, building after building, doing it up right. The place is gorgeous, twenty-six rooms all beautifully decorated in a unique style that we call the Don and Rick touch.

When the Garnet Inn, a local landmark in downtown Center Harbor, came on the market, Rick and I developed and funded a plan to convert the inn into housing. But a sewer moratorium sidelined the deal and probably saved our necks, as the recession came and the housing market collapsed. The original part of the older of the two buildings dated back to about 1820. Apparently Rick and I were the only ones in the world who thought those buildings were beautiful. It was a tough day in 1995 when they were torn down; I felt like I had failed a friend. In the years since, I've found myself thinking that if only I'd done this or that differently, I could have saved those buildings.

When a chain of movie theaters in this area was gobbled up by a bigger chain, the Plymouth Theatre, a small-town movie house from 1930, was closed. Of course Rick and I fell in love with its Art Deco lines and decided that we had the smarts to make it a viable business. For once we were right, and since 1990 we've operated one of the few small-town theaters left in New England.

If we can ever raise the five million dollars needed, we'll have in Kimball's Castle a forty-room inn that will be known throughout the country. This regional landmark was abandoned in 1960 after its owner died. Thirty years later Rick and I gained an option to buy with the idea of creating a first-class country inn and restaurant on the site. Nothing is ever easy in life: after nine years and seven hundred thousand dollars of investors' money, we still haven't broken ground. And as part of this project we took ownership of the 1901 Lakeport train station, which was about to be torn down. We moved it to a temporary site, where it sits without its roof, waiting to be moved to Kimball's Castle and turned into guest rooms.

Rick and I opened the Shaker Inn at the Great Stone Dwelling in 1998. You can imagine how it would have struck you to come along the lake and see this magnificent structure in 1841, when everyone was living in little hovels. Our guests actually stay in the museum. Anywhere else, you would peer at the rooms across red velvet ropes. Here you get to use the drawers and touch everything.

I've been in love with old buildings and the stories of the people behind them since I was a kid. We always lived in wonderful big old houses. Being the youngest of four boys, I was always last to pick a bedroom and always got what everyone else considered the worst room in the house, way up in the attic. I would have these fantastic big garret rooms with soaring ceilings and big arch windows, servants' rooms and old servants' bathrooms. I had a great time decorating these rooms and playing in them.

While I was majoring in American history at the University of Maryland, I interned with a local preservation group and saved my first building, the 1909 Montrose Schoolhouse in Rockville. After working for several years as a reporter, I decided to ditch financial security and become my own boss as a partner in Historic Inns of New England. I've served on the board of the New Hampshire Preservation League and helped to found a group promoting heritage tourism in the Lakes region of New Hampshire. In 1996, surrounded by friends and family, I married the neatest guy in the world in a ceremony at Kimball's Castle.

Mark Sammons

Now director of the Wentworth-Coolidge Mansion in Portsmouth, New Hampshire, Mark Sammons was until recently "chief cook, bottle-washer, and curator" at the Newburyport Maritime Society in Newburyport, Massachusetts. He has worked at Strawbery Banke Museum in Portsmouth, New Hampshire (Strawbery Banke is the city's original name), and at Old Sturbridge Village and Hancock Shaker Village in Massachusetts. Sammons lives in Kittery, Maine, with his partner, David, in an 1806 house that, he is happy to say, was rehabilitated by someone else before they bought it.

BY THE AGE OF NINE OR TEN, kids have seen enough birthdays and Christmases go by to begin to develop a sense of the passage of time, a sense of history. When I was that age, my parents moved us from Schenectady, New York, to the Berkshire Hills of western Massachusetts. The two-hundred-dred-year-old church we had attended in Schenectady made little impression on me; I was too young to comprehend it. But I quickly grasped that our house in Massachusetts was one hundred years old, an impressive number to a kid just turning nine. My mother and a friend of hers went around the house knocking on walls, hoping to find a covered-over fireplace as a friend of theirs had found one. I was greatly intrigued.

In about 1965 my mother and I made our first visit to Old Sturbridge Village, an outdoor history museum in central Massachusetts. On that glorious spring day time seemed to stand as still as the motionless columns of smoke above the chimneys. The unpaved roads, the livestock, vehicles, and clothing all created a sense of other-worldliness. An early teen and incipient nerd, I was beguiled by the atmosphere of the place. For years afterward I drew the floor plans of buildings I had seen there and did sketches of furniture out of the souvenir photo booklet I bought.

This fantasy-of-the-past phase gave way to a new reality in the spring of my junior year in high school. A chance conversation at a Sunday school picnic landed me a summer job with the Berkshire County Historical Society, indexing historic buildings over an area of three or four towns. The last week of school I was carrying around a two-foot stack of books on architectural history; to complete the effect I should have had a safety strap on my eyeglasses and a pocket protector. Today those who knew me then assure me that I was not only weird but unbearably boring. In any case I plowed through those books and worked hard.

My mother was fond of quoting Auntie Mame's remark that "the whole world is a banquet and all the poor bastards are starving to death." My parents saw to it that we gorged: my siblings and I were saturated in Baroque music at home and at Tanglewood, in post-Impressionist painting at the Clark Art Institute, in contemporary dance at Jacob's Pillow, and dinner-table conversation that encompassed Tudor politics, theology, the Civil Rights movement, the war in Viet Nam. Like kids everywhere we assumed this home life was normal.

All this and a college summer job at Hancock Shaker Village have shaped my interest in social history and interdisciplinary study. A deep flaw in history museums today is their lack of breadth of background knowledge and range of inquiry. A well-done restoration or exhibit should allow free motion in connecting the local to the regional, national, and international, with cross-references beyond the obvious aesthetic and technological connections, to encompass literature, philosophy, politics, religion, even sex and sexuality. If history isn't used as context for making decisions today, why bother studying or preserving it?

From its beginnings in the nineteenth century, historic preservation in America has been shaped by gay men. It's obvious that we've been busy in the private sector during the recent decades of urban gentrification, but we've also been a major influence in history museums. I've been a history-museum professional since 1975. As a starry-eyed teenager I hoped to enter the curatorial field because of my appreciation of beautiful old things and the romance of the past. However, after college I entered the educational and administrative wings of the field and have remained there. This has shaped my perceptions considerably, so that I see objects, buildings, and landscapes as documents from which to understand, interpret, and teach a larger social history.

Through the 1980s, my former partner and I restored three Victorian houses in small mill towns in central Massachusetts and northeastern Connecticut. Doing serial restorations was not our intention. We were biding our time until we could afford a rural house. We purchased affordable houses that were in good historical condition as well as good physical shape. We removed later accretions, mostly post–World War II asbestos siding, aluminum storm windows, partitions, fake hardware-store paneling, and the like, leaving us with a house that was historically intact and in need of scrubbing, surface work, and painting. This meant we could get fine results on a shoe-string budget. When we would read about couples who spent fifteen years restoring a house, we recognized the advantages of being well informed in our choice of property. (This was usually expressed in uncharitable remarks like, "Why didn't those morons do their research before they bought!") As we polychromed the exteriors of these houses in appropriate colors, our neighbors often took note and began trying the approach on their houses. Two of our houses were in Southbridge, Massachusetts, a town fighting a declining economy, so I can't say our work inspired the blossoming of a restoration district. But our third house was in Putnam, Connecticut, also in economic decline, and our restoration work there did cause the neighborhood to perk up.

All my professional jobs have involved conducting preservation, interpreting scholarly restorations, and promoting the value of the built environment as context for understanding how we came to be what we are today. I've also been researching and writing social history. At Sturbridge I worked on the history of education, religion, politics, law, banking, and rural commerce. I worked on a lot of subjects at Strawbery Banke as well, but I'm most pleased to have collaborated with a community member to compile a three-hundred-page resource book on local black history from 1645 to 1970. In working on this project I made a point of calling attention to parallels between the experiences of black Americans and those of other minorities, including Jewish and gay Americans.

Gay people preserving straight history is akin to me, a suburban white boy, doing a black history project. But while gay people are simply *expected* to preserve straight history—after all, we've done it so well for so long—we are usually dismissed if we suggest that gay history be included. Even with properties that originated with gay men. Consider Beauport, Henry Davis Sleeper's house in Gloucester, Massachusetts, now owned and operated by the Society for the Preservation of New England Antiquities. There's no doubt that Sleeper was a major decorating queen: he single-handedly defined the look of interiors decorated with American antiques. Yet on my recent tour of Beauport it was never mentioned that Henry Sleeper, who's been dead for decades, was gay. Why would the truth be considered invasive or irrelevant?

Before it was state law in New Hampshire, I asked the board of Strawbery Banke to add sexual orientation to the Equal Opportunity Employer paragraph of its handbook. When they asked if I was making the request because of problems with other staff, I said, no, I was doing it to protect the institution from future bigotry. I asked them to contemplate the losses if everything done here by gay men were to disappear at the snap of a finger. Comprehending the scale of those contributions, they made the change.

Is preserving civil rights a form of historic preservation? Looking at the Constitution, I'd say yes. Looking at the grim realities of the past centuries, I'd say it's an *innovation!* When the Portsmouth city council held a public hearing on a proposed gay civil rights amendment, I presented myself in my best WASP ethnic costume (navy blazer, gray flannel trousers, boring necktie) and asked what I as a local historian might bring to the consideration of the issue. I cited the role of bigotry in the city's history, as attempts were made to limit or intimidate minorities. Three-quarters of the council was of Irish descent, so I illustrated my remarks using the Irish experience and noting the extraordinary contributions the Irish have made to the local culture. I suggested that we learn from the past and establish equal civil rights, liberty, and justice for all. I even caused some inadvertent hilarity by "coming out" as part Irish, a fact long suppressed in my own family's lore.

Design-Minded in the Mid-Atlantic States

THE MID-ATLANTIC REGION IS HOME to the enterprise typically deemed the origin of the historic preservation movement in the United States: the rescue of George Washington's estate by the Mount Vernon Ladies' Association of the Union in the 1850s. Another group of mostly women launched the Association for the Preservation of Virginia Antiquities in the 1880s. In the 1890s the Daughters of the American Revolution spearheaded the restoration of Independence Hall.

These culture-keeping ladies of the late nineteenth century had male collaborators, among them Henry Chapman Mercer. Born in 1856 in Doylestown, Pennsylvania, Mercer manifested a deep reverence for the past from a young age. Like many others, his interest in the material culture of his native region was stoked by the nation's centennial, with the grand exposition in nearby Philadelphia. The handsome young bachelor helped organize the Bucks County Historical Society in 1880 and became an ardent collector of whatever old things appealed to him—a miscellany of objects from the seventeenth, eighteenth, and early nineteenth centuries: quilts, signboards, clothing, pottery.

As Mercer was rummaging through a junk dealer's mass of obsolete tools one day to find a pair of old-fashioned fireplace tongs, it occurred to him that he was looking at a trove of archaeological evidence of preindustrial culture. Cast away for a generation or more, often in favor of mass-produced implements, these objects were disappearing as inexorably as had the tools of early humans thousands of years ago. Driven by the conviction that even the most prosaic artifacts were important links in Pennsylvania history, Mercer began scouring eastern Pennsylvania to make a systematic collection of such objects. In 1897 he issued a descriptive catalog of more than seven hundred items, *The Tools of the Nation Maker,* to accompany an exhibit at the Bucks County courthouse. In scientific fashion the catalog described each object and its Old World origins, specified the donor, and reported the folklore associated with its use, such as superstitions, songs, and rituals. With this carefully categorized and labeled exhibit and catalog, Mercer established himself as a pioneer in the sophisticated use of objects to portray the history of everyday life among ordinary people.

By 1914, having collected more than fifteen thousand objects of historical interest, Mercer turned his energies to making a museum building in Doylestown. He designed it around the collection and built it of reinforced concrete, with tiers of galleries around a high central atrium. Boats, wagons, baskets, cradles, gristmills, and other large objects were suspended above the courtyard and groups of smaller objects, from apple parers to anvils, were arranged by type in their display compartments below. The museum reflects the love of curiosity-clutter, the passion to preserve, and the mania for typology that characterized Mercer's Victorian-era imagination. Convinced that by studying its tools one could chart a culture's course, Mercer collected as many examples of each tool as he could find and displayed them in chronological sequence.

While the never-married Henry Mercer was engrossed in collecting and museum building in Doylestown, James Denholm Van Trump was growing up in Pittsburgh. Born in 1908, the artistic Van Trump was a shy and solitary student of his native city's history and architecture for the first half of his eighty-eight years. But with the destructive tumult of urban renewal in the 1950s, he metamorphosed into a visionary preservation pioneer, awakening his fellow Pittsburghers to their city's history as manifested in its architecture and landscapes. The activist in Van Trump emerged in 1953, when he issued a lonely cry to save Pittsburgh's soon-to-be-demolished city hall. He began to pour his long-accumulated knowledge and passion into poems, articles, and books on the buildings, architects, gardens, and communities of his home region. A founder of the Pittsburgh History and Landmarks Foundation, he became a local celebrity through his preservation ministrations on radio and television.

Having found his calling, Jamie Van Trump blossomed into this "Father Pittsburgh" role with enthusiasm and flair. He let his hair and side whiskers grow long and sported the hip, priestly garb of a turtleneck adorned with a cross on a gold chain. "The past is part of the life of the land, and we are interested only in preservation for life's sake," he declared. "The human heart desires the past which is, in the end, the anchor of man's dreams and his remembering."[1] Van Trump proclaimed his devotion to the past and to the past working in the present. "Many of the architects of the twentieth century are saying, 'Throw the past out and we will start all over again!' Everyone wants to *create*. As I see it, the architects should be doing rehabilitations as well as new creations. We live in a kind of cultural continuum, like a chain. We need a constant going back and forth from the present to the past. We have to have the past from which to move on."[2]

The historical/cultural continuum about which Van Trump was so impassioned captured Joseph Svehlak's imagination in childhood. First-generation American of Czech heritage, Svehlak has been a resident of New York City for most of the years since he was born in 1940. "Starting in 1957," he says, "I began to witness the destruction of so many fine old buildings. I began to question the stability of my known world, as areas that had meant something to me and my family—whole neighborhoods, including the streets themselves—were given over to modern development. My history was being obliterated before my eyes."

Svehlak found an outlet for his passion to preserve in the 1970s, buying and restoring three working-class row houses in the Brooklyn neighborhood where he grew up. "I was very interested in helping to save the neighborhood from further decline, and my old houses weren't the only things that needed fixing. There was a drug problem in the neighborhood, and city services needed improving. For more than fifteen years I was a community activist involved in preserving and promoting the neighborhood. I started the big neighborhood house tour: it got hundreds of people to come into the neighborhood each year, so they would find out about the community and some of them would eventually buy a house there."

Now a licensed tour guide, Svehlak leads tours for the Municipal Art Society—Grand Central Terminal, Rockefeller Center, the Flatiron District, Manhattan's Civic Center, Brooklyn Heights. "Not only am I doing architectural history; I'm doing social history: what old city neighborhoods were like, what's happening currently, and how things can be preserved and have a new life. Am I more sensitive to my environment because I'm gay? I don't know, but I do know that I enjoy making my tour-goers aware of what's around them and how fragile our built environment is. So I'm still an advocate for good city planning and design. To paraphrase Winston Churchill, we make our buildings and our buildings make us. Preserving one's environment is, in a way, self-preservation. Preserving a sense of place and our history and trying to hold onto some of the values that we had. In my last year of Catholic grammar school, I thought I wanted to be a teaching missionary. I guess I'm doing my missionary work with my tours."

A generation younger than Svehlak, Paul Daniel Marriott has been with the National Trust for Historic Preservation since 1993. He directs the Rural Heritage program, wrote *Saving Historic Roads,* and organized the first national conference on historic roads. Marriott's experience with the National Trust suggests that the longstanding design- and preservation-minded alliance of straight females and gay males thrives: "There's a joke at the Trust, that it's staffed by lots of gay men and divorced women," he says.

"If you look closely, it's not far from the truth. Like the design field, preservation is full of gay men."

The four individual narratives that follow illustrate the close relationship between historic preservation and design sensibilities. Urban preservationist Ken Lustbader pays close attention to how things are looking in his New York City neighborhood and advocates planning and design that respect the city's complex and many-layered historical fabric. As a child, artist James Nocito was enchanted by the historical layers of his Pennsylvania hometown, "a rich Colonial past overlaid with the more recent history of coal mining." Nocito remains fascinated by the aesthetics of layers: "decomposing surfaces that look like they're peeling away, old patinas, and lacquers that look like they've been worked over by time." Architectural historian Dwight Young's love of elegant design leads him to his current collecting passion, ocean-liner memorabilia. Architect Greg Kinsman says, "Gay men I know who have preservation interests and values similar to mine have a strong concern for visual aesthetics."

Ken Lustbader

Ken Lustbader was born in 1961 and grew up in a suburban tract house in Valley Stream, Long Island. From 1994 to 2002 he worked at the New York Landmarks Conservancy, a private nonprofit preservation organization based in New York City. As director of the Sacred Sites Program, Lustbader was "the church person," providing technical and financial assistance to religious properties throughout the state. He now works as a preservation consultant.

AS A CHILD I HAD A GREAT INTEREST in buildings and architecture, sketching floor plans of three-bedroom suburban houses and building Lego and balsa models of houses on Saturday afternoons. I was fascinated by our relatives' incredible old homes in Brooklyn and was unaware of any similar buildings in my neighborhood. The old main street in Valley Stream was dramatically altered in the 1950s when they built a shopping mall right behind where we lived. I was intrigued by photographs that contrasted the old and the new. At the orthodontist's office I discovered a children's book about a family that finds a run-down old house and renovates it. The illustration at the end of the book is a view from above, showing the house all cleaned up and the roof patched. I went through that book over and over.

At Vassar College I took courses in art history, architectural history, and drafting. But I never really thought that I would be an architect or do anything in that regard. After finishing a bachelor's in economics, I worked in my family's retail shoe business, in which I had worked since high school. We were very busy through the 1980s, opening stores in downtown shopping districts in New York City and New Jersey.

Working on the nineteenth-century buildings in which we were opening stores, I sometimes found myself exploring the upper floors that had been sealed off years before, when the staircase was ripped out to open up more retail space on the first floor. It was fascinating to climb through a small access hatch into a second-floor space that was like a time capsule, with the old store fixtures and counters and cabinetry and signage stashed away. I would stand there trying to imagine the original configuration of the space, how it had been used, and who had been there before. This detective work was far more emotionally compelling for me than was installing our store's new nylon carpet and cheap paneling. Nor did I get aesthetic satisfaction from ripping out the old storefront and putting up our giant twenty- by ten-foot sign, which covered the second-floor windows.

After seven years of this work I couldn't see myself in the retail business for the rest of my life. I had friends in preservation who had gone to Columbia University, and I had a hunch that maybe I could do it. When I was thirty-one, I had a meal with a friend—we've called it my epiphany dinner—at which I made the decision to apply to Columbia's master's in historic preservation program.

I started at Columbia thinking I would become a building conservator, but I had a professor who was very enlightening: Historic preservation is not about bricks and mortar, he said. It's a radical profession that can convey social history. He stressed how the documentation of buildings had to expand beyond the architectural mode of placing values on structures. We discussed the presentation of African American history and the development of Chinatown in New York, where the buildings were not built by the Chinese, but are layered and have Chinese-style lettering and so forth.

I was perturbed to find that the New York City Landmarks Preservation Commission's designation report for Greenwich Village didn't say anything about gays and lesbians, just "bohemians." Although I understood that it had been written in 1969, I got a bee in my bonnet: With all these walking tours of the Village, whose history are they really presenting, and what are they omitting out of ignorance? I did my thesis on the issues of how to use the built environment to convey the history of gay people, people who were covert because of police suppression and societal pressure but who clearly had their meeting places. George Chauncey had written his doctoral thesis on gay life in New York (the basis of his book, *Gay New York*), so I was able to get a lot of information from him about the locations of bars and restaurants and other meeting spots before World War II.

This was in 1992 and 1993, just before the twenty-fifth anniversary of the Stonewall Rebellion, so there was a great deal of interest in the topic. No one had really written about preservation and gay history before. After my thesis was completed, I helped a group called REPOhistory, who were putting up signs in the Village marking such places as the site of the Stonewall Rebellion in 1969 and the site where, in 1966, activists pushed the limits of the state law that made it illegal for bartenders to serve openly gay customers. The REPOhistory signs could stay up for only six months because of city rules, but it was an affirmation of the ability to convey gay and lesbian history through the built environment. I also worked with the Organization of Lesbian and Gay Architects and Designers (OLGAD) to produce a map of sites of significance to gay and lesbian history and did my own walking tours for OLGAD, the Greenwich Village Society for Historic Preservation, and the Municipal Art Society. We also started working on getting Stonewall listed in the National Register. It's now a National Historic Landmark.

I'm the keeper of my family's history. When my parents moved recently, I took possession of all the family photographs. My grandparents came
from Poland and Austria around 1910. That's as far back as I know. I have a
few late-nineteenth-century images of my great-grandparents, but when I
asked my relatives about them, they couldn't tell me anything. There's no
sense of historical continuity in my family, and my parents and brother don't
understand my historical interests.

I'm Jewish and grew up in a very Jewish community. Though my upbringing was very secular, I have developed great affection for old synagogues
and churches. Many of them are so magnificent and monumental. But the
part of the job that I like the most is the connection that these buildings have
to people—the people who worship there and care for the building, the people
who are running the soup kitchens and day-care centers, being community
anchors. We get calls from people throughout the state, wanting to save a
house of worship that's been abandoned. But most of our work is with small,
active congregations who want to know how to maintain their heavily used
buildings and don't have the know-how or funding.

"You think I'm just dealing with buildings," I joke with my lover, a
psychotherapist. "I deal with people's personalities all day, just like you do.
I'm a social worker for people and their buildings." There's so much psycho-
drama connected with buildings, especially religious buildings, people's sacred spaces. I think of my role in preservation as an educator and facilitator.
I build relationships with people and teach them how to appreciate something old, how to look at it differently, and how to take care of it.

You find a lot of gay men in preservation, just as you do in social
work. Perhaps so many of us are drawn to preservation because it's much
more fluid and intuitive and emotional than pure architecture. In preservation there's a level of connection to buildings and neighborhoods that's
more visceral and connected to understanding people. Preservation is about
community, context, and who was there before. There are so many of these
cultural and associational histories. After decades of preservation based on
architectural significance, people are recognizing the complexity of these
issues and pushing the boundaries of preservation. I deal with synagogues,
for example, that are not very significant architecturally but that have associational histories of incredible value. Similarly, my boss wrote a letter of
support for getting the site of the Stonewall Rebellion into the National
Register.

There has been talk at the Landmarks Preservation Commission that
their new designation reports will include relevant gay and lesbian history.
There's even been discussion about going back and rewriting the Greenwich
Village designation so that it expands on "bohemians" to specifically cite gays

and lesbians. (I find it rather ironic that gay men, a group whose history has been so undocumented, play such a major role in preserving American architectural and social histories.) My dream is to make a documentary on the gay history of Greenwich Village from the perspective of the built environment. One of my professors at Columbia once asked if I thought the Village has been so well preserved because so many gay men have lived there for so long. Though I can't answer that with certainty, I do know that I'm on the board of my Greenwich Village co-op because I want to have a say in how things are running and how my neighborhood is looking. And many of my fellow board members are also gay.

James Nocito

Born in 1960, visual artist James Nocito grew up in the coal-mining country of northeast Pennsylvania. *Found Lives: A Collection of Found Photographs* is a small volume of human images selected by Nocito from the thousands of abandoned photographs that he has gathered and preserved through the first decades of his adulthood. "What were these people doing?" Nocito asks in the book's introduction. "What were their relationships to one another? Who was behind the camera and what was he or she seeing at that moment? These pictures reveal their secrets slowly or not at all."[3]

AN ECCENTRIC FRIEND THAT I MET at a summer arts program in high school gave me my first found photo. I really liked her, but she was a bit of an outsider and very neurotic: she read Camus, was obsessed with Sylvia Plath, and wore her grandmother's sweaters. Even so, I found it truly strange that she would fixate on this picture of a person she never knew, someone presumably dead. It was a picture of a foreign-looking soldier, stern and proud beyond his years and height, both comical and frightening. It was an object whose value had expired, as meaningless as a stranger's memories. Yet there was a humanity about the picture of that little guy that was haunting to me.

I began to wonder: How did he manage in the war? How was he treated by the other soldiers? Did he return home? Was this picture taken before he left home or after he returned? Asking myself those sorts of questions got me going on collecting more pictures, really taking a good hard look and seeing what's going on in them beyond the first glance. I would find them at garage sales, secondhand stores, flea markets, antique stores. Every once in a while I'd hit a mother lode with a photo album, but mostly it was one here and one there over many years. I got more and more avid about collecting them, and now I have tens of thousands organized in different categories, boxes and boxes of them.

While I was trying to figure out what to do with my pictures, I spent a lot of time with them, often coming up with stories to go with them. But when I first put the book together, I wrote only a title for each picture. One of the comments I got as I sent it around to publishers was that there was nothing to read. That made me realize that I really did have stories for all those people; I just hadn't written them down yet.

Growing up, I liked to pore over our family photos, but when I was twelve we lost that box of pictures in a flood. They were mostly of my immediate family, a few of my parents when they were children, and of my grandparents. I remember my mother saying after the flood, "Everything else is just stuff, but the *pictures*—we've lost the pictures." I think that's part of what drew me to collecting photos, wondering about the people in them, seeing what stories I could create, what gaps I could fill in.

On her dresser my mother had a picture of her father, who had passed away when she was quite young. Because he was dead long before I came around, it was always a very powerful little image in its round frame. Especially when we lost the rest of the pictures, it became an important icon. It was never mentioned, but it was imbued with so much meaning and value, you wouldn't dream of moving it from its place.

We lived in a 1960s tract house and didn't have a lot of money, certainly no fabulous antiques. My folks bought new things; new was good. You knocked down old houses; you trashed old furniture. My father was first-generation Italian American: you assimilated and you got new stuff because old stuff was just going to break. My mother had more of a sense of tradition, and she had some things that had been passed down to her.

I bought some old magazines at an estate sale near our house. Just the fact that they were old was enough for me. There was some kind of connection I was making when I was in the presence of something old, something with an accumulation of history or wisdom inherent in it. I'm not quite clear on what that connection was, but I really did seek it out. I had the same feeling about the few old things that my folks had, a chair and some jewelry of my mother's and some old coins of my father's. But it always seemed like I could never really get my hands on much of it. There was such a scarcity of that sort of thing, which only made me pine for it more.

There weren't any antique stores around, except for one about ten miles away, in Kingston. Too young to drive, I would have had to get a ride, and I could never manage that. Riding my bike that far would have been kind of ridiculous, but I tried, then gave up, and turned around. If I could just get myself to an antique store! Somehow I knew that it would be the place for me, that I would find all the answers there. In high school I finally made it to the one in Kingston, where I bought some keys and magazines. It turned out to be a little junkier than I had imagined.

The pickings were so slim where I was brought up. I wanted to find an arrowhead more than anything in the world, and it seemed like there just weren't any more to be found. Finding an arrowhead would have been a moment of that electricity that happens even now when I find photographs. The same as when I would find a fossil or a nice quartz when I was little. This may sound weird, but it feels something like a divine intervention: this thing I'm finding is meant for me. When I come across a picture, it still feels that way. So, when I find a photograph I'm not just connecting with history and with the people in the photo; I'm connecting with something in my own childhood.

I started keeping a journal when I was in sixth or seventh grade. I still have them all, God help me, and I still keep a journal. When I was growing up my journals were like scrapbooks. I drew and painted in them, pasted in poems and pictures of artworks or nature that I would cut from newspapers and magazines. And I've collected quotes since I was young, when I would put them together in books.

There's a picture in *Found Lives* of two boys standing in a stream, glowing in the sun. I found that one during a trip to Hawaii. At the only antique store in all of Kauai, there were four snapshots sitting in a little dish, and this was one of them. I nearly fell over. On that same trip I found a book of quotations with the lines from Wordsworth about being "apparelled in celestial light." That photo and those lines were just meant to be together. It was that wonderful feeling you get when it's all been prearranged, fated.

The place where I was raised had this dichotomy of a rich Colonial past overlaid with the more recent history of coal mining. I was really drawn to the Colonial part, and the old hitching posts that I'd see around were a tie to that period, like the old houses. I wanted to possess one of those hitching posts, something authentic, a remnant of a very different time.

I loved that my paternal great-grandmother was with us for so long. She died when I was in college, a teeny-tiny Italian relic who spoke very broken English. When I was in high school and would go to her house to visit, she would shower me with kisses. After a minute or two of conversation her vocabulary would be exhausted, and we would just sit together without talking. I had never experienced that with anyone else, the comfort of being able to just be silent with someone.

I also liked spending time with my grandmother, who lived across the street from my great-grandmother. We would cook raviolis together. I liked her old stone house because of its hand-built qualities. My grandfather, who died before I was born, built much of it himself. There was a canning cellar with jars of weird stuff that seemed like they had been there since the days of Mussolini. I loved that the place was old and that it had been around so long, but it was a little spooky because it was so raw, and it had an aura of hypermasculinity that was off-putting. I knew that deer had been dragged through the yard, gutted and butchered, and there was a special shower for the men down in the basement. It was pretty hardcore Italian male, a scene that I knew I wasn't really party to.

During my college years in Pittsburgh I was intrigued by archaeologi-cal excavations. The paintings I did then looked like they had been hacked away or scratched out: I would pile on a whole bunch of paint and excavate the surface until I came up with something. Today the passage of time and the nature of memory are important themes in my artwork. I'm really drawn to layers, decomposing surfaces that look like they're peeling away, old pati-nas, and lacquers that look like they've been worked over by time. I'm also attracted to scenes that could have been painted today or two hundred years ago. I'm drawn to that in life, too—contemporary landscapes where every-thing you see could have been there two centuries ago. I've found these seemingly timeless places in the forests of Pennsylvania and in remote coastal areas of northern California.

My boyfriend, Sal, gets a bunch of flowers from the farmers' market each week and puts together arrangements for the house. Invariably the one that comes out best is the bathroom arrangement made of the leftover cut-tings. He just kind of puts them together in a little vase (he collects old art pottery), doesn't really fuss over it. For his birthday recently I secretly did a painting of each of Sal's weekly "leftover" bouquets for a year and put them in an album. There was something about collaborating with him in that way that I enjoyed, creating a record of his evanescent endeavor, tracking the passage of the seasons. I was marking the passage of time and gathering memories that might be lost. Which is really what collecting the photographs is all about. I'm giving these abandoned, leftover, "worthless" pictures an-other life, noticing things in them that had been overlooked, finding all kinds of meaning in them.

The photographs that totally get me are the ones with the person's handwriting on the back. There's a picture in *Found Lives* of two women dancing together, and on the back of the picture is written "1930" and this note: "My guest for seven weeks who returned to her home in Havana, Cuba, for Thanksgiving. She is a rare delight—." The woman who's looking at the camera is presumably the writer of these words. She looks kind of prim, with her little collar and sensible haircut, and she lives in a place that reminds me of Pittsburgh. It's autumn in 1930, the leaves have fallen from the trees, and there's some snow on the ground. Into her dour world comes this tall, thin woman who wears a cape and dances with her in the backyard. God, what a wonderful treat that must have been! And here's this beautiful record of when these two dear friends got together.

Dwight Young

Born in 1944, Dwight Young grew up and went to college in Lubbock, Texas. With a degree in English literature and American history, he taught English for two years overseas, then returned to the United States. He lives in Washington, D.C., where he works for the National Trust for Historic Preservation.

I'VE ALWAYS BEEN A HISTORY BUFF. My grandmother was a great saver of family photographs, and I enjoyed looking at them with her. I often asked my grandparents to tell me about their own lives, what they remembered and what they had experienced. My grandmother told me the same stories over and over, but I still delighted in hearing them.

The part of Texas where I grew up was relatively new and raw. Lubbock wasn't even founded until around the turn of the last century, so it seemed very new to me. I liked the idea that there were places that had a much longer recorded history. When I came back from overseas, living in Richmond, Virginia, was a real watershed experience, my first intimation of the connection between history and place. It was the first time I'd ever lived anyplace where I was surrounded by tangible connections with events that I'd read about in history books. The state capitol in Richmond, the church where Patrick Henry delivered his "Give me liberty or give me death" speech, Civil War battlefields—being able to visit and physically touch those places was a life-changing revelation.

One morning I drove out to the battlefield at Beaver Dam Creek, the site of fierce fighting during the Seven Days Campaign that raged around Richmond in the summer of 1862. I stood there with a guidebook in my hand, and I could *see* it. Right here, next to this mound where I was standing, were the Union trenches. And over there was the hillside where the Confederates had charged out of the woods, running down the slope to the creek, firing their rifles and yelling in the summer heat. I could see it all; it was real.

Another day I went to Saint Paul's Church downtown and, after a few minutes of searching, found the pew I was looking for. I sat in it and thought: This is where Jefferson Davis was sitting on a Sunday morning in 1865 when someone crept in and told him that Petersburg, Virginia, had fallen and Richmond was doomed. Right in this building, here on this very spot. The fact that I could see and walk through these places, could touch the nicks and grooves where history had bumped against them, impressed me enormously. I'm convinced that this is one of the most important reasons why we choose to preserve old buildings and neighborhoods: These places permit us to have tactile encounters with the past. History stops being just an idea, a scrap of story, or a page in a book and is transformed into a thing with solidity and texture, something you can connect with, something you can touch—a brick wall, an iron railing, a pane of glass, a grassy trench, a church pew.

For a time in my youth I loved the idea of becoming an architect, but I had a very rarefied idea of what architects did. After finding out that they had to do much more than sit around and sketch buildings that somebody else then translated into bricks and mortar, and that it involved a working knowledge of things like engineering and mathematics, I quickly determined that it was not the career for me. I became a building watcher rather than a building designer. Then one day in east Tennessee, where I was working as a hospital administrator, I read in the newspaper that a team from the University of Virginia was coming to the county I lived in to do a survey of historic architecture. I was astonished. I had no idea anyone did that for a living, and I thought it sounded wonderful. So I got a master's degree in architectural history at the University of Virginia.

As soon as I got my degree, I was hired as director of the city preservation agency in Mobile, Alabama. After a year there I was hired in 1977 by the National Trust for Historic Preservation to open their southern regional office in Charleston, South Carolina. I've been with the Trust ever since, in a variety of jobs. Currently I'm sort of the utility writer at the Trust, and I love it. I write speeches for the president, newspaper and magazine articles, press releases, and brochure copy and that sort of thing, in addition to my column in *Preservation* magazine, "The Back Page."

I think I'm genetically predisposed to be a collector, though I'm not even sure anymore that I'm really a collector. I think I'm just an accumulator. I love secondhand books and antiques of the past century, from the turn of the century through the 1940s. I collect all kinds of stuff, especially pottery, but my current passion is ocean-liner memorabilia. I delight in finding artifacts from the great liners of the twenties, thirties, forties, and even fifties, particularly paper: menus, letterheads, passenger lists, that sort of thing. One of the two big ocean-liner memorabilia shows of the year is taking place in Maryland this weekend, and I'm already getting shaky and slobbery at the thought.

So much of the ocean-liner stuff is so beautifully designed, and there's a wonderful quality to the artwork in the menus and the letterheads. Also, I love the pieces that passengers have scribbled notes on or passed around the dining table and had everybody sign their names to. There are collectors of paper ephemera who demand that the items they acquire be pristine, but I'm always delighted by things that have been written on. The names don't mean anything to me, but I love having that connection with a moment when somebody picked up a pen or a pencil and wrote his or her name on this piece of paper, which I'm now holding in my hand.

I'm also intrigued by these things because they represent a world that is absolutely vanished. There were fleets of these ships crossing the ocean and now they're *gone*. I regret having missed out on ocean-liner travel: I came along too late and was born too poor. But I have drawers and boxes full of things that link me to that world, a world that's as fully and finally vanished as the eighteenth century.

I've sometimes wondered if it's dishonest to call myself a preservationist, since I have never done rehabilitation work on an old building, but I've decided it's not. I'm perfectly content and justified in urging other people to do that work while realizing that it's not part of my nature at all. I have a low tolerance for plaster dust and that sort of thing. I have friends who glory in it, who enjoy the rehabilitation process so much that as soon as they finish a house they want to sell it and move on, do the same thing all over again. I find that wonderfully inspiring and totally appalling. Fortunately for our architectural heritage, there are lots of people who are not only willing but eager to do that.

My first job with the National Trust was fabulous. It gave me an excuse to live in Charleston, which is one of the great cities in the country, and it legitimized what I would otherwise have done for fun—traveling around the South looking at old buildings and talking to people who were trying to find ways to save them. It seemed inevitable that in every southern town I'd go to, the people who were showing me around would take me to the home of a gay man in the community. He was typically the florist or undertaker or something like that, and his house was frequently the most lavishly decorated or it had the longest historical pedigree. My hosts would want me to see it because it had been so beautifully restored, it was so well cared for, and all that sort of thing. I got the sense that the South was populated with an enormous number of gay men living quiet, largely closeted lives in these wonderful old houses. Such a person might have a reputation in the community as being artistic or cultured, strange, different, but he was tolerated and maybe even thought of affectionately as the town queer, for lack of a more genteel term. Everybody knew he was "that way," but that didn't matter as long as he didn't bother people. And anyway, hadn't he done a wonderful thing with the old Jones house. He'd made it beautiful.

All of this was going on before I really recognized my own gayness. I was married and had children and was living a pretty "straight" life (with great big quotation marks, because I knew what was going on in my head, though it wasn't going on anywhere else). I looked on these preservationist men that I was meeting pretty much as their neighbors did: as rather endearing curiosities. My feelings of kinship with them came later, when I acknowledged that I was gay and realized that these men were my brothers, all over the country.

It isn't exactly news, though we've sometimes treated it as if it were a secret best left undiscussed, that gays have traditionally been in the vanguard of efforts to revitalize historic neighborhoods. In city after city the first sign that a shabby block might be on the brink of rebirth has been the appearance of new residents driving cars with pink-triangle or rainbow-flag bumper stickers, emblems of gay pride. And if you go on many historic-district house tours, chances are you're no longer surprised to find that the beautiful Victorian row house you've been admiring was restored by a male couple. Could it be that gay men have an intrinsic preference for older neighborhoods, just as they have a gift for biting wit, an ear for show tunes, and a knack for knockout window treatments?

I don't go out much on weekends, but whenever I do there's almost always a moment when a gay man says or does something that strikes me as thoroughly witty or delightful or outrageous, and I'm immediately seized by the thought, God, the world is so lucky to have gay people in it! What a gray, dull, cotton-wool place it would be if we weren't here. Many people still aren't ready to recognize that we're *wonderful,* but I think more and more people are recognizing that having us around is a good thing. Not only for the general level of wit and humor but also in more tangible ways, like neighborhoods made into more beautiful and livable places.

Saving old buildings and neighborhoods is something we do because we need to. I love old buildings just because they are so good to look at. I'm fascinated by the materials and the intricacy of detail and the workmanship and all the things that make them different from the buildings that were put up before them and the ones that have been put up since. But beyond that visual delight, I believe there is a fundamental need in the human psyche for some assurance of permanence and continuity. Saving old buildings and neighborhoods is an enormously effective way to make that continuity manifest in the places where we live.

Greg Kinsman

Greg Kinsman is an architect who lives in the Shenandoah Valley and is currently employed by a preservation organization in Washington, D.C. In his job he helps private owners of historic buildings and farms figure out how to preserve them. (All persons in this narrative have been given pseudonyms at the subject's request.)

I GREW UP ON SEVERAL FARMS in northeast Ohio in the 1950s and 1960s. My father would buy a farm and make improvements to it, then sell it and move on to another farm. In addition to the farmhouses in which we lived, my parents would buy, fix up, and sell other houses, some from the mid- to late-1800s. My brother, sister, and I were the slave labor to help with the grunt work on weekends. But I enjoyed going into those old houses and hauling out the junk, cleaning things up, painting. Sometimes I'd find little treasures, antiques or old newspapers or books. My sister and brother, both younger than I, were often too busy with sports and Scouting to be of much help, but I had the time. I often went to auctions with my parents and was always wondering, what's our next adventure?

One of the oldest of these investment properties was from the 1840s or 1850s, a big Greek Revival house on a large corner lot in the county seat. There were lots of houses from the 1820s through the 1850s in the area and a lot more from after the Civil War. I was aware of these things as a child and was fascinated with the older farmhouses and the older sections of the cities and some of the smaller towns in the area. I loved to draw designs of individual houses or little cities. Sometimes I would draw real houses, sometimes imaginary ones.

After undergraduate architecture school in Cleveland, it was on to Boston. While attending night classes at Boston Architectural Center, I worked as the office boy in a major firm that had a great interest in finding new uses for old buildings. They restored the exterior of Faneuil Hall Marketplace and did a massive restoration of the Hotel Vendome in the Back Bay. A large French Second Empire building, it had been one of Boston's luxury hotels in the late nineteenth century and had survived hard times in the mid-twentieth century. Though I was not yet an architect, I got involved in building the design model for an addition to replace a portion of the hotel that had collapsed as the result of a horrific fire.

From Boston I moved to Maine, where a small firm had hired me to be their draftsman. We worked in a grand old ice baron's house along the

Kennebec River. But before long I was back in Ohio for graduate study in preservation at Ohio State. I got a lot of summer contract work through the Ohio Historical Society, doing architectural inventory surveys. I would travel around and photograph buildings, write up the architectural descriptions, then do research on them in the county courthouses. I documented hundreds of buildings this way. Some of the projects were the result of some stupid freeway going through, so I had to do the inventory work on several different corridors while someone else did the archaeology. One project was for a proposed power plant site along the Ohio River. It was disconcerting to be preparing what felt like postmortem reports on old buildings that were not yet dead.

After graduate school I was a regional historic preservation officer in a rural area of north-central Ohio. It was wonderful working in those seven counties. I did lots of inventory work and National Register work, focusing on the county seats, trying to get the major centers documented, but I was also struck by the incredibly beautiful farms throughout the counties. Like a circuit preacher I did a lot of public speaking: Rather than tearing everything down, why don't we think about keeping some things? Identify them and figure out if they have intrinsic value, then figure out if they can be rehabilitated, and then try to do it.

I went to work for the National Park Service, then got into private-sector practice in San Francisco, then moved back east to begin my current job. I had friends in the Shenandoah Valley and was interested in finding a home here. I fell in love with a mid-nineteenth-century Greek Revival house in the downtown historic district of this small town. The house was move-in-able, but the kitchen and bathrooms needed redoing, and the interior finishes and features have needed a lot of work. I've tried to locate the best-skilled people to do it.

I've always had a sense of being somewhat apart and, because of that, being able to evaluate what things mean and if something has lasting value and is worth keeping. How intelligent was the design, what sort of materials were used, and what was the quality of the handwork that went into making the thing? I want all three of these elements to be at a high level. And then there's the sense of history, the documentary aspect of an old building or object being a witness to a particular time or a series of times and having some story to tell.

Many of my friends are gay men who are devoted architectural preservationists, or they're antique collectors of some sort, or both. I don't know whether it's looking back and trying to recapture something, or just appreciating something that's survived. The crowd I run with in town, we've been talking about starting a special twelve-step program that I have termed

Antique and Art Collectors Anonymous. We're all fetished about something. I collect bronzes, one of my friends loves silver, and another is a fan of original paint finishes. A good friend here in the valley loves to buy total wrecks of cars, junk-pile things, and restore them. He is absolutely meticulous. He also does houses.

Gay men I know who have preservation interests and values similar to mine have a strong concern for visual aesthetics. Think of the "bachelor" artists moving into neglected urban neighborhoods, finding the abandoned or disused buildings, and creating something beautiful out of them. San Francisco is one of the key places where gay guys have been doing this. Back in the 1970s and 1980s, there was a "tart, fluff, and flip" routine out there. You would buy a dog of a house, tart it and fluff it, then flip it, sell it for a profit, and move on to the next one. Lots of guys were doing that, including some of my old friends.

There are lots of gay men who fall in love with houses. Among some of my friends, taking on an old house and carrying it forward really means something. A friend of mine in Cleveland is a real hands-on guy who's been taking on dogs of properties in older neighborhoods, inner-city areas that were more or less forgotten. He's the urban type. My friends Mike and Jim here in the valley are the rural type, buying and restoring dogs of abandoned houses way out in the sticks, houses that no one has lived in for decades. The reality of what gay men do with old buildings is finally being acknowledged by the mainstream preservation movement: the real doers of the movement are not just little old ladies in tennis shoes but also gay men in 501s.

In the fall of 1998 my friend Timothy and I made an appointment to see a house that we had been curious about for some time after seeing an ad in the local real-estate magazine. It was on a country road on the way to Mike and Jim's eighteenth-century stone houses south of here. The exterior was rather plain, and the place looked a little tired, but the interior was absolutely astounding, with late Georgian/Federal woodwork that was just incredible. It was a typical five-bay, center-hall, two-and-a-half-story, gable-roofed house with end chimneys and a handsome cornice. Inside were incredible paneled fireplace walls and a massive staircase that went all the way to the third floor.

The house was built about 1801 for a Scots-Irish Presbyterian widow, and its last owner was also a widow. It was an extremely well built house with solid brick walls. Though it was very restrained on the outside, the lady who built it obviously wanted a very stylish place inside. Timothy and I went to see it as more of a lark than a real-estate venture, and we both fell in love with it. But I was being cautious and rational because of the economics. They were asking $225,000, and the house needed a lot of work.

We spent much of that autumn examining the house and its seven-acre grounds, which included the eighteenth-century, two-story stone springhouse, the slave kitchen and quarters, the remains of the boxwood hedges, and the slave cemetery at the back of the property. Mike and Jim fell in love with the place, but Jim was already working on his third house. He said, "This one's for you, Greg." When I would bring in my contractor friends, they would roll their eyes. They could see only the expenses and the effort.

With the help of an appraiser we made an offer around Thanksgiving that was well below the asking price. It was accepted. In exploring the contingencies we determined that the water was not potable, the septic system was a big mystery, the slate roof was failing, the electrical system needed work, and the heating system was laughed at by our contractor. So there was much more that we would have to deal with. We withdrew our offer in January 1999, and through that winter we went around and around on what our next offer would be.

On Easter Sunday I decided to drive by the house. Coming down the road, I was shocked to see sky where I should have seen the roof of the house. There had been a fire. It was so horrible, I couldn't look at it; I had to keep going. I got back home and just sat, stunned. Timothy came out from Washington the next weekend and wanted to drive by the place. I told him I would never go down that road again. I was so emotionally wrapped up in that house, imagining it, thinking about designs—how to do the various rooms, the systems, what to do with the outbuildings. It was as if the building had become a person, a man with whom I was infatuated, and now he was dead and badly mutilated. I knew every part of him, but I never realized a relationship with him. I'll sometimes wake up at night walking through the rooms of that house, seeing every detail. My lost place that I never really had.

I have lots of photographs of the place, but I can't look at them. I'm going to give them to the county historical society. The last widow who lived there was an active amateur genealogist, so there's a file cabinet filled with her stuff, including thick files on the house. The property was one of those early grants at the beginning of European settlement. The house was noted in the National Register as having one of the most significant wood interiors in the county, incredibly well preserved. The woodwork was highly and finely carved, and it had been gently handled through its entire life.

One of those almost-virgin survivors that had come down to us, the house had been carefully preserved by the ladies who had owned it. The 1950s widow did very little to it, a new kitchen and bathroom in a small wing that she added on, electrical wiring, and a heating system. Timothy heard that the fire was caused by an electrical malfunction. Later the story in some circles in the area was that a disgruntled relative started the fire. I don't know the true story. The autumn before the fire, a back door at the house was repeatedly kicked in. The real-estate agents were hardly concerned, but it seems to me now that someone was sending prospective buyers a message: "Danger! Don't come here!"

For a while I felt an incredible sense of failure for not taking on the house and carrying it forward. It had survived almost two hundred years, and the work that we were going to do should have carried it through at least another century. But I might be dead if I had been living in the house at the time of the fire. So there were conflicted feelings of guilt, remorse, regret, and relief. I felt anger too. Anger at myself and anger at the absentee owner, who had spent nothing on the property in the years since the widow had died and left it to him. And anger at the real-estate people who did nothing to secure the house. If they had really wanted to sell that property, they could have advertised it in the *Washington Post* or some of the preservation periodicals, and it would have been snapped up right away, probably at the asking price.

Don't go looking for a beautiful old house unless you're ready to move quickly. I was trying to be cautious and rational about it, because it was a big chunk of change for me: I offered $170,000 but figured that at least $100,000 more would have to go into it right away, unless I was willing to camp in it and do things gradually. Camping indoors is how Mike and Jim do many of their properties, but they have more fortitude than I. My method is to think through the project in terms of the design and systems, work with the contractors in problem solving, and then my major job is to write out the checks. To be truthful, gardening is the most satisfying work for me, because I can see the beginning and the end of a project in the same day.

When I was in high school, I worked on genealogy, tried to get the facts of my family down as best I could determine them. I talked with my grandmother and uncles and aunts, asking them who was what to whom. I wrote to various places, gathering data, and tried to put it all together. My great-grandfather was a rather successful dairy farmer in Ohio and Pennsylvania from the late nineteenth century into the early twentieth. There's an old photograph of his family, he and his wife standing in front of their beautiful brick Federal-period house of two and a half stories, with center hall, five bays. My great-grandfather once lived in a fine house just like the lost house I almost rescued.

To the Rescue in the Atlantic South

PROBABLY THE MOST FAMOUS GAY PRESERVATIONIST in America is Georgia native Jim Williams. A central figure in John Berendt's best-selling book, *Midnight in the Garden of Good and Evil,* Williams died in 1990. Born sixty years earlier in a small town near Macon, young Williams was smitten by old-fashioned things. In his teens he rode his bicycle in search of antiques. He would buy old oil lamps, mirrors, and pieces of furniture, fix them up in his workshop, then sell them by advertising in the local paper. Wealthy women from Macon were known to get Williams out of school so that he could take them to the house, where he sold antiques out of his bedroom.

Even as a teenager, Williams realized that much of Georgia's heritage was being destroyed, with many abandoned old houses being torn down or allowed to go to ruin. Recalling his exploration of one of the first houses to grip his imagination, Williams wrote, "Few places have held such a powerful psychic intrigue for me. . . . Where were these souls once vibrant and so alive? . . . Where was continuity?"[1]

About 170 miles southeast of Williams's hometown, Savannah lay moldering through the 1940s. The old center of cotton commerce had been growing shabby for years before Williams was born. With the proliferation of automobiles after 1910, the city's gracious public squares were often targeted for elimination in favor of uninterrupted thoroughfares and more parking space. Many of its great houses were badly deteriorated, and the privations of the war years intensified the toll. In 1946 Lady Astor likened Savannah to "a beautiful lady with a dirty face" when she visited the city.

Williams fell in love with scruffy Savannah. He moved there in the summer of 1952 and opened an antiques shop. He was twenty-one, the city was filled with blighted architectural masterpieces in need of rescue, and there were only the faint beginnings of a preservation effort. "In those days," Williams said, "people like me, with a love for taking old houses and putting them back into shape, were considered a little eccentric."[2]

"The old part of town had become a slum," said one of Savannah's preservation-minded women. "The banks had red-lined the whole area. The great old houses were falling into ruin or being demolished to make way for gas stations and parking lots, and you couldn't borrow any money from the banks to go in and save them. Prostitutes strolled along the streets. Couples with children were afraid to live downtown, because it was considered dangerous. One thing we did do, we got the bachelors interested."[3]

Williams was one of the city's bachelors, confirmed as well as concerned, but he would have scoffed at the suggestion that his interest in revitalizing old Savannah was sparked by the women of the city. He had refurbished antiques and sold them to the ladies of Macon as a teenager, just as he was selling antiques and interior design services to the citizens of Savannah from his shop on East Broad Street.

Savannah's nascent preservationists were riled by the razing of City Market in 1954 to make way for a parking ramp. When Davenport House, a rundown rooming house at the time, was targeted for demolition in 1955, Historic Savannah Foundation got started. The official story in Savannah is that seven ladies—outraged, courageous, and fiercely resolved—joined together to save the 1820 Federal-style house and found the organization. As is typical, the uncommon men who worked with the ladies have been edited out of the story.

Jim Williams worked side by side with the women of Historic Savannah Foundation as they scrambled to rescue many old buildings, with very limited funds. With local businessmen declaring downtown doomed, most banks refused to extend financing on downtown property. The demand for distinctive old Savannah gray bricks to use in new suburban construction helped keep the wrecking ball swinging. "Georgia Fawcett and I had many a tearful meeting," Williams recalled. "What house shall we save next? How? How much money did we have? How much money could we borrow? We used every dollar we could to preserve multiple houses."[4] Even if there weren't enough funds to restore a building right away, acquiring it and making sure the roof and structure were sound would see it through to better days.

Williams's own architectural preservation work began in 1955 and saved more than fifty houses over a period of thirty years. "All existence is rehearsal for a final performance of perfection," Williams wrote.[5] He strived for perfection in his restoration work, doing whatever research was needed to achieve authenticity, selecting appropriate materials from his huge accumulation of architectural elements that he had salvaged from doomed buildings and stashed away wherever he could find storage space. Through the 1960s Williams continued to reinvest his real-estate profits, buying, restoring, and selling dozens of old Savannah houses.

"There can never be a suitable replacement for a living historic city," Williams said. "It gives its inhabitants a sense of well-being and security that only an old section can create."[6] His own example prompted others to get involved in rehabilitating blighted buildings and neighborhoods. "By the early 1970s," John Berendt writes, "couples with children came back downtown, and the prostitutes moved over to Montgomery Street."[7]

"Voices from the past speak to me," Williams wrote in his fifties, recalling his response as a fourteen-year-old to a white-columned antebellum house he encountered while traveling with his parents. "Our journey continued but my mind hesitated, reflecting on vibrations clearly received from that mysterious mass."[8] Such vivid vibrations drew Williams to many a restoration project. "Some people are blessed with the ability to see beauty even when that beauty has been tarnished or besmirched," said one of Williams's friends. "Jim Williams had the extraordinary talent to see potential beauty in an enormously wide spectrum of art objects, antiques, buildings—and people. Just let him near a painting, a piece of furniture, a house, or a person whose beauty had become obscured by the vicissitudes of time and life, and he would instantly and energetically begin, as if by magic, to make that beauty apparent to those willing to take a moment to look."[9]

By the time artist Jack Richards moved to Savannah, its rescue had been underway for almost thirty years. Born in 1952, Richards grew up in a small Illinois town. "When I saw the city of Savannah, I really fell in love," he says. "It was absolutely seductive. Within a matter of months I was down here painting and found a place that would sell my work on consignment. I lived in several lovely apartments in the historic district and became acquainted with Savannahian architecture. I got involved with Historic Savannah Foundation as a tour guide. Then, because of my interest in spiritual concerns and because Savannah has so many legends, I developed my own walking tour, 'Ghost Talk Ghost Walk,' with the help of Margaret De Bolt, the author of *Savannah Specters and Other Strange Tales*.

"I've always been interested in older people and their ideas, in 'oldish' things and restoring them. Bernice Coleman and her husband, Floyd, lived in the oldest house in Georgetown, Illinois. It was an 1852 American Gothic structure, in beautiful condition, and they had some of the nicest antiques. Everybody in Georgetown knew I was a little odd, but Bernice and Floyd were not so judgmental. Both my grandmothers had died when I was two, so the Colemans were like surrogate grandparents. I was very inquisitive. They taught me a lot about quilts and how to look at things and determine their age. The first thing I bought from them, when I was sixteen, was a beautiful wingback chair with a hassock, upholstered in a tufted brocade velvet that's really lovely. And I bought a flax wheel for $125. Lord knows I couldn't afford that at the time, but I had to have it. I've used it a lot in the past thirty years to spin flax into linen thread. I weave the thread into what I call my prayer cloths—intimate, shamanistic pieces of work that I've needed to do now and then, when I've had something to work through.

"I'm one of those people, like a lot of gays, who are drawn to history, art, aesthetics. I love to look at things, to study how they were made and why they are beautiful, and to restore things. My grandfather was a furniture doctor and had a little shop where I would work with him during summers and holidays. It was wonderful to listen to my grandfather as he worked over an old piece of furniture. As he rubbed it with a special kind of oil, he would say, 'This wood is coming alive again because I'm putting my energy into it.'"

Bob Page's penchant for restoration led him to put his energy into founding Replacements, Ltd., "the world's largest retailer of old and new china, crystal, silver and collectibles." From a sprawling facility in Greensboro, North Carolina, Page and his staff help to make things whole again. The company's warehouse and showroom contain millions of pieces in thousands of patterns, many of them discontinued. Thousands of pieces arrive each week from the company's network of freelance pickers around the country, who scour estate sales, flea markets, thrift shops, and auctions. Some items need to go to the company's restoration department before being offered for sale.

Born in 1945, Page grew up near Greensboro and became part owner of an antique shop in 1978. After he found some pieces of china that a customer was missing, she recommended him to her friends, and the requests kept coming in. "There are a lot of people out there who are really looking for some of these older patterns," Page says. "It was grandmother's or Aunt Sally's china and they inherited it, or they got it years ago when they got married. It's very sentimental to them. There's no greater feeling than when you get somebody on the phone, or they walk into our showroom, and they say, 'I've been looking for that for twenty-five years!' Sometimes they have tears in their eyes."

China collector and show-tune enthusiast Richard Jost commented that the remarkable involvement of gay men in historic preservation "would seem to argue for the existence of a preservation gene, which I would guess is located very near the Broadway show-tune gene." Perhaps no gay man in America offers more compelling evidence of the proximity of those two genes than Jerry Herman, the composer and lyricist whose career brought the world celebrated musical productions, from *Hello, Dolly!* to *Mame* to *La Cage aux Folles*. Herman started writing songs as a child but decided to study architecture and interior design, his other loves, in college. Though he completed only one year of design school before his show-tune destiny prevailed, he never lost the urge to design and decorate.

In the mid-1980s, Herman began a relationship with Marty Finkelstein, who was involved in architectural design and restoration in Philadelphia. Finkelstein had never been to Key West, one of Herman's favorite places. "So we flew down to Key West for a long weekend and I showed Marty all the things I loved," Herman writes, "the little bridges, the tree-lined streets, the charming old houses. There is something very romantic about the ambience and informality of Key West."[10] Finkelstein was captivated by the place and soon moved there for good. Many gay men had made the move before him: though Key West has only about thirty thousand residents, it has several thousand historic structures and more preservation organizations than Miami.

Key West became Herman and Finkelstein's common ground; its needy old houses became their rehab ventures. "The preservation society loved us," Herman says. "A lot of people buy these old Victorian houses and jazz them up, but we honestly restored them by keeping the integrity of the original design. Some of the houses we did were no more than falling-down shacks, so we rescued them and created elegant new exteriors for them." The couple rehabilitated eleven Key West dwellings. "In a way," Herman says, "doing houses is like doing a Broadway musical, only without the chorus girls. You have to love the property and give it all your time and concentration. And if you want to make the work interesting you have to keep trying something new. You have to make it a challenge for yourself."[11]

The persistent urge to rescue and rehabilitate is evident in the five individual stories that follow. Allan Gurganus sees "something potent about taking a beautiful, broken, preexisting form and making it once more whole." Myrick Howard directs Preservation North Carolina, calling it "an animal shelter for buildings . . . the poor dogs that nobody else will love." John Anders, preserver of forgotten literature, sees his passion for the North Carolina historical novels of Inglis Fletcher and the New Orleans writings of George Washington Cable "as a way of saving them from oblivion." For serial house restorer Robert Barker, who fell in love with and rescued his first desperate old house at age eighteen, "it's quite a thrill to take a place that's really been altered and get it back to what it was originally, . . . the way it was meant to be." Cranford Sutton longs to see his highway-sundered Georgia hometown revived, a strong sense of community rekindled. In the meantime Sutton channels much of his restorative energy into several vintage automobiles and his century-old family home.

Allan Gurganus

Born in 1947 in Rocky Mount, North Carolina, writer Allan Gurganus lives near Chapel Hill. His novella, *Preservation News*, gives a portrait of Tad Worth, founder of the Society for the Salvation of Historic North Carolina Architecture, in the words of Worth's friend and right-hand collaborator, Mary Ellen Broadfield. Occasioned by Tad Worth's death from AIDS at the age of forty-three, the profile says that Worth was involved in saving "over fifty-seven homes and public edifices." He would drive around North Carolina in his pickup, looking for old buildings to rescue, and then spent "his own inheritance saving houses he then practically gave away to others, homes he never really lived in except to work on them."[12]

MY FIRST IDEA FOR WRITING *Preservation News* came from hearing about a tragedy in Washington, D.C. Many staff members at the National Trust for Historic Preservation were dying of AIDS. One after another, it seemed a whole chain of the coming young men in the field went down to the disease in its early years. I thought, what an amazing subject. To me it recalled the Civil War, those boy generals who perished young on horseback. I've always seen the quest to save properties as something heroic and noble, in the ways we were once told wars were necessary. It seemed to me I had fallen into an immense and beautiful contradiction: young men's exits and old houses' resurrections. It was a subject destined to be ignored, ruled out of bounds by the persistent homophobia of our culture.

There's some magical relation between gay men and restoration. You can always tell an urban neighborhood in transition by that harbinger of change, the corner Art Deco shop opened by two gentleman friends. This store must have lots of padlocks to keep people from breaking in. Of course, there's no money in there; there's nothing but stylish Bakelite! But such shops always indicate a neighborhood being recalled to life. Just as miners once took canaries down into the mines, knowing that if the songbirds died of the gas then everybody had a few minutes to get the hell out. It seems Art Deco pottery must be the early warning-sign of incoming life. Gay pioneers rush in where wise men only tread with armed guards. Selling 1930s gewgaws and reupholstered furniture, the pioneering couple wanders in—aware of the architectural possibilities, sniffing out incoming prosperity, and willing in some extremely brave way to put their own lives on the line, to live out an aesthetic vision, to fight militantly for a sense of beauty. That seems to be one thing gay men were lavishly given when the breeding instinct was taken away.

Old houses forever fascinated me. In my earliest memory I'm on the porch of one. I drew them a lot. I started out to be a painter. The first story I ever wrote, the first I ever really showed anybody, concerned an old lady in a deteriorated mansion. I'm sure she was heavily influenced by our eighth-grade reading of Miss Havisham. But I'm forever interested in where my characters live, what their interior setting looks like. It seems a defining, clarifying frame for every character.

I furnished my childhood room as a kind of James Bond Oriental fantasy. There was a long, low, slatted wooden bench, a mounted Buddha's head set on its far end. Over it, off center, scroll paintings. I was a very advanced little stylish person for eight; I believed myself to be Cole Porter. I was doing all this very much alone. I got my look out of junk shops or from the back of Momma's *Woman's Day* or through catalogs. I'm touched to remember these first attempts. Of course, your taste changes and enlarges and complicates. But a deep love of artifice and tall true tales, those were all there from the start.

I have a collection of about 450 masks. I also gather Federal mirrors; I find these—the more liver-spotted the better—extremely beautiful. Also Central and South American religious carvings, life-size saints. And paintings. Whatever. Somebody asked, "What do you collect?" and I said, "What have you got?" Two of something is a pair, three is a collection. I've tried to beat some of my dozens of objects into submission; I've made many shelves in this house so that the quorum clutter is a little less terrifying for strangers.

Like all southerners my father's tribe came stuffed with compulsive genealogists. My paternal grandmother especially seemed to know a great deal. She could tell the same forty stories over and over again, sometimes with a new detail thrown in, so they'd be worth listening to. It was our finest liturgy. So, I grew up with that sense of self-regard, with stories that included the black people who'd forever worked for our family. It was not just us but the whole supporting staff, the years of pets and livestock, the war, the weather—it all went into our personal family history, History itself did.

I always kept my great-great-grandfolks' photographs in sight. As a kid, I labeled all the pictures. I'm very grateful for that now that both my parents are dead. All the information I know is written on the backs of things. We have drawings and photographs from the early nineteenth century, family images, books written by family members. All those things seem very important, charged. I have my great-great-grandfather's crystal inkwell, one I still use. Magic powers, I swear.

My first memory is of sitting on my grandmother's porch when I was eighteen months old, in the lap of some adult rocking a rocking chair. I sat looking out at the sidewalk before the house, watching my three-year-old cousin ride her red tricycle up and down in the beautiful sunlight. I remember thinking, gosh, that looks like so much fun, but it'll probably be much too complicated for me to ever figure out. But the larger part of the memory is missing, the way it is from dreams. I mean: the is-ness of the rocking chair, the assumption of a lap to sit in, and the immense mayoral presence behind me of this big Victorian house. I felt, literally in my first memory, that the house was both my protector and my sponsor. Almost as if I were resting safe in the lap of a lion, staring out at the world, defended and defined.

In hindsight, of course, that place wasn't quite the castle I'd believed. It proved a perfectly adequate, gingerbreaded, middle-class Victorian house from the 1880s. But for me starting out, it seemed the emblem of everything that was secure and steadfast and historically continuous in the world. This home that I live in now, at the age of fifty-two, is a self-conscious replica of that first house. I'd done a long, roundabout search for a place to renovate and redefine. This time I'd be both the kid on the porch *and* my own grandparent, the sponsoring organization. Those of us who are obsessed with restoration often have some one homeplace in mind. It's one we're seeking to restore, either a great and lost house, or some architectural standing in the community that we didn't quite have, a family that we somehow aspire to. But that's a kind of restoration, too, if only the restoration of a fantasy.

Tad Worth is a flawed person with a large preservative vision. His greatest gift is how he enlists other people's talents. He surrounds himself with gifted folks who maybe don't quite understand how gifted they really are, not till they come into contact with Tad. It's like Christ calling the apostles. Some happened to be tax collectors, others fishermen, but each could claim a larger capacity than he even knew—till such gifts engaged communally, then spiritually. A huge sense of collective mission can be articulated by a single articulate, impassioned person. "Salvation" can mean saving both an edifice and the soul of the person who does such saving.

Mary Ellen Broadfield describes the basic root word of "religion" as meaning "to regather" or "to bind up again." There is something potent about taking a beautiful, broken, preexisting form and making it once more whole. Just as a lot of gay people I know are endlessly adopting broken-legged cats and hurt birds, we seem to have a tendency to identify with those down-at-the-heels, the bypassed, the formerly beautiful. We are the kindest of strangers! I've just described Tennessee Williams's work in a nutshell. To see the heroism of aesthetic face-saving, the rigged and foredoomed struggle. We also have the theatrical skills and color sense, the wickedly perfect taste plus what my mother used to hideously call "the people skills" to do exactly that rebinding, that regrouping, that refining.

A sense of texture, a glorying in color, a knowledge of art history and therefore of design, all these rank among the millions of powerful gifts we bring, replenishible, to the culture. Just as there are postage stamps that celebrate the contributions of black Americans and Jewish Americans to the vitality of American culture, I look forward to the day when the charity and scope of gay Americans are similarly acknowledged, celebrated. Our culture is endlessly, determinedly marginalizing us.

One reason the country has seemed so dispirited and coarse and shoddy and lurid and out of control these last fifteen years: 150,000 boys who were designers and visual arbiters, editors and writers, got ripped asunder by AIDS. They really formed a kind of refining filter for the nation. That's why we all now feel a rising level of shoddiness and sewage in our culture; it was once held back by these guys. Men who would stay late at the office to see a project through, for no reason better than they wanted it to look beautiful, they expected things to be fair, they didn't want the newspaper's questions to sound cheap and mean and tacky. I am convinced that everybody in the culture, straight or gay, sensitive or boorish, none-theless *feels* this sea change. The reason for it has not yet been sufficiently articulated. A postage stamp is needed!

Crucial that the narration in *Preservation News* should be a straight woman's vision of a gay man. We get her take on his great contribution. Gay men and straight women get on well: both groups are interested in men, of course. We're also both given the tasks of prettying up, setting the table, making the meal and centerpieces, the house-and-home skills—tasks that straight guys are often not all that interested in and therefore are all too willing to delegate. But it's fascinating to see how powerful these talents can become, and how people who are put into subsidiary, secondary positions of power can wield their power in such ways that it changes local commerce. Such folks can let the local government recall that this is a historical town, one nobody ever noticed being especially historical before. The aesthetic role can radically alter the landscape. And has. Daily does.

There are benefits that go with the jeopardy of being childless and legally unable to marry. Such seeming lacks often enrich the larger community. They don't just show up in our tendency, as somebody said, not to propagate but to decorate. We step so easily into the role of rememberer, storyteller, saver of tribal lore. And when we move into a great house—a house with a great history, meaning a long one—our being movie queens, legend buffs, mythomaniacs helps us understand that we haven't bought just the bricks and mortar. We've assured our short mortal term in the house's stewardship. What comes free with a historic home is its history, the story of the people who've been there before.

Part of the genius of preservation is that it lets one see one's own place in history's larger parade. Nobody who's buying a house built in 1757 thinks that he's getting it all for himself and forever. If you understand history, you realize that you're just "the current owner" as they call it in carpentry circles. You understand you're preparing a place for the next person in line, and the next; you feel there is an element of accountability, a responsibility to preserve what's beautiful, what's so handsomely been there. So you shore up the leaky roofs; you make it acceptable unto the second and third generation. And there's a narrative responsibility that goes with owning an old house, a need to ensure the record can be passed along.

My own place was built in 1900, which is new by the world's standards. It rests next to a cemetery where one of the signers of the Declaration of Independence is buried. I know every single person who ever lived in my home, by name and repute and occupation. I hadn't even got unpacked here when people started bringing me pictures of "Doc" Durham, the man who built it in 1900. So I've become the archivist-historian, at least of my own house. I feel extremely lucky. What's touching is how the village where I live came to me with my own house's stories. "We thought you should know . . ." That's one of the best things about reclaiming an old property—along with the nightmare of plumbing and the endless rewiring and the battle with squirrels, you do get the stories and whatever weird found items you can lay your hands on. I found a child-sized hangman's noose dangling in the basement, found a burned spot in the attic, which nobody knew what-all had happened. There was a horde of World War II soldierly toys hidden behind one brick. I found notes, bills, pieces of paper, and cryptic love letters. Bits of eighteenth-century ginger jars broken in the garden. These are the dream-stuffs that a novelist feeds on.

I had a little cottage in Chapel Hill, ten miles away. I couldn't really afford a great house in Chapel Hill, so I wandered as far and as close as I could go, to the next town. Happily I got here just before this burg was discovered. The village is beautiful. It was originally the state capital in the 1750s, and it's got a great layered mythological sense of itself. But it was sort of blessedly down at the heels, which makes it like Charleston and Savannah till recently; poverty plus gentility plus inertia is what really preserved those towns and this one. The rumor is John Rockefeller considered making this town his eighteenth-century town-museum. When the local farmers nobly turned him down, he went on to found Historic Williamsburg.

When I started looking for my own home in North Carolina, I first looked at Federal places. I found most were already on the National Register. That meant I could do very little to them except choose a proper citrus yellow for the foyer. Some were in such bad shape, I couldn't afford to hire the structural engineers required to fully save them. When this place opened up, a block away from a beautiful tripartite Italianate Federal house I'd had my eye on, it seemed perfect, because it's not on the Register. I haven't changed the exterior footprint of the house, but I've had far more license to make the interior mine, by using William Morris paper and by literally painting the Elgin Marbles on the walls. I probably couldn't have risked that if I owned a house with a longer history, a finer pedigree.

My two favorite moments in American architecture: 1810 to 1820 and 1910 to 1920. The family-oriented domestic architecture that arrived, a promise, just before the first war remains one of our great high points; it's totally unpretentious, it's foursquare and commodious; it assumes five or six children, at least. Everything is extremely well built in heart pine. Plus it's right on the cusp of late Victorian cottage architecture, with daring Arts and Crafts coming in. Such houses strike me as extremely beautiful, with all sorts of serendipitous details like my porch's Moorish arches. I feel very, very lucky, rocking out there, the squire, reading and writing, being left alone by neighbors and the squirrels.

Part of my joy in this house: I throw a big Halloween celebration every year. Trick-or-treaters swarm into the front three rooms; we have sinister-comic tableaux vivants going. It's almost gotten out of hand, the numbers of ghouls seeking a sugar high and a free thrill here. But the whole community gets engaged. It's a tiny symptom of how the village reaches out to us, and how we, with our theatricality and crazy, try-anything gameness, give so much energy back.

The ecology of beauty, of holding onto what is assuredly gorgeous in this world where everything seems to be endlessly improving itself out of existence, that contains its own kind of wisdom. Brave, just to say, "I accept janitorial duties for this small patch of ground." I have an acre here. The house and its trees and their shadows soon dictate what the garden can and cannot be. You are really lining yourself up with certain inherent principles, with the often-inconvenient forces of good. I recall this sometimes when I'm at the coast: I see how sea birds at rest face into the wind so their feathers won't be constantly ruffled. You somehow line yourself up with the ley lines, with whatever geometry and commerce made a place beautiful two hundred years before you ever found it. By honoring that, by bringing it back to a fuller order and life, you somehow discover your own. There is a moment when habitation becomes cohabitation. This house, yours in sickness and health, till death do you part.

Myrick Howard

The Society for the Salvation of Historic North Carolina Architecture in Allan Gurganus's novella *Preservation News* is a take-off on the real-life organization known as Preservation North Carolina (PNC). Myrick Howard has been director of the group since 1978, when he was twenty-five. He and his partner, Brinkley Sugg, live in the Cameron Park neighborhood of Raleigh.

Its creative use of a revolving fund has made PNC a pioneer in saving endangered historic properties. The group secures an option to purchase a building over a given period, ranging from several months to several years. This shields the property from destruction while PNC lists it in its quarterly magazine as "available for restoration" and makes other efforts to find a preservation-minded buyer. When that happens, PNC facilitates the transfer of the property and consults with the new owner in rehabilitating the structure. Hundreds of historic properties in North Carolina have been handled through the revolving fund.

When a textile company closed its mill at Edenton, on the Albemarle Sound, PNC took on a task more daunting than brokering individual buildings. It was determined to create a new life for the old forty-four-acre mill village, which includes the mill building and fifty-seven houses.

I FEEL STRONGLY that the gay community has made great contributions to our cities and towns as pioneers in revitalizing downtown neighborhoods and districts, contributions that should someday be recognized by the straight community and by gays themselves. I wish *The Advocate* would do a series on the contributions of gays to modern society, rather than yet another interview with yet another cute, gay-friendly movie star. No doubt I would be outvoted on that one. The contributions of gays may be obvious to some of us, but lots of folks, including many gays, don't get it. And there's a real hesitation to even talk about it. Back in 1987 or so, I wrote a chapter on local preservation for a book called *The American Mosaic*. When the editor deleted my paragraph about the role of gays in revitalization, I gave him a choice: leave the paragraph or dump the whole chapter. One of the first reviews of the book referred to that contested paragraph as an example of how the book was breaking new ground.

When I had dinner with leaders of the National Trust for Historic Preservation recently, they ticked off a list of preservationists who they felt were good prospects for the Trust's upcoming capital campaign. I pointed out to them that their list was 100 percent gay. They had no idea! For a number of years I've advocated to my colleagues in North Carolina and to the National Trust that the preservation community needs to recognize the role of gays in preservation. And to solicit their financial support, especially in planned giving. Two incomes, generally no heirs, often a passion for historic buildings: any fundraiser should perk up his or her ears at that combination. A substantial percentage of PNC's planned-giving Heritage Club is gay. With good planned giving gays have a special chance to influence the futures of their communities in a way that families with children don't.

I grew up in Lakewood, a working-class neighborhood in Durham, in a substantial bungalow built by my grandfather in 1916. During that period I saw urban renewal tear down the buildings where I went to grade school, where the barbershop was, where my father bought his car. There was an area with fine mansions, the homes of major Durham industrialists. Those houses were particularly striking to me, and they were torn down when I was ten or twelve years old. I have vague memories of my father and me standing behind the Benjamin Duke mansion as it was being demolished, and of my grandmother saying what a shame it was. Ben Duke's house was on a beautifully landscaped four-acre site that an insurance company wiped out to put up an office building. On the site of another house they built a motel that has since been torn down, and in another case the demolition made way for nothing. Racial issues were coming to the fore in numerous ways during that period, and much urban renewal in Durham as well as all across the country was racially motivated.

Recently, when my mother moved out of her house into a retirement facility, I brought home with me the boxes of family photographs going back two or three generations. It was kind of weird to go through them and see how many of them were labeled in my own handwriting. I have some vague recollections of sitting down with my mother and going through them when I was a teenager. And I stripped and refinished several family pieces of furniture when I was in high school, a Victorian oak bed and dresser and some chairs, things that had been painted in the 1920s.

At Brown University in Providence, Rhode Island, I took walks all around College Hill, up this street and down that one. I didn't know what I was looking at, but I was fascinated by the wide variety of structures and styles on the Hill, one of the earliest historic districts of its kind in the country. What the heck do you do with a degree in history? I went on for planning and law degrees. I really enjoyed my courses in urban design and historic preservation, and I had a strong environmental interest. I had a real aversion to the throwaway nature of our society, particularly then, in the mid-seventies, and that has remained very strong. Preservation North Carolina has a

bumper sticker that's been real popular: "Historic Preservation: The Ultimate Recycling."

I grew up with stability and continuity and a strong sense of place. A
big part of my decision to stay in North Carolina rather than go to work with
the National Trust in Washington, D.C., was a North Carolina thing: I feel a
real connection to this state. And preservation is fundamentally local. The
closer you are to being local, the more you're really doing preservation. In
this job my familiarity with the places and people of North Carolina is almost
more important than my knowledge of historic preservation.

I view preservation extremely broadly. It's not just about saving one
building here and one building there. It is really about the fabric of our
lives—the places where we live now, where we grew up, where we're going
to be in the future. I believe North Carolina's history is important to its people,
and that the built environment should be preserved for variety, for continuity, and for education. We need to do more to teach children how to look at
the buildings around them so there will be a strong interest in preservation.
I'm concerned with how North Carolina looks, and preservation is one way
to shape that look.

If you have any regard for history and the development of our communities, if the physical fabric is not there, the memory is gone. It's like tearing
up the photograph of somebody. Unless the person is eminently famous, the
next generation will never know about him or her: the connection is gone. I
consider the buildings like the photo album. Without that photo album, stuff
just slips out of one's consciousness. You go two or three generations, and
they're completely forgotten.

Sometimes the connections are purely personal, and sometimes they
have real social dimensions. The places where the sit-ins took place during
the early Civil Rights movement, for example. If those places were gone, our
connection to those events would be very different from when you can see
the lunch counter and the stools. And if you want to talk about something
that happened 150 years ago, it's even more important that the place remain
and that there be some tangible connection.

The biggest part of PNC's operation is trying to find buyers for endangered and usually pretty pathetic historic houses. Pathetic in the sense of
poorly maintained. We refer to our organization as an animal shelter for buildings. We deal with the poor dogs that nobody else will love—houses, churches,
school buildings. The thing we're into right now is mills and mill villages,
which is hugely beyond what we've been accustomed to dealing with.

Glencoe, in Alamance County, is our second mill village. The mill closed
in 1954, so it's been basically a ghost town my entire life. Fascinating place.
About 65 of the 101 acres we bought is raw land along the Haw River. Just a

beautiful site, rolling hills going down to the river. There's the dam, the lake behind the dam, the rapids, and the mill race. The city parks and recreation board wants the city to buy the land along the river for a park, and we'll sell the thirty-five mill houses and mill separately for private redevelopment, under covenant. Glencoe will be a restored mill village, almost a museum village, with condos and the mill and a park. People can look back fifty years from now and think, what a wonderful place. I'm just tickled that we're headed in that direction.

Right now our organization owns about a million square feet of mill buildings and about seventy-five houses. We're running some fairly serious risks by doing this, but my intuition, which I rely on real heavily, is saying we're doing the right thing and it's going to work just fine. We'll look back on it five years from now and say, gosh, that was easy. Yeah, right! The first mill village we did, the one down in Edenton, it's kind of funny how the local folks are now saying it was a dumb natural. The hell you say. I remember when the board was sweating bullets about the thing. Nothing dumb natural about it. It was a hell of a lot of work, but it has worked out fabulously well.

Through the years at Preservation North Carolina we've had quite a few situations where I or someone else would go into an old house and not feel good about the place. I mean have an unsettling reaction that has nothing to do with the house's architecture or condition. There have been situations where a couple of different folks have gone into the same house and had similar reactions along those lines. I think there is something to be said for some sort of connections in these houses that go way beyond just the wood and the bricks. Spiritual connections.

I've lived in the Procter house since I bought it in 1979. It was built in 1911, a nice two-story late–Queen Anne house, lived in by the Procter family from about 1921 until Mrs. Procter's death in the mid-seventies. When I bought it, about two years after Mrs. Procter died, the downstairs bedroom ceiling had been lowered below the tops of the windows with an acoustical tile ceiling and the room was peach with a peach shag carpet. Period piece. I bought the house with the notion of doing pretty much a total renovation.

One night I was reading in bed, in the peach bedroom, and the door to the front hall opened—just affirmatively *opened*—right beside the bed. I had a very strong feeling of some presence coming into the room. It was an eerie but calming sort of presence, with a sense of "Things are fine." Then it left, but the door stayed open. I pretty quickly assumed it was Mrs. Procter, who had died two or three years earlier. That experience made me want to learn more about who lived here, what type of people they were. Mrs. Procter apparently was very involved in the movement to get Mother's Day designated as a holiday. From everything I've heard about her she was a very nice, warm person, but a pretty determined lady.

One day, a woman I had known for many years said to me, "You live in the Procter house, don't you?" I said yeah. She said she had lived there for a few months, right after Mrs. Procter died, and that she had had a weird experience there after Mrs. Procter's death. I asked her to tell me about it. "Well," she said, "I was in one of the downstairs rooms . . ." "Let me guess," I said. "The peach room with the peach shag carpet." "Yeah," she said, "it sure was. The door opened and Mrs. Procter came in. She told me every-thing was fine, then left." "That's so weird," I said. "The same thing hap-pened to me."

I've had a small handful of experiences with what one might consider ghosts or other-world spirits. PNC had an office in a house in Raleigh, the Caveness House, which we had bought to keep it from being torn down. One night I was having dinner with someone on my staff and with a board member who is fascinated with this sort of thing. The board member asked if I had seen or heard or felt any ghosts in the Caveness House. The only thing that had happened, I told him, was that a number of times I had been working upstairs, late afternoon, early evening, and I would have sworn that someone came in through the dining room door. Just the sense of hearing a door open and shut and somebody coming in downstairs. When I would go down and look, the door would be locked. It had happened a number of times, and I hadn't given it a whole lot of thought. That's the only thing I've had happen, I said. My staff person looked absolutely ashen. "My God," he said, "I've had the same thing happen!" It turns out that several of us had heard that dining room door open and shut, a door onto the side porch, always in that 5:45, 6:30 time period. We decided it must be Dr. Caveness coming home from work.

I've heard all sorts of ghost stories. Several of the houses that we've worked with have been pretty well known in the community to have spirits. We worked with a house in Goldsboro where there had been a number of incidents. Nothing harmful, but a strong sense that Miss Gertrude Weil was still around. Often the spirit is of someone who's pretty intense. A couple of houses that we've had some association with, where murder or something like that has taken place, have had some sort of unsettling spirit. But in most cases it's pretty benign. Some folks will kid around and say that if a building they work on doesn't have a ghost, they're disappointed. Frankly, I like the notion of having ghosts. I'd like to think that I'd stick around for a while and check on things periodically.

John Anders

Born in 1948, John Anders grew up in coastal North Carolina. Since 1985 he has lived in Lincoln, Nebraska, where he received a doctorate in American literature at the University of Nebraska. "Before I came to Nebraska, I had read extensively in Nebraska and Great Plains literature in the hope of one day coming here," John Anders says. "Now, I'm reading nothing but North Carolina books in the hope of someday getting back home."

I COME FROM AN AREA OF THE COUNTRY rich in history and the preserving instinct. New Bern, with its colonial governor's palace, and Beaufort, a three-hundred-year-old sea captain's town, surround me with antique buildings and their abiding mystery. Some time ago I got involved in trying to save an old house in Havelock from being destroyed, my only venture into hometown politics. And a friend of mine once owned the oldest house in Beaufort, unofficially dated at 1698. Although unlivable, it was still usable for storage and play. He recently sold it, and it has been restored to a semblance of its former beauty. But even in its dilapidated state, it had a singular appeal; I was always thrilled to be around it, however ignorant I may have been of its meaning.

But despite an inherent southern propensity to be mesmerized by the past, my involvement with architectural preservation has always been that of an observer, whether watching it happen around me or seeing it in the pages of *House Beautiful* or *Southern Accents.* I am more actively involved in the preservation of literature. Reading forgotten authors is one of my passions. My particular favorites are the French writer Pierre Loti and the American George Washington Cable, the father of modern southern literature and the writer responsible for first putting New Orleans on the literary map. I read about, write about, and talk about these authors whenever possible as a way of saving them from oblivion. I try to find their books in either first or early editions, copies that have the look and feel of the past. I enjoy immensely their antiquated styles and lost language and delight in their intricate plots and strange patois. I am also drawn to authors who celebrate the past and its enduring symbols. Writers like Willa Cather, Sir Walter Scott, Walter Pater, and Elizabeth Bowen—especially her novel *A World of Love,* which is, in part, a paean to the presence of the past in our lives. All evoke in their fiction something beyond nostalgia.

My most feverish reading of late has been the historical novels of Inglis Fletcher. I've known about them all my life but never read one till last summer. I drove around four counties back home looking for them. There are twelve in all, often referred to as the Carolina Series or the Carolina Chronicles, and I'm building multiple sets, including the many paperbacks and the signed and limited first editions. They all concern the English settlement of North Carolina, from the earliest attempts at colonization in the 1580s to just after the Revolutionary War. With a storyteller's imagination, Fletcher combines the panorama and pageantry of the historical novel with the colorful history of North Carolina. In doing so, she recalls some of the most romantic figures of the age: Charles I, for whom the Carolinas were named; Charles II and his "natural" son, the Duke of Monmouth; and later Bonnie Prince Charlie and the Scottish heroine Flora MacDonald.

Not a native North Carolinian, Inglis Fletcher happened upon her Carolina subject while doing genealogical research in California. She intended to write a novel of American pioneers following a great river west. Instead, having traced her family to eastern North Carolina, she kept them there, along with her other characters. She felt that no one had written of North Carolina the way she intended to, a way that would stress the state's distinctive character and interpret its history more as a response to place than as a series of events.

Inglis Fletcher chose the town of Edenton as her fictional center and moved there in 1944. She used Edenton's old buildings, such as the Cupola House, the Chowan County Courthouse, and Saint Paul's Episcopal Church, as settings for her novels, and its surrounding countryside—the Carolina pines and pocosins—as background to their action. Perhaps the most famous historic house in Fletcher's novels is Tryon Palace in New Bern, just a few miles from my home. Designed by John Hawks as the residence of the royal governors, it was considered his crowning achievement in colonial America. Like Versailles was to the French, Tryon Palace was to North Carolinians a source of discord and contention on the eve of revolution. In *Raleigh's Eden* and again in *The Wind in the Forest,* Fletcher describes the crowds on the front lawn, celebrating its completion. She has them eating barbecue, a true North Carolina tradition.

Finished in 1770, Tryon Palace was destroyed by fire in 1798. In the 1950s it was completely rebuilt and furnished with period antiques, following the original architect's drawings and Governor Tryon's household inventory. While lovely to look at, nothing at Tryon Palace is authentic except, I think, the stables and a few bricks in the kitchen's foundation. The restored gardens were modeled after those of eighteenth-century English country houses. Then in 1991 some of the palace's original garden plans were found in a library in Venezuela. It turns out that the original landscape designer, Claude Sauthier, had been strongly influenced by a man who was himself a pupil of the designer of Versailles. Thus, the garden style at Tryon Palace is now believed to have originally been more French than English. Talk about digging something up! Unlike Colonial Williamsburg, which also has reconstructed historic sites, Tryon Palace has the reputation of being a "beautiful fraud." This latest embarrassment, if not a preservationist's worst nightmare, is, nonetheless, what Henry James would call an aesthetic headache.

In the summer of 1983, at home in North Carolina, I was preparing to drive up the coast to attend a performance of *The Lost Colony*, the outdoor historical drama based on the play by Paul Green. Inglis Fletcher never wrote a novel of the lost English colonists, but she was certainly inspired by the story. So was I, partly because I had a black-haired, blue-eyed boyfriend who played one of the lusty, leaping Indians in the production that summer. Back in the seventies, I had gone to see *The Lost Colony* with some friends, and we were invited to a cast party after the performance. (The highlight of the party was a magnificent specimen of a man who had played the leading Indian role that night. As I remember it, he reveled in showing us how to remove his body paint.) Looking at a map to plan my route to Roanoke Island, I noticed the town of Nebraska, North Carolina, near where I was going. Since Nebraska was much on my mind at the time, I saw it as a good omen and made the short detour to see it. I mention this for two reasons. First, because I never knew before that time that there was a Nebraska, North Carolina, and, indeed, I've not found it on any map since. Second, because one of the first books I bought after coming to Lincoln in 1985 was a used copy of Fletcher's *Lusty Wind for Carolina*. I bought it more out of homesickness than any desire to read it at the time.

Reading Fletcher, I hear names of people and places I've known all my life. So prevalent is the myth of Blackbeard in eastern North Carolina that as many places claim an association with him as they do with George Washington up in Virginia. In her own telling of Blackbeard's story, Fletcher preserves his legend as convincingly as the recent discovery of his flagship, the *Queen Anne's Revenge*, which sank off the coast of North Carolina in 1718, just two miles out from Beaufort. While no treasure was found, other items have been recovered—a brass bell, a blunderbuss, and a twenty-four-pound cannonball—all exhibited at the local museum. I saw them when I was last home and thought it a lucky accompaniment to *Lusty Wind for Carolina*.

Willa Cather was not a historical novelist, at least not in the popular sense, but she had a historical imagination. During her first European tour, in 1902, her mood was at times particularly inclined to historical fiction. After visiting Chester, England, which she deemed "the quaintest and most picturesque of all English towns," she wrote, "One can understand, lying a morning through at the foot of the Norman tower, why there are Maurice

Hewletts in England. The temptation to attempt to reconstruct the period when these things were a part of the living fabric of the world is one that must necessarily assail an ardent imagination."[13]

I have in my apartment a small green table with the paint chipped and worn away. Upon it is a bust of the Apollo Belvedere, roughly scarred as if recently excavated. Looking at these objects helps me think about the past and its preservation, for there are many ways to connect with the past, whether the culture of the ancient Greeks or the house next door. And that connection, that continuity, however and wherever we find it, is what keeps our spirit alive. Though Inglis Fletcher's place in the archives of North Carolina history is secure, I'm doing what I can to help save her from near oblivion, as the Cape Hatteras Lighthouse was recently saved by picking it up and moving it to higher ground.

Robert Barker

Born in 1929, a native of Long Island, New York, Robert Barker first visited Charleston, South Carolina, when he got out of the army in 1953. He fell in love with the place and finally moved to Charleston in 1977. Barker works part-time as senior architectural interpreter at Drayton Hall Plantation. "I have no intentions of quitting until they put the lid down on me," he says. "Every day I meet new people, they're excited about the place, and I get such a thrill out of showing them the house. It's so great, and there's such great history there."

MOTHER SAID I BROUGHT HOME my first treasure when I was seven, a Christmas tree somebody had thrown out, and I never stopped after that. I started collecting antique furniture at a very early age, bringing home things people put out for trash pickup. And the people whose lawns I cut would have stuff in their attic or garage they didn't want, so I lugged it home. Mother never criticized anything I dragged in, except maybe the Christmas tree. With money I earned, I would buy porcelain and other things. A big leaf-shaped majolica dish was one of my earliest purchases.

"You want to get into everybody's attic," Mother said, and I did, hoping to find treasures up there. I remember a Victorian tufted chair that I thought was just the greatest thing that ever happened. Mother thought it was awfully rickety, but she went along with me. I had a great love of old trunks, small trunks with humped tops and big iron handles on the ends. The best of the lot I gave to a museum years ago. One was covered with all leather, another with leather studded with brass nail heads. I had a couple of old sea chests too. My hometown of Port Jefferson, Long Island, was a seaport and a shipbuilding town, so these things were around and not too expensive in those days. I might pick up a nice little pine sea chest for ten dollars. I'd refinish it (today that would be a crime, but in those days it wasn't), and then I'd live with it for a while, and then I'd find something else I wanted more and I'd sell it. I've never stopped collecting. I like eighteenth-century and early-nineteenth-century furniture, and I'm very partial to blue and white Canton. I don't have a big collection, but what I have I'm very proud of, and I'm always hunting for another piece. It's gotten hard to find anything that's within my reach.

I grew up in a house from about the 1830s that my parents had restored around the time I was born. Mother appreciated lovely old things and had bought some furnishings at the big estate sale when they moved in there. By 1930 we were broke, so there wasn't much buying after that. When my father died in 1941, we had to leave that house, and my mother had to go back to work.

I always loved houses. As a child I would draw little plans of houses, some very grand, with ballrooms and the whole works. I started restoring my first house in Port Jefferson when I was eighteen. I had gone to look at an early house that I was interested in, but it wasn't for sale. On the way home I went through this big old Greek Revival that was standing there with the doors open, and I thought, this is for me! It was in rough shape, desperately in need of restoration, and I just fell in love with it and conned Mother into it. We were renting at the time. I had inherited some money, so I had enough to buy the house, but that was about it. The place had been vacant for a good many years when I got it. I didn't know any better; I just thought I could do anything.

The great big monster of a house was missing about seventy window-panes, so I soon learned how to putty windows. The last tenant had not drained the water out of the heating system, so I had endless broken radiators and pipes. I dismantled the old radiators, put in new gaskets that I'd made, and put them back together. There was a big sag in the house's center wing, so I was jacking that up and the plaster was falling off the walls. I had no idea how to do these things, so I just went ahead and did them. That house was my learning house, and I played with it for a long time. Over the years I redid a lot of my original work.

I studied interior designing at Parsons School of Design in New York, but after two years there I went into the army. I should have gone back to Parsons, but instead I worked off and on with a friend who had a design business, and I just got carried away with my houses. Mother and I lived in my first house until 1963, when I sold it and bought another one in Port Jefferson, a huge thing with ten rooms on the first floor. It hadn't had any care in many years, but it wasn't in such bad shape as the first. I made a profit on the first one, so I had a little money to work with. I had no thought of turning around and selling that second house right away, but a friend in real estate said she could get me a big price for it. So within a year I got that house together and sold it. My third house in Port Jefferson was one I'd known and loved all my life. When I was in school, a friend of mine lived there. It came on the market, and I decided I had to have it. I did that one over pretty quickly too, sold it, and moved on to the next one, a huge early Victorian thing. Big rooms and high ceilings, it was a great house, and I had a wonderful time doing it. I stayed in it nine years and ran a summer guesthouse there.

After doing four houses in Port Jefferson, I came to Charleston in 1977, did two houses here, then went back up to Long Island for three years, and did two more up there. The first was a 1720 farmhouse that had been altered several times. I got it back as near as possible to what it had been, replaced the center chimney and three fireplaces, moved the stairway back to where it came from, and took up all the oak floors to get back to the old wide boards. That was a great house. I did one more big Victorian in Long Island purely as a business deal. I had no intention of staying there. I wanted to get back to Charleston.

When I bought my first house in Charleston, 2 Wragg Square, I was just about the only white person in the neighborhood. It was a gorgeous, big Greek Revival house that had been made into six apartments. I converted it back to a single-family house. It's quite a thrill to get a place that's really been altered and get it back to what it was. The architect who designed these houses had something in mind. You can see the changes that have been made, you know what was there, and it's really exciting to get it back to what it was originally, the way it was meant to be.

After about two years in Charleston, I was walking one day with a friend and saw another place that was on the market, on Wall Street, and I thought, *God, I've got to have that house!* Within one day I sold 2 Wragg Square. The house on Wall Street was marvelous, a vastly different sort of look. It's what we call a single house here, the end of the house facing the street and a piazza leading to the door. Someone had turned the whole downstairs of the main part of the house into one room, eighteen by thirty-eight feet. There was also a wing that had been kind of cut up. By moving walls and raising ceilings I got a twenty-one-foot dining room with a ten-foot ceiling, and a small kitchen, small bedroom, and bath for my mother on the first floor. I had two bedrooms and two baths on the second floor. It's a wonderful house and in a very nice area. I once tried to buy it back, but the price had gone through the roof.

I'd get a house done, and then I'd see another house and think, *God, I'd love to do that one!* The only way I could afford to do it was to sell one and move into the next. Mother and I would live in them while I was doing them. She always said that by the time I got the sawdust out of the dresser drawers, we sold the house and moved. Which is just about the truth. My second house in Long Island we moved into in the fall, and in December we had one whole side of the building torn off, covered with tarpaulin, with no heat except a fireplace and a wood stove in the kitchen. When I did the 1720 farmhouse, Mother was up in her eighties and had to climb a ladder to get upstairs to bed because I'd torn the staircase out. She was a great sport, and when I needed somebody to hold up the end of a two-by-four, she was there.

I did five more houses in Charleston, plus the one I'm in now. My real-estate agent is a good friend. She's sold me all my houses and sold all my houses for me, and when something great comes up she calls and says, "I've got a key. Do you want to take a look at it?" Not that she's trying to sell it to me. She just knows I love houses. Of course, sometimes I've succumbed, but every time another one comes up, I have to go see it.

Charleston is a charming old city that just attracts gay men. There's a very large gay community here, and the populace seems to tolerate us. All my gay friends here are very proud of their homes and take good care of them and love to entertain in them. One of them remarked that students move into the city's low-income areas first, for the low rents, and then gays buy the places and restore them and the prices go through the roof. That's about the truth of it. Gay men move in and do the work themselves, even if they've never done it before. Straight couples have to get a contractor to do everything. We gay men find out how to do it ourselves, and we help each other.

Cranford Sutton

In recalling his work with the southern regional office of the National Trust for Historic Preservation, Dwight Young says that "it seemed inevitable that in every southern town I'd go to, the people who were showing me around would take me to the home of a gay man" who was exceptionally preservation minded. If Young had gone to Willacoochee, Georgia, that man would have been Cranford Sutton.

Sutton was born in 1936 and grew up in Willacoochee, a farm market town in south Georgia. In 1925 his parents purchased the house in which they and their only child would live. He now lives there by himself. In compiling the house's history, Sutton noted that the structure was built of Georgia pinewood in 1899–1900. To commemorate the first hundred years of the large, two-story house, he rehabilitated its exterior in the late 1990s.

Sutton worked as a music teacher, band director, and guidance counselor, mostly in a public school district near Willacoochee. Now retired, he has served on a regional development committee and is a leader in the town's volunteer library program and its local history group.

WILLACOOCHEE DATES FROM 1889. When I was growing up in the 1940s and 1950s, it was pretty well self-contained, the center of the universe. We had two train lines running through here, north-south, east-west, twenty-four hours a day. Our downtown storefronts were the old-fashioned brick fronts with plate-glass windows that turned inward, inviting you in the door. We had a movie theater that operated the whole week long, with Saturday night late show and Sunday afternoon matinee. I would park the pickup truck downtown at two o'clock on Saturday afternoon just to have a parking place on the front street, because by dark everyone from the surrounding countryside had come in to buy their groceries and visit. It was a huge gathering each Saturday. We young people had many activities and two cafes, one with a piano. We would play and sing and dance there and walk and ride up and down the front street.

My parents had a strong work ethic, and I was raised to work. We farmed, and my father was a rural mail carrier, which ensured a good income. I was raised with the idea that you must take care and you must preserve, that it is important for things to be kept orderly and in good shape. My mother insisted on this house being kept clean and in excellent order and repair. Some things were too nice to be used all the time. "We don't use that until Sunday," my mother would say.

Long ago I was aware that this town was special and that my role in it was to be something of a caretaker. I was raised with the idea that we are stewards of our farmland and forests. And this old house was to be protected and cared for. I developed an attitude of stewardship with things and also with people. People were also to be treated respectfully, formally. Even at home, my parents corrected me if I referred to an adult by his or her first name. My parents were elderly when I was born, and I was trained to be very courteous and kind and very careful with everything. I think that's one reason I became a counselor. And after retiring from my career as a teacher and counselor, my intention in becoming a massage therapist was to find another way to help people heal.

Willacoochee had about a thousand people when I was a child. Now we have about twelve hundred. But the town's character has totally changed. We've had so many of our older people die, a whole new group of people have grown up here, and new people have moved in. Everyone's locked in their homes with their TVs and VCRs, their cable and computers. Their attentions are turned away from the town, and many of them travel out of town to work. Willacoochee is now a bedroom community and a mobile-home manufacturing center. Everyone drives eighteen miles to Douglas to shop at the Wal-Mart.

There was a strong sense of community here in Willacoochee and a sense of history. Several of us here had talked about doing something to save that history. In 1996 we began to meet informally, and out of that grew a group called the Warp and Woof of Willacoochee History, Incorporated. We've had as many as fourteen in the group, nine or ten women and five men. Now we're down to four or five members, of which I'm the only man. A pitiful little spark, but I'm thankful it's still going.

The city council has given us the historic Willacoochee Women's Club building, a log cabin built by the Civilian Conservation Corps in the 1930s. The Women's Club was organized in the late 1920s and lasted until the 1960s. So we're in a falling-down log cabin, trying to get a grant to reconstruct the building to serve as a local museum and welcome center. The Warp and Woof has become the only civic club in town, the pseudo-chamber of commerce, and the conscience of the city council. We've done a census of the old Willacoochee cemetery. We've acquired microfilm copies of the four Willacoochee newspapers that were published from 1900 through 1930. We've gone into the school and given talks to the young people about our activities and some of the facts we have established about Willacoochee's origins.

Because we have such a sense of the past and remember how Willacoochee was, at times we find ourselves trying to recreate that. Each year we have an Easter banner parade. We've asked each church to partici-pate in making banners, and we now have about thirty-five, most of them made by people in our history group. The ladies have sewed quite a bit, and I've made quite a few banner poles. We recruit people to carry them at the sunrise service on Easter Sunday.

"Let me live in a house by the side of the road and be a friend to man." Like Thoreau, I pride myself on keeping an open and inviting door for many visitors, local and distant. There's always been a strong sense of living pres-ence in this house. It has never failed to be my center. I really hope I get to die at home. My mother wanted to, but we could not arrange it. The house contains the same furniture that my parents bought. The only thing of any significance that I've added is a concert grand piano. Other than that, it's like it has always been, the same early-marriage furniture that I love so much. I've had to repair or reinforce every piece of it, all the chairs and bedsteads and tables. I love this place and have a duty-bound commitment to it, but sometimes I get so sick of the constant work. One should be twenty-nine years old and have a million bucks to repair and restore one of these old houses. I have felt many times that if it wasn't the old home place and center of my growing up, I would simply pack and sell, run away!

It's kind of a given that gay men are good at cooking and decorating. That I did not get. I wire, I plumb, I do cars. I grew up with a yard full of old cars my father used on his mail route. You couldn't buy cars during World War II, so you had to make do. We couldn't afford to go on a vacation, but we could always buy car parts. That was almost as good as Christmas to me, to come home with a box of brand new parts to put on the car. And car repair was probably the only area in which my father and I really connected.

I have five automobiles, and these days my main passion is their care and repair. I got so tired of working on the house; I just recently gave up the idea of redoing the upstairs and went off and bought myself another Cadillac. A lot of my gay friends can talk car, but they're not interested in actually working on them. They don't want to get their hands dirty. I really enjoy it; if my hands are busy, my head shuts off and I can be at peace.

Highway Corridor Z, as they call it, goes from Columbus, Georgia, where the state's main military base is, to Saint Marys, Georgia, where the nuclear submarines are based at Kings Bay. This four-lane military highway came through all these small towns and destroyed their serenity and safety. With truck stops at each end of town Willacoochee has become just another little place you have to slow down. We've had people killed and injured in accidents, and we've lost a sense of community. We're a highway-divided town. Not far from here Wal-Mart's distribution center is pumping out six hundred semis a day. Plus all the other trucks that use this highway as a connector from I-75 to I-95. I'm not seventy-five feet off the road, so all of this has spoiled sitting and visiting on the porch, which covers about two-thirds of my house.

All the problems now faced by Willacoochee and other small towns along Corridor Z could have been prevented if our city, county, and state officials back in the 1970s had possessed wisdom and foresight. Bypasses could have been constructed within short distances of the towns, allowing travelers to see what they might enjoy stopping at and visiting. At a regional meeting with officials from the Georgia Department of Transportation back in the 1970s, I was the only person to protest their plans for this highway coming directly through the center of our village.

I see in the future a revival of these wonderful small towns. I envision an exodus from the sprawl of today's traffic-choked cities to places like Willacoochee, where walking or biking to the post office, to the grocery store, and to visit others is safe and revitalizing. I believe that we all have within us the capacity and energy to heal our differences, to coexist, to be teachers, learners, and doers together. This is what I strive for, and I'm so thankful that I have been given the opportunity to work and heal here in the wiregrass country of south Georgia.

Domophiles Out West

SEATTLE IS HOME to one of the largest concentrations of gay men in North America, so it's no surprise that the city has achieved an outstanding record in architectural preservation and urban conservation in recent decades. Larry Kreisman has played a large role in this accomplishment. A native of New York City, Kreisman completed a master's degree in architecture in Seattle. Working in the city's urban conservation division introduced Kreisman to architectural preservation. He did research for the city landmarks program and produced his first book, *Apartments by Anhalt,* about the work of a designer-developer who arrived in Seattle in the 1920s and built apartment buildings unlike anything the city had known before. By the age of thirty, Kreisman knew that he wanted to work in preservation.

"As I grow older, I become more convinced that I was born out of time—that all my sensibilities set me on the stage of life a century ago and it was only a quirky accident that brought me into the world in 1947. I probably would have been much happier if I had been born in the late nineteenth century and had grown up in a world of Beaux Arts designs, with a lot of character from ornament and decoration and grand spaces. I have always maintained a romantic, sometimes nostalgic view of the world—a conviction that things were more beautiful, more expressive, and better crafted back then. It has become one of the great pleasures of life to surround myself with furniture and decorative arts that evoke the ambiance of an earlier place and time."

Through the 1980s and 1990s, Kreisman produced more books about historic architecture. They included *Art Deco Seattle* and *West Queen Anne School: Renaissance of a Landmark,* which chronicled the life, decline, and rebirth of a building that the school district planned to demolish and that was transformed into residential units in the early 1980s. *The Bloedel Reserve* documented a private estate on Bainbridge Island. *The Stimson Legacy* examined the architectural projects built by one family, from the Midwest to the West. *Made to Last: Historic Preservation in Seattle and King County* was published in 1999, the second edition of Kreisman's 1985 book, *Historic Preservation in Seattle.*

Living in Seattle's Ravenna district with his partner, Wayne Dodge, Kreisman is program director at Historic Seattle. He helped found the tour program of the Seattle Architectural Foundation and directed it for twelve years. He writes design features for the *Seattle Times* and is involved with the International Coalition of Art Deco Societies. During his six years as historian with the Seattle Landmarks Preservation Board, Kreisman exerted his most direct influence on his adopted city's architectural integrity.

"I do not negate progress, new buildings, and the need to accommodate new growth and activities. But it has been my job to constantly remind city agencies and private developers that for every step forward, it is not necessary that something valuable be lost. To conserve means to be moderate and prudent, to keep from being damaged or wasted. It connotes a respect for the past and a cautious approach to accepting the new or the different. To be conservative prevents the loss of the character-defining built features that make Seattle unique.

"In my writing and teaching and the architectural tours I've developed, I try to make residents of this city more aware of their built environment and help them learn to think visually. I want people to have a grasp of architecture and design, what buildings are like, why they stand up, why they look the way they do. And that it's important to retain them so that we have a collective history, a collective memory. I want them to go away from their tour with a sense of pride in their city and an appreciation of the value of these things, so that they can spread the word."

A world away from the Emerald City, Cliff Schlothauer fosters civic pride in his New Mexico hometown. Like many of his kind, Schlothauer's love of old things started early: By the age of seven he was scavenging for "antiques" in an old dump on the farm where his family lived. "There were bits of fine porcelain, which I assume came from the main house, and broken Mexican pottery from the Hispanic laborers, and many other things. My father let me keep my collection in the maid's quarters."

Schlothauer grew up in Las Cruces, New Mexico, just north of the Mexico border. He now lives with his mate, Ron Donaghe, in a 1913 Craftsman-style adobe house in the city's Alameda Depot district. "Being a small, poor town, Las Cruces didn't have much to begin with, so what has survived is very precious," Schlothauer says. "We have lost so much, but there are still structures to save. When I purchased this house in 1991, it was the blight of the neighborhood. In the years Ron and I have lived here, it has become the best-looking house on the block. With all we have done to renovate it, we've helped to raise property values on our street. If I were to come into a great amount of money, I would renovate more houses in this neighborhood and entice more historically minded homeowners to move here. Because of my interest in this district, my brother and his wife have purchased a home next door and are in the process of renovating it. They have three children and so are adding another generation to the district."

"Living in this part of Las Cruces, I feel a sense of permanence and stability," Schlothauer says. "It gives me feelings of happiness and comfort to know that my father grew up playing in the park down the street where I now see children playing and neighbors walking. We enjoy a wonderful feeling of community that the rest of the city does not have. I shudder when Ron and I drive through some of the newer, wealthier sections of the city and am thankful for where we live—for our mature trees, the patina of age, our not-so-perfect sidewalks, and the many other irregularities. Our district has endured time and turmoil and is still here, mostly intact."

Thanks to Robert Frost and Ralph Bolton, the Witter Bynner House in Santa Fe, New Mexico, is still standing. With the idea of opening a bed-and-breakfast inn, the couple bought the place in 1996. A well-known poet in the early twentieth century, Witter Bynner (1881–1968) first visited Santa Fe in 1921. He bought a three-room adobe house on the edge of town, built in the mid-1800s. Through the next several decades he added on, creating a rambling villa of thirty rooms in Spanish-Pueblo Revival style. Bynner acquired adjacent lots and landscaped extensively.

"The house was basically sound but needed immediate attention," Bolton says. "There were cracks in the top of the adobe walls, and if rain kept penetrating those cracks, it wouldn't take long for the house to collapse into a pile of mud. The bank agreed to lend us the money to buy the property only if we took an extra two-hundred-and-some thousand dollars to do the immediate restoration, which we gladly did. We replastered the outside with three coats, reroofed and rewired, and replaced rotting viga ends and inappropriate windows installed post-Bynner. We've also restored the gardens and walkways, which were famous in Bynner's time, and rebuilt the adobe wall that surrounds the property."

While Bolton and Frost operate the Inn of the Turquoise Bear, they continue to restore the place, guided by their ongoing research. "We were fortunate enough to locate a gentleman who knew Bynner and who helped us document what the house looked like before," Bolton says. "He showed up one day with about thirty invaluable photos, mostly of the interior. People who knew Bynner have been giving back things that belong in this house. An ancient Chinese vase is back on the mantel exactly where it is in the photos from the time when Bynner was here. The gentleman who gave us the photos brought the vase to us one day. 'It belongs in this house,' he said.

We know where the furniture that Bynner had is stored away, and we're trying to get the owner to either donate it or sell it to us. We've obtained some vintage photos of Bynner by Ansel Adams. A painting of Bynner by Henriette Wyeth went to a museum in Roswell, New Mexico. We would like to commission someone to make a copy to hang back where it once hung. We haven't located Henriette's portrait of Bynner's lover, Robert Hunt, which hung in Bynner's study. Witter Bynner was himself a preservationist, much involved in setting up Santa Fe's preservation ordinance. He deserves better than to fade completely into obscurity."

Domophilia is a key trait among preservation-minded gays—the love of houses and things homey, a deep domesticity. Just as Larry Kreisman, Cliff Schlothauer, Robert Frost, and Ralph Bolton are dedicated domophiles, so too are the individuals in the profiles that follow. Jay Yost, ever enchanted by old houses, describes undertaking the massive job of rehabilitating his childhood favorite in his Nebraska hometown. Forever fascinated with old houses and what happened inside them, Ken Miller reflects on his career in interior restoration in Colorado, which includes the revival of his own Queen Anne house in Denver over a twenty-year period. Growing up in Missoula, Montana, Gilbert Millikan admired the Queen Anne house where his surviving partner, David Richards, now lives. The couple resurrected that house and several others in the neighborhood since 1975. Comfortably settled in a 1907 house with his partner, Charles Fuchs, Seattle resident Richard Jost believes "most gay men have a strong streak of the romantic in them and can live it out vicariously by being associated with these fine old homes."

Jay Yost

Born in Red Cloud, Nebraska, in 1957, Jay Yost is one of the young-est members of the board of governors of the Willa Cather Pioneer Memorial and Educational Foundation, based in Red Cloud, Cather's hometown. "Few Americans seem to realize what a treasure they have in Red Cloud, a veritable little *ville musée*," A. L. Rowse wrote.[1] Gay men have been a devoted presence among those appreciative few since the Cather Foundation was established in 1955, and Yost is a solid link in that lineage. Jay Yost lives in New York City with his partner, Wade Leak.

WHEN I WAS GROWING UP, our family's idea of fun was getting in the car and driving somewhere. Most of our forays consisted of touring our home-town and the rest of Webster County, discussing who lived in a certain house when and what connections we had to those folks on one side of our family or the other. As my parents regaled us with stories of a home's now-departed inhabitants, I couldn't help but imagine what those houses and farmsteads looked like when their owners were young and ambitious and proud of their small piece of Western civilization on the prairie. It was these rides that planted the seeds of my fascination with seeing how things had been. My craving for imagining the past was further encouraged in the late 1970s when my history-crazed sister gave me a copy of *Webster County: Visions of the Past,* a wonderful book that chronicles the architectural heritage of each of the county's sixteen precincts.

When I lived in France in 1980, after college, Paris was in the midst of cleaning the exteriors of all its buildings. It was just amazing to see things going from "before" to "after." Even as a kid I was always wanting to fix things up, make them look good again, make broken old things work again. I've always been meticulous and anal-retentive. There was an irregular, empty lot catty-corner across the street from where we lived, where the road jogged a little bit, with hedge apple trees behind it. I would mow it and put in little plantings, and there was a log in the middle of it for visitors to use as a bench. I called it Pooh Corner, a quaint little natural setting I created and tended, like an English garden.

I've always been captivated by old houses, and there were three or four really beautiful ones in Red Cloud that I remember loving as a kid. Of course, they're gone now. While they were being torn down, I would wander around in them after the wreckers had left for the day, trying to picture what had been where. One great old house with a mansard roof had huge bowed wooden beams, like somebody had bent the wood. I couldn't believe they were tearing it down.

Fascinated with an Eastlake bedroom set of my grandmother's, I tried to imagine what kind of house it would have been in. I started picking up a few antiques when I was in high school. By then I had my own bedroom, so I kept my antiques there, including an Eastlake table and mirror. It was mostly junk that I would fix up, things I would find at garage sales or be given by old ladies who didn't want the stuff anymore and knew I liked it. I was a big plant freak too. If you know how Victorian rooms used to look, filled with lots of plants and stuff, that's how my bedroom looked. I had forty-some plants in there.

My father had a meat-packing plant, so I usually worked there, but one summer during high school he had me work on landscaping the yard full-time. I really got into it. We built a deck, laid brick walks, built terraces in the higher part of the backyard, constructed a small barn. I also envisioned a secluded little patio with a fountain, but it was never built. I was creating little rooms outside, imagining how people would relate to those spaces. That's how I always thought about houses too—how a house made you feel, whether intimidating or cold or comfortable. I didn't like newer houses; they made me feel like I was cooped up inside a trailer.

I was always a bit strange. In high school I went out for football for a couple of years, then refused to because I hated it. I joined Pep Club: one guy and fifty-five girls. I wore neck scarves and wooden beads, coordinated my outfits, had my hair done in an Afro, and was the only kid in Red Cloud wearing earth shoes. I'm sure my parents must have been dying a thousand deaths, but they never said anything. I got really involved in the church, was a Jesus Freak for a while, going to both the United Methodist and Assembly of God churches. It was pretty wild. I even spoke in tongues eventually. By about my junior year in high school I dropped the Jesus Freak thing, but I spent much of my senior year going to Methodist church meetings. Being a minister was one thing that I always tested high for.

Growing up in Red Cloud, I loved to attend the Cather events, with all the academics and other people coming into town. You could always spot the Cather people, as we always referred to them, walking around like alien invaders. I would go to the spring conference. I'd pad around the museum. I'd go to the dedication ceremony when the Cather Foundation would acquire another building. In junior high I was thinking how cool it was that they were buying these old buildings, protecting them until they could restore them. Wherever I go, I gravitate toward this stuff. It's something that just keeps following through.

On April Fools' Day in 1996, I bought my own old house in Red Cloud. It's at Ninth and Seward, a block from where I grew up. When my parents would work late on Saturdays, my sister and I stayed overnight with the old widow who lived in that house. She would have a couple of widow friends come over on Saturday nights to watch TV. The house was kind of creepy and smelled a little like a nursing home, but it was also really cool: it had staircases both front and back, and one of the stairway windows had red glass panes, so that everything was red when you looked outside. The place also had a big old barn, a carriage house.

I must have had another life as a Victorian, because I'm just way too attracted to everything that has to do with the period from the 1880s to World War I. When I was a little kid, running my fingers over the etched glass in those two front doors, dashing up the stairs, looking out that red window, I tried to imagine the original owners, what kind of life they had there. I thought how cool it would be if I could have a life like that and how wonderful I would feel if I lived in a space like that, with all the woodwork and moldings, chandeliers and fireplaces.

Years ago I told my babysitter that I wanted to own her house some-day. In the early 1990s I sent a letter to remind her of my interest. When she started to lose it to Alzheimer's, her daughter-in-law called me. I ended up buying the place for five thousand dollars, which is what the land is worth. The house was in such bad shape; anybody else would have just torn it down. Most people think I'm crazy to have bought it, but it's cited in the National Register as one of the three most significant houses in Red Cloud. I just thought it would be horrible to lose it. It was built in 1888 by Charles W. Kaley. There are three Kaley houses: an older one from the late 1870s, my house right beside it on the corner, and another built across the street in about 1907.

The house is being worked on slowly, slowly, like everything moves in Red Cloud. It took several thousand dollars to clear all the trees that had grown up on the property. Then they put on a completely new roof, but before they could do that, they had to rip out all the original chimneys and rebuild them, because the mortar had turned to dust. The siding and trim need a lot of work before the house gets a good paint job. A new foundation is the next big project, before we start any interior work. We did get the three stained-glass attic windows repaired: I want to illumine them with lights that will go on automatically at night.

The house is an uninhabitable shell, without heat or water or electric-ity. The heating was so inefficient that it would have cost several hundred dollars a month just to keep the pipes from freezing, so we had everything shut off. Then the barn collapsed under heavy snow, and the city ordered me to tear it down. Unfortunately the electricity ran to the barn first and then to the house, which shows how old the wiring was. Anyway, once you have the electricity cut off, you have to be up to code in order to have it turned back on. So now I'm screwed. As soon as we get the foundation in, we're going to start doing internal systems. There's a little outbuilding, perhaps the washhouse or cookhouse, that we redid recently, so that's cute now. It was in as bad a shape as the barn, but it's much smaller, so it was a lot easier to do. I'd like to rebuild the barn and make it into a living space.

I still think of Red Cloud as my home. Once we're retired, I tell Wade, we're going to live in the house for a month in the spring and a month in the fall. Assuming my siblings and I won't have my parents' house after they're gone, we can all get together at the Kaley-Yost House, and there will be enough room for everybody. The rest of the year I would rent it out to Cather scholars or other people who have a Cather connection, or to people who want to visit Red Cloud to get away from it all. I had made previous attempts to buy old houses around Red Cloud. My sister and I were going to buy one of the biggest houses in the county, north and east of town, but the owners decided they didn't want to sell the abandoned place after all. Then I tried to buy the Wick Cutter House, a small house at Ninth and Cedar. When the Charles Kaley House came up, I felt like fate was telling me that I had to do it.

A building is kind of your history, and once you lose the building, you lose the memories. I've written letters to the Red Cloud newspaper, saying that every time I come home, they've torn down another piece of my past. Saying that if you take away all the old buildings, you're really taking away people's history. Pointing out the soulless quality of Republican City, a town up the river about thirty miles that was relocated and built anew in the 1940s, when they put in the dam. The buildings there lack character and dignity. They don't embody people's shared history; they don't make people feel good about themselves.

We don't really own these old buildings; we're just stewards of them. Recently a tin cornice was removed from one of the buildings next to Dr. Cook's old drugstore, across the street from the Red Cloud Opera House. It was a safety hazard, and they couldn't get anybody to fix it, so they cut it into three pieces and took it down. When I was home, I noticed that it was missing, asked where it was, and was told that it was in the alley. I called the guy who owns the property, and he agreed to store it in the basement of the building. I'm getting the shop class at the high school to fix the cornice as a class project, and I'll raise the money to repair the parapet wall that it's attached to.

Red Cloud had a National Register survey done back in the 1970s, which designated four historic districts in the town as well as all the individual sites. For years I pushed for Red Cloud to adopt a historic preservation ordinance, even offered to help draft it. Now that the town has one, I'd really like to work with the historic preservation commission to designate local landmarks and districts and to get a more potent version of the ordinance adopted. Right now, all it does is delay demolition. It needs to ensure that any alterations to historic structures are historically appropriate and that inappropriate structures can't be built in designated historic districts. I found out, for example, that a new church is to be built behind the historic Saint Juliana Falconieri Catholic Church. Talking to the guy who owns the lumberyard, who designed the new building, I learned that it's going to have wood siding and a metal roof. I tried to let him know that it's important that the color of the roof be dark, so that it doesn't stand out when you're looking at the old church.

Around the turn of the last century one of the local newspapers published several little picture books of Red Cloud and gave them away to their subscribers. I've had them enlarged on color xeroxes, laminated, and bound. I gave copies to the library, the high school, the museum, and the Cather Foundation, so people can see how these houses used to look. A lot of what's needed in Red Cloud is just education. Many people like having old buildings around; it's important for more people to realize that they need to work for them.

Soon after I purchased the Kaley house, a niece of theirs lent me a turn-of-the-century photo postcard of the home showing a beautifully maintained Queen Anne house with her great-uncle and great-aunt sitting proudly in their horse and buggy on the lawn. I had the photo enlarged, and the detail is such that you can clearly see the nail holes in the skirt of the fence behind them. You can't ask for much more when you're trying to restore a gem of an old house.

Intrigued by the postcard of the Kaley House, I began collecting other real-photo postcards of scenes from Red Cloud and surrounding towns and of old opera houses in the region. The quality of many of these images is amazing, since the negative originally produced was often the same size as the postcard itself. Visual history of this quality allows us to see much of the world that Willa Cather saw growing up—the same world that she, while sitting in her New York apartment decades later, vividly recalled in her Nebraska novels. These photos also demonstrate how incredibly lucky we are that the buildings Cather knew are still in existence and how we can help to assure the town's future by ensuring that we save its past.

Ken Miller

Ken Miller was born in Denver, Colorado, in 1947. After completing
an undergraduate degree in history he served in the Peace Corps in
Iran, then returned to the United States, and completed graduate degrees in religion and Middle Eastern studies. Following a fellowship in
Egypt, Miller moved back to Denver. There he met Larry Lyons, his
lover and business partner, who died from AIDS in 1992.

ONE DAY IN THE MID-1970s, traveling from downtown back to my
mother's place, where I was living at the time, I drove through a section of
Denver that I had never experienced. When I was growing up, there were
areas of the city you didn't go to, streets you didn't cross. I never understood
why; that was just the way it was. But here I was, driving through Swallow
Hill, one of the older sections of town. Denver at that time had just the
slightest inclination toward urban revitalization and preservation. These things
may have been roaring on the East and West Coasts and in Chicago, but in
Denver they were barely surfacing.

Living and traveling abroad, I'd been exposed to so much historic architecture. I had actually become more interested in the architecture than
in my academic studies. As I drove down this street in Denver, passing one
decaying Victorian building after another, I was absolutely captivated. When
I looked over at an incredible terrace, I thought, I want to live there. That
was the first place I went looking for an apartment, and they had one for
rent, so I moved in. The building was home to a lot of hippies and other
marginal types, and everybody formed a wonderful little community within
the building. It was the perfect environment for me, and I became absolutely enamored with American architecture of that period. I knew nothing
about it; I just knew that it engaged me.

I met a gay man who had gotten into decorative painting on the
West Coast, and he invited me to get involved in that work with him
during what proved to be his brief stay in Denver. That was my introduction to preservation. We worked in an old Victorian home in the Curtis
Park area, one of the first districts in Colorado to be put on the National
Register, an intact neighborhood abutting the downtown. I realized there
was something going on here that I not only enjoyed but was excited by
and wanted to learn more about. At that time in Denver there wasn't anybody who knew a damn thing about interior restoration, so anything that
we wanted to do had to be researched. With my academic background I
was well suited to that.

Within a few months I asked another gay man with whom I had become acquainted if he might be interested in going into business with me. Maybe there was some potential there. Both of us had nothing, so we had nothing to lose. We jumped into it head first, neither of us with any academic background in preservation or art. This man who became my business partner also became my lover. So Larry and I had a unified and very focused life. We survived financially by pooling whatever minor resources we had and putting all our effort into promoting and doing what we could with this crazy idea, dealing primarily with restoring historical interior finishes and design.

I met Larry because he lived in the same building, the fabulous Queen Anne terrace in the Swallow Hill area. We eventually moved in together, and then when that building was sold, we traded work for rent and moved into an 1880s sandstone house that was on the other side of the city but still in the inner city. By that time we were so completely immersed in the Victorian environment that there were no alternatives. I would not consider living anywhere else. I tell people that I've lived in all the great slums of Denver. Of course, now they're so yuppified that you couldn't get near them with three hundred grand, but back then it was a different story.

The late 1970s and early 1980s was the period of the West's great oil boom, so there was a lot of money. People who weren't necessarily preservationists were getting involved in property development in a Wild West kind of way: nobody knew about these parts of town, but the buildings were good deals, and, what the hell, what have we got to lose? So Larry and I began doing projects for some of these people. Of course, we palmed ourselves off as experts even though we didn't know a damn thing about most anything. We would tell people that we knew all about it, then come home and try to figure out how in hell to do what we had just promised. I named our business The Grammar of Ornament, after the book with that title.

One day we were just driving down the street, and there was a fabulous 1920s kind-of Beaux Arts house that had been donated to the city as headquarters for the adjoining botanic gardens. A sign out front said that a ceiling restoration project was being funded by the Colorado Historical Society. Larry suggested that we stop in, and, to make a long story short, we talked ourselves into the job. Our experience has been that if we don't know about something, we'll find someone who does. The person who ran Historic Denver lived at the other end of our block, and through her I got in touch with a guy who worked for the National Park Service and also did paint color analysis. We asked him if he would help us. People were very gracious, understanding that we didn't know what we were doing but respecting our desire to learn and to do things correctly.

After that project we went back to doing private homes when they were available. There were periods when we had nothing, when we had to take second jobs, and then we managed to get a project at the United States Mint downtown. Unfortunately at the time of Larry's death we were at the threshold of our most successful period. In the years since, I've been the recipient of the fruits of our labor up until that time, and the inheritor of Larry's drive and commitment.

The house that Larry and I purchased in the Curtis Park historic district was almost completely derelict. But it was the size and style we wanted, and we could never have afforded a house like this already renovated. We got into it like a couple of guys on a tree-house adventure, with totally unrealistic expectations about money and time and effort. Thank God, we were ignorant. We moved in and began the process, which I thought would take five years. My, how time flies. I've been here for a little over eighteen years, and just last year I finished the interior.

About a year after we got into this house, the oil crash hit, the economy went flat, and we saw people losing things all over. People had moved into these big old houses, mortgaged themselves to the hilt, borrowed massive amounts of money to renovate, and then lost everything. Larry and I decided that the house had to be done with cash and that we would do as much of the work ourselves as we could. We were not going to jeopardize our home by borrowing money, which we couldn't have done anyway.

I was never trained in preservation, and I had no art training whatsoever. Why did I end up doing this? From my earliest memories I was always fascinated with houses and what happened inside them. Two things that were extremely important to me as a child: One Christmas I got an absolutely fabulous toy gas station, one of those little 1950s metal things with the cars and ramps and garage doors. A couple of years later I wanted a miniature house. Well, of course, there was only one way to describe it then: a dollhouse. I got it, and I don't remember anyone freaking out about it. After all, I hadn't asked for dolls.

Most of the houses in the area where I grew up were built from about 1900 to about 1920. They were what we call Denver Squares. Contemporary houses didn't appeal to me because they didn't have a past. We lived a block from my grandparents, so I formed a very close relationship with them and loved spending time in their home. My grandmother had begun collecting antiques from the time she was first married, about 1917, so she had old pieces and the stories that went with them. I would spend a lot of time hanging out with her: Tell me about this. Where did you find this? What does this mean? She had collected and maintained an enormous amount of family history, letters and artifacts that went back to 1815 and earlier. All these things fed my interest. Now I've become the repository of all that stuff, which I'm currently farming back out to the relatives.

I've always loved history. As a five-year-old I was cutting things out of the newspaper that had to do with old dynastic families. Good Lord, I could hardly even read. I did a lot of yard work in the neighborhood in the summers, and any money that I earned I would spend at antique shops with my grandmother. I became fascinated with a type of pressed glass that was a ruby red color. I didn't particularly care what the object was; I just loved the color. When I would go to the Saturday movie matinees, I was obsessed with movies that had anything to do with lost cities or people finding treasure. I was always fascinated by the past, anything old, anything hidden, anything unrecognized.

For more than ten years Larry and I were the preeminent interior restoration consultants in Colorado. There was no one else doing it, so we ended up working on all the major preservation projects in the state. Eventually they played out, and there hasn't been a lot in the years since. Around the time Larry died, we had begun a major shift away from preservation. Now I deal almost exclusively with very high-end residential projects.

Preservation has all sorts of wonderful things about it, but it doesn't pay shit. No one ever has any money. They can have a ten-million-dollar project, and by the time they bring you in, they say that they ran over budget on everything else, so all they have left for you is ten bucks. That may be fine when you're young and if you're willing to live the starving artist lifestyle, getting along by the seat of your pants. But I was never interested in leading a bohemian life. We needed to go where there was money.

Now I design and execute painted period interior pieces: eighteenth-century Adam ceilings, Louis XV ceilings, Tudor Revival things. So, I've left preservation in the strictest sense, but what I do is still part of the historical continuum. There's nobody in the state of Colorado qualified to do what Larry and I used to do. Now they have to haul someone in from New York and pay through the nose to get restoration stuff done.

Nobody around here would ever study with us; no one was ever interested in learning to do what we did. Out here in the rootin'-tootin' West, men do not get involved in my profession. They may get involved in preservation, but being an architect is the only way that is socially acceptable. Otherwise, you're too artsy-fartsy and suspect. I got so tired of women, only women—and I'm not a misogynist—but I just wondered, isn't there a *man* out there who's interested in this? What's the problem? Do they consider this effeminate? You go to the East or West Coast and that doesn't play anymore, but in the West it still does. It's not regarded as a manly thing to do. You're a "fop decorina," as we say.

Larry and I poured ourselves into the revival of a late 1880s Queen Anne house, one of America's icons of family, heritage, tradition. In my family and social circle, everybody wanted to come to our house for Christmas and other holidays. Our involvement in preservation has involved us in the resuscitation and safekeeping of all our pasts. This house and a handful of houses around it were scheduled to be demolished for a telephone switching station. I've wanted to make sure that whenever I give up this house, it would never occur to anybody to demolish it. Of course, demolition is legally impossible now.

Denver destroyed most of its downtown through urban renewal. They leveled blocks and blocks of our history to make room for parking lots. It went on in the 1960s and 1970s and 1980s and 1990s; they're still doing it. Now, if it's Victorian, it's safe. But if it's a magnificent International style building from the 1930s, they don't give a damn. Tear it down. Destruction in Denver is an ongoing thing because the city is so pumped-up on money and its sense of self. That's pretty typical of Western cities, and Denver has done that ever since it was founded.

We lost the downtown. All we had left were the neighborhoods. Thank God, the block I live on has been city landmarked. Because of the economic boom and downtown development, and because this area is a ten-minute walk from the middle of downtown, our property values have gone through the ceiling. As a self-employed person, I see this as my retirement. It's one of the few times that I can say, boy, it was a crapshoot and I won on this one. But I have no intention of leaving this house until I cannot physically maintain the property. I'm an inner-city rat. When I visit people who live "outside," I get creepy-crawlies after a few hours away. I want to return to my neighborhood, my culture.

Gilbert Millikan and David Richards

Through the 1950s and 1960s and into the 1970s, Gilbert Millikan witnessed the destruction of many historic buildings in his hometown of Missoula, Montana. Seeing the potential of the elegant old Queen Anne house on Raymond Avenue, he and David Richards purchased it in 1975 and began to restore it. Twenty-three years later, the couple hosted an open house in celebration of the showplace's centenary. The brochure they produced detailed the house's history, stating that "what you see today is a Victorian masterpiece, thanks to Gilbert, who has successfully preserved and enhanced the unique and picturesque property with the hope that all who succeed him will maintain and enhance the property for the next one hundred years."

DAVID AND I HAVE KNOWN EACH OTHER since we were kids. My aunt was married to David's great-uncle, which makes us shirttail relatives. We were both born and raised in Missoula; I was born in 1936, David in 1926. My roots in this area go back to around 1899, 1900, when my mother's parents came here from Nova Scotia and New Brunswick. My father's parents came from Georgia and Kansas to Stevensville, the oldest community in Montana, thirty miles south of here. David's great-great-something-or-other-grandfather signed the Declaration of Independence.

After David graduated from college, he went out to Hollywood, where he spent the greater part of eleven years writing for many television shows. We became reacquainted after he returned to Missoula in 1965, and we've been partners in life ever since. Everybody in the community knows about us, though we've always tried to maintain a low profile. But it's obvious that we're a couple when we've been together for more than thirty years.

David is the inside man: he does the designing, carpentry, painting, decorating, and cooking. I'm not much in the kitchen or with a hammer and saw. My priorities are out in the garden. David has worked as an architect these past thirty-plus years and has designed many fine homes in Missoula. He designed the new garage and sunroom addition to our house and the gazebo so that they harmonize with the original house. He's not quite as intrigued by the old as I am, but he goes along with what I like.

I've always been fascinated by old dwellings and places like Virginia City, our ghost town here in Montana. Missoula was never very interested in preserving its old buildings. I saw a glorious mansion destroyed by the wrecking ball because the citizens here wouldn't approve a bond issue to save it. The house and grounds were offered to the high school, which was adjacent to it. Part of the city block on which it sat could have been used for a running course, and the mansion could have housed various school activities. Or it would have made a magnificent public library. But in the 1960s big old houses like that were seen as white elephants, so it ended up being demolished. I was devastated when it was torn down, but with my energies focused on running my floral business, dealing with the public sixty hours a week, I never joined a preservation group or got out and protested as I should have.

For twenty-five years I ran my shop in the same corner of town where I grew up and where my dad started in 1932 with a little market. There was a wonderful Queen Anne house directly behind my business, but the lady who owned it let it deteriorate over the years until finally it was torn down. And then there was the most elegant Victorian house in Missoula, the Greenough Mansion, situated on a huge parcel of land with stables, a beautiful gazebo, and ornate wrought-iron fencing around the property. The family had traveled all over the world and collected many fine things. There was a French room and an Indian room and on the third floor a huge ballroom. The Greenough Mansion had to go because it was in the path of the interstate highway. One of the heirs had it moved to another part of town. I was happy that it was not demolished as others had been, but it wasn't restored very well. It survived as a restaurant until fire destroyed it in 1994.

As a child I was fascinated by this house where David and I now live. I remember admiring it and wondering who had lived in it. Sitting on an acre of ground with a little stream running through, it was the last old house in town with space around it. Over the years, as Missoula grew, most of the big houses were built right next door to other houses. But here, ten minutes from downtown and from my shop, I felt like I was out in the country. An elderly woman who had lived in this house from 1920 until 1949 gave us several photographs of the house in that era.

The family who lived here for several years before us had done quite a bit of inside work, including the slow, tedious job of stripping paint from the interior woodwork and restoring the wood to its natural beauty. But much of the place had fallen into disrepair. It needed foundation work and rewiring, it was underheated and needed insulating. That's how things began for us here, and we discovered that it needed many other things as we went along. You always get into the unexpected redoing an old house, and it generally ends up costing at least twice what you originally thought it would, sometimes much more.

We eliminated the wire fence that ran across the front of the property and replaced it with a white picket fence more in keeping with the house. We added a paved circular driveway and sidewalk so we could use the wonderful, grand entrance at the front of the house instead of coming in through a side door as previous owners had done. Even with its 1960s shag carpeting and garish wallpaper in hues of orange, green, and cream, the house was livable when David and I moved in. We put up with that look for several years because there were so many higher priorities.

Back in 1890 William and Carrie Raymond purchased 120 acres in the Middle Rattlesnake Creek area of Missoula, much of which was an apple orchard. By 1898 they had saved enough to buy a Victorian catalog house, for which they paid $3,750. The materials were shipped in from Tennessee, the house constructed, and it was immediately a showplace. The street we're on was named after the Raymonds, but I've been debating whether or not this should be called the Raymond House, considering that they lived here only about three years. I had imagined a romantic tragedy: he built the house for his bride; she died; he was broken-hearted and sold the place. But our local historical officer sleuthed through the files of the *Daily Missoulian* and discovered that the Raymonds' divorce made front-page news in the early 1900s. William Raymond was a philanderer, it seems, and she caught him and filed suit against him. Rarely in those days did a woman sue for divorce and the husband contest it. But Mr. Raymond did contest it, lost the case and the house, and left town. Mrs. Raymond sold the place a year later.

Over the years the property was divided again and again until when we bought it there was just slightly more than an acre. The grounds were suffering from decades of neglect, with weeds and brambles, overgrown bushes and trees that we had to cut down, and old stumps that needed to be removed. We left the century-old spruce and pine trees and a wonderful gnarled mulberry that was as pretty without its leaves as with them.

Much of the paint was peeling when we bought the house, so we brought in a crew with heat guns one summer to strip the exterior down to bare wood. Then we started over again with painting it. It still requires retouching every year or two, which is one of the reasons we went to a totally white look instead of creating a Painted Lady. White doesn't fade, so you can do touch-up more easily. I get color accents with vegetation and all the flowers and container gardening that I like to do. My great passion has been the garden, where I grow many plants that I knew and loved as a child, including some of my parents' and grandparents' favorites: lily-of-the-valley, phlox, Shasta daisies, and some of the shrub roses that my Grandma Millikan grew.

After three more years David and I will have been in this house the longest of any of its owners. And we have done the most to restore it, taking some artistic license but always in keeping with its Victorian style. I've always lived in older homes. In the early 1960s I bought a house in the University district, a place that was constantly a work in progress, like this one, though it was not a showplace. David and I did a lot of the work while we

were living there, redesigning, redecorating, and adding two nice apartments. I liked the feel of the neighborhood, close to the university, with
boulevards lined with maple trees and alleys running through the blocks to
separate neighbors, so you'd get a bit more privacy. We lived there until we
bought the Victorian, then rented out the property until we sold it in the
mid-nineties.

Now we own a duplex and an artist's studio adjacent to us, plus all the
houses in the adjoining block, which are rentals. One is a brick house nearly
as old as ours. Its floor plan wasn't much, and we wanted to make it into a
nice rental, so David designed a new interior. We gutted it and started new,
but the exterior of the building still looks as it did when it was built. We
could have torn it down and built a new house for less than we spent redoing
it, but it's a wonderful old house of the same era as this house, and I really
wanted to keep it.

I've always been a collector. I collect antique jewelry of the period in
which our house was built—stickpins and brooches, mourning pins, hair
rings, and bracelets. I have cigar cutters and lorgnettes, a wonderful beaded
Tiffany bag, another that's embroidered. There's a whole history of the era
in those small things. We've kept the front parlor of the house furnished as
a vintage Victorian parlor, with a beautiful set of antique Victorian furniture
that includes a sofa, love seat, his-and-hers chairs, side chairs, and an antique desk and marble-top tables. The room has French pocket doors, so it
can be closed off as they often did a century ago when the room was not in
use. The rest of the house is a real potpourri. We didn't want the entire
house to be a Victorian period piece with a lot of heavy Victorian furniture
that you see so much around. The rooms in this house are actually quite
small and would have been dwarfed with those kinds of furnishings. Besides,
when my mother died she had some nice furniture from the early 1920s,
like her china closet and dining-room buffet, and some of those things are
nostalgic to me.

Richard Jost and Charles Fuchs

Richard Jost and Charles Fuchs met in Denver, Colorado, in 1981, and now live in the Wallingford district of Seattle, Washington. Jost, born in 1954, grew up in suburban Syracuse, New York. Fuchs was born in 1943 and grew up on a farm near Humphrey, Nebraska.

RICHARD JOST: CHARLIE AND I have always lived in older homes. Indeed, we both feel more comfortable in older homes and would not consider living in anything contemporary. Our current house, built in 1907, still retains most of its original layout and feel. Our furnishings are mainly pieces that were handed down to us from our families and would not fit into a contemporary design. We were the ones in our families who expressed an interest in having the pieces of furniture that no one else wanted because they were seen as too heavy or old fashioned. When we have purchased furniture over the years, we have made sure that the style fits in with the older pieces we already own.

My interest in collecting old furniture began at a very young age. I seem to have always been scavenging discards from the neighbors or haunting Salvation Army stores for odd pieces of furniture that attracted me, even as I was trying to cram it into my childhood bedroom. I vividly recall the day of my grandmother's funeral, when my grandfather took me up into the attic of their house in Syracuse and told me that I was to have two pieces of furniture that were stored there: a brass and marble plant stand that was a wedding gift to a great-aunt in 1900 and a Gothic Revival chair, which had been in the family for a long time. I still have both pieces in my home and treasure them. My grandfather told me that I was the only one in the family who would appreciate these things.

Why did my grandfather give them to me? Certainly most adolescent boys were not collecting antique furniture, so even then my interests (which had always been very divergent from those of most of my peers) were on a decidedly different course. As my realization of my gay identity grew stronger, so did my interest in historic preservation and design. Did my grandfather sense this in me even before I might have been fully aware of it myself? Did he know that I would take good care of these pieces of family history for him and that to pass them on to anyone else would be a waste? I'll never know for sure, but I do know that his actions helped me to realize that this interest of mine was okay, which opened many new opportunities for me.

In college a study-abroad program allowed me to spend a year in Paris. I was a history major, and a strong part of my desire to go to Europe was my wish to enrich my grasp of history and have an opportunity to see the wonderful architecture that I had been reading about. It was a very fulfilling year, during which I spent most of my weekends taking day trips around the French countryside, visiting chateaus that were open for tours. This continues to be my favorite form of travel and touring, visiting historic homes and studying period design.

I have been a member of the National Trust for Historic Preservation for many years and have always had memberships in the local historic preservation societies wherever Charlie and I have lived, including Denver and Seattle. Since moving to Seattle in 1992 I have become involved in the Seattle Architectural Foundation, a group devoted to enhancing public understanding and appreciation of the city's architecture, primarily historic, through guided tours and lectures. I now serve on the tour board and help organize the tours.

My interest in architecture and design brings me a great deal of satisfaction and has enriched my life beyond measure. I collect books on preservation and design and am constantly adding, subtracting, or moving around furniture within the house to come up with a new design. Lucky for me, Charlie is very patient with all this and lets me indulge myself without too much complaining. How all this fits into my being gay is somewhat a mystery to me. But many of the volunteers at the Seattle Architectural Foundation are gay men, and that has usually been the case in other historic preservation groups that I have been a member of. It would seem to argue for the existence of a preservation gene, which I would guess is located very near the Broadway show–tune gene.

Perhaps so many of us gay men gravitate to historic preservation because it is linked to a certain romantic past. The mansions and historic homes represent an idealized past where romance seems to be inevitable. I think most gay men have a strong streak of the romantic in them and can live it out vicariously by being associated with these fine old homes. It is also certainly true that there is a design element in historic architecture that speaks to many of us and that we are trying to preserve the best of the past just because there is something beautiful about good design itself, no matter what the time period.

For me historic preservation and friendship are bound together. Many of my friends are gay men I met through membership in preservation groups; with others we simply discovered that we had a shared passion for preservation and that brought us together. In Denver in the mid-1980s it seemed that all the gay men Charlie and I knew were buying old houses and fixing them up. Dinner conversations were all about paint colors, period fixtures, and faux finishes. I remember my friend Dale, now deceased, who used to make scrapbooks for his own pleasure with articles on architecture and historic preservation clipped from the *Washington Post*. Last year I spent a long weekend in Newport with my college roommate Michael, touring the great houses and soaking up the local color.

Charles Fuchs: I collect John Deere antique tractors, the old ones that are started by cranking the flywheel. It's not that I want to go back to the times when these things were made or when I used them in Nebraska. In fact, I've spent much of my life trying to escape from those times and places. But old tractors evoke for me strong and nostalgic memories of my own working on the farm and the simplicity of small-farm life. I now value my life in a big city, but my journey began with those machines. The old two-cylinder John Deeres were used at a time when a farmer was close to the land and could understand how his tractor was put together and how it worked. Today's tractors, gigantic earthmoving machines, are almost certainly a mystery to the person inside the air-conditioned cab. "Homesteads" of today look more like industrial dumping grounds than they do places for aesthetic enrichment. Orchards, gardens, shelter belts, milking barns—these are things of the past. They're not functional; they don't make money.

Back in Nebraska I got acquainted with an old farm neighbor who lived with his sister and never married. He began taking photos when he was sixteen or seventeen. The last time I visited him, when he was still living on the farm, he showed me his original camera, which he still used, an old 120 bellows-type that he bought from a Sears catalog. For something like eighty years he wandered around the countryside taking pictures, mostly of parades and often of weddings or social occasions. His house was a museum. Only in recent years did he get a telephone, and I'm not sure he ever had a TV. Water came from a windmill on a hill behind the house, and heat was provided by a cook range in the kitchen and an oil stove in the living room. A closed-off pantry next to the kitchen served as the refrigerator. He farmed with horses as late as the 1950s, when he quit farming and rented out the land. He and his sister took care of their parents until they died at an old age.

The original house his parents built he kept painted and trim, though no one lived in it for many years. He lived in the "new" house next door. Avidly Catholic, he had a collection of photos of what must have been every Catholic church in Nebraska and many from neighboring states. He also had a collection of matchbooks and key chains, the kinds of things businesses would give away as gifts at Christmas. Something of a hypochondriac, he religiously took vitamin pills and patronized about every chiropractor within a day's driving distance. I'm sure this man was gay, though his times and his religious background prevented him from ever really knowing what he was.

I need to go to the hospital to have a hernia taken care of. I've been telling everyone that the surgeon recognized it immediately as an EFM hernia: excessive furniture moving. Twenty years of helping Richard arrange and rearrange his heavy furniture. Richard and I are interested in such different things that we complement each other, in an odd sort of way. We're both interested in old furniture, but he's constantly playing with his old china, about which I know little. Richard collects china and has acquired too much of the china his mother and aunts had. I don't know what he plans to do with it all. But I genuinely enjoy looking at china with him, and he accompanies me to look at antique tractors, about which he knows little.

I also collect old typewriters, mostly the beautiful black monsters designed for simplicity and enduring performance, like locomotives. When I type on one of them, the neighborhood knows it! The typewriter that I use regularly, given to me by my father in 1959, still works well, not only because it was well made but also because I've valued it and taken good care of it. It's more than an inanimate object; I think of it as having a personality. I shudder to think what will happen to it when I am no longer able to use it or care for it. I think I know: It will become an orphan, sold to some auction house, which will in turn sell it for junk—landfill.

Richard is fond of saying that when he met me, I didn't even have a bed, that I slept on a pile of rags. A couple of years ago, when we happened to be wandering around Harrod's in London, looking at the Royal Doulton china, I commented on some pattern that I liked. That stopped Richard in his tracks: he just couldn't believe that a Nebraska farmer would say such a nelly thing. On the other hand, when he goes with me to tractor exhibitions, he's exposed to a world that is both amazing and amusing to him. We've wandered around antique stores in tiny towns in Kansas, Nebraska, Iowa, and Missouri, places that he would never have found had it not been for me.

Whenever we go to antique stores, which I very much enjoy, I have the feeling that I am picking around in someone's private history. At one time these objects were given as gifts and taken home with great pleasure. I have a painted glass egg, "Easter 1909," that my mother won at the one-room school she attended in rural Nebraska. Often she told me how thrilled she was as a little girl to win that treasure and how carefully she held it on the sleigh ride home. Will it ever find another custodian as careful as she?

Richard and I have pictures and pieces of furniture that others in our families didn't want. They're important mostly because of the family history and stories that go along with them. We treasure these things, but we're unsure what to do with them. Richard has nephews and nieces, but our feeling is that they would not be much interested. I have no close relatives to whom I could tell stories told to me by my father. For example, my father had his appendix taken out on our dining-room table in 1919. Richard sometimes reminds me that dinner guests need not know of this event, but I find myself telling these stories to some of our visitors. I'm a little sad that the stories will probably end with my death. We gay men collect and preserve this stuff, but we often have no one to pass it on to. I've given some thought to writing the stories and the histories on little sheets of paper and pasting them behind the photos or stuffing them in the legs of tables. That way, someone at another time and in another place will know.

California Conservative

LIKE MANY GAYS WHO CAME OF AGE in the 1950s and 1960s, Roy Little and Jim Raidl left their hometowns and gravitated to San Francisco. They met in 1971 at a gay bar in a part of the city that was just beginning to go gay. Many rundown Victorian houses in that area were becoming available, cheap, as blue-collar residents left the neighborhood for the suburbs. What had been known locally as Most Holy Redeemer Parish would become known as the Castro, after the landmark Castro Theater, a 1922 Spanish Gothic movie palace.

"I always wanted color," says Roy Little. "From the time I was three years old, I knew that I was going to be an artist." In 1973 he and Jim Raidl found an outlet for their domophilic artistry: a dreary four-story Victorian on Hartford Street, in the Castro. "The house was in good condition, but nothing had been done to it since it was built just after the turn of the century," Little says. "There were so many possibilities. It was a virgin house with no fancy stuff about it, and we wanted it fancier. So we worked on making its presentation better. We started playing with color, restored the textured wallpapers, added rosettes to the ceilings. We did all the stained glass in it after we learned how to do that." Within a few years Little and Raidl's Queen Anne house became a showcase of antiques and interior design, and the couple operated an antiques shop for several years.[1]

Roy Little and Jim Raidl were caught up in a crusade of urban revival that had started years earlier in another part of the city. "In the 1950s and 1960s, an almost invisible movement of middle-class gay men began buying faded Victorians in Pacific Heights," writes Randolph Delehanty in his San Francisco guidebook. "Then 'Lower Pacific Heights' (the blocks south of California Street) drew buyers, then Dolores Heights, then Noe Valley, then the Castro." The 1970s saw a renewed surge of restoration in San Francisco, as newly arriving gays refurbished old houses: "Many young gay men and gay couples made their living by buying, restoring, and then selling Victorian houses," Delehanty writes, "only to buy more faded real estate to propel the process further."[2]

In their books on the Victorian Painted Ladies of San Francisco, Elizabeth Pomada and Michael Larsen document the richly colorful results of this exceptional burst of architectural redemption. Though the books do not mention gays explicitly, they offer coded acknowledgment: Pomada and Larsen describe the city as a shelter for "one of the world's greatest collections of individualists" and as "a unique and magnificent setting that attracts creative people, people who take pleasure in color and design, as well as artists of all kinds for whom design and color are an essential part of their personal and professional lives." They dedicate their books to "the legions of the faithful who have fought with words and actions to save the Victorians" and to "the artists, homeowners, painters, and color designers who are transforming San Francisco into the most colorful city in the world."[3]

Since their construction in the last half of the nineteenth century, many of San Francisco's thousands of ornate, multicolored Victorians became drab and dilapidated, targets for urban renewal's bulldozers. Scrap-metal drives during the two world wars stripped away much of their wrought-iron ornament, and many were doused in battleship gray Navy surplus paint or covered with asbestos siding. Gay men have been at the forefront of San Francisco's colorist movement from its beginnings in the early 1960s. They saved many of the city's degraded Victorians in distressed neighborhoods, buying them "VOV"—vacant, open, and vandalized—and camping out inside while getting going on rehabilitation. For many, interior restoration proceeded slowly, perhaps one room each year. The exteriors were the first things to be revived, returned to their original polychromatic splendor.

Legions of gay men from throughout the country became acquainted with San Francisco during World War II, and many of them made it their home when the war ended. Gay historian John Loughery states that apartment buildings in various parts of the city underwent "queenizing" in the 1940s.[4] More gays from throughout the country gravitated to the Queen City of the West in the 1950s, seeking refuge during the national homophobic frenzy. It was during the psychedelic 1960s that gay men's artistic and restoration sensibilities began to burst forth in San Francisco. Local writer Herb Caen told of a little old lady who had been following the progress of two painters working on a Victorian for several days. Seeing that they were starting to apply a fourth color, she yelled, "Now you boys stop dropping acid—you've got enough colors up there already!"[5]

One of San Francisco's pioneers in the Painted Lady revival began in 1963 with a combination of intense blues and greens on his Italianate house. Some of his neighbors loved it, some detested it, but before long many of them were repairing and repainting their own houses. "It only takes one good flower to make everyone want to fancy up," commented another early color designer. "Gardening tools appear, the street gets swept, windows are cleaned. The people in the neighborhood don't change, but now they have something to be proud of, to respect, and none of the newly painted Victorians ever gets graffiti or abuse after they are finished."[6]

Gays may be readily glimpsed among the band of evangelists preaching the gospel of color and renewal: Two men move into a grim gray house in 1962, unpainted in sixty years. After restoring seven houses on his block, a man finds the street renamed in his honor. A color designer says his work is most satisfying when he's working on degraded properties because he can contribute to neighborhood renovation. A man describes his Victorian home, a perpetual work in progress, as a personal statement against the lack of ornamentation in modern culture. A mansion that was to be torn down and replaced by condominiums is turned into a bed-and-breakfast by two men. The profusion of individual restoration enterprises gave rise to organizations like Victorian Alliance and San Francisco Victoriana.

Lee Liberace was another craver of color and renewal, and in the earliest years of San Francisco's Victorian revival he was working similar redemptive magic in Los Angeles. Beneath Liberace's flamboyant show-business facade beat the heart of a quintessential gay preservationist: "I feel that all these beautiful things I live with have been placed in my care to look after," the popular musician wrote in the 1970s. "They don't really belong to me; they belong to the world . . . somewhere, somehow, they had been abandoned or not cared for. Then I came along and saw a broken chair or an unwanted dog or a forgotten antique that cried out to be saved. The reason I have so many dogs—I have fourteen altogether—is because the majority are animals that no one else wanted."[7]

Liberace claimed that all his homes were structures that would have been torn down if he had not rescued them: "Anyone can build a house if they have money. But to take something that is going to be destroyed and is dying, and make it live again—that is a very special thrill for me."[8] His third Hollywood dream house, for example, was a badly deteriorated mansion built in the 1920s and long uninhabited before he purchased it in 1960. Liberace biographer Darden Asbury Pyron writes that "the deterioration actually pleased him. He loved redeeming the unlikely, mending the broken, reclaiming the forgotten, recovering the abandoned."[9]

"Liberace always loved the shoddy, the secondhand, the unpolished, the unfinished," Pyron writes. "He preferred things the world rejected—run-down houses, broken furniture, stray dogs, and, not least, human flotsam. He told a reporter, 'I've always liked to take something that is ready to be destroyed, decadent almost, and prove that it can have another life by restoring it.' The reporter observed, 'He has saved houses, pianos, vintage automobiles, old movie props. He has saved a pound's worth of canines. . . . If, you find yourself thinking, he's had his occasional troubles with people, it's probably because he's wanted to save them, too.'"[10]

"I admire beautiful things, obviously, but I admire even more seeing some ugly duckling things become beautiful," Liberace wrote. "Sometimes it's very difficult to help people in such a direct way, most of them are very sensitive to change. But you can always help a piece of furniture."[11] Lee Liberace exemplified the close vocational relationship between religion and preservation, a deeply rooted calling to rescue diminished things and make them whole and beautiful again. "I once thought I ought to become a priest," he wrote.[12]

Growing up in New York in the 1940s and 1950s, Kent Warner found his calling in the glorious, glamorous world of music and costume, stage and screen. As a child Warner collected 78-rpm records, phonographs, telephones, and radios. With the advent of long-playing phonograph records, his love of musical theater led him to buy original cast albums. He would listen to them over and over, building miniature stage sets complete with lighting and costumed figures, moving and changing them as the record played.

By twenty-one Warner was in Los Angeles and working for Berman's Costume House. When Berman's purchased the old RKO studio wardrobe and decided to discard most of it, Warner moved quickly to save what he could, including garments worn by Ginger Rogers and Fred Astaire. At Berman's, Warner developed his knack for locating seemingly unfindable old costumes and his reputation for "liberating" some of the choice things he found. He was known as Lana Lift among some of his friends, and the mid-1960s was a prime time for Warner's lifting: movie studios were being bought by corporations that had no particular interest in the vast accumulations of the old wardrobe, prop, and publicity departments. Costumes, script drafts, key books, musical scores, press books, and publicity photos were being incinerated or buried in landfills. Warner salvaged as much as he could.

A connoisseur of movie memorabilia, Warner was most drawn to preserving clothing from the best movies of the 1930s, Hollywood's golden age. He studied his favorite movies so that he knew which costumes to look for. Because he adored Ginger Rogers, he worked especially hard to find her costumes. Judy Garland was another of Warner's idols. When he went to work for the Metro-Goldwyn-Mayer auction in 1970, a year after Garland's death, she was very much on his mind, especially in her role as Dorothy in *The Wizard of Oz*.

MGM had just been sold, and decades of warehoused props and costumes were about to be liquidated. As the designer of displays for the MGM star-wardrobe auction, Warner scavenged among the hundreds of thousands of costumes to help the liquidators prepare for the sale. More than anything, he wanted to find Garland's ruby slippers. "I think *The Wizard of Oz* was the ultimate representation of home, family, solidarity, well-being, security," Warner said. "At the same time there was this madness and fantasy of Oz. All I can think of is the heels clicking and Judy saying, 'There's no place like home, there's no place like home.'"[13]

Warner discovered at least five pairs of dust-covered ruby slippers on the third floor of one of seven costume-crammed buildings. He put them all in his duffel bag and took them home to examine. He determined which had been worn for dancing (they were quite battered), which were used in medium and long shots, and which had been worn by Garland's stand-in (they were a different size). The pair that had been kept in pristine condition for use in close-up shots was the pair that Warner kept for himself, the take-me-home-to-Kansas pair. Eventually he displayed them in his home on a spotlighted pedestal. "He took them out of the case and showed me the bottoms," said one of Warner's boyfriends. "He showed me where Judy tapped her heels together. They had little, circular scuff marks. He said they were worn only in that scene. I almost fainted."[14]

Kent Warner died from AIDS in 1984. While Hollywood burned and buried much of its history through the 1960s and 1970s, Warner was among the first to work for its preservation. "Kent was the greediest person I ever met," said a fellow collector. "I was always grateful he was stealing. He certainly saved costumes that would have been thrown away. But his greed got the better of him. He would steal a dress and sell it to buy a chandelier. But a lot of things were saved like that."[15]

In San Diego, Jeffrey Shorn and Charles Kaminski were among the first to be concerned with preserving the area's modernist buildings. Natives of New York, Kaminski was born in 1946, Shorn in 1944. Both worked as architects in the Peace Corps before they met in New York City in 1974. The couple were lured to San Diego from their Central Park West brownstone in 1975, when they were informed of a vacancy in a Rudolph Schindler–designed complex of beach cottages. So began their protective relationship with El Pueblo Ribera, the beautiful twelve-unit complex of concrete and redwood cottages from the 1920s, designed by the Viennese architect. Within a year of moving in, they attempted to protect the site from insensitive changes by getting El Pueblo Ribera designated as a historic district. This controversial venture sparked in the couple an even deeper interest in the area's historic architecture.

"For all the architects there were in San Diego, no one gave a damn about historic preservation," says Shorn. "It was just being born as a movement here. The Historic Sites Board had just been created. There was no preservation consciousness, only developer consciousness: level everything as quickly as you can, just for the land. The landlord who had called us so nicely in 1975 did not want El Pueblo Ribera designated historic and ended up throwing us out. But just recently I got to rebuild one of the units there that had been completely destroyed by fire. So we're still fighting little battles for Pueblo Ribera."

"We're not necessarily involved with the Victorians or the Craftsmans, which most people associate with preservation, especially in San Diego," says Kaminski. "We've tried to get people interested in the early modernists, like Schindler and Richard Neutra and the later modernists like Louis Kahn. I've called Jeffrey the chaperone for the Salk Institute, designed by Kahn in 1961. It was a very young building, but it needed to be designated historic because there was a proposal to expand it."

Jeffrey Shorn established the first historic preservation course in San Diego and has been involved with the city's Save Our Heritage Organization, its Historical Resources Board, the Balboa Theater Foundation, the La Jolla Historical Society, and the California Preservation Foundation. Charles Kaminski has been his steadfast collaborator. "By our natures we find value in the past and would like to be part of preserving it," says Shorn. "We seek to learn from the past in order to create for the future, while sustaining the historic fabric of our cities in the present." Still, Shorn says, "Southern California is the automobile's world. Even San Diego's downtown is not yet a real downtown. Chuck and I want a sense of space and place, walking amongst buildings. We're thinking maybe we would like to live in an older culture, go to Europe for a while."

"We want a smaller scale, more intimate spaces that are tangible and touchable and have a touch of history," says Kaminski. "Maybe it's a gay gene that makes that happen: We're the 'between' people. Think of Jackie Kennedy and Philip Johnson joining together to save Grand Central Station—the ultimate queen and the ultimate queen's queen."

The "between" people whose stories follow carry out their culture-keeping missions in a state noted for its attraction to things new. At home since 1965 in his painstakingly restored Victorian row house, Nebraska native Richard Reutlinger contends that "if a bunch of auslanders like myself hadn't moved into San Francisco, none of this would be left. The basic native San Franciscans didn't care." Gerry Takano's twenty-five years as a preservation architect have led him to hold a similar view: "Seeing the potential of old buildings to be attractive, gay men are not afraid to go into marginal areas and fix them up. I have found that this gay sensibility is very much out there, in every community." Architect and planner Jeffrey Samudio got involved in city planning at eighteen, when a block of historic buildings in his Los Angeles community was threatened with demolition. Within the next several years Samudio declared a dozen city landmarks. "Of the people that I got to know who were early into preservation here in L.A., most were misfits . . . eccentrics," says historical consultant Jim Wilke. "I was fortunate to develop friendships with a lot of gay men who liked old stuff."

Richard Reutlinger

Since 1886, when it was built for businessman Henry Brune, a handsome Italianate row house has stood at 824 Grove, between Webster and Fillmore Streets, in the Hayes Valley district of San Francisco's Western Addition. In 1965 Nebraska native Richard Reutlinger rescued the languishing place when it was seventy-nine years old and he was twenty-nine. The two are well into their fourth decade together—an affectionate and sustaining collaboration of High Victorian vision and just good fun.

MY GREAT-GRANDPARENTS WERE PIONEERS in Nebraska, where they helped found the little town of Fullerton. When I was young, I spent a lot of time with my grandparents, my mother's parents, and was fascinated by the stories they would tell me about pioneer life. When I was about ten, my dad built a cabin at a lake near our hometown of Lexington, Nebraska. My parents were not especially interested in anything historic, but the cabin was a very primitive thing, with a coal stove in the kitchen and kerosene lamps. I thought it was just great, recreating the pioneer life that my grandparents had told me about. I practically lived out there at the lake every summer.

About that time my sister married a man from Kansas whose mother had furnished her whole house with Victorian furniture. That was the first time I'd ever seen anything like that, and it really turned me on. After one of our visits down there, I went to a secondhand store in Lexington and bought a dresser, my first piece of Victorian furniture. I also bought some of the early Victorian-era artifacts that fascinated me, especially kitchen gadgets like apple peelers and other crazy mechanical pieces.

I had a pretty close relationship with my grandparents. I was the only one with any real interest in the family artifacts and photographs, so as people died off I inherited things from them. My great-uncle Lynn, who was kind of the archivist for my mother's side of the family, left me a lot of stuff. Fortunately, he had written names on the backs of all the photographs going back several generations. Uncle Lynn was a very gentle man, almost effeminate. (Grandpa always referred to him as Aunt Lynn.) I think Uncle Lynn was gay. He was a pharmacist like his father, and his drugstore, which survived until the late 1950s, was pure 1910—marble-topped soda fountain, wire furniture, mahogany paneling. He and his sister lived together for fifty years in the same town as my grandparents, so I spent some time with them in the summers growing up.

I got involved with music early on, took accordion lessons, and then started teaching accordion. Aunt Louise, my mother's sister, was a very entertaining woman and a good ragtime pianist. When she would come to visit, she'd play all this great music for me. I really got hooked on that musical era, which almost coincides with the Victorian era. Vacationing in California with my folks one year, we visited the Cliff House in San Francisco, which had a large collection of player pianos, orchestrions, and other mechanical instruments. I was absolutely entranced by them: they sounded just like Aunt Louise! And so back home in Lexington, I sold my Lionel electric train to a friend and bought a player piano from the local furniture dealer for fifty bucks. I had it delivered to our cabin at the lake before my folks knew anything had happened. That was the beginning of my mechanical instrument collection. We had tons of fun with that piano all the years I was in high school and college, until I left Nebraska.

We often went to Colorado for vacations, and I visited a lot of the old mining towns—places like Central City, Georgetown, Leadville, and Cripple Creek. It was really fascinating to see those places that had just sat there for so many years, pretty much intact, having had nothing much done to them. I was very interested in mining history and read books by Lucius Beebe and Charles Clegg about the nineteenth century, about railroads, about San Francisco, and books on Colorado history. I subscribed to the *Territorial Enterprise,* published in Virginia City, Nevada, and edited by Lucius Beebe. It was a very flamboyant newspaper, with lots of Nevada history. By the time I was living in San Francisco, I was pretty well versed in the history of this city and of Virginia City, Nevada, which funded so much of the development of San Francisco. It was such a lavish era—the architecture, the food, the entertainment, everything—and I was just caught up in it and loved it all.

I worked in Yellowstone Park during college summers and would hitchhike all over the place on my days off. That's how I made my first visit to Virginia City, Montana, an abandoned mining town that had been bought up and restored, or at least arrested in its deterioration. The old stores were stocked with period merchandise, and the homes were furnished so it looked like the residents had just stepped out, leaving everything in place. Virginia City had a big influence on how I eventually went about putting my own house together: I wanted to have all the small things, the day-to-day stuff that people would have used at the time.

Alaska in the mid-1950s was sort of the last frontier, which appealed to me romantically, a throwback to all the pioneer stories that my grandparents had told me. I thought it would be great to live up there and left Yellowstone with the idea of going to Alaska. But I was broke by the time I got to San Francisco, so I decided to stay in the city until I had enough money to go on.

I soon fell in love with San Francisco and that was the end of that. I've never been to Alaska, and I've never been homesick for Nebraska.

Shortly after I moved to San Francisco, I got interested in theater organs. We had a huge Fox Theater, one of the big five, which seated over five thousand people and had an absolutely glorious French Renaissance interior. It was in good shape and was still being used as a movie house when the film studios were forced to divest themselves of their theaters. The Fox was offered to the city as a performing arts center, for about $1.2 million, and the city rejected it. That's when I got involved in my first preservation project, trying to save the Fox. We got it on the ballot twice, and both times it was turned down by the general populace. By the late 1950s, early 1960s, so many native San Franciscans had moved to the suburbs, and the city really suffered because of it. Buildings were left to deteriorate, and people just weren't interested in preservation. Ultimately the Fox was torn down. It was just incredible that a place that beautiful went.

The Western Addition was solidly Victorian when I moved to San Francisco in 1956, block after block of wonderful gingerbread houses. They looked kind of bad because they had deteriorated and hadn't been painted in years, but they were in good shape structurally, and the neighborhood was still intact; nothing had been torn down. I couldn't believe all this crazy, fanciful architecture, and I had no idea that within ten years most of it would be gone. Redevelopment didn't really get going until the mid-1960s, but it was already planned at that point. This was basically a black and low-income neighborhood.

There were lots of antique/junk shops in a five-block stretch of McAllister Street, just a few blocks from where I live now. Because so many people were moving out of the city, those dealers would get stuff by the carload and just stack it up to the ceiling in their shops. If you bought something, it would sometimes take them a day or two to extract it from the stack. My first purchase was a big gilt-framed pier mirror. I just loved those shops and was over there every weekend, seeing what I could find that I could afford that would fit into my apartment.

After living in a Nob Hill apartment for about two years, I moved to a four-room cottage on Nob Hill. I furnished that place totally in Victorian. Then in 1962 I bought a six-room working-man's Victorian on Elizabeth Street in the Mission district. The facade was nice, but it had nothing going for it inside, and it was in bad shape. I didn't have much money, but I had helped some lesbian friends rehab a couple of houses, so they helped me. I had that place for about three years and learned a lot of general skills, carpentry and plaster patching and floor sanding. It had three bedrooms, so I rented out rooms to help make payments.

When I got this house on Grove Street, it was structurally sound, but there was major damage throughout the place. I worked on it for close to nine months before I could move in. I would wake up on Elizabeth Street, go to work at the accounting firm all day, come directly to Grove Street and work until midnight, then take the bus back to Elizabeth Street. This went on for months. In the meantime, I found a buyer for Elizabeth Street, two guys who had come out here from Boston. They didn't have any furniture, so it was fine with them that I continued to live there with them for a while.

The Grove Street house had been the black Antioch Baptist Church for twelve years before I got it. During that time they had taken out the central furnace and installed oil and gas heaters throughout the place. But they didn't vent them, so all the ceilings became coated with a gummy residue. Getting ready to paint, I was in the dining room scrubbing the ceiling, when all of a sudden the old paint started to flake off the picture rail. I found that the upper rail was gold leaf and the lower one was silver leaf with little copper flowers. I also discovered that some of the woodwork that had been painted over had originally been grained to look like walnut or other woods.

My basic premise when I first got the place was to get it cleaned up so it was livable, then rent out rooms to help with the mortgage payments. I learned a lot as I went along, and the idea of putting it totally back into period came to me gradually. When I first had the place, people would talk about all the lost arts: nobody did plaster cornice work, carving, stenciling, gilding, graining, or marbleizing anymore. It wasn't until the mid-1970s, with the bicentennial, that people really got interested in these things again, and young people could make a living at them. And so all these arts reappeared. The Artistic License group here in San Francisco, a guild of these artisans, is an outgrowth of that revival.

When I bought the house, I knew that it was well designed, but I didn't know that it was architect designed. That revelation came about ten years later, when a friend happened to find my house listed in the October 1886 issue of *California Weekly Architect*. It was designed by Heinrich Geilfuss, a well-known architect in San Francisco in that era. Finding out that it was architect designed added a lot of luster to the reputation of this house. I got hooked on the whole era and decided I wanted to put it back as close to period as I could. Some of my early restoration work I've redone as I've learned more. I've been extremely fortunate over the years to have very fine craftspeople work on this place. And the house has good bones to work with.

I had gotten some Turkish Victorian furniture, very comfortable armchairs that are built on wire and wrought iron frames. Burlap is stretched over the frame and everything's built on that, and of course the burlap eventually rots out. I couldn't find anybody who could redo those chairs, so I decided to try an upholstery class, which turned out to be a lot of fun. I kept going for five years, twice a week, so I reupholstered quite a bit of furniture. It would take me a semester to do one of those chairs because they're so involved. The instructor was a wonderful little old Englishman who knew all the old techniques.

The upholstery on the 1870s love seat in the master bedroom is original to the piece. It has seven kinds of needlework, including portraits of Queen Elizabeth and Sir Walter Raleigh. My theory is that the upholstery was so flamboyant, it got covered up early on and stuck away for years, and that's why it survived so well. The first time I saw the piece, in the mid-1960s, it was in a shop down near San Jose. I was fascinated with the piece, but whatever they were asking for it was a lot more than I could afford. Several years later it showed up in a shop in Marin County (there couldn't be two like it!), and again it was more than I could afford. I think the third time I saw it was in a shop in San Francisco. The fourth time, in 1975, was in a five-floor antique emporium down on Market Street that had a big sale every year. The first week was 10 percent off, then 20 the second week, on up to 50 percent. I had taken a neighbor down there during the 50-percent-off week to see a sideboard that I thought was just perfect for his dining room. He bought the sideboard, and as we were walking down the stairs to the first floor, there on one of the balconies sat that love seat. I asked if the price was half off, they said yes, and I said, "It's mine!" Sometimes you're just meant to have things. I used the colors in the upholstery to choose the colors for the whole room.

I love to find original textiles and work them into things. The valances in the master bedroom, velvet with appliqued designs, were in a parlor in a house here in the city that was going to be torn down. So I bought the valances and the red damask wall coverings, which turned out to be pretty fragile. I had to glue them to plywood panels before putting them on my walls. The drapes in the master bedroom are old theater curtains that I found in a junk store on McAllister.

Probably 90 percent of this house has been furnished out of Butterfield Auction Gallery. I would also check regularly in a number of shops, and the dealers would call me when they found something they thought I might want. I had running accounts with several of them, because rarely could I afford to pay the whole price at once. And we used to have a couple of really wonderful flea markets here in the Bay Area. I attended them religiously every Sunday morning, with a couple of other guys here in the neighborhood who owned a big house over on Alamo Square. Every couple of months we'd go around with a big truck and pick up all our acquisitions and take them to our respective houses.

That was part of the fun of this neighborhood. When I bought this house, I knew the two guys who owned the house next door. In fact, it was they who tipped me off to this house being on the market. I lucked out that the place was in such bad shape; most people didn't want to take it on. And I didn't realize that the neighborhood was quite gay. The larger neighborhood was predominantly black, but the immediate neighborhood, particularly this block, was almost totally gay owned. The guys right next door to me came from other western states, and quite a few of the guys down the block were from the Midwest. I don't think there was one who was a native San Franciscan.

After buying this house in the summer of 1965, I met two guys down the block a little bit further who had a really beautiful house. They invited me to their big New Year's Eve costume party. I'd stored a lot of my stuff from Elizabeth Street in the ballroom downstairs here, until I could move into the rest of the house. So a bunch of us came over here and raided the drag trunks down there, got all done up, and went to the party through the freezing cold. New Year's Eve that year was on a Thursday, I think, and I didn't get back to Elizabeth Street until Sunday night. We just kept going back and forth from one party to another on both sides of the street in this block. It was a great neighborhood to live in.

A lot of gay people down this way and all around Alamo Square had established the Alamo Square Neighborhood Association in the early 1960s. It was a very viable group by the time I moved here. We really had to get organized, because we were all slated to be torn down; this area was supposed to be redeveloped. We went after the Federally Assisted Code Enforcement program, and I believe we were the last residential area to get FACE funding before Nixon cut out all the money for it. We had to get the whole neighborhood organized. It was not a deal where you could just do individual buildings; it had to be the whole neighborhood. We had a lot of absentee landlords to convince, and we had a lot of poor blacks who didn't understand all the ins and outs of the program. So we established a citizens' advisory committee to work with them, so they would get their maximum benefits. I was on that committee for several years.

Most of the buildings in the neighborhood were structurally sound. Many of them didn't look good because they hadn't been painted in years, and the wiring and plumbing systems were failing, but the FACE program addressed all that. Once we got the program going, around 1970, it took about three years to get everything done, and it stopped redevelopment from coming into this neighborhood. I've contended for years that if a bunch of auslanders like myself hadn't moved into San Francisco, none of this would be left. The basic native San Franciscans didn't care. It was all just old buildings to them. The redevelopment agency asked the black community what they wanted, and they wanted new housing because the old buildings were just slums to them. And so they got new, and most of those new buildings are already falling apart, they were so badly built.

In the late 1970s a bunch of us decided that we should lobby at City Hall for historic-district status, to protect the architectural integrity of the Alamo Square area. Historic-district status protects only the exterior of the buildings, and we did not try for control of color, but there were some who opposed *any* control over their property. Like the FACE program it was a long fight, but we were ultimately successful in 1984. I was treasurer of the group, and holding a porno night at my place was one of the ways we raised funds for the project. One of my neighbors at the time produced quite a lot of still and movie porn, so it was a rousing success.

When I got my first apartment in San Francisco, I really wanted a piano. I thought maybe somebody in San Francisco would have a player piano that I could rent. There was a funny little piano store down in the Tenderloin area, with a player piano in the window, but whenever I went down there on lunch hours the place was closed. Then one night, when I was walking home from a movie, it was all opened up. It turned out that the two guys who had the place operated the piano department in the City of Paris department store. That's where they were during the day, and they used this location to do repairs. I introduced myself and asked if they would let me rent the player piano in the window. They wouldn't, so I bought it.

It turned out that the two piano guys were gay, and we became good friends. I was fascinated with everything about pianos. When they got in a reproducing grand piano, I was just entranced: it reproduced all the performer's musical dynamics as well as the notes. Artists like Rachmaninoff and Rubinstein recorded for the manufacturer. I really wanted that instrument. They said they would take the upright player back as a trade-in, but I still had to come up with about a thousand dollars. I was twenty at the time and couldn't get a loan until a friend cosigned for me. That reproducing grand was the beginning of my mechanical instrument collection in San Francisco. I'm a founding member of the Automatic Musical Instrument Collectors' Association, which got going here in the city in 1963. We now have about sixteen hundred members internationally, an interesting bunch of people, probably a third of them gay.

It was in Virginia City, Montana, that I got hooked on Fotoplayers. The summers that I worked in Yellowstone and went up there, there was an old stone stable that had been turned into a theater, and in the orchestra pit was a Fotoplayer. I'd never seen one before. The first time I went to see a production there, a guy came out in top hat and tails and went down in the pit and did some fiddling around, and all of a sudden incredible amounts of music were coming out of that machine. And I thought, *Oh, I've got to have one of those!* Fotoplayers were used to accompany silent films in small, neighborhood theaters. They have two piano rolls, so you can switch from one type of music to another, and you can reroll one roll while you play the other. And they have lots of pulls and pedals for the various sound effects—drums, cymbals, train whistles, horses' hooves, all that sort of thing.

I bought a big Fotoplayer from a fellow collector in the early 1960s and stored it in the garage on Elizabeth Street for a year before I got Grove Street. One of the things that really appealed to me about this house here on Grove was the big room downstairs, right at ground level, which was built as a ballroom. It's easy to move these big instruments in and out of that room. I also had a smaller Fotoplayer-like instrument, made by a different company, which we used in Little Theater productions. For about six years, until the time I bought the Grove Street house, I was very involved in the Little Theater in San Francisco and Sausalito. We would do nineteenth-century melodrama in the summertime, with vaudeville acts, in order to make some money so the winter theater could do serious stuff and lose money.

I joined the Victorian Alliance in 1973, a year after it was founded. It started out as a homeowners' group, to share house-restoration ideas and craftspeople and products. Then we got involved in the bigger picture of preservation in San Francisco, trying to save the City of Paris department store. We lost the department store, but we saved its rotunda as part of the new Neiman Marcus store, which would not have happened had we not fought them for four or five years. We're always writing letters to the landmarks board, giving small grants for various restoration projects, such as stained-glass windows in churches, and we have a scholarship fund to help people who want to take classes in interior design, particularly nineteenth-century. We've sent a couple of people to the Victorian Society of America summer schools. It's an interesting, volatile group of people and a lot of fun. We're a smaller group than San Francisco Architectural Heritage and not so high-society.

I've never seen myself as a scholarly collector. I just bought things I liked at the time, and in the last ten years I've learned so much about them. Until the last fifteen or twenty years, there was very little scholarly research on Victorian architecture and interiors. Architects and museums used to turn their noses up at the Victorian era. All that ornate stuff was seen as so distasteful and unrespectable.

I really enjoy opening my house to tour groups. It's pure theater when you come right down to it. But to me my house is just home. I never thought of it as anything so important, because a lot of my friends have Victorian houses too. They may not be as heavily into High Victorian as I am, but it's a style I like living with. In the last few years a number of people have talked to me about doing something to leave this house intact, as a house museum or something. I'm pursuing local landmark status; the house has never had that, even though we're in a historic district. Paul Duchscherer, who's been active with the preservation and restoration community for years, says that the house is an important example of early restoration work, before it was generally done. And a couple of other big-time collectors of Victorian stuff (whose quality is much better than mine, because I can't afford what they can!) have talked to me about the importance of my furniture collection and that I've put together a whole period interior. So maybe I need to establish a nonprofit Friends of the Brune-Reutlinger House or something like that. Hopefully, I have a few years to work things out.

Gerry Takano

Gerry Takano worked for the National Trust for Historic Preservation in the organization's western office in San Francisco from 1996 to 2000. Since then he has returned to private practice as an architect and planner. Living in San Francisco with his partner, Michael Stick, Takano is involved with Friends of 1800 Market and the National Japanese American Historical Society. Friends of 1800 Market supports the preservation of the San Francisco's architectural heritage, especially buildings and sites important to gay, lesbian, bisexual, and transgender history and culture.

A LOT OF GAY MEN REALLY DO have a sense of good design, a good aesthetic sense. Whether or not it's politically correct, I believe that stereotype is the truth. There are major differences between gay men and straight men, very different ways of living in and viewing the world. Seeing the potential of old buildings to be attractive, gay men are not afraid to go into marginal areas and fix them up. I have found that this gay sensibility is very much out there, in every community.

I was born in 1948 and grew up in Honolulu's Nuuanu Valley. Most of the houses were New England–style, wood construction, built in the early part of the twentieth century by the descendants of missionary families. My family is very working-class Japanese American, and we moved in there after many of those families began relocating to suburban neighborhoods. So I was around older buildings as a child, but I was also intrigued by urban renewal's radical transformation of old Honolulu. The city was being heavily developed in the 1960s, so a lot of historic buildings were being demolished, and nobody seemed to care. Because Hawaii had recently become a state, people just assumed that the new "mainland" growth was better, which was typical throughout the country. And in an isolated place like Hawaii, we were thirsty for change: new ideas, new things, new buildings, new developments.

In the early 1970s I attended Syracuse University to study architecture. It was a period of intense preference for modernism and fashionable antihistoricism. It wasn't until I was living in Boston's South End that I really developed an appreciation for historic buildings. That's where my connection to preservation began to click. The South End had a reputation as a seedy, dangerous place with many derelict old buildings, but the area's promise was slowly being realized by those who chose to live in the inner city, especially gay men drawn by the outstanding vernacular architecture. After acknowledging and accepting my gay reality, I broke off plans to marry a woman and moved into a brick 1860s townhouse flat on Appleton Street. I was near the gay bars of choice at the time and just up the street from a market run by a tough, burly gay man.

While working in the planning department of a large engineering office, I studied the impact that major development projects were having on old buildings and neighborhoods. Doing an urban design study of downtown Leominster, Massachusetts, really got me excited about historic buildings, their undiscovered qualities, and untapped potential. Many people in Leominster couldn't see any merit in what they had and thought I was totally off.

Gradually I began meeting a lot of people in preservation. One gay man who was very much involved in Providence, Rhode Island, really influenced me to see the potential of neglected industrial and residential areas of urban centers. I've never been that interested in opulent mansions; I've always focused more on the undiscovered vernacular sorts of buildings.

I was in New England for six years and was very happy there, but there was a recession and work dried up, so I went back to Hawaii at the end of the 1970s. I got a job with a state agency in charge of redeveloping several hundred acres in the industrial part of Honolulu. There was a strong emphasis on consolidating parcels of land for new buildings and complexes, so I tried my best to identify and document some of the more important historic structures that were threatened by this development. It was frustrating because people had very little sympathy for a lot of those old buildings.

I joined the Historic Hawaii Foundation, became a board member, but even there I was frustrated by the indifference to buildings and places that represented working-class Hawaiian life. These kinds of cultural resources were rapidly being destroyed by post-statehood development. Hawaii was just not a preservation-friendly environment at the time. Like the continental United States it was evolving into a generic environment of sprawling new development.

After my urban redevelopment work with the state of Hawaii, it was difficult to adjust to designing resort architecture in the private sector. Preferred designs often ignored the existing fabric, the cultural and social layers, and the historic resources themselves. Our international work especially troubled me because our clients preferred designs of American prototypes, totally disregarding their own rich cultures and what was originally there. In Java, Indonesia, for example, a client requested that we build an equestrian center, boutique hotel, and single-family residential subdivision on the site of three hamlets, rice paddies, and clove and cinnamon groves.

I promote historic preservation that represents the broader spectrum of America's history. We're doing a great job of preserving significant symbols for mainstream, majority America, but a lot of work needs to be done to

make sure that other groups are represented. Other fragments of our complex American story need to be told, interpreted, and linked. The perception is that preservation is elitist and reactionary, but that doesn't need to be the case. Even though it's been heavily Eurocentric in this country, preservation is really a universal field. It was another gay preservationist in Hawaii who helped me to understand and be confident in my own direction: a queer, working-class, Japanese American Buddhist from Hawaii, I am as much a preservationist as anybody else. I want to be around more people whose vision of preservation is inclusive. My greatest satisfaction comes from working with grassroots groups, currently in the Bay Area.

Other people can do the legalese and public policy aspects of preservation much better than I can. My background is design, the visual part of the world and its relationship with the complex and fascinating dynamics of culture, society, and time. Preservation is really about loving particular places and the history that's connected to them. It's about transformation, revitalization, and change in our existing order. And it's about bringing community back, which includes the physical places of community, the built environment. I'm sort of a romantic, so I love working with people who have passionate, rooted connections with historic buildings. If it doesn't affect you in your heart, there's no real connection.

Jeffrey Samudio

Jeffrey Samudio was born in the Los Angeles area in 1966. He studied architecture and planning at the University of Southern California, where in 1993 he helped to originate a program of historic preservation courses, the first such program in California. In 1987 he started an architecture, planning, and preservation firm, Design Aid, with a fellow student. Through Samudio's teaching the language of good design and preservation is now part of the graduate real-estate program at USC. "For the first time, I've got the right audience in front of me: real-estate developers." Samudio is cocreator of a book of early photographs of Los Angeles architecture, part of Arcadia Publishing's *Images of America* series.

I GREW UP in the historic northeast L.A. railcar suburbs of Mount Washington, Eagle Rock, and Highland Park. These communities were settled mostly by midwesterners, especially Presbyterians from Indiana, Ohio, and Iowa. So there was a heavy influence of midwestern traditions, values, and building types in the area. Occidental College, which is at the center of these communities, was established by the Presbyterians.

From the 1880s to the 1920s, wealthy families came out from the Midwest and East Coast in droves and settled in Pasadena, just up the Arroyo Seco. They built summer houses in these hills, where they could catch the breezes from the ocean. Later, with the influence of the Arroyo School and a myriad of artists, the plein-air movement began in this area. It played a major role in attracting the early civic and cultural boosters of Los Angeles and socially progressive people. So you had a very curious cross-section, people with strong midwestern values living in the same neighborhood with bohemians.

Teddy Roosevelt wanted to make part of this area a national park because of the natural beauty of the arroyo. Unfortunately the local boosters of this idea didn't get their act together before it was all developed. But now it's a genuinely wonderful area to live in. Eagle Rock Valley and Highland Park Valley are surrounded by hillsides with housing stock that's quite eclectic, ranging from large mansions to duplexes to regular old suburban tract houses. Being some of the older suburbs of Los Angeles, they were among the first to go through integration in the 1960s. When I was a kid, they were considered one of the most integrated areas in California. I live now within the area defined as Eagle Rock, which was an independent city until it was gobbled up for water, like most communities around L.A.

I grew up the youngest of four boys in a very poor family. The day I was born was the day my mother received her divorce papers. The five of us lived in a tiny one-bedroom duplex. But we never felt poor because we lived in a community that was very diverse and tight-knit, and being in the center of the Los Angeles region, there were always things going on. We were obviously the most needy family on our block, so we were sort of watched over and taken care of. It was an area where openly gay and lesbian people could live, so I had a very positive upbringing. My babysitter was a retired makeup artist from Paramount Studios who had been a famous L.A. drag queen in the 1920s and 1930s.

I'm third-generation Hispanic American, by way of Mexico. Samudio is a Basque name. My mother was born and raised in Manhattan. The first Mexican restaurant in New York City, El Chavo Español, on Charles Street, is now a city landmark. My grandparents ran it as a private club, a speakeasy. My great-uncle used to make gin in the bathtub of an apartment upstairs. You name it; we've got the characters in our family—bootleggers, entertainers, psychics, whores. They moved out here after the war, as so many easterners did, because Los Angeles was a very urbane and cosmopolitan but lower-density version of New York. At that time L.A. was a fairly compact city, with the largest transit system in the country. That was dismantled soon after their arrival. My mother never drove until she was well into her fifties, so I grew up in a household that didn't own a car. But we were in one of those old streetcar suburbs where you didn't really need one. Buses provided us with excellent public transit.

Early on I realized that I lived in a pretty remarkable area that had quite an interesting history. Because we didn't own a car, I was never stuck on freeways. Instead, I was stuck on city buses, which traveled slowly through the enormity of L.A., all its different neighborhoods. I would spend weekends taking different bus routes all over the city with my brother. It was a real hoot to just go out and get lost somewhere. It was a whole day's journey to go to West Los Angeles or Westwood or the UCLA area or Santa Monica. It was another world, and a completely white world, which was not something that we were used to. And Pasadena, right next door, gave us a real sense of old California and the influence of old money on a new region. Greene and Greene's Arts and Crafts–style Gamble House was at the top of the arroyo, close enough to ride my bike to.

Not having a car, I was always very appreciative whenever we would go on trips out of the neighborhood; I would devour everything I saw. I was not like any other kid. I spent a lot of time by myself, building enormous cities in the backyard or garage. I spent every dime that I earned trying to replicate in model form things that I saw around me. I had quite a photographic memory for cities. Mostly I focused on buildings, and I would always have trolley-car lines and multilevel freeways. Off in my own little world, I guess I always knew that I wanted to go into architecture or urban planning. The grown-ups must have thought, "He's a very old soul who still has a lot of designing to do."

Myron Hunt's incredible connection with Occidental College was a great influence on me. He designed every building at the Eagle Rock campus between 1912 and 1943. More than three hundred acres, it's a rambling campus in sort of a refined Beaux Arts Mediterranean Revival style that completely takes advantage of the hillside location, with stunning views. And Sparkletts Water Company, a great Moorish Revival structure, was right below my elementary school. And, lo and behold, all but one of my elementary teachers were openly gay; they would bring their lovers to school events. It was the 1970s, man, and everything was cool.

My block was about one-third retired couples, one-third Ozzie-and-Harriet families, and one-third gay, ranging from retirees to young bikers. There were plenty of kids to play with, but I would usually spend a good portion of my time by myself reflecting on what I saw around the city and building my model cities. I had no interest in playing softball on the weekends. I would much rather have breakfast with the retired couples on my block, straight or gay, getting them to tell me about their lives and the history of the area. I would much rather sit with my friend Betty and her husband and her sister and hear stories about the Union Pacific Railroad suburbs and how the West was exploited by the railroads. We had a few veterans on my block, and I loved to hear their stories about things like traveling on the *Queen Mary* from New York to England during World War II. My mother and her family had taken the *Queen Mary* from Europe to New York in 1939, before the war started, so it was fascinating to hear the luxurious side of it from my mother, then how the ship was transformed for military service, and then brought back to life, to the glory of its heyday, just down the freeway at Long Beach.

Even though it was just seven miles from downtown Los Angeles, Eagle Rock was still a very isolated place. From the top of the hill above my house you looked down on the massive skyscrapers that were growing, but Eagle Rock still had the appearance of small-town America. We had our Carnegie library, the city hall where all kinds of gatherings were held, a beautifully designed park structure by Richard Neutra. We had architectural influences from Mediterranean, Spanish Revival, Arts and Crafts, all the way to the International style. And the memory of a couple of Rudolph Schindler homes that were lost to a freeway that encircled the valley. But the place was pretty much the land that time forgot.

My adoptive father passed away about a year ago. I took care of him the last thirteen years of his life, after he had a stroke. A Japanese American gentleman who grew up in the very segregated plantation culture of Hawaii, he was a Los Angeles city gardener for nearly thirty years. In retrospect I can see that he was gay, though I don't think he would have defined himself that way or even understood it. A lot of repression there. It was a chance meeting; he sort of fell in love with me when I was about one year old and took care of my brothers as well. Everybody thinks that he and my mother had a thing going, but that was definitely not the case. He was in love with me as a son figure, and I with him as a father figure. He would take us on trips to all the wonderful towns and cities up and down the California coast. By the time I was in my teens we were getting more money, so we made annual pilgrimages to New York in the new family car. I would spend whole days just walking around Manhattan, taking in the great city.

The architect Ena Dubnoff was my instructor the first year at USC. I lucked out. If I'd had one of the male instructors I would never have survived. Ena was very motherly, a feminist of the strongest bent, but she never lost that wonderful soft side. She was much more nurturing than the hard-edged male architect assholes. Which is another reason why I didn't go into regular architecture. Preservation was a much kinder, softer, and gentler environment.

When I was eighteen, in my second year at USC, Eagle Rock's old jail and a whole block of historic buildings from the teens were threatened with demolition for a mini-mall. This was about 1985, the beginning of the mini-mallization of Los Angeles, the same boom that everybody else in the country tasted at the time. We saw the writing on the wall: rampant development was finally coming into this little Arcadian community that we all cherished. About 150 people were at a community meeting, really angry and trying to figure out how to stop mini-malls from proliferating. The developer agreed to work with me and others on an ad hoc committee, so we agreed to his request to hold off on submitting the historic landmark application.

At seven o'clock the next morning I got a phone call from Kathleen Aberman, a woman I had met the night before who would later become my surrogate mother. "They're tearing down the buildings!" she said. "Can you come by and help me stop them? I'm going down there right now." I went down to the site immediately, and half the buildings were already demolished. I got really angry. Kathleen, this very fashionable, gutsy lady who had parked her new Jaguar right next to the trash truck so that debris was falling all over it, was up on the roof of this building, getting arrested. Our city councilman was really scared that there was going to be a riot, and he couldn't deal with housewives rioting, so he announced L.A.'s first mini-mall moratorium and that the city would create a specific plan for Eagle Rock. At eighteen I was appointed to the planning advisory board and was one of the founding members of the Eagle Rock Association. We did an architectural survey of the area to identify valuable sites and to systematically declare them landmarks.

I declared my first city landmark when I was about twenty. (That building was the only one in Eagle Rock that was burned during the Rodney King riots in 1994.) By the time I finished undergraduate, I had declared a dozen landmarks. One of these buildings I can see from my front porch, a four-story house, the last Women's Christian Temperance Union home for wayward women. When we found out it was closing and scheduled for demolition for a large apartment complex, we saved it. The publicity surrounding our saving it at the very last minute helped us find a new owner for it. It has been fully restored as the headquarters of the Greater Los Angeles Association for the Deaf.

The Eagle Rock Association has really set wonderful standards for our community. Now nobody comes into this part of the city without calling five or six of us to serve as an ad hoc design review board, and we're about to become an official design review board. I can honestly claim to have killed about three dozen inappropriate developments in our community and to have saved about a dozen really remarkable historic properties, all but one or two of which have been fully restored. A few years ago I coined the marketing phrase for this area, "L.A.'s Hometown." Hollywood loves filming here whenever they need a shoot for a quiet little midwestern town. It's awfully good revenue for revitalizing historic buildings.

To do preservation in Los Angeles you have to emphasize diversity, economic development, viable economic use, and ownership and empowerment by all cultures in a neighborhood. You talk about historic resources as maybe the third or fourth thing down the list. Instead of sounding like debutantes from the Society for the Preservation of New England Antiquities, talking about this lovely building and who built it and who lived in it, you have to work with a lot of really nagging social issues. Especially after the Rodney King riots, that became incredibly clear. The first building that I designated a landmark is a perfect example: the kids in the neighborhood knew that the old Victorian house was owned by a bunch of whiteys, and who cares about them, so they burned it.

At twenty-eight I was appointed architectural historian for the state historical resources commission. That catapulted me to a whole different level of politics, sort of the state cultural police. Much more than I ever could on a local planning commission, I began to understand the power of policy to affect the built environment, cultural values, how our culture views itself, and what will be left in a hundred years to reflect our lives. I was the youngest person ever appointed to this position, but I'm used to hanging around an older crowd. Viewed as a young whippersnapper, I got really active on a few issues, helped rewrite the state's preservation master plan, and took part in the great debate on the detrimental effects of sprawl.

Being openly gay gave me a lot of power in what I was doing, because nobody messed with me as I suggested revisions to the state's preservation master plan, to recognize marginalized groups. So now, as funding comes down the pike, gays and lesbians are plugged right in there as a deserving bunch of guys and gals.

We recently had major hearings on where preservation is going in California and how it should be funded. Half the room was gay, and I was shocked that so many of them got angry at me when I mentioned gay men's involvement in the revitalization of the Castro in San Francisco. Several years ago we got a grant from the National Trust to create a cultural map of gay and lesbian historic sites in Los Angeles, much like the maps that had been created in New York and Boston. Things like where the Mattachine Society first met in the late 1940s and the location of the bathhouse that George and Ira Gershwin owned in the 1920s. I had to defend myself to a lot of gay friends in preservation who I thought would have been completely supportive. "Gay culture and history? *What* culture? *What* history? Why are you doing this, Jeff—drawing attention to *bathhouses?*" I was hearing from my younger friends a lot of conservative attitudes that I would have expected from closeted older guys. I thought, it's part of our cultural history, guys. Get over it. Get over *yourself*. See a therapist, quick.

I've always been haunted by the area that I grew up in. Even though my office is in Hollywood and most of my social life is in West Hollywood, I still live here in Eagle Rock. It's a nice little repose and a taste of reality. I live in a wonderful old 1912 Craftsman. When I was eighteen, I took my college housing stipend and went in with my brother to buy this house. My brother has since moved on to suburban hell, but the entire family considers this house the family house. It has a huge arroyo-stone front porch with a swing chair and the American flag flying: Mom, Chevy, and apple pie all rolled into one.

I never tire of preservation. I never consider what I do, work. It's fun. And then to teach architectural history and theory and design. My offices are in Whitley Court, which is sort of Preservation Central in L.A. Five major firms in an old residential bungalow court in Hollywood, the leading consultants for cultural resources in Los Angeles. Christy McAvoy, the owner of the largest firm, is the person who taught me how to deal with city hall and how to identify historic resources when I was a teenager in the Eagle Rock Association. She attended my swearing-in to the state historic resources commission and can claim to be my preservation mother.

Jim Wilke

Jim Wilke's great-grandfather settled in Los Angeles in the late 1800s. Born in Santa Monica in 1962, Wilke lives in Los Angeles and works as a historical consultant. "I advertise my services in a resource directory for filmmakers. If they need to know where to get a stagecoach or a vintage refrigerator, or what kind of food goes on the table for *The Age of Innocence,* I can tell them."

WHEN I WAS A TEENAGER I collected old phonographs. It was a very curatorial thing: I had one, then I wanted to get another kind, then I wanted to get a different type, and then I wanted to get the same kind but by a different manufacturer. My big collection of records started when I got my grandmother's record collection. There was something visceral about listening to the popular songs of 1905, hearing sound that had been made back then.

I had that collection for a while, but then I realized it was kind of kooky to have all those things in the house. I wasn't running a phonograph museum, and my friends didn't want to come over for a phonograph party. And I began to realize that objects can't satisfy unless they're something that you can really use, like an old car. If it's not practical to use, then it's clutter. So I sold them.

My parents didn't really object to my collecting, but they didn't encourage it. It wasn't usual; it wasn't average. Teenagers don't go collecting old phonographs. My parents always knew I was unusual, and like most parents they very much wanted me to be as normal as possible, to help them present to the world a normal family. Everything that they liked was modern, and everything I liked was old. But now my taste runs pretty modern. I've still got old Craftsman furniture, but I've got modern things as well. I don't want to live in a period house. I could do it easily, in a curatorial sense: assemble it room by room, with the right magazines and books, the right arrangement of things. But that's for set decorators. I don't want to live a replica life.

Some of the Victorian houses around here are rather kooky restorations, and their interiors are equally kooky, not very well done. They don't really know much about Victorian, so they get a funny sofa and stick it in. No one really lived like that. But I've known some gay men who have restored older homes to within an inch of their lives and have made very accurate replicas of the past. They knew what life was like in the past; they understood and enjoyed the past. None of them were ever really going anywhere in terms of jobs or careers, but their knowledge of the past was priceless.

Intuitively they knew so much about the past lifestyles of "just plain folks," as one of them put it.

Roger was the king of being "just folks." I got to know him when I was seventeen, and his interests and knowledge were very much a siren for me. I met him at the Doo-Dah Parade, our annual Pasadena parade of kookiness. I was with a friend in his old car, and Roger had an old car and was dressed just right and impressed me. I was invited to his house. A good number of his friends were there, gay and straight, male and female. They were all characters, and in many ways they were misfits. Roger had a great house. The furniture was from as far back as the 1840s, but it was an 1890s house as it might have looked around 1920. Everything worked, including the gaslights. It's now in the care of the Pasadena Historical Society.

I was really uncomfortable with traditional fagdom, but I was fortunate to develop friendships with a lot of gay men who liked old stuff. Roger was one of those people who wanted to see buggies go by when he stepped outside. I remember, in a book published in the 1970s, a picture of a man in high collar, period clothes, standing before a wall filled with piano-roll boxes. I think there was a phonograph there too. You could tell it was serious with him; he wasn't just your house-museum docent dressing up. I've always felt a very strong emotional and sexual attraction to men like that—the idea of undressing such a man, removing a lot of things. I've had such a strong interest in old stuff myself since I was a kid that anyone who was like that, I wanted to know about him. I wanted to get into him, to figure out how he worked, to know the secret, to see. Of the people that I got to know who were early into preservation here in L.A., most were misfits. Bunker Hill, a downtown site that was once covered with mansions, was all rundown and slated for destruction by the 1960s. The types who wanted to preserve it were not Waspy, blue-blazer types, Dorothy Chandlers or Lady Bird Johnsons. They were all funky folk, mainly eccentrics, and older people who had lived in the area all their lives.

I've never really gotten along with most people socially. Trains were my friends. I have liked trains since I first saw *Petticoat Junction* on television when I was four. I didn't care about the show; I just watched it for the train. I've always liked only the very early wood-burners, from back in the days of the Civil War. They're not fast; they're not high-charge muscular. They are slow, grand, high, and beautiful machines—magnificent, really—their physical proportions, the concept of the culture that built them, and the colors. They were not just big black things; they were opulent. I'm also interested in stagecoaches, wooden ships, and other vehicles that all have that one thing in common: large, spectacular, slow, gracious beauty, like a really incredible float rolling down a street.

It was after I had been working as assistant curator with the Autrey Museum of Western Heritage that I rekindled my love of trains by going to a museum that had restored several early examples. I started attending railroad symposiums and met an entirely new crop of people, including my best friend, a gay man who is the editor of a locomotive and railway preservation magazine. In 1993 and 1994 I got to redo the colors of two replica steam engines at the Golden Spike National Historic Site at Promontory Summit, Utah. They're essentially steam-powered Mayflowers, interpretive things. They had been painted red by a Disney artist in 1978, so they looked like toys, things that should be under a Christmas tree. The original color schemes had since been discovered, and with some help from friends at the Smithsonian and the National Park Service, we repainted the locomotives.

It's not just an interest in railroads but, I would like to think, a way of preserving history. It feels good to see people go up to the steam engines and ooh and aah, smell them and watch them run, and see that one's burning wood and the other's burning coal. One of the engines that we repainted in Utah was named the *Jupiter,* originally built in upstate New York in 1868, standard wood-burning, beautiful machine. Bright red, as by the Disney artist. We redid it according to a newly found newspaper article that described it as being blue and crimson. I had a whole squadron of die-hard railroad historians against this blue engine, even though we found tons of evidence.

My interest has not been on the inner workings of steam engines as much as the outer trappings, the beauty of the color and ornament, period aesthetics. I know how they work, but boiler pressures and shaft lengths have just never interested me, and I'm not mathematically inclined. A gay colleague of mine in Ohio is just the opposite, almost all technological. Paul, a gay friend, is really into railroad track. When we look at a photograph together, I'll say, "Ooh, look at that engine!" and he'll say, "Ooh, look at that track!" If there's anything aesthetic about track at all, I don't know, but Paul sees a certain type of switch or a certain height of rail and, boy, he's into it. Another gay friend of mine is really into museum conservation and preservation, and another is into the ornamental aspects of locomotives, like I am. A friend of mine in Pennsylvania just sent me fragments of an 1856 locomotive. That's the kind of fraternity we have.

I'm taking my 1975 Scout apart bit by bit, cleaning all the little parts, and putting it back the way it ought to be. I drive it around too. I think it's a cool-looking car. It's orange and has oversized white wheels with big tires. I just like the guyness of it. I mean, it really looks like a giant Tonka truck. They're great cars, made out of steel, but what they really are is the biggest boy-toy you could get. They're not very common, so we Scout drivers acknowledge each other on the street.

I like to take it apart and see how it works, and then it's a big challenge to put it back together again. I'll shell out the dollars to have someone repair the transmission for me. But I do simple things like take off the door panel, get the rockers back in shape, clean up the risers, replace parts that are missing. I love to get away from my desk and get my hands dirty doing that kind of stuff. One of the first things was cleaning off all the junk that previous owners had put on it, paring it down to what is genuinely real, then taking that apart to see what's underneath it, then putting it back together, like a house.

In the 1950s a lot of people collected Model A Fords. Mostly they were people who had driven them when they were younger. But the prizes for the restored Model A's were usually based on the number of accessories they had, like whitewalls, things that the average Ford never had. The way the Fords really were was not the way the owners or judges really wanted to remember them. You see the same phenomenon today with over-restored Chevy Bel Airs and with hyper-cutesy old houses, the Laura Ashley kind of past. Some of these Victorian houses have been so dolled up. They were never like that.

Generations of Gentlemen Keep Cooksville, Wisconsin

JUST AS MANY U.S. CITIES are subject to gay men's restorative ministrations, so too are many much smaller settlements throughout the country. One such place is the unincorporated village of Cooksville, Wisconsin, a quiet rural crossroads community of fewer than one hundred people near Madison, the state capital. Since 1911, very early in the American preservation movement, Cooksville's early buildings and other historical documents have been a focus of the gay passion to preserve.

Cooksville is one of many settlements that sprang up in Wisconsin in the 1840s and 1850s, when venturesome residents of New York State and New England moved west. Though its chances of becoming a larger city ended when the railroads bypassed it, Cooksville didn't disappear. It just stagnated. Seventy years after its first settlement, most of the original houses in the village were still standing, and few others had been built. Eventually dubbed "the town that time forgot," quiet little Cooksville possessed a mid-nineteenth-century frozen-in-time ambience that attracted gay men of several generations throughout the twentieth century.

It was a spinster who got things going. In 1910 Susan Porter bought one of the early brick houses facing Cooksville's public square, as a summer home. A teacher in Racine, Wisconsin, Porter had grown up in the village. During her first summer there she hosted a party at her quaint house. Some of the guests came from Racine, nearly ninety miles away, and one of them was Ralph Warner. Born in 1875, Warner was in his mid-thirties and, like his friend Susan Porter, a never-married teacher. He was enchanted by the sleepy, verdant village and the idea of owning one of its old brick houses. Porter told Warner that the house next door to hers was for sale. He purchased it and named it the House Next Door.

The house Ralph Warner bought in 1911 was a small, square, two-story structure made of local vermilion brick. Blending elements of the Federal and Greek Revival styles, it was a modest showplace built about 1848, when Cooksville's speculators still harbored dreams of growth and prosperity. By the time Warner bought the house, it had been sold five times and had weathered many years as a marginally maintained rental property. He paid one hundred dollars down and committed himself to a five-year mortgage of four hundred dollars.

Warner hired tradesmen to level floors, rehang doors, repair plaster, put on a new roof, repair chimneys, and open the bricked-up and plastered-over fireplace. Many windowpanes and a few sashes had to be replaced. Some shutters were broken, and everything needed paint. Layers of wallpaper had to be scraped off. With help from a Cooksville neighbor woman and one of his manual arts students from Racine, Warner spent much of July preparing the house for his first guests. "We began with painting, papering, and cleaning upstairs," he wrote in his diary. "Paul painted woodwork and floors. Mrs. Savage helped me with the papering at first, but I soon felt I could do it much better alone (or, that is, with Paul's help), as her way was not mine. She was not particular whether things matched or not."

By the end of July the properly papered rooms were ready to be furnished, and it was time for a housewarming party, attended by two dozen Cooksville women. During the next month Warner hosted about a dozen guests, a small beginning for the enterprise that became the creative focus of his middle-life: In his old-time house furnished with his long-accumulated antiques, Warner served luncheons, dinners, and teas by reservation only. The first few summer seasons at the House Next Door were short and the guests were few. But things took off in 1917, and for fifteen years, typically from late spring through mid-autumn, Warner's old house and garden kept him very busy. Garden clubs and other (mostly) women's groups were frequent customers, as were society types from nearby cities and towns looking for an exclusive and unique automobile outing.

Warner did no advertising, and there were no signs identifying the House Next Door. He wanted his guests to learn of it personally, through word of mouth, and to experience it not as a restaurant or museum but as his home, a gathering place for kindred spirits who found romance and beauty in the things and ways of the olden days. Sometimes he would dress in black broadcloth, fine faded waistcoat, and high top hat to greet his guests. Often he would play his old square rosewood piano with its thin, harplike sound. The guests might sing, and, if he was in the mood, Warner might join in. Old English ballads were a favorite. Occasionally Warner provided bed-and-breakfast accommodations.

Meals at the House Next Door were neither gourmet nor strictly 1840s fare, but Warner enjoyed cooking and brought his artistic eye to it. For two women visiting one day he served a simple meal of an omelet with currant jelly, a freshly picked salad of tomatoes and lettuce seasoned with herbs, an aged cheese flavored with mustard and garlic, and dessert of baked custard and coffee. As his guests ate on old pewter, which gleamed against the shining mahogany table, Warner admired the look of the golden omelet on the dark blue platter. "The cream Wedgwood plates were never quite right until I got the ivory handled knives," Warner remarked to the women. "They brought everything together, and the ivory pepper pot saved the situation."[1]

One of the earliest and most knowledgeable antique collectors in Wisconsin, Ralph Warner began gathering old-fashioned things as a child, starting with family pieces from his grandmothers and aunts and other old women he got to know. Through his twenties and early thirties he gathered, repaired, and stored many antiques in anticipation of finding just the right house for them and himself, and he acquired much more thereafter. "I begin to think I draw things to me like a magnet," Warner exulted in his acquisitions notebook. Antiques were important to him not only for their beauty and value but for the people, places, and events associated with them. "They tell me things," he said.[2] True to his house's age, Warner at first furnished his rooms with late-Empire and early-Victorian furniture. But his rooms were dynamic spaces, frequently rearranged, and through the 1920s he sold most of this more ornate and massive furniture and replaced it with simpler eighteenth-century pieces.

The House Next Door was a dream come true for Ralph Warner, but he was ambivalent about engaging with the world in such an intimate way. He was bright, sociable, and talkative, a creative homemaker and gardener, a gifted pianist. He was also quite effeminate in voice, mannerism, and essential nature, and his complexion was badly scarred as a result of childhood smallpox. "I wish those who come to do so because they have been told of my collections by mutual friends, and to arrange for their coming by a note addressed to me," Warner told a reporter in 1926. "Other visitors I cannot hope to give time to, even when they come from long distances, as is often the case."[3]

Magazine and newspaper articles about Warner and his Cooksville home brought many strangers calling. "The most remarkable thing about The House Next Door is its owner," declared a 1923 article in *House Beautiful*.

> The story of how the man dreamed the house for years, collected much of the furniture to go into it, and finally acquired it and with his own hands made it the charming place it is to-day has a legendary sound. It wouldn't be so much of a story, or so interesting perhaps, if Ralph Warner were a woman; it certainly wouldn't be if he were a wealthy collector and had the house as a hobby, or if he were a shrewd business man and used it as a money-making proposition. But Ralph Warner is the direct opposite of these things. It is not

easy to catalogue him at all, except to say that he is—in the broader meaning of the term—an artist. . . .

Paying guests who come for the first time to the house insist that there must be a wife or a housekeeper somewhere concealed. If they accept the flawless housekeeping as Mr. Warner's own, they challenge the delectable food. Confronted by proof, they are still skeptical about the dishwashing. Later, when they hear the man who has both prepared and served their meal play beautifully at an old piano, they are in a state of mind to believe anything. The enchanting old-fashioned garden, the linen-weaving, the hand-wrought copper bowls, the hooked rugs of original design—all these are further evidence that the most remarkable part of a remarkable house is its owner.[4]

When a visitor asked, "Where is *Mrs.* Ralph?" Warner gave an evasive reply that was no doubt well rehearsed: "All the ladies nowadays belong in the tomorrows and next days. I've never found one that fitted into my land of long ago."[5] Reporters often hinted at Warner's queerness. They described him as an artist, a musician, "a very pleasant, romantic gentleman," a "delightfully temperamental antique collector." They likened him to Henry Thoreau at Walden Pond. "He was a bachelor and he was different," observed one writer toward the end of Warner's life. "He always puttered around the house—cooking, making hooked rugs, collecting antiques and the like. Strolling around the village in his white pants, he always had plenty of time to talk when the farmers were busy with their chores. . . . He would mop his brow with a silk handkerchief delicately and say, 'Death, it's so *wahm!*'"[6]

The writer of a 1933 *Ladies' Home Journal* piece titled "Wisconsin Witchery" made similar winking observations. She enthused about Warner's homemaking and gardening and deliciously frugal cooking but described him (without naming him or Cooksville) as a monkish recluse: He was living in one of the prim, half-ruined witch-houses of a little old forgotten settlement, with old women's bodices, petticoats, and dresses hanging on the door pegs as if discarded yesterday. She stated that Warner's hard-working farmer neighbors regarded him as a harmless curiosity, though they were not quite sure of his harmlessness: his tangled garden grew strange medicinal herbs that in earlier times would have assured his burning at the stake. "A young man of this sort may well find himself a little lonely sometimes," she observed, "lost in the middle of the Wisconsin wheat fields."[7]

This article, with its fanciful illustration depicting Warner as a young blond hunk serving a meal to two ladies, brought an effusive letter from a lonely young man in rural Oregon. Harold March, a college student, confessed to being so charmed by what he read in the *Ladies' Home Journal* that he had requested Warner's address from the author. "I'm not the gushing type," March declared, "and so it is difficult for me to really say to you what is in my heart. The things you have done in reality I have only accomplished in the secret places of my soul." March mentioned that he had several pioneer things from his grandparents, who had crossed the plains and settled in southwest Oregon in 1852, and that he was starting an herb garden. He told Warner about his travels in California the previous year, during which he had his first experience of bohemian life, and a visit to San Francisco. "I have never encountered another such delightful place—the true home for the bohemian," March wrote of San Francisco. "I got the finest meal of my life in a shabby little restaurant, a remodeled carriage house at the foot of Russian Hill."[8]

March implored Warner to accept his friendship and to write and reveal more about himself and the history of his Wisconsin village. Warner began his carefully composed reply by cautioning Harold March not to be misled by the magazine illustration. "Would I were a beautiful blond boy. Never was blond or beautiful and now not young and really almost bald. Sorry if this is spoiling an agreeable something for you. You would however like the little house and the tangled garden and possibly the owner if you forgot the story and the picture."[9]

"I am not married," Warner continued, "so have not that responsibility, nor the care and expense of children." But he wanted March to know that he was not a recluse: the joy of his summers was that his house was a meeting place, not only for his stream of scheduled guests but for the boys of the village, who would stop by to get Warner to join them in the swimming hole at the creek. Later in the summer the boys would lend a hand at his cider press, and he would give them pony rides. Likewise, Warner welcomed the attention of the young man from Oregon: "I'm sure I should enjoy your friendship and perhaps the time will come when you will travel my way," he wrote. "I should enjoy seeing you and making you an omelette." He closed his letter to March with greetings "from a he-witch of Wisconsin."[10]

Within several months of this correspondence, Warner suffered a stroke that left him greatly incapacitated for the rest of his life. He lingered as long as he could in Cooksville, then went to live with a friend in the Chicago area, and finally with his sister in Florida, where he died in 1941. As Warner's life was ending, one of his friends remarked on the relationship between the man and his house: "No one could enter that front door without feeling that he was stepping into 'yesterday,' a yesterday complete and alive in spirit. Coupled with the material side of the house and its garden was something of a happy philosophy which Ralph Warner gave to all who knew him; and which still lingers, in essence, about the House Next Door. He firmly believed, as he had often expressed it, 'My house will keep me.'"[11]

A few years after Ralph Warner's final departure from Cooksville, the House Next Door was sheltering gay men of a younger generation. Indiana native Chester Holway, born in 1908, had traveled widely throughout Wisconsin in the1930s. Picturesque, historic towns had a special appeal for the young journalist. Holway had heard of Warner and the House Next Door, had visited Cooksville, and was captivated by the idea of owning an early house in the village, where he could live as a country gentleman. Following Warner's death in 1941 Holway purchased the House Next Door and its dusty contents. It was the most renowned and desirable house in the village.

After serving as an officer in the U.S. Army Air Corps, Holway returned to Cooksville in 1945 with Texas native Marvin Raney, ten years his junior, the man who would be his life partner for thirty-five years. The couple were soon consumed by the work of rehabilitating their new place. The house needed relatively modest repairs and refurbishing; simply getting it opened up and lived in made a big difference. It was a staggering task, however, to restore the formless and impenetrable half-acre garden to something of its appearance in Warner's time. But by the summer of 1947 at least parts of the garden were deemed a suitably groomed backdrop for snapshots during a visit by Holway's mother and by Raney's mother a year later.

Raney and Holway got to know the woman next door, a cousin of Warner's friend Susan Porter. Cora Atwood had inherited Porter's summer house and carried on the Cooksville Old Settlers traditions, including the annual reunion. A founder of the county historical society, Atwood compiled many notebooks from the scrapbooks of news clippings and other ephemera kept by local women. When she died, Raney inherited her collection of local history materials and continued to add to and organize them.

When he wasn't gardening, Raney was likely to be researching the history of Cooksville, compiling biographies of the village's early families, buildings, and businesses. He spent many hours in the county courthouse, tracing back the deeds to every piece of property and using census records to determine who was living in what house when. He enjoyed poring over the country correspondent columns in old newspapers; their gossipy reports helped to bring vanished Cooksville residents to life. The director of the Wisconsin Historical Society expressed an interest in seeing Raney's history when it was completed. "Between you and Mr. Holway," he wrote, "Cooksville seems to boast an unusually high percentage of articulate historians."[12]

Raney safeguarded village census records, business ledgers, and school rosters. He compiled the genealogies of scores of families in Cooksville and the surrounding region. Raney was interested in more than just the raw data of names, places, and dates. He was charmed by the atmosphere, neighborliness, and old ways of the village—the persistent custom of husbands doing the household shopping at the Cooksville store, for example. He wanted to create an intimate portrait of daily life in early Cooksville and continued to gather and study the rather scarce materials that would help him do it.

Elton Breckenridge first visited Cooksville in 1938 and fell in love with it. In 1952 he bought a five-acre lot across the road from the House Next Door, perhaps inspired by the example of his friends Raney and Holway. On the property stood a small, century-old oak frame structure, which had been first a one-room house, then a farm shed. In the 1920s the woman who owned it had it moved there from a block east, saving it for sentimental reasons.

An instructor of interior design at the School of the Art Institute of Chicago, Breckenridge had lived in an old mansion on Oak Street in Chicago from the mid-1920s. With his arrival in Cooksville he became the village's most overtly eccentric resident, one of several Chicago transplants who gave the phrase "Chicago people" a distinctly artsy/queer connotation among the locals. He wore a decidedly bad wig, loved decorating Easter eggs and delivering them in baskets to various households around the village, and despite his Chicago commute never learned to drive.

Over the years Breckenridge helped Raney and Holway with their domestic projects, and they returned the favors. Digging the basement and building a foundation for Breckenridge's small house and a new wing was their first major collaboration. The man who was hired to move the old structure onto the new foundation was appalled that anyone would spend money on such a shack. "There are very few of these houses left anymore because nobody sees," Breckenridge remarked in later years. "My home points up what can be done with a thing that people regard as worthless."[13] He refinished the original pegged oak floor, some of the planks nearly two feet wide. He built a fireplace using brick from the blacksmith shop that had stood on the property. He was so pleased by the zebra-stripe look of the exposed riven lathing on interior walls that he decided to leave it exposed.

Breckenridge's style of decorating and furnishing was attuned to aesthetic harmony and personal whim rather than period consistency. A seventeenth-century Italian trestle table, a French crystal chandelier, American pine cupboards, louvered cherry closet doors from Chicago mansions, Venetian glass mugs, a platter by Picasso, a patio teacart by Matisse's grandson, pieces from the Art Institute's castaway section—Breckenridge wove them all into the dynamic fabric of Breckhurst, his telephone-free Cooksville retreat.

When Breckenridge sold his creation in 1976, the original house was just one of seven rooms, as Breckenridge had continued to design and build additions. He created the landscape so that every window looked out onto a striking scene—a white stone Victorian bust set within a half-circle hedge of trimmed Chinese elm, for example. Near the house he developed an elaborate and intimate garden in the style of old Italian-English gardens. There were flowering crabapple trees, many varieties of clematis, meticulously clipped hedges of arborvitae and hemlocks, Italian sculptures, a fountain and a lily pool, and many intimate places to sit. At night he illuminated the garden with candles, Viennese lanterns, and iron lanterns of his own design, made by the Cooksville blacksmith. He had many bird feeders and left a large portion of his acreage undeveloped as a haven for wildlife.

"Elton was in the tradition of the sensitive, artistic resident who is concerned about the beauty of Cooksville, its tranquility and quaintness," says village historian Larry Reed. A gay antiquarian and his wife wandering around Cooksville's streets one summer weekend found themselves drawn into Breckenridge's garden, though they had never met him. After they had been strolling around awhile, a shutter door opened, and Breckenridge stepped out of the house. "How nice of you to enjoy my garden," he said. "When you're finished, please come inside."

On a June weekend in 1953, Marvin Raney and Chester Holway joined with four neighboring households in opening their house and garden as part of a fundraising tour sponsored by the Mothers' Club of the Cooksville school. The two were closely involved in planning the event, which represented Raney's big debut as village historian. The five tour houses were chosen because they were about one hundred years old, they were either in their original state or had been restored, and most of their furnishings were the same age as the houses. Raney prepared a mimeographed tour booklet including a brief account of Cooksville's development and biographies of the five houses. Only a few hundred tourists were expected that weekend, but thirteen hundred showed up. This success was reprised a few years later, and Raney and Holway continued to open their house to small groups as Ralph Warner had done—though without meals, period costume, or musical entertainment—allowing many women's clubs to tour the premises as part of their outings.

By the time of the 1953 house tour Raney had opened his first business enterprise in their old barn. Cooksville House was "a fey shop, if there ever was one," observed a local reporter, who described Raney as "an engaging young man with no visible means of support, who shudders slightly when the word 'work' profanes his presence. (Unless, of course, it be caring for the plants and flowers of the formal gardens behind the house in which he lives.) He does not have a telephone in the house because they bother him."[14] Raney's shop was dedicated to selling things handcrafted in Cooksville, "with some of the craftsman's heart in it, and a little bit of the beauty of the old village."[15]

A local weaver and ceramist produced much of the shop's merchandise. Raney wove rag rugs and began venturing into the antiques trade.

While Raney immersed himself in Old Cooksville, Holway was working in Chicago much of the time and living with his mother near the city. Raney was kept busy as a historical consultant and antiques expert, speaking and writing on porcelain and pottery. A longtime member of the county historical society, he worked with it on many projects. He established the society's archives and was a key consultant during its restoration of historic buildings. If people had questions about Cooksville history, they turned to Raney. If people had something related to the village, they gave it to Raney. He had become the keeper of the community's history and seemed to relish that role. It was Raney's research that formed the basis for Cooksville's listing as a historic district in the National Register of Historic Places.

By the late 1950s Raney and Holway's Cooksville presence was attracting younger gay men with similar leanings. With Raney's encouragement Chicago native Bill Wartmann bought the long-vacant and disintegrating Sayre-Osborn House several miles east of the village in 1959. Wartmann moved there from Madison with his lover, Michael Saternus, and they began a meticulous restoration of the place. "There were at least three or four gay people living in tiny Cooksville at that time," Wartmann recalls. "I said to Marvin, 'I knew we were organized, but I didn't think we had a whole town!'"

Around the time that Wartmann and Saternus moved into the Cooksville orbit, Eric Lieber (pseudonym) discovered the village. He was driving a drinking buddy home from Madison late one night, and that friend happened to be Raney's nephew who was living with his uncle. "Two or three o'clock in the morning we came to this wonderful old house at the corner of a village square," Lieber says. "That was my introduction to Marvin Raney and Chester Holway and this small town that had maintained its integrity over the years without too much modernization. I became fascinated by the place, by what was going on and the people involved. I wanted what these men had, not only the old houses and the antique stuff but also the type of life they were leading and the intellectual things they were doing. My own experience growing up in New York City had never exposed me to that country-gentleman sort of thing. My friendship with Marvin began when I told him that I was gay and that I presumed he was. I would come out to Cooksville on weekends and help in Marvin and Chester's garden. That was the beginning of a long and dear friendship with those two men. I became sort of their protege. This kind of mentoring was especially critical in the old days, when things were more closeted. Marvin and Chester were my mentors intellectually and provided emotional stability through the rough times."

Lieber bought property in Cooksville in 1963, when he was in his early thirties, and moved there in 1967. The child of German-born parents, he had grown up in a tenement house in the South Bronx. "We had no roots in this country, nothing to tie yourself to. We had no history; I felt more European than American in attachment and language. I was looking for roots: owning a piece of land, which seemed impossible to me growing up in New York City, and buying a gravesite in the Cooksville cemetery. How critical that was to my well-being and still is."

By 1971 Raney was in business once again, selling antiques at the Only Yesterday Shop in an old granary building near the village. Chester Holway was retiring from his Chicago business and planning to become a full-time Cooksville resident. And the village's gay population was continuing to grow. Another Madison couple had bought an early house facing the village square. Though Raney and Holway fretted that these new arrivals would blow their cover, they were pleased that the house was being properly restored. While Bill Wartmann continued to work on his old house east of the village, his former lover Michael Saternus staked a claim in Cooksville by purchasing the landmark Congregational church building. Saternus began restoring the exterior of the 1879 building with the help of his new lover, Larry Reed. Within a few years Saternus and Reed purchased the Van Buren House across the street from the church and began its rehabilitation. The small Greek Revival frame house had been vacant and deteriorating for twenty years.

With a new generation of gay men earnestly engaged in Cooksville's preservation, Marvin Raney died in 1980, shortly after Chester Holway suffered a stroke. That year Saternus and Reed moved into the House Next Door to help care for Holway and his home. They lived there for six years while working on their Van Buren House, which they moved into in 1986, the year Holway died.

Michael Saternus was another of Cooksville's "Chicago people." Born in 1936, he grew up on the city's near-west side. Very visual and artistic, he studied architecture at the Illinois Institute of Technology, then moved to Madison, Wisconsin, in the late 1950s, where he studied art. Shortly before AIDS ended Saternus's life in 1990, he thanked Bill Wartmann for awakening in him a passion for restoring historic buildings. What Wartmann had done about thirty years earlier, toward the beginning of his ten-year relationship with Saternus, was to saddle them both with a barely inhabitable wreck of an old house out in the country near Cooksville. It was in those circumstances that Saternus discovered his own desire not only to make the structure sound, waterproof, and warm but to do it in a way that respected the house's period integrity.

Working on the Sayre-Osborn house with Wartmann through the 1960s was Saternus's restoration apprenticeship, with Marvin Raney as chief mentor. But the house belonged to Wartmann, and when their relationship ended, Saternus looked elsewhere for his own redemptive focus. He found it several miles west, in Cooksville, when township officials decided in 1971 to sell the building that was originally the Cooksville Congregational Church. Built in 1879, the church was largely idle and in disrepair after a scant thirty years of ecumenical use. In 1939 the building was shorn of its spires and belfry to serve the township as a meeting hall for twenty-five years. Then it sat vacant for several years before township officials decided to sell it.

The old church building was Cooksville's most prominent architectural landmark. Saternus wanted to save the pale, stripped-down structure and put it back the way it was meant to be. His sealed bid of $2,250 won him the property. For twenty-five years Marvin Raney and Chester Holway had been witnessing the relentless disintegration of many of Cooksville's early buildings and had been unable to do much more than create documents of their diminishing lives. With Saternus putting down roots in the village and planning to restore the landmark church, historic Cooksville's chances of survival must have suddenly appeared much greater than Raney and Holway had ever allowed themselves to imagine.

Saternus envisioned creating a local history museum in the former church sanctuary. But museum making would have to wait until the outside of the building was restored. Raney supplied photographs and documents relating to the building's early appearance. Knowing exactly how the original belfry and four spires looked, Saternus constructed reproductions of them in his church-basement workshop. At a nearby antique shop he found a bronze bell close in size to the original. On a fall day in 1974, with his partner Larry Reed and many neighbors and friends gathered, Saternus saw the ninety-five-year-old building regain its nineteenth-century silhouette as a crane operator hoisted the five new structures into place. A few strategically placed smears of Vaseline helped to slip the balky belfry snugly onto its base.

The clapboard siding and original doors, long painted white, were returned to their original light brown with dark brown trim. The wooden entrance porch, which had been replaced with a concrete one, was restored. A document from Raney's archives indicated that the windows, now clear, had originally been stained glass. This was confirmed when the chancel window, which had been sided and plastered over, was uncovered and the original stained-glass window was still in place. An antiques-dealing Cooksville couple gave Saternus remnants of some of the other original windows and one of the original pews. Though badly deteriorated from many years in their garden, the pew would be invaluable as a basis for the eventual crafting of reproductions.

"When I moved to Cooksville," says Eric Lieber, "the Congregational Church was just an old square building with no steeple, an eyesore that needed to be either torn down or fixed up. When I saw Michael's designs for it, I thought it would be a nice addition to the village. The good old Norwegian farmers around here wondered why anybody would invest money in something frivolous like restoring the church. But they seemed rather pleased that it worked out—maybe didn't say as much, but they seemed to be proud of what the community was doing. Michael used the village as a showplace for his work."

By 1975, with the church's exterior restored, Saternus and Reed were looking for a home of their own rather than continuing to rent. They considered making their residence in the church basement but decided to try to get a proper house. In a carefully composed letter to the absentee owner of the long-vacant 1848 Van Buren House near the church, Saternus expressed his concern about the condition of the small house and his desire to buy it and restore it as his residence. Within a year Saternus and Reed owned the place.

In addition to Saternus's full-time employment as an architect, the massive and compelling job of restoring the Van Buren House meant there was no time to work on the church's shabby interior. Still, the tall and stately profile of the brown building at the village's main intersection continued to attract praise and publicity. While Saternus worked on the church, Cooksville residents stopped by to watch. As some of them were inspired to restore their own buildings, Saternus found himself in business. In addition to his own church and house, he got involved with many architectural restoration projects around the village and throughout the state. From his stashes of old doors, windows, shutters, and other items, he was able to supply his neighbors with replacements that helped them maintain the original look. He charged only for architectural drawings, not for advice, and loved to teach on the subject. With Reed working as preservation coordinator for the Wisconsin Historical Society, the couple developed an old-house workshop. Saternus's detailed written and photographic documentation of his restoration work made it easy for students to see the process happen, step by step. His "before and after" slides were inspiring.

"I think Michael Saternus was, like me, a big-city escapee looking for roots, someplace he could attach to," says Eric Lieber. "At first, when he was living down the road with Bill Wartmann, Michael was sort of in the background, very quiet and subdued. He may have had all the artistic talent in the world, but you didn't know it. Then all of a sudden he blossomed from a very shy, reticent person to somebody who had opinions, who seemed to have found himself and his voice: he would get up in front of people and speak about historic preservation. One or two successful projects turned him around. When he was working on something, Michael was the most focused person I ever knew."

As Michael Saternus blossomed at midlife, the rehabilitation and restoration of Cooksville's historic buildings began in earnest. "Cooksville's been lucky," Saternus said. "It's had a history of sensitive people, intelligent, artistic people who cared about its past and the aesthetics of the place."[16] Through the 1970s and 1980s, Saternus secured his place in that impassioned and quirky lineage.

The three individual narratives that follow present the accounts of contemporary gay men with Cooksville connections. William Wartmann gives an impassioned portrait of the rich blend of impulses—artistic, romantic, connective, redemptive—that led him and Michael Saternus into the Cooksville orbit in 1959. Reflecting on his adopted Cooksville, Al Garland remarks on the tremendous creative and physical energy that he has seen many gay men pour into the rehabilitation of things of beauty. Just as Saternus was introduced to Cooksville by his lover Wartmann, Saternus introduced his new lover, Larry Reed, to the village in 1971. Even as Reed celebrates more than ninety years of gay-propelled preservation in Cooksville, he is working to ensure that his own curatorial vision for the village persists well beyond his own lifetime.

William Wartmann

Born in Chicago in 1936, William Wartmann moved to Madison, Wisconsin, in 1958. He was an art teacher and Michael Saternus was an architect during most of the decade they were together as lovers. In 1973 Wartmann quit teaching and opened an antique shop, Wartmannia. He lives near Edgerton, Wisconsin.

I WAS RAISED in an immigrant neighborhood in Chicago, a slum. At the age of eleven I slept with a revolver under my pillow. People were violently attacked on the streets, mugged and raped occasionally, and there was always a sense of fear. I remember at eleven years of age listening to the Metropolitan Opera every Saturday on my Silvertone radio, and that gave me a great deal. And I played with dollhouses a lot; I could establish a sense of order—no confusion, no violence, no anger. I attempted to do that in my parents' home as a boy and eventually with Michael, in our apartments and in our home here in the country.

My father was a gentle man, but he had suffered from a tremendous depression and was schizophrenic. My mother was an alcoholic and a *rage*oholic. I was the little man who was always supposed to take care of everything. I think I've always known that I've been on the outside of society, even as a child. And my way of handling things is often to involve myself in a kind of magical thinking, to alleviate the pain, loneliness, and anxiety that I always experienced. I listened to the radio a great deal. One of my great loves was "Let's Pretend," with Billie Burke, and there was "Captain Midnight" and a whole series of stories. I spent a lot of time with that wonderful, comfortable green eye of the great big radio that my parents had.

I had an interest in architecture very early and spent a great deal of time as a child walking around looking at buildings. We lived at 2142 West Monroe Street, in an area of the south side of Chicago that had many old row houses. I went to a school that was maybe a couple of blocks from my house, but it seemed like a long way. I would study the various houses; I think some of them were Renaissance Revival, some Romanesque, some a pastiche of German and Greek, and I found them very interesting.

One Christmas when I was about ten I received all sorts of wonderful gifts, but nothing that I really would have chosen. An archery set and straw target, a pigskin football, a catcher's mitt, a fielder's mitt, a boxing bag on a stand, and boxing gloves. I think my father was attempting to curtail the feminine side of me. I always knew that I was different, and my mother would wonder where I came from.

My father wanted to reestablish a relationship with me. When I was twelve he took me to Kroch's and Brentano's and asked me if there was a book I would like. I saw Miller's *American Antique Furniture,* a Philadelphia high-boy with flamed finials on the cover, and I thought it was the most beautiful thing I had ever seen. I think the book was $15.95, and he bought it for me. With the typewriter I got when I graduated from grade school, I started categorizing furniture on index cards: Sheraton, Chippendale, Duncan Phyfe, Empire. I would think, oh, if someday in my life I could only own one antique.

Many weekends, from about age eight until about thirteen, my mother and father took me with them to look at real estate. Eventually we bought a home in River Grove, a suburban area of Chicago. From that point on I wanted to work out an environment that would be beautiful. I tried to do it to the best of my ability, and at thirteen, fourteen, fifteen, I made decisions that were very naive and aesthetically pretty horrible. My mother and I would go to look at furniture at Wiebolt's in Chicago. They had a sale on lamps, so we picked out lamps for our house, a colonial base with a shade of swirled and twisted satin. They were seconds, a little dented, but we brought them home and were so thrilled. Somehow that was the beginning of a sense of arrival.

My parents' home was a very large house, a rooming house. I did a lot of remodeling, learned to use a hammer and nails, tore out walls. I was thirteen, fourteen years old, and I worked like a man, to exhaustion. I would read *House Beautiful* and stuff like that and always try to improve the house. My concept was that if you had certain things, then you would have harmony and peace.

My mother was from Croatia; my father from Germany. My father went to the eighth grade, and my mother went to the fourth grade; she could barely write. So I realized that I had to go to school; I had to try to take hold of my own life and make something out of it. I went to Oak Park–River Forest High School, a very wealthy high school at that time, because I was interested in art and I knew that I had to go to a wealthy school because art and music instruction of any caliber was only given at very wealthy schools. I had a wonderful art teacher there who opened up all sorts of doors to me.

Many Saturdays and Sundays in my high school years I would go down on the El and spend the entire day at the Art Institute of Chicago. At that time, the institute had a series of rooms, French and Italian and English. I spent most of my time in the English townhouse. I got to know the guards, and they would let me look under the furniture to see how things were put together. It allowed me not only to survive but to have hope, because I didn't want to go home. Yet on the other hand, I wanted to go home and make things right.

My father was a laborer, my mother ran the rooming house, and I was going to a high school in which 98 percent of the kids went to college. I had to figure out a way to get to college, but there was no money for it. I decided to work on an art portfolio; *Scholastic Arts* magazine always gave an art scholarship. And I had to get away from the house. My mother would say, "You stay in this house; it's a goldmine! We have seven bedrooms at ten dollars a piece, seventy dollars a week. You come back here when you get through school and paint in the basement, use that as a studio." And I thought, I'm not going to do that. I'll look like a classic old fruit, living there with my mother, doing my paintings in the basement.

When my mother would say I was wasting my time, that I wasn't going to be worth a goddamn, I would say I've got to get out of here. Saturdays and Sundays I would get on the El and go down to the Loop, sit on my little campstool on Michigan Avenue and Rush Street, and do drawings and paintings. Drawings of Cyrus Hall McCormick's mansion, which was at 675 Rush Street, and William McCormick's mansion, and Mrs. Blair's mansion, and Edith Rockefeller McCormick's mansion, which was near the Drake Hotel.

The house at 675 Rush was forty-five rooms, and the caretaker gave me the key so I could wander through the empty house. It had a staircase on which six people could walk abreast at the base. It had an elevator and a beautiful library with ebonized wood and Japanese woven straw wallpaper. It had a grand hallway and a swimming pool in the basement. It had a mansard roof with a tower. I would sit up there and draw and look at the whole city. I spent my weekends inside those empty houses, trying to learn things, trying to get out of what I was in, trying to become part of what I thought was the way things were supposed to be.

I got a full four-year scholarship to Illinois Wesleyan University in Bloomington. It was not an easy experience for Bloomington or for me, because I really knew who I was in many ways, and even in the 1950s I was going to be who I was. I'd been going to cocktail parties on Rush Street in Chicago when I was fourteen years old, and now I was going to this university in the middle of a cornfield. I had my hair in a widow's peak like Audrey Hepburn and wore Italian boat-neck shirts and sandals. Looking at me, people in Bloomington didn't know whether to shit or go blind.

I worked as a house servant for a Bloomington family; I lived on the third floor in an unheated apartment. When I was interviewed for the job by an octogenarian woman, she asked me if I smoked. I said yes, I do. She asked me if I drank. I said, yes, I do. She asked me if I went to church. I said, no, I don't. I thought, this is crazy, but I'll be damned if I'll lie to some old lady. She looked at me and said, "You have the most beautiful brown eyes. You remind me of my husband. You may have the job."

In my attic apartment I arranged and rearranged furniture and built my dreams. When the Bloomington Country Club was redecorating, I bought a wing chair, a nice reproduction, for five bucks and carried it on my head about three or four miles to where I lived. Along the way I would sit down in the chair in the cornfield and smoke a cigarette. People driving by would practically go off the road.

There was always the idea that I wanted to be an artist, a painter, and I had to have shelter. How was I going to do it? I thought that the only way I could ever own a house was if I bought four trailers, one at a time, and put them all together in a square and then created a courtyard atrium garden. I could make each long, rectangular area some kind of period room. Then I thought of living in an old schoolhouse. Or maybe when they tore down a Queen Anne house, I would be able to save the attic part, have it lifted off the house and set up on legs so that I could park my car underneath and walk up into it.

After I graduated from college, I stayed in the area and worked as an art teacher. Then I fell in love with a beautiful girl in Bloomington who happened to be at the University of Wisconsin in Madison, so I followed her there. I worked very hard on my graduate degree in painting. Back in Chicago in the summer I went to a gay bar and met a very handsome young man named Michael. I was determined that I was going to get him to be my lover that night, so I had to work fast. He had quit his job at Sears Roebuck, so I convinced him to go to graduate school in art at Wisconsin. Michael Saternus and I got an apartment in Madison, three rooms for thirty-five dollars a month. It was in the Greenbush, which was really a mess but the kind of neighborhood where everybody just sort of coexisted, Italians, Jews, and blacks.

Thursday night was garbage night in Madison. Someone would throw out a chair; I would carry it home to our apartment on my head. If it was too heavy, I would ask Michael to get on the other end. Michael was terribly shy and hated to carry furniture down the street; he would be blood red all the way home. But I insisted that we go out every Thursday night. We were gonna get it, whatever it was. I would refinish three or four of these things and take them to an antique shop and trade them for one good piece. And so I would upgrade myself. I developed a surrogate family of antique dealers and learned the business from them.

Eventually Michael and I were forced to move because of what was euphemistically called redevelopment. By the time they started tearing the buildings down around us, we were in a larger apartment, six rooms. We had sanded all the floors and had white walls and antiques and art objects. The redevelopment department sent two young social workers to our apartment to try to help us prepare for the move. A lot of street people were sleeping in the hallways on the first and second floors of our building. I would just step over them, saying excuse me, and go up to our apartment on the third floor, where we had all these antiques and china and chandeliers and oriental rugs and objets d'art and a large German Shepherd.

When the social workers came upstairs for our appointment, I was wearing a black floor-length, moiré bathrobe, smoking a black, gold-tipped Russian cigarette in a jade cigarette holder, and holding a glass of sherry with a hazelnut in it. We were listening to Boccherini. I said, "Do come in," and when they stepped through the door, they practically fell backward, they were so disoriented. It was light and airy, very much like any place that Michael and I ever lived; eventually they were beautiful places. And so we were told that we were going to have to move.

Long before I purchased it, I heard about this house in the country from a Mr. and Mrs. Middleton, who were antique dealers. They said, "Bill, there's this wonderful great big house with Egyptian woodwork"—actually, it's Georgian, not Egyptian. "You have to go and look at it, and get it." And so I thought, well, I'll buy that house. Michael and I didn't have two nickels to rub together. While I continued filling up our apartment, Michael kept asking, "What are you going to do with all this furniture?" I said we were going to move into that house in the country. "What house in the country?" The one the Middletons were talking about. "Where?" I don't know, I said, but I'll find out.

I had also heard of Marvin Raney, a man who lived in Cooksville who was a collector of china and porcelain. He was a friend of Ellen Anderson, an antique dealer who was also a friend of mine. I used to go to her shop in Madison on a regular basis to look at her things and learn about antiques. She said Marvin was a wonderful, brilliant man who knew a great deal about china. One day I drove out to Cooksville, and I saw this man on a ladder, smoking a cigarette in a cigarette holder, cleaning the gutters on the two-story part of his house. I stopped and said, hello, my name is Bill Wartmann. I understand that you collect porcelain and pottery. "What are you interested in?" he said, the cigarette holder in his mouth going up and down as he spoke. I told him I was interested in Leeds and soft-paste Queensware and salt glaze and Spode. He practically fell off the ladder. He invited me into his home and showed me part of his collection, and we got along splendidly.

I said that the Middletons had told me about a house that was for sale. Marvin said, "Yes, the Sayre-Osborn House on Caledonia Road. I'll show it to you if you come by tomorrow." The next day Marvin and I went out and looked at the old house. Just me; Michael was not interested. It was a twelve-room house built in 1852. A basement wall had caved in, there was snow in the living room, and a lot of the windows had been broken. Kids would come in the house and smoke pot and make love and whatever you do when you're young. I thought it was beautiful and Marvin said that it would be a wonderful place. I didn't know how to get the house, but I knew I was going to try. A man who had an option to buy the house was planning to install aluminum siding and picture windows. He can't do that, I said. He'll destroy it! You have to keep the integrity of the house. I asked the Sayres, the people who were selling it, to let me take two of the doors and refinish them. If you sell me this house, I will make it into something really beautiful and you'll be very proud. Let me show you.

I took the doors back to Madison, dragged them up three flights of stairs to our apartment, and refinished them. They had eight to ten coats of paint on them, and there was buttermilk paint, which is just a son of a bitch to get off. I had to use paint remover and SOS pads mixed with bleach. But I refinished the two doors and took them back to show the Sayres, and they were very pleased. When their other deal fell through, I told them I wanted to buy the house on land contract. I was teaching art in one-room schools two days a week and going to a psychiatrist three days a week; I had had what might be considered a nervous breakdown. Naturally, I had no money. Michael said, "Don't you dare buy that house." I was supposed to put a hundred dollars down, but they accepted fifty. This was in 1959.

Michael had studied contemporary architecture under Mies van der Rohe in Chicago. He didn't know a great deal about Classical or Colonial or Greek Revival architecture, and he certainly was not interested in old houses. But I fell in love with this house. As an itinerant art teacher I would occasionally drive by here, and if it was at night, I would come in with a lantern and sit in the dark. The doors would bang in the wind, there would be snow on the living room floor, and I would be thinking about where I would put a grandfather clock. I was into fluff and cosmetics; we were going to create ambience. We'll get a couple of this and a couple of that, and we'll hang this and we'll hang that, and we'll sweep the floor and that will be it. Well, Michael came from engineering and architecture, and before I know it we've got the pieces of this huge house all numbered, and we're taking it apart. We're young and think we can do anything. And we're trying to make a compromise: he doesn't care how I decorate as long as I work with him on the structure. But I didn't know shit about structure.

The first year we spent in trenches eight or ten feet deep, rebuilding our foundation by hand. I had no money, so I bought a cement mixer from Sears Roebuck without a motor. We're young; we can turn the crank by hand! We mixed concrete forever and hauled it in buckets. The first thing we did was put in the footings for the fireplace. The back wall has caved in, we're not certain if the house is even going to stand up, but we're putting the fireplace footings in, which are four or five feet deep. Eventually we got a motor for the cement mixer and built the three-story fireplace.

While working on our fireplace we had some blue-rinse group of women who came to tour the house. We cleaned it up as best we could and had candles and things like that. They didn't really understand why we were doing what we were doing and must have thought we were mad. One of the things that they were most concerned about was which of us slept in which bed. We were young and energetic and in love. One day I wrote the date on a piece of wallboard, then wrote: "We are two homosexual men working on this restoration. When this building is torn down, we hope you find our signatures. Michael J. Saternus and William J. Wartmann."

Michael and I had different points of view in the beginning, but we both wanted to create beauty and order. One of my intents was that this house would be a safe compound away from Madison. I came out here almost monastically. I was afraid that we wouldn't give up the 602 Club, where some gay people would go every night to have drinks, a very insidious thing. By getting Michael and me away from the city and the 602 Club, I thought we would be safe. I thought I could control Michael, keep him involved and occupied with the house, and alcohol wouldn't be a problem. Every week on Friday night we would go to Edgerton to do the laundry and eat, and then I would go shopping at the antique stores there and buy stuff to put in the shop I planned to open.

So we continued to work on this house and got it put back together. Michael and I lived here for about ten years, under extremely distressing conditions. For many years there were no walls or finished floors; everything was numbered and taken apart, then put back. I would pretend that the aluminum foil on the insulation was English tea paper. That way I could get through the evening. One day I had just finished reading a Flannery O'Connor story about Bible salesmen when I heard a knock on the door. I came running down the stairs and threw open the door. The young Watkins salesman looked in and said, "Oh, no one lives here." He saw only two-by-four studs. I said, What do you mean nobody lives here? *I* live here. "Is the lady of the house in?" he said. I'm the lady as well as the man of the house, I said. "But you can't live here," he said. "There are no walls." The paintings are hung, all the furniture is in proper place, there just aren't any walls, I said. No problem.

Michael and I thought we would get this house done, and then we would go into nearby Fulton and buy those homes and fix them up. It was a perfect site, with a river, an old church, an old school. It would have been wonderful. But people didn't see then what we saw. I think gay people often see with different eyes, a different sense of beauty. As I always say to people,

once we move into the neighborhood, it always gets better. If I were a young man now, I would go homesteading in inner-city Chicago, buy a house for a dollar.

I considered Michael the brains and me the brawn, in many ways. And he considered me the expert in certain areas, researching historic details or picking out furniture. This house has about twenty-five windows, and each took forty hours to restore. I tried very hard not to break the fragile old glass. When we discovered that the front door had had sidelights, I was able to find an old door with sidelights in a house that was contemporary with this house and was being razed. We also got a staircase and balustrade from that house. We wanted to keep this house sort of basic Georgian. By rights the pumpkin pine woodwork should be painted, but I didn't want to be painting it all the time.

I'm very nineteenth century—chocolates, flowers, sonnets, music, candlelight. In some ways Michael thought that I was quite mad. I probably was, probably still am, according to the standards of the culture. I loved Michael to a point of madness. As a child my favorite song was from *Snow White*—"Someday My Prince Will Come." In one sense Michael was my prince; in another sense he was my demon. It's a miracle that we stayed together for ten years.

Al Garland

Al Garland grew up near Detroit, Michigan, and moved to Madison, Wisconsin, in the 1960s to attend the University of Wisconsin. Within a few years he and his partner, Richard, discovered nearby Cooksville. Both Al Garland and Richard are pseudonyms.

AT AN EARLY AGE I had an appreciation for old things. We were poor, but my mother had a china cabinet with pieces of ruby red etched glass, hallowed treasure. I remember the great tragedy when one of my sisters broke a hurricane lamp. You'd have thought the world had come to an end. I still have a lot of the stuff that was in that old china cabinet and furniture from our original home.

I had a rather romantic dream about buying a big, old rambling farmhouse, so Richard and I looked around in all directions and came upon Cooksville one Sunday afternoon. We stopped at Eunice Mattakat's antiques store and asked if she knew of anything for sale, and she sent us to Marvin Raney. Marvin was terribly courteous. He was very fetched by Richard, I found out subsequently. He walked us across the green and showed us this place, which had a huge, clumsy, ugly porch on the front, as well as an ignominious TV tower, just horrible. Marvin was saying it had a lot of potential, but I turned up my nose. So we went to look at several places off in the country. Then I read *In Cold Blood* and decided I did not want to live out in the wide-open country, distant from neighbors. This house began to look much more appealing.

Marvin introduced us to Michael Saternus and Bill Wartmann. Michael was this immense, handsome devil who hardly ever said a word. He smiled a lot and drank a lot and was gorgeous to look at. And he was terribly enthusiastic about restoration, even though he and Bill were living at Wartmann's place on Caledonia Road with no north wall and no west wall. They would go to a movie house to get warm. Michael checked out the house Marvin had showed us to make sure that it was structurally sound and all that. I think he was just humoring us, but we felt as if we had gotten expert advice and decided to make an offer. I made what I thought was a ridiculously low offer, and I'll be damned if the seller didn't accept it, right then, cash. We really lucked out because we got it for nothing.

We started spiffing up the place almost immediately. Our first project was sort of a promise that Michael urged us into: to restore, as close to the original as possible, the front elevation of the house. So the three of us began, and some of my lesbian friends came and helped to tear off that awful front porch. It was sort of a community effort. Lots of people, straight and gay, were so pleased when they saw what we were doing and helped us.

Next was the restoration of the three rooms in the front of the house. We ripped up every damn floorboard and straightened things out, then started on the woodwork. Even though we knew that the wood was painted originally, we decided that we liked the patina of the old pine too much. Then we stripped off all the wallpaper and repaired the walls and ceilings as best we could.

Michael did most of the carpentry. We often felt guilty throughout the restoration because Michael spent so many hours working on our house, from hauling the filthy old furnace out of the basement to building cabinets with old wood. He loved to spend weekend after weekend tinkering with that. I think it was about this time that he decided that he really wanted to specialize in restoration. Richard and I worked hard too, but we didn't know what we were doing. I was Michael's gofer.

Then Wartmann and Michael told us—and I remember how shocked I was—that the lovely kitchen had to go. It was a lean-to that stretched all the way across the south side of the house, windows on every side and wonderfully cozy. But the roof was bad, and it was on a concrete slab. So that was the next project. Our plans grew beyond simply replacing the kitchen to building an addition. We decided to contract that out but did all the work that we could ourselves, to save money. And always recycling, as did Michael Saternus, every board, every nail, everything.

We ate over at Marvin's practically every night when we were without a bathroom and kitchen. And Marvin would wander over frequently to see what was going on, what progress was being made. He was good advice and was grooming Michael all the while, teaching him what was appropriate and what wasn't. Marvin came up with original photographs showing how the front porch should be. He was the dean of the village and a great buddy. There were, God, how many bottles of gin that went down in this house during that period.

Chester worked in Chicago and seldom came to Cooksville because he was living with his mother in Hammond, Indiana. When his mother died, he announced he was moving back here, which sort of shook Marvin up because that meant he could not carry on in his old curmudgeonly ways. Chester immediately started having things done to their house, like modernizing the bathroom and kitchen, and that didn't go over well with Marvin. Chester wasn't as sensitive as Marvin would have liked about details. I remember the great fight, and Chester saying, "I'm simply *not* going to have an antique bathroom!" For so many years Marvin had been the ruler of the house. Suddenly Chester came back, and Marvin couldn't say a word because the house belonged to Chester, and he could do whatever the hell he wanted.

Chester said that one day he simply got fed up with all the crappy old cracked china that Marvin had, so he went to Marshall Field's and bought a new set of dishes.

When I was hauling furniture and china and linens back from my childhood home in Michigan, Marvin was the consultant. Is this worth anything? Shall we throw this out, or shall we keep it? Marvin had a great deal to do with the way the interior of our house looked, what was appropriate. When he had his shop, he would tell us, "I have something that's very good and very nice and that you should have." Richard and I have a magnificent tapestry and many pieces of furniture that came from him.

We saw a great deal of Marvin and Chester in those days. Every weekend they were here or we were there. After we had been living here for a while, a friend of some friends who was studying to be a landscape architect came out on successive Sundays with his lush of a lover to map out our garden. All the while Marvin and Chester sat back smugly and maybe smarting, because it didn't occur to us that this was just the kind of thing that they loved to do and were experts at, because of their own garden. So we had them look at the plan, and they modified it, discreetly and delicately but substantially. They would say, for instance, "You need gray dogwood. We have lots of that. We can give you all the gray dogwood that you want." They were very generous because they wanted to pass on to us certain lovely plants. Gardening was the cement that held Marvin and Chester together. By the time we had moved here they had started to neglect their magnificent gardens, but Marvin used to work in them all day long. It was fun to see them talk together about items in their yard. They, of course, knew everything by its Latin name and had their little botanical in-jokes.

Marvin was terribly bright and cultivated his curmudgeonliness. He had no patience with phony people and was very opinionated but very informed. He read the *New York Times* from cover to cover every damn day of his life. Chester was a businessman who was also very well informed, but not as well informed as Marvin, which would cause some sparks once in a while. Chester was kind of a dandy. He used to have his hair tinted and was careful about his dress, whereas Marvin couldn't care less and would wear any old rag.

Marvin was cautious about the idea of Richard and me moving into the village, but it appears that Chester was the one who was uptight about it. He didn't want Cooksville turning into a faggots' haven. They were a wonderful pair. Chester and I grew to be very close friends, as did Richard and Marvin. Richard admired Marvin a great deal as an intellectual, and Chester and I simply had a lot of fun; we traveled a fair amount together. Chester became much less uptight about being gay because we had gay parties and gay friends as visitors frequently. Chester would come to our notorious Thanksgiving drag parties, but Marvin wouldn't.

Marvin's concern about Richard and me buying this house was probably that he didn't want a bunch of flaming fairies over here. It was about 1968; you just didn't flaunt it. We weren't effeminate, so there was no reason outwardly to think that we were anything but a couple of regular joes, particularly since we mixed cement and built foundations ourselves. People might say, "Isn't that nice, two young men are restoring that house." Most of the straight people in the village welcomed us with open arms. Total strangers brought us housewarming gifts like a cake or a pot of stew.

There have been bachelors around Cooksville for a long time, and there is a long tradition of gay men taking the lead in preserving the village, fortunately always in a very quiet and subdued manner. We've always been very pleased about that. Mineral Point has long been a nest of fighting, bitching gay people who are more flamboyant than here in Cooksville. In Mineral Point you see a lot of Chicago types who have moved in, with dyed hair and excessive jewelry and effeminate manner, which pretty immediately identifies them as gay people. That hasn't happened in Cooksville. There have been a lot of gay people around here, but we've never thrown it in the face of the straights. And although we were screwing around with each other early on, there was always a rule that you don't mess with any of the straight men in the village.

When we first met Michael, he was so shy and timid that it was painful, and at the same time he was hot as a pistol. Michael had met Wartmann as a graduate student in Madison, and they were up to their eyebrows in that place on Caledonia Road, so he already had a passion for restoration. He had come to know Cooksville, was enchanted by the village, and saw the possibilities, and with encouragement from Marvin and Larry he decided that the village was his project. Michael would do anything that he could to convince people to restore in Cooksville. It was a passion, and he was completely devoted to it. He came out of his shell, had more confidence in himself as an authority, and knew what he was talking about, be it restoration or opera or whatever.

Gay men are very sensitive to beauty. It's perhaps a hackneyed stereotype, but I believe in it—I simply know it. It's an aesthetic capacity, an appreciation of beauty in old things, the grace of a lovely, older house with elegant details. And when gay men are interested in something, they give it their all, tremendous amounts of creative energy and physical energy. Not many straight people would do for this house what we did for it.

Larry Reed

Larry Reed was born in Green Bay, Wisconsin, in 1939. After serving as a naval officer during the Vietnam War, he returned to Wisconsin and immersed himself in theater as a graduate student, playwright, actor, teacher, and eventually as a preservationist.

TWO PASSIONS OF MINE, theater and history, have been intertwined in my life for a long time. In 1971 I was completing graduate school at the University of Wisconsin, writing a dissertation on how American playwrights have made dramatic use of American history. Meeting Michael Saternus at the Pirate Ship, a gay bar in Madison, was the beginning of a very serendipitous sea change in my life. Michael was an architect, but especially a restoration architect and architectural historian. He introduced me to an aspect of history that I had not been much aware of: the buildings and structures from the past that surround us, and how they can enlighten us, improve our quality of life, and help us to understand who we are and where we came from.

When I met Michael, he had just purchased the Cooksville Congregational Church and had started to restore its exterior. Michael's association with Cooksville began in the 1960s, when he and Bill Wartmann were restoring a historic house several miles east of the village. Before I met Michael, I had never heard of Cooksville. In 1973 we moved into a rental house near the village. I was teaching playwriting and theater history at Beloit College and writing a one-woman stage play based on the diaries and letters of Fanny Kemble, a British-American actress of the mid-nineteenth century. We moved into the House Next Door in 1980. All the while, especially on weekends, we worked on the church restoration.

When I first saw the Van Buren House across the street from the church, it was a sad sight: long-abandoned, a gray ghost. But Michael and I were busy on the church and didn't pay too much attention to it. We planned to turn the basement of the church into our residence and restore the upstairs nave. Then the light bulbs lit up in our little heads: rather than live in the church basement, here was a house just across the street—tiny, cute, manageable looking. Marvin Raney called it a little duckling of a house; I think he meant ugly duckling. It was in very bad shape, no paint on it, vegetation growing wild, a real eyesore. More than that, it looked like it was going to fall down. But it was a duckling with possibilities: it could be turned into a swan if you gave it a little attention. Marvin Raney and Chester Holway helped Michael get in touch with the woman who owned it, who was living in California, and in 1976 she sold the house to us for seven thousand dollars. A lot of the local reaction was that we were taking on an impossible task. Some people said we were crazy to bother with such a simple little house that was falling apart and should be bulldozed.

So we had two restoration projects going across the street from each other, the church and the house. We spent most of the effort on the house. Under Michael's guidance I was becoming an amateur preservationist and amateur architectural historian. Then suddenly I found myself becoming a professional preservationist when I was hired in 1980 by the state historical society to be its local preservation coordinator. For seventeen years, until I retired, it was my job to preach preservation throughout Wisconsin, to arouse communities' interest in their past, and to assist their preservation efforts.

Michael Saternus was an audacious visionary when it came to old buildings. He led a lot of us, happily, down the primrose path to preservation. "There's never a building that you can't rehabilitate, no matter how bad the shape it's in," he would say. "There's always enough there that you can preserve it and rehabilitate it." Looking back I think that's true, basically, but at the time it was my ignorance and naiveté and innocence, soon lost, that led me into the partnership on the Van Buren House. But having seen Michael work on the church for five years, I had every confidence; he had the vision, and he was a damn hard worker. Especially on weekends he loved to work on the church and the house, much to my frustration sometimes. It seemed that Michael would rather be working on the house than doing almost anything except going to opera in Chicago.

It took us ten years to rehabilitate this house. We pulled the whole thing apart, numbered everything, then put it back together. Neither of us wanted to live in a museum, but our guiding principle was to save as much of the original house as possible, knowing we were going to add a modern addition. I pulled nails out of old boards so they could be sanded and refinished. I cleaned the old mortar off hundreds of old Cooksville bricks so Michael could use them to build the new fireplace. We built our relationship while we were rebuilding this house. Working side by side, sharing in the vision and the planning, sometimes complaining and sometimes making mistakes, it mortared and nailed our relationship together. The house turned out beautifully and so did the relationship, though, of course, each had its flaws and weaknesses here and there.

As I became more skillful at what I was doing, Michael trusted my judgment a little bit more. We talked about the design, where to put the bathrooms and the bookshelves, what kinds of furnishings. I was the one who decorated the house—chose the paint colors and did the painting, decided where to place the furniture and the antiques, where to hang the pictures—but always with Michael's okay. In a partnership one person has to lead in some areas and the other person in other areas. If you're lucky, things work out without too many arguments. I think our biggest disagreement about the Van Buren House had to do with the location of the washer and dryer. I won out on that one.

Michael worked on many other restoration projects besides the church and the Van Buren House, some for pay and some not. He was an artist, and in architecture he was creating art that was permanent and useful. Michael was practical, so architecture was the perfect form for his creativity. I don't know how he learned to think of architecture as music in wood and concrete, how to make it useful and beautiful at the same time, but he had those skills. His love for historical architecture had to do with his love of the old, the craftsmanship, the fine details. He could read historic buildings and understand them, appreciate their styles and how they were put together, why they had this kind of molding and that kind of reveal. He was a collector of antiques, artifacts as well as buildings, and he truly appreciated them.

After more than twenty years working on preservation and restoration in Cooksville, Michael died in 1990. It was a great loss. The village needed somebody to take the lead in carrying on its preservation traditions, which extend back through the whole twentieth century. If you're interested in something, people will turn to you, depend on you, and give you the mantle and all the materials that go with it. And so the mantle was dropped on me.

A lot has been done in Cooksville, but much remains to be done. I see myself continuing the tradition, preserving the architecture and the great wealth of historical materials that have been passed down to me: photographs, artworks, speeches, letters, genealogical research, diaries, recipes, and other things that record the history of the area and of Cooksville in particular. A lot of this material was gathered together and passed on by people I didn't even know. Who donated it to Susan Porter, or to Ralph Warner in the 1920s, or to Marvin Raney in the 1950s? People were giving material to Michael in the 1970s, and they're still giving things to me now. Many of them are descendants of the early settlers who came here from New England, New York, and the British Isles in the mid-1800s. It all needs to be put in some kind of order to create an accessible and useful Cooksville archive, maybe housed in my house or church. An exhibit of some of the more interesting material would be a good project, and I've thought about creating a publication of some kind to give a picture of life in Cooksville over the last 150 years.

Until now it has just been assumed that somebody would pick up the ball as the keeper of Cooksville history. It was left casually to the goodwill of history buffs and lovers of Cooksville. The times are such now that we have to be a little more formal. In 1999 we formed the Historic Cooksville Trust, to help private property owners preserve and restore the historic buildings and the natural setting. With the pressures of development, the mobility of our society, and the new technologies, you have to create formal structures to deal with change—make sure that it's the kind of change you want and exert some control over it. With the Trust's assistance, rather than leaving it up to God knows who is going to follow in our footsteps, all of us in Cooksville will be more confident that the traditions will carry on.

In 1996 I finally finished the restoration of the church interior, a long haul from 1971. I have no particular heirs that I want to pass the Van Buren House and the Cooksville Congregational Church on to. I might be willing to have the Historic Cooksville Trust take charge of these properties, if not as owner perhaps as holder of preservation easements on them, so that no awful changes can be made. For those of us who want somebody watching over things in Cooksville when we're no longer here, the Trust could help preserve the buildings, the archives, and the artifacts. We have lost properties because individuals made the wrong decisions: the last blacksmith shop was demolished before we had an ordinance to protect historic buildings. Things like that could happen again. Even though we have laws on the books in the township to protect Cooksville, they're not foolproof. And there are historic properties in the outlying areas of the township that are not protected by ordinance, so there's still work to be done.

I feel a real responsibility to Cooksville because it has been so good to me. But more than that, it's just a human responsibility to preserve and understand and celebrate our history. If we don't, we're not much different from the lowest animal, just grunting our way through life, then gone. The past gives us a sense of what life is all about; it helps us gain a vision of the future. Without that sense of the past I think we become a little less human, a little more ruthless. Even Cooksville, this one little flyspeck on the map of the world, can teach us something about human nature and the human condition and what keeps us going. You can't live in Cooksville without feeling a sense of history, consciously or not. The past is accessible in this village in a way it isn't in many other places. That's what preservation is all about.

Singular Preservationists in the Midwest

IT'S NOT UNCOMMON for those with a fervent drive to collect, restore, and preserve old things to see their passion as something of a disorder. Commenting on the serial house restorations in which he continues to immerse himself, a gay interior designer in Indiana asks, "Is this a hobby or a disease?" Calling himself "a collector from way back," a gay interior designer in Wisconsin lists the kinds of antiques he favors: blue-and-white china, crystal, cobalt glass, ruby glass, green opalescent glass, cloisonné, porcelain dogs, French bronze, Toby pitchers, Nipponware. "Collecting is almost a little illness with me," he says. Of another Wisconsin gay man's drive to rescue and restore old houses, a newspaper says, "You could call it a mission or a compulsion."[1] Steve Dunham says he was "particularly loony about two very different things" as a teenager in Toledo, Ohio, in the mid-1950s: "derelict Victorian houses and buff, good-looking boys." This adolescent looniness led him to photograph his favorite mansions in the city's Old West End, which were beginning to be demolished.

The introduction to this chapter presents portraits of gay midwesterners whose preservation-minded endeavors mark them as eccentric to one degree or another. Robert Neal and Edgar Hellum, pioneering keepers of early Wisconsin history, lead off this singular pack. A generation younger than that small-town duo, Chicago preservationist Richard Nickel lost his life while battling the beauty-obliterating forces of urban renewal. Another generation later, aesthetic packrat Alex Davidson devotes his life to gathering and warehousing lovely objects of the past.

Robert Neal was born in Mineral Point, Wisconsin, in 1906 and grew up in that moribund mining town. Miners from Cornwall, England, started arriving in the lead-ore region of southwest Wisconsin in the 1830s. They soon built their one- and two-story Cornish-style limestone cottages near the mines, in the shelter of a ravine. This early settlement was called Shake-Rag-under-the-Hill, so the story goes, because miners were summoned to their midday meal by the waving of a cloth. When the growing town became known as Mineral Point, only the street of early houses retained the name Shake Rag.

Robert Neal learned about the old days and old Cornish ways from his grandmother, his father's mother. He was intrigued by the decrepit limestone cottages on Shake Rag. "As far back as I can remember, I had always been interested in the old houses. When in high school I often thought of buying one of these old houses, though I did not know what I would do with it. My early interest lay more in their artistic possibilities and the things that could be done with them than in their historical meaning."[2]

Bob Neal's father ridiculed his interest in old things, but Neal found a mentor and kindred spirit in Will Gundry, who lived in the family mansion on one of the highest hills in Mineral Point, where he had grown up. Wealth amassed by Gundry's father built the house and permitted the elderly bachelor to collect fine antiques, build a large personal library, and maintain many acres of gardens. He worked in business in London for a few years and became an accomplished pianist, but fortunate for Neal he chose to live mostly in Mineral Point.

Will Gundry was Neal's aesthetic father; Mrs. Somerset Maugham was his aesthetic mother. Neal first connected with the prominent socialite in the spring of 1928, when, on Gundry's recommendation, he was hired as general handyman in her exclusive interior decorating shop in Chicago. Neal was the oldest of three children whose mother had died when he was seventeen, and he had stayed dutifully close to home to help raise his sister and brother and run the household. At twenty-one he had graduated from high school but had not gone to college and was ready to get out into the larger world. With his eye for color and design and his interest in antiques and interiors, Neal saw working for Syrie Maugham as a way to get an education and open new avenues beyond his hometown.

After two years in Chicago proving that he was capable of much more than dusting, waxing, and moving furniture, mending veneer, and washing windows, Neal was transferred to Maugham's shop in New York City, where doing window displays was part of his job. When the economic collapse of the early 1930s forced Maugham to close the Chicago and New York locations, Neal was thrilled to be asked to work at her flagship shop in London. After seeking Will Gundry's guidance on whether or not to go, Neal boarded a ship for England in the spring of 1933. But the charm of working for Syrie Maugham in Depression-era London soon wore thin. "I really feel that a good rest is the thing that I need," Neal wrote to Gundry, "and outdoor work and labor, as I am sure it would do me no end of good. Had I the funds I would buy my house on Shakerag and work in getting that in shape. I think that would get all this out of my system."[3]

Neal returned to Mineral Point in the summer of 1934. Unemployment was widespread, people were leaving town, and the place was becoming very shabby. The newly established Work Projects Administration had begun demolishing some of the first houses to be abandoned, the decaying stone cottages on Shake Rag Street. In Neal's childhood there had been more than twenty of the stout old houses on that street, and suddenly it seemed possible that none would be left. The stone from walls a foot and a half thick was being sold for use in new foundations or retaining walls or as landfill.

The summer of Neal's return to Mineral Point, Edgar Hellum heard about the old houses being demolished and came looking for vintage building materials to use in fixing up his 1840s house in Cooksville, Wisconsin. Hellum ended up finding Bob Neal as well. Of Norwegian heritage, Edgar Hellum was born in Stoughton, Wisconsin, in 1906. Reading, flower gardening, and cooking were early interests. As an artistically inclined teenager Hellum met Ralph Warner of the House Next Door in Cooksville, just a few miles from Stoughton, in 1923. "Ralph Warner had the most beautiful garden and was the first to influence my interest in food and antiques and restoration," Hellum said. "He started my education, my curiosity, and got me off on the right foot. He was old enough to be my father and had been around enough that he knew antiques. There wasn't anybody I knew at that time who had anywhere near the knowledge of antiques that he had."[4]

From high school graduation in 1924 until he met Bob Neal in 1934 was a period of wandering exploration for Hellum. He tried college briefly, worked at various jobs, dabbled in sculpture, took night classes at the School of the Art Institute of Chicago. Realizing that he didn't have enough talent to make it as a professional artist, he went home to Stoughton. Ralph Warner was happy to have Hellum back in the area and advised him to buy a house in Cooksville, but Hellum had more wandering to do before settling down. By the time he returned, Warner had had an incapacitating stroke that left him almost unable to speak. That fall Hellum bought the ramshackle ninety-year-old Cook House in Cooksville from the county for two hundred dollars.

From the fall of 1933 through the spring of 1935, Hellum continued to live in Stoughton and worked off and on at fixing up his small, early-1840s frame house, the oldest in Cooksville. During the summer of 1934 he stayed with Warner at the House Next Door and took care of him. One day, when Hellum returned from a day of antiquing with his mother, Warner was eager to hear about the things they had seen. "*What-what-what-what-what-what?*" he said excitedly in his stroke-impaired manner. "You want to know what we saw?" "Yes!" Warner exclaimed. Among other things Hellum told him about a set of six chairs for twelve dollars, which he had decided not to buy because their cane seats were missing. When Hellum drew a sketch of the chair design, Warner cried out, "Oh, *yes-yes-yes-yes-yes-yes!*" "You think I should have bought them?" "Yes!" The next day Hellum drove back and bought the chairs. "He was teaching me," Hellum said. "They were chairs from about 1840. Ralph worked with wood in the classes he taught in Racine. That's where he did his own furniture repair at first. So that's what I did."

Hellum showed Neal around Cooksville. Seeing Edgar's old house there and being introduced to Warner and the House Next Door bolstered Neal's determination to buy one of the old Shake Rag houses. In the spring of 1935 he phoned Hellum in Stoughton: "I've found a house, but I don't know what you can ever do for it, it's so bad." Before long, Hellum made the seventy-mile trip to Mineral Point to inspect it and reassured Neal of its potential. Hellum moved to Mineral Point to live with Neal and to help him restore the abandoned two-room limestone cottage. It was filthy and disintegrating: a century of freezing and thawing had left the south wall ruinous, leaning more than a foot. They paid about one hundred dollars for the property. Then it was time to figure out how they could earn enough money in Mineral Point to support themselves and repair their house.

They scavenged for old building materials and hauled them back to 114 Shake Rag, accumulating a reserve supply of stone, lumber, brick, and other materials. "We kept salvaging stone all the time, wherever we could," Hellum said.[5] The couple's queer enterprise made them the butt of jokes, but that was nothing new to either of them. "The prevailing opinion was that we were nuts," Neal said, "that we should presume to take something that was fit and ready to be torn down and spend time and money and energy to fix it up."[6]

Will Gundry admired the couple's enterprise, but wanted Neal and Hellum to live in a proper house up in his part of town, not in a shack down on the Shake Rag. "Mr. Gundry was a country gentleman, with a little cut moustache," Hellum recalled. "He invited us up for dinner on the weekends that first summer—'You boys work so hard, and I'm afraid you don't eat well enough.' We got to his house for six o'clock dinner and it was two minutes to, so we sat in the car until it was six o'clock. He opened the door, clicked his heels, shook our hands, and welcomed us in. I didn't know that kind of living, all that finesse, and was much impressed with it."

By September 1935 their house on Shake Rag was restored to a condition that allowed Neal and Hellum to show it. They invited Gundry and his sister down as their first guests. "I never thought I would be taking tea on the Shake Rag!" Gundry said. Insisting that Neal and Hellum's house should have a name, he presented them with a list of suggested Cornish names from which they chose Pendarvis.

Neal and Hellum decided to open an antiques shop, sell some of their things, and serve tea to raise money to continue their work on the property. One September afternoon two women saw their sign and stopped to investigate. One of them, a columnist for a Madison newspaper, devoted much of the next day's column to enthusing about her Mineral Point discovery. At great length she described the quaint old house and its furnishings, the charming young men who restored it and lived in it, and the delightful tea they served.[7]

As a result of this glowing publicity, a stream of people began to make their way to Pendarvis House for tea and saffron cake. With tea at fifty cents a head, plus whatever antiques they sold, the place started to bring in some money. But cold weather soon brought an end to their procession of visitors. With only wood heat in the fireplace and water freezing in the pipes, Neal and Hellum lived in their two rooms at Pendarvis that first winter.

Needing more room and wanting to save more than just one of the old houses, Neal and Hellum soon decided to pay $450 for the three-story stone-and-log house thirty feet to the south, to which they gave the name Polperro. Then, for $275 they bought the two-story stone cottage a few feet to the north of Pendarvis, which they named Trelawny. They intended to make Polperro's ground floor into a shop where chair caning, weaving, and other crafts would be taught, and they would live upstairs. Trelawny would serve as their office. But all these plans seemed years from fruition. It was a serious stretch for Neal and Hellum to make the monthly payments on their three properties while still making progress in restoring the houses. They kept selling antiques, serving tea, and selling homemade saffron cake and plum preserves to visitors and by mail order.

Glowing articles about the two boys at Pendarvis House began to appear in newspapers around the region. "Two young men with the soul of an artist, and a vision, have remade one of the most antiquated and ill kept houses into a delightful art shop," one paper reported.[8] Soon they began serving meals of traditional Cornish foods, especially a meat-and-potato pie called pasty. The front room of Pendarvis became the dining room, which seated twenty at tables covered with red tablecloths and set with tea-leaf ironstone dishes, bone-handled knives and forks, and old glass goblets. "When we started here we went around and gathered a lot of the old recipes from the Cornish cooks, the older generation," Neal said. "It was from my grandmother who came over here in 1847 from Cornwall that I learned how to make the Cornish pasty."[9]

To enchanted outsiders Neal and Hellum were tireless and charming artist-artisans with an eye for beauty and tradition. But to many in Mineral Point they were a couple of crazy kids. A Mineral Point newspaper trumpeted Neal and Hellum's accomplishments during their first year in business and called on the city to help rehabilitate the Shake Rag neighborhood.[10] Few rallied to the cause. There was jealousy of Neal and Hellum's success in achieving so much on the slummiest street in town. In addition, although Pendarvis House's old-fashioned charm was rooted in local and humble tradition, it was not a business that catered to locals. It was pricey, and Neal's personality imbued it with haughty, discriminating airs. Pendarvis House guests were generally sophisticated folks from elsewhere who wrote or phoned ahead for reservations. And then there was the queerness of the whole thing: two thirty-year-old bachelors living together, serving high-class tea in a low-class cottage.

"We were sort of the laughingstock of the community," Neal said.[11] It was common in Mineral Point, when Neal and Hellum were mentioned, for a person to twirl an index finger at the side of his head, indicating that the two were pixilated—crazed by the pixies. "How are things going out on the Shake Rag?" people would ask facetiously, and Neal and Hellum would say that they were doing the best they could. "We then divorced ourselves from the city," Hellum said. "We stayed out on our end of the street and did our thing."

Doing their thing comprised a daunting range of tasks, but being queer had its virtues, and versatility was one of them. Both Neal and Hellum brought many talents to their work and developed many more on the job: hauling rock, mixing cement, laying stone walls and terraces to create courtyards, stairs, and garden spaces; landscaping, digging garden, reestablishing native plants; laying shingles. Then, after showering and dressing for the house, they would tie on aprons and go to work in the kitchen, baking, canning, cooking, and serving Cornish foods.

Neal and Hellum's life together worked well enough for them, but it proved disconcerting to some of their Pendarvis House guests. Hellum recalled two women who visited: "One of them said, 'But you boys do all the work!' 'Yes,' I said, 'each morning I scrub the floors on my hands and knees. Then I arrange all the flowers for the tables. Bob assumes the responsibility in the kitchen. I've got the meat all cut up, the potatoes and onions peeled, and he puts the pasty together.' 'Well, you both should get married, have wives,' the woman said. 'But what a drudge it would be for them,' I said. 'But that's what women are for!' she said. Before long, they sent the names and pictures of two women for us to write to. For Bob they picked a real good-looking one. The one for me wasn't so good-looking, but they said she was a real good cook."

"The restoration was a struggle from the beginning, because there was so much repair work to be done," Neal said. "The way we earned our money was serving meals. We needed lumber, mortar, sand, carpentry help, a mason. Over a period of time we developed the ability to carry on alone. What we had to our advantage was youthful enthusiasm. There were times when we thought we would never get finished. You would start to repair a baseboard. When you got that out, the floor joist would be rotted out. You might as well repair that while you have the baseboard out. Then you take up the floor and find out that some joists are resting on dirt, so you take out the dirt to get ventilation. Then you dig through the wall to put in vents. What you get into in repairing a baseboard has got into a major job."[12]

Neal and Hellum's financial pinch was eased in the late 1930s when, out of the blue, Gordon McCormick of the Chicago industrial family informed them that he wished to finance the restoration of Polperro.[13] The pixies were working magic. As the prospect of America going to war loomed larger, McCormick urged Neal and Hellum to get their estate plans in order and to come up with a strategy for safeguarding their Mineral Point properties in the event that they would be called into service. Both Neal and Hellum wanted to serve in the military, but both were rejected for medical reasons. Undeterred, they took food-service jobs at a Wisconsin military base. Neal ran the kitchen, and Hellum ran the pantry.

Pendarvis House was closed in 1943 and did not reopen for business until 1946. Over the next twenty-five years the tiny restaurant prospered and attracted national critical acclaim. "And so—with cooking, with people, with restoration, with the gardens and everything else—I found my pattern," Hellum said. "That was the thing about Pendarvis: we didn't do it for money, and we didn't have any money. I told Bob, 'If you want to go to the opera, get a fruit jar and keep puttin' it in so that when the time comes to buy your season ticket you've got the money.' But we had found our pattern, and we were enjoying what we were doing."

The winter months in which Pendarvis House was closed gave Neal and Hellum time for other projects. Neal wrote the first visitor's guide to historic Mineral Point in the 1940s, and the two hosted community development meetings by their home fireplace. They wanted to keep the old town as it was, but to revitalize it. Though many locals were dismissive of the pair's enterprises, others followed their lead and fixed up their houses and gardens. Neal and Hellum offered their services as consultants in architectural restoration, landscaping, and interior decorating, and Neal gave talks to women's groups on interiors and antiques: porcelain, pottery, glassware, and woven coverlets. Hellum favored woodworking, restoring old furniture, and crafting new pieces in his workshop.

Neal and Hellum had more time to go antiquing during the months when Pendarvis House was closed. They were always looking to "high-grade," a term Hellum picked up from Ralph Warner. "Bob and I weren't antique dealers," Hellum said, "but we kept peddling pieces of furniture because we kept high-grading. Bob would say, 'There's a set of chairs better than what we've got,' so we would peddle the six chairs that we had and replace them with something better." Neal was a persistent high-grader even with Christmas decorations. "We always had a Christmas tree, and with Bob it had to be a certain kind of tree," Hellum recalled. "We sometimes ended up with three or four Christmas trees in the yard, stuck in the snow, because we'd find a better one."[14]

The 1950s were Neal and Hellum's golden years at Pendarvis House, which was busy from spring through fall. "In the quiet atmosphere of the cottages with their adjoining courtyards and gardens," Neal wrote, "one may experience the intimate repose that comes from a touch with the past."[15] By the early 1960s the Shake Rag complex included the first three houses, two guest houses, and a row house that they restored and named Tamblyn's Row. "The old style cottages, like the old time people, are dwindling," Neal said. "All these little cottages were built with care and anxiety in the long summer evenings. The Cornish people tilled their little gardens and planned for the days when these little cottages would be left to their children. But their children scattered to the ends of the earth and their homes were desolate and forgotten."[16]

"What we have attempted to do here at Pendarvis is to save a lot of local things from being lost or going out of Mineral Point," Neal said. Pendarvis became a repository for documents, artifacts, and relics related to the history of Mineral Point, much of which he and Hellum donated for the founding of the Mineral Point Room at the public library. Neal, who founded the Mineral Point Historical Society in 1939, was a saver both sentimental and scholarly. He kept the hair from his first haircut, when he was three, and his first Christmas card from Hellum, mailed from Stoughton in 1934. He was the sort of compulsive saver who would gather fragments of old newspaper that had been used in framing a looking-glass, put them in an envelope, and label it "1839 newspaper pieces from back of small Empire mirror."

Through their nearly fifty years together, Hellum was Neal's right-hand man in the saving of Mineral Point history. "We told the guys at the city dump," Hellum said, "'Any furniture or papers or pictures or anything like that that comes to the dump, don't burn it up. Have one of the guys bring it out to our house first.' We saved hundreds of old photographs that would have been burned up. We'd take them to our good friend Laura Nohr, and she and her mother identified many of them. So now people come to the Mineral Point Room and find out their backgrounds, who their uncle was or who their grandparents were."

"That all of this belongs to time, and to the generations yet to come," remarked a friend of Neal and Hellum's after seeing their restored cottages.

Thirty-five years after they began to save the old houses on Shake Rag Street, Mineral Point became the first city in Wisconsin to have a historic district listed in the National Register of Historic Places. Neal was instrumental in making that happen and in developing local regulations to protect his hometown's historic buildings. By this time Neal and Hellum were ready to retire from running their Cornish restorations. They sold the Pendarvis complex to a foundation, which then turned it over to the Wisconsin Historical Society to be operated as a historical site. With the decision to hire a married couple as caretakers of the site, the mainstreaming of a remarkable work of pixilated vision had begun.

Born in 1928, Richard Nickel was in his twenties when his native Chicago embarked on massive demolition in the name of urban renewal. As thousands of slum properties were razed, many buildings designed by Dankmar Adler and Louis Sullivan were lost. Sullivan was the preeminent artistic inspiration of Nickel's life. As more and more of the architect's buildings were threatened with destruction, Nickel documented them by photographing them exhaustively and drawing detailed floor plans. And he salvaged as much ornament as he could haul away: terra cotta, limestone, wood, and metal. At first his goal was simply to save whatever beautiful fragments he could, to keep Sullivan's work from becoming landfill. Then came the idea of creating a Sullivan ornament museum.

In his book on Nickel, Richard Cahan credits him with starting "the first vigorous, hands-around-a-building preservation campaigns in Chicago that inspired a mass movement throughout the country."[17] Wearing tie and jacket, carrying a placard asking "Do We Dare *Squander* Chicago's Great Architectural Heritage," Nickel was part of a small group that protested the planned demolition of the Garrick Theater Building in 1960. Another man's sign read, "Mayor Daley Destroys Buildings as Hitler Destroys Jews." The protesters gathered petition signatures, wrote letters to the city's newspapers, and got others to make their views known to the mayor, the landmarks commission, and the papers.

Letter writing was Nickel's preferred method of activism. Shy and soft-spoken, he was loath to speak at public hearings or to engage in sign-carrying protests. It was the apathy of others that compelled him to engage in those activities. Uninterested in politics, he put little energy into getting legal protection for Chicago's landmark buildings. But he did take time out from photographing and salvaging to write scathing letters to architects whose alterations had compromised the integrity of Sullivan's buildings: "Oh, it's so God-Damned hopeless," he wrote to one. "You don't deserve to polish Sullivan's shoes and here you are bastardizing his buildings."[18]

"People say rightly of me that I'm too fussy," Nickel remarked, "but if you're not analytic over everything, then soon enough you're a slob and anything goes." Regarding the rehabilitation of the Auditorium Theater, his purism caused him to grouse that "if it isn't as Adler and Sullivan left it in 1890, in essential character, then it's better to be abandoned."[19]

Despite the depth of Nickel's bitterness about the unrelenting, numbing demise of Adler and Sullivan's architecture in Chicago, he maintained a resolute focus on his mission: definitive documenting and salvaging and bearing witness to the passing of his city's beautiful old buildings. In the late 1960s Nickel made regular rounds to check on the thirty-some Sullivan structures still standing in Chicago.

The first death knell sounded for Adler and Sullivan's Stock Exchange Building in 1968. Nickel was cynical and weary after a decade of preservation battles mostly lost, but he couldn't stay out of the Stock Exchange fight. He wrote impassioned protest letters and took part in sidewalk demonstrations. Beginning salvage work in the building's trading room in the fall of 1971, he told a colleague, "I think it is sort of like a holy room. The more you are in here the more you are in awe of it."[20] He suggested that they save not just pieces of the room but the whole room; it was eventually installed and restored in Chicago's art institute.

"Ah, the world gets weaker and weaker, dumber and dumber," Nickel remarked in 1971. "The good people get knocked off, the good buildings get smashed, the lofty values wither." He kept going back to the Stock Exchange Building, to salvage ornament and just to be with a dying masterpiece. In the spring of 1972, while on a solo visit to the demolition site, Nickel was killed when part of the building collapsed on him. "I had met Richard Nickel, oh, maybe a month before it happened," Studs Terkel said. "The way he talked, oh God, about beauty and past and history and how we must hang on to some things and continuity and all that stuff, I guess you'd have to say he was crazy."[21]

Getting acquainted with Alex Davidson (pseudonym) and seeing his home is my closest personal encounter with preservation's unruly shadow side. Having ventured into Davidson's rough inner-city neighborhood one wintry November afternoon, I knocked at the side door of his grandiose but very scruffy mansion. Davidson soon opened the door and invited me in, and I was alarmed to find myself in darkness when I closed the door behind me. Little daylight made its way through the covered windows and crammed, high-ceilinged rooms of the first floor. Following Davidson's voice and moving sideways to avoid running into objects stacked along the walls, I felt my way through the clogged hallway to the stairway, then navigated a narrow path to the second floor, being careful not to knock things over. In the dim light I discerned mostly dusty stacks of stained-glass windows leaning against the walls of the stairway and landings. Davidson explained that an automatic timer would turn some lights on, but not until five o'clock. The tightly packed stacks of his accumulation prevented him from getting at the timer to adjust it.

Davidson's bedroom was the warmest room in the house, maybe fifty degrees, and his bed was the only open space in the house, so we agreed to talk there, sitting cross-legged at either end of the mattress. Piles of old newspapers, magazines, books, letters, and bills surrounded the bed. An electric space heater hummed nearby. Most people are ants, Davidson declared: undeveloped, unaware, satisfied with conventional lives. If not for the truly creative among them, the artists and artisans and those who preserve their beautiful works, the lives of the ants would have no meaning. "Most people are content just to live a mundane existence, follow the path of least resistance. To do something creative takes a lot of work and sacrifice. It's nice to keep a house at seventy degrees, but that would be deathly expensive in an old, inefficient building like this one. With this house sacrifice means a much colder temperature. But at least the gas company doesn't get the money."

Most of Davidson's modest income as a teacher gets funneled into acquiring beautiful old objects and restoring them as he finds the time. His clothing is threadbare, his self-care marginal. He considers himself to be in the same league as the artists and craftsmen who created those objects: he is the medium by which the lives of their creations are being perpetuated. Davidson drew my attention to a newel post ornament, hand carved in chestnut, which he had placed prominently in a corner of the bedroom, as one might position a religious statue. It was a handsome figure of a standing woman, though her forearms had been broken off and lost. He had gotten it for six hundred dollars at a recent auction and was considering whether or not to restore the splintered arms.

"With America's great pool of immigrant craftsmen, abundance of virgin timber and other materials, and tremendous wealth and exuberance, lots of incredibly beautiful, well-made stuff was created in this country in the late nineteenth century. Much of it endured through the first several decades of the twentieth, but with the prosperity that followed World War II came a desire to get rid of all this cluttered-up junk. Those of us who went against the grain, who saw the beauty in these things, believed that they shouldn't be lost. When these things are gone, you can't bring them back. Generations yet unborn will never have the opportunity to see them. It was the beauty of this old stuff that prompted the few of us who cared about it to save it. In those early days of salvaging you were seen as just a lost soul saving some 'interesting' but worthless junk.

"Even as a child I had a particularly strong interest in design and old things. Visiting my grandmother in the 1950s was like time travel. Everything in her house seemed to be frozen in time, virtually intact from 1926, the year my grandfather died in a horse-and-buggy accident. She still cooked with a wood-burning stove, had an isinglass heating stove upstairs, a wind-up Victrola, no radio or television. At four, five, six years old I was fascinated by these things and asked her what it was like living in the old days, without electricity, cars, radio, and other modern conveniences.

"My parents didn't encourage my interest in these things, especially when I started finding old stuff and bringing it home. My first antique purchase was a brass kerosene lamp, Success Manufacturing Company, seven dollars at a florist shop in the neighborhood. It was very dingy, but I polished it up, put kerosene in it, and tried it out. Boy, did it stink! I would go to antique shops around the city, returning home on the bus with small things like ornate brass doorknobs and piano rolls, even some nice big stained-glass windows with lots of swirly glass. When they tore down the old buildings at the main intersection in our neighborhood to widen the streets, I salvaged square-cut nails and ornamental hardware from a wood-frame church. From another building I saved a couple of stained-glass windows and some ornamental tinwork. Through my teenage years I found bigger and better pieces. I scraped together fifty dollars for a beautiful overmantel from a mansion that was going to be torn down; that meant a lot of lawn mowing at two dollars a lawn.

"My salvaging was more limited at first because I had to get things home on the city bus, but once I got my driver's license Mom's car got spirited away from time to time. One day I came home with some terra cotta from the waiting room of a train depot that was being demolished. I didn't know what terra cotta was, but I knew this piece was beautiful. It was so heavy; I had a heck of a time getting it in the trunk. Mom got very upset when the back bumper scraped the driveway. Her car was definitely not going out on any more salvage runs.

"The campus where I went to college was expanding, and a lot of old houses nearby were coming down. In one of those vacant houses I discovered a beautiful door with etched glass, nice trim, and a mechanical doorbell. The owner said I could have it, so I carried the door back to my dorm room. Porch columns and cobblestones followed, and I ended up paving the floor of my room with old bricks. For twenty bucks I bought the beamed ceiling, paneling, door casements, and everything else from the library room of another mansion. The fireplace tiles from that room are now around the fireplace here. By the time I bought this house, I was in my mid-twenties and had stuff stored in the basement and attic of my parents' house, in a semitrailer, and in a vacant store building.

"If you really understand the times in which a house was created, then you'll have a restoration that echoes in harmony with the original makers' ideas. About ten years after I bought this house, an old lady who came to see it one day said it looked like I'd moved some of the furniture around. When I asked what she meant, she told me that the man for whom the house was built was her uncle. She was born in the late 1890s, about the time of the house's construction, and had visited here as a child. She said there had been an automatic piano player, a push-up Pianola, at the piano in the music room. Without any photographs or other information as to how things had been originally, I had furnished that room with those same things and had virtually the same kinds of furniture in almost the same arrangement as it had been when she last saw the house around 1918. I had recreated it so accurately that she just assumed that the house and its contents had sat unchanged since her last visit seventy years earlier. She thought I had just rearranged a few things! In fact, the house had been used as a hospital, then an office building, and then a rooming house before I bought it."

Mechanical musical instruments are Davidson's special passion. Insisting that vintage music is the thing that brings a historic home to life, he led me back downstairs and played two rousing pieces on an antique Aeolian Orchestrelle, "The Flying Dutchman" and "El Capitan." In the dim, closely packed rooms he pointed out two more of those massive machines, plus player pianos, music boxes, nickelodeons, Victrolas. In his years of restoring these instruments he has learned to cast and plate metal parts, to repair veneer and stained glass, and to carve wood. He says that he'll need to do some casting and plating to restore a parlor stove he bought recently for about three hundred dollars. But two vintage slot machines purchased just yesterday seem to be in good condition.

"You've only seen the tip of the iceberg," Davidson says. "I've got the whole terra-cotta facade of an old movie theater, probably four thousand pieces, stacked under my front porch."

The individual narratives that follow give candid portraits of gay men whose preservation-mindedness is infused with a singularly eccentric passion. Dana Duppler describes his zealous plan to rescue, restore, and preserve modest and often unappreciated vernacular buildings from the early-nineteenth-century settlement of the Upper Mississippi Valley. Elsewhere on the spectrum of architectural aesthetics, Joe Johnson and Ron Markwell tell of becoming possessed by their mission to restore a grossly disfigured Queen Anne–style mansion. In Minneapolis, Robert Seger's penchant for preservation finds its release not in high-style houses but in stylish, "high-drama" household appliances of the past half-century.

Dana Duppler

Born in 1949, the oldest of six children, Dana Duppler grew up on a farm near Paoli, a small town near Madison, Wisconsin. With a vision to save early-settlement buildings from the state's nineteenth-century lead-mining days, Duppler founded the Lead Region Historic Trust.

A SENSE OF INTERCONNECTEDNESS AND COMMUNITY is strong with me, and I've always had an interest in history: how my community developed, where the settlers came from. I'm three-quarters German, one-quarter French, and I traced my family back to the settlement period. The Germans came to the area in the early 1850s, the French followed a bit later. Historical buildings and personages are all intertwined, all part of the big picture. I've got a good collection of real early photographs, all identified and properly cared for, of buildings and people in the Paoli area.

As a kid I always liked old things. My grandmother gave me a kerosene lamp and a little crock jar that you beat eggs in, and a lady in Paoli gave me some more stuff. A lot of people would give me photographs in frames. My room was piled full of it. Ma thought I was out of my mind. I didn't ever go to an antique shop or show, nothing like that. Wouldn't have had any way to do it. But something about auctions intrigued me. I went to one in Paoli with my folks when I was maybe eleven or twelve, but I didn't go to one on my own until I was about twenty. Since then I've gone to thousands of them. In the seventies I did it to furnish the place where I lived. Now I do it more to acquire things to sell to make a profit. To keep myself going I do a little antique and art buying and selling on the side, anything that's handmade that has artistic character, with some age. Folk art, architectural art, weathered building pieces that had some design in the first place, to which nature has added the patina of a hundred years.

The house I currently live in, Fischer Hall, is an 1850s house of some character that has been familiar to me all my life. The building was named after William Fischer, one of the longtime early occupants. There was a dance hall upstairs, where the school had their plays and where town meetings were held. My grandfather and my dad went there to vote; I remember going up there with them a couple of times. We always drove by it, and the old couple that lived there were cousins of my grandfather, so I would stop down to see them when I was a kid. I always really liked the building, and it just seemed like it was the place that I should be. Something intrigued me about the style of the large old house. Italianate brackets are really the only ornamentation, and each bracket has a turned acorn; that artistic design must have caught my eye when I was a little kid. All my life I can remember those brackets.

Fischer Hall was really the community center of Paoli. There was a store on the first floor and a tavern in the basement. The people that ran those businesses had their living quarters on the west side of the building. Later they added on and started a cheese factory, so there was a lot going on in there. The last year it was used for the township meetings and voting was 1955. I bought it twenty years later, and when I got done restoring it in 1982 I had a big party upstairs. We got in a good old string band and a couple of half barrels and cheese and had a real good time. I've done that almost every year since; second Saturday of June I get the band in there and have a dance. And on Friday nights between April and October, groups of contradancers use the hall maybe a dozen or fifteen times each year. So it gets some good use.

When I bought Fischer Hall in 1975, I intended to restore the building eventually, but I had no funds and no knowledge of hands-on restoration. I had visited a lot of historic house restorations though, and probably the one that interested and motivated me the most was Pendarvis in Mineral Point. I knew the history of what had happened there, that what was there was good, and that somebody with foresight had made it happen. But I never imagined that I could do something like that. By 1978 I was ready to go at it but still had no knowledge and no way that I could do anything. At the time I was running a precision machining shop in Paoli. I had heard of Mike Saternus in Cooksville, so I called him up and asked if I could hire him to look at the building with me and give me some direction.

Saternus walked through Fischer Hall with me and pointed out features that he considered of worth. What he showed me on that first visit was how to look at the building, how to think about it, and how not to put my feelings about the building onto it, but to let it speak for itself. To respect the designs of those who originally built it and to respect the uses and adaptations that had occurred in the building over time, which had gained some significance in their own right. Built in the 1850s, Fischer Hall had had some additions and modifications in the 1870s and again in the 1890s. Initially I thought they should be reversed, but after talking with Saternus I could see why they were important parts of the building. So he helped to form my thinking very early on. He did some drawings for me, to replace a missing cupola and doorway and to rework the porch, and over the next three or four years I had relatively frequent contact with him. He showed me the great Greek and Gothic Revival houses in Cooksville. I read and reread every book on historic architecture that I could find.

I had gradually become aware that Wisconsin's development began in the southwest lead-mining region and that the first settlers there had come from the southern and eastern parts of the United States, the Carolinas, Tennessee, and Missouri in particular. They brought with them to southwest Wisconsin some of the vernacular building styles that had developed in other areas of this country and that were influenced by the Federal or Greek Revival or Gothic Revival styles. As I traveled to auctions in southwest Wisconsin in the early to mid-1970s, I would see these buildings in the old mining towns. I started to build a body of knowledge about styles and forms and vernacular types that I saw there and that I didn't see anywhere else in the state.

In the early 1970s things were just starting to get going in Mineral Point, although Pendarvis had been done years before. There was a mindset there that something was of value in their built environment. But I saw that once you got outside of Mineral Point, or Galena, Illinois, there was really no interest in preservation. Lots of good things were just going completely to hell, and there wasn't anything I could do. I was tied up with my machining business, and I had no skills with my hands outside of that. I did some hands-on work on Fischer Hall but hired most of that work done between 1978 and 1980, then started to learn to do finish work myself.

I first saw the Prairie Spring Hotel, forty miles from Paoli, in 1982 and talked to the owners then. Complete nutcases, both of them. I couldn't buy the building because I couldn't do anything with it, but I could see that it was really important. From my readings and observations I figured this building had to be one of the oldest around, probably early 1830s. I kept working on the owners, primarily to prevent them from destroying it.

I sold the machining shop in 1984; I liked the work, but I wanted to take a break. So I went to Wiota, one of the early lead-mining settlements, thirty-eight miles from Paoli. For two thousand bucks I bought a little saltbox house that dated to about 1840. It was in a hell of a shape, but I had started to develop some carpentry skills and had practiced on a couple of buildings that I bought and resold. I felt like I was ready to do something in the lead region on a more serious scale. So I poured a bundle of money and time into restoring the little house in Wiota. I didn't need a second house to live in, so I rented it out when I got done with it. But I got familiar with Wiota and the early buildings there. I found that most of them had already been destroyed but that the last remaining half-dozen examples were significant. And I got to know Shullsburg a little better and Hazel Green and Dodgeville. I could see that there was so much there and no appreciation for it at all, just totally unrecognized.

If it's a primitive log cabin, everybody loves it. If it's Frank Lloyd Wright, you're supposed to love it. If it's Queen Anne, you're supposed to really get into it because it's the limit. And barns have a mystique about them, especially round barns. Jeez, some people genuflect in front of a round barn. I like them too, but I don't go completely nuts about them. But historic preservation traditionally has been focused on the buildings that were built by the richest segment of the population. Around the Midwest, when you think of a historic restoration, generally speaking, you think of Italianate, Queen Anne, Second Empire, Stick-style buildings. Grandiose, high-style, mansion-type houses, lots of gingerbread and trim and bullshit. This is okay; I mean, these are significant buildings.

Vernacular buildings are the common, utilitarian structures built by average people who didn't have a lot of money. But if you really start to look at what's out there, you find that even these people of moderate means were influenced by the dominant styles of the period. The little one-and-a-half-story saltbox house I restored in Wiota is a vernacular house. But if you look at it carefully, you see that the builder had seen Greek Revival, and with his limited knowledge and tools he put some simple classical detailing on it. It's bare bones, but it's there. You see that in just about every building, in one way or another.

I thought these vernacular things were of some worth and that maybe historic preservation should cover a broader field than just the wealthiest 5 percent of the population. That maybe we should look at what the middle class built and what it said about their lives and look at what the miners or the common laborers built and how they lived. Occasionally you'll see a vernacular building nominated to the National Register, but not very damn often.

By 1990 I had bought and restored two buildings in Wiota and one in Shullsburg. My funds were getting pretty slim. I started to realize that if the work I do is going to endure beyond me, and if these buildings are going to be used as teaching tools to change the perception of what historic preservation is all about, there has to be some type of organization to hold the properties and some type of management group that is knowledgeable about them. And there has to be some money. I was influenced by the model of the Society for the Preservation of New England Antiquities. If donated dollars were available to acquire and restore a building, and if it could then be leased out for any money at all, even two hundred bucks a month, that building should be able to support itself. If you escrow, say, one-quarter of that money over the years, the money will be there when the roof needs to be replaced, when the furnace goes to hell, when it needs to be painted. If the proper management structure could be developed, with people trained in how to interpret, care for, and manage these buildings, the buildings would take care of themselves. If you could just get the money together to buy them and restore them.

I visualized setting up an organization that would raise funds, acquire properties, and restore them under my direction. Maybe twenty-five years down the line the organization might own twenty or thirty buildings, there would be no debt, a substantial cash flow, trained people, and I could just lie down and die, and somebody else could take it over. So, in 1992 I incorporated the Lead Region Historic Trust, and that's the concept that we work on, that buildings are purchased and restored, hopefully given a use similar to what they were originally intended for, that the organization would derive income from them, that we would develop a staff and go some place. And we're on the road.

Dean Connors came along in 1994 and underwrote the cost of buying the Prairie Spring Hotel, moving it, restoring the exterior, and all the other costs. Almost a hundred thousand dollars. I could never thank him enough for making that happen and for validating what I'm doing. The Prairie Spring Hotel is a rare, early example, a museum piece, not a building that we'll ever lease out. It's relatively untouched on the inside, and we'd like to preserve it as much as possible like it is. To make it a house that you could live in, you'd have to tear out all the hand-split lath, all the original plaster, the layers of wallpaper that talk about its history. And then, living in it, you would expose it to the risk of destruction from using electricity in it and heating it. Obviously, nothing is guaranteed forever; a tornado could wind through there, and we could lose it. But good curatorial management of that building says that the site and the building are there for study and exhibit. I'm looking at not just the next fifty years, but the next five hundred, so that's going to be up to somebody beyond me. The paint job is going to be renewed every five to seven years, the roof you're going to replace every twenty years, and you're going to tuck-point it once every fifty or sixty years. But you aren't going to need to do the radical interventions we did to get it structurally stable and to get it moved.

There are still buildings that I don't know, but I've tried to get to know what's around. Most of them are in southern Iowa County, Lafayette County, and the very southern part of Grant County, because of the heavy mining. There are some really good, early ones in Dubuque that don't compare to anything else, but they're almost certain to be lost. We won't have the money to get them before it's too late. In Galena everything's pretty safe, but everything in the immediate area outside of Galena has been destroyed. It's just amazing, the stuff that I've seen purposely burned and destroyed in the last five years.

They destroyed a great little Greek Revival in Hazel Green that probably would have been the best example of the style anywhere in the region. It was a tiny house but it had everything, and one day they just bulldozed it and put up a modular home. I could have killed that bastard. I had talked to him so many times; I'd talked to his wife: "I'm always interested, here's my name and number." He had said they wanted to build there someday. I asked if he would consider another lot in town, and he said he would if he got a price for this one. I said, well, we can talk. Seemed to be all right. But the day I heard about it, it was too late; he already had it down. That one I really hated to lose.

In Jenkynsville, down in the southwest corner of Lafayette County, there's a Georgian-influenced vernacular stone house that has a fantastic interior. God, is that a great building. It's small, but it has a presence. You drive off the road quite a ways to go back to it, and it's on a little bit of a knoll and there's a stream in front of it. It's a dandy. Dean Connors had a part in getting that building, which was probably the toughest one of all. These people were living out of state, and if you called and asked about that house, they'd swear at you and hang up. Complete assholes. I called them once, explained that I was just wanting permission to drive up and look at the house. "Fuck you," click, dial tone. Something about people wanting that old stone house just pissed them off.

I had taken Dean down there and showed it to him, and after the Prairie Spring Hotel was moved, he said maybe he should try to buy the Jenkynsville place. I said it was going to be tough, explained how they wouldn't even discuss it and would cuss people out. Dean said he would try a different approach, use a realtor and an attorney and just say that he was a doctor looking for acreage in southwest Wisconsin, preferably with a river running through it. Never mention the house. They were real nice and polite to Dean, sold him the whole farm. He succeeded in saving a significant building for us by tricking them.

I've been up and down the Mississippi from Saint Louis to Dubuque a lot of times, every town on both sides of the river. The river towns were settled real early. You look at some of the towns that have been there a long time, like the Quad Cities, Muscatine, Burlington, Fort Madison, Hannibal, Quincy. Quincy's really loaded. The first area to get settled would be closest to the river, in the section that is now usually the downtown. And if you look behind the commercial buildings, sometimes there's a little house that escaped destruction. Or if you look a block back, sometimes they'll be there. I can see that every one of those towns has got a couple really neat ones in it yet, but none of them have been restored or really recognized even. They're lived in by people who have no money at all, the house is in a hell of a fuckin' shape, and there's shit all over the place, but you can see that they're real early buildings. Canton, Missouri, is a real small town that's got some really neat early things because nobody ever had the money to change them. I drive through there, and I just wish there was something I could do.

I think it's unfair that these early vernacular designs have been so overlooked. My desire to restore them has to do with their artistic appeal: people have screwed them all up, and it would be nice to get them back in shape.

Some of them are really rough, just a terrible mess, but when you get done and you look at it and you see it the way it's supposed to be, the way it was meant to be, and it's just been a hell of a looking thing, you know that the community is going to appreciate it more, and it can serve the purpose that it was built for.

Somebody asked me once what kind of experience is needed to do what I'm doing. I said it isn't experience at all; it's magic. I don't know what drives me. It's something that interests me, it's something that I can do and that I enjoy, it gives my life a value, and nobody else is going to do it. In other words it's something that's cut out for me. And it might be an example that other people learn from. Is it a compulsion or an obsession? I don't know.

Joe Johnson and Ron Markwell

In 1885 a twenty-three-room cream-colored brick mansion was built on the main street of Delavan, Wisconsin, for a wealthy farmer. Milwaukee's leading architect of that era designed the showplace in the Queen Anne style with Eastlake details. With its opulent exterior painted in greens, reds, and creams, it proclaimed that Alexander Allyn was a success.

In the 1920s young Earl Vaughn admired the Allyn Mansion while walking to his piano lesson each week. But in the decades after Vaughn finished high school and moved away, the Allyn Mansion underwent ravaging changes. Stripped of its tower, balcony, porches, and porte-cochere, it was used as a nursing home in the 1950s and 1960s, then as a furniture store through the 1970s and into the 1980s.

Back in town for a visit years later Vaughn saw that two of the Allyn Mansion's ornate cast-iron urns were still in front of the shabby place. "The whole front yard was a parking lot, blacktop, and here were these perfectly wonderful urns with their bases half buried in it," he says. "I had to get a pick axe and dig them out, but I made up my mind that they were going to be inside my station wagon that evening." An antique dealer in Illinois, Vaughn took the urns home to Rockton and wove them into the landscape of his old stone house.

The Allyn Mansion's redemption was orchestrated by Missouri native Joe Johnson, born in 1940, and Kentucky native Ron Markwell, born in 1936. By the time the two met in 1977, they were both established in their teaching and antique-collecting careers: Johnson was close to filling two houses with Victorian furniture and accessories. They loved to travel, visiting house museums and staying in old-house bed-and-breakfasts.

Markwell and Johnson bought the Allyn Mansion in 1984 and began its meticulous restoration. They tore out walls that were not original, replaced original walls that had been torn out, stripped paint, refinished a staggering amount of woodwork to a proper Victorian shine, and restored ornately hand-painted ceilings. Finding the architect's original drawings for the house in a basement safe, they reconstructed the elaborate tower, balcony, porches, and porte-cochere and replicated the original exterior color design. Within two years of buying it they deemed the place habitable enough, and their financial need great enough, to open several bedrooms to the public and begin doing business as the Allyn Mansion Inn Bed and Breakfast. For another five or six years they and their guests inhabited a work very much in progress.

Ron Markwell: Joe was living near Delavan, in a historic house that I helped him restore on weekends. Whenever we'd come to Delavan to shop, we'd use any excuse to come into the furniture store just to look at what remained of the Allyn Mansion. Despite the many horrid changes that had been made to the exterior, and all the tacky furniture they had for sale inside, the house still held its own. We knew the place had once been spectacular, and it still had much to recommend it: the structure was solid, the big mirrors were still here, the nine magnificent Italian marble fireplaces were in perfect shape. Six of the largest gaslight chandeliers were still in place, and one of the original hand-painted ceilings was intact.

Joe Johnson: But we had no idea of ever owning it. After the furniture store closed in 1983, I'd drive by and think, "Have a good look, because the next time you come by here this is going to be a blank spot." I was sure it was going to be bulldozed. It had been on the market for a decade, and most of the locals thought it was an eyesore that should be torn down.

Markwell: Every time we came in, I felt the house *pulling* me and saying—

Johnson: "Clean me! Clean me!"

Markwell: "Help me! Help me out here! I'm an important piece of history. Save me!" This place almost fell into the hands of the town's rooming-house queen. I looked at this house as an underdog, as I do a lot of beautiful structures that need to be saved, shunted off by society at large. In bringing something like this back, we're thumbing our noses at society: "Look! You didn't care about this, but look what can be done when you're willing to spend the time and the money." Of course, we didn't truly understand all that it would take to bring this house back.

Johnson: When I look back at the "before" pictures, I don't know how we did it. I don't know how we had the guts. But once we worked with it a while, we realized that we're more owned by the house than we own the house. We got possessed with the whole thing.

Markwell: It's become our life, our life's work, an obsession. Even early on, when we still had our full-time teaching jobs, we weren't really interested in that work anymore. This is what we wanted to do. And we did it gladly, because the old house responded so well to kind treatment.

Johnson: When you get into a project like this, if you don't get possessed by it you're going to walk away in six months. We've been sort of commandeered by this house. It won't turn us loose. We are really obsessed with making the house right.

Markwell: We've always felt that our ownership transcends just having our names on the deed. We're stewards for future generations, seeing to it that this structure stays around. And we probably know more about the Allyn family than anybody else in town. Owning a place like this almost dictates learning about the people who created it, what they did, how they lived here, what happened to them.

Johnson: Something odd about this house: It's very formal and could be intimidating, but within a half-hour of getting here most of our guests end up hanging out in the kitchen, saying they're ready to move in. A feeling of warmth seems to envelop people here. Even being alone in this house is great—it's not like there's something scary moving around upstairs. If there are spirits here, they're kindred ones.

Soon after we bought this place, a woman who stopped by said she knew where the original urns from the front of the house had gone. "Considering what you're doing for this town," she said, "I'm going to see that you get them back." The urns belonged to a guy she knew who used to live in Delavan. When she told me that he lived in Rockton, I said it would be easy for me to stop by and see him when I was driving to Iowa to visit my parents. "Oh, don't do that!" she said. "He's really rather eccentric. He'll probably kick you off the property."

Heading for Iowa one day, I couldn't resist at least driving by his house. And sure enough, there were those urns sitting out in front. Something about my impulsive nature, I suppose, but I walked right up and rang the doorbell. When this guy came to the door, I said, "I've come to get my urns." He said, "I *knew* you would be coming!" He invited me in, introduced me to his mother who was living with him, and showed me around the house. He was very formal.

"About those urns," he said. "I felt guilty about taking away something that was original to the property, but I really think I saved them from the dump. I know they belong to the Allyn Mansion, and I'll see that they get back there someday. For now, I like them where they are."

Since that first visit, Ron and I have become close friends with Earl. At a party here he mentioned that he knew of two large urns that would be just perfect for the front of the house. "But you've told us that *your* urns are coming back to the Allyn Mansion," I said. "Well, you can't have too many urns!" he said. Later, I discovered that Earl has about a dozen urns around his place and that it's in his will that the Allyn urns are to come back to the mansion.

Robert Seger

Robert Seger was born in 1963 and grew up in East Brunswick, New Jersey. It was after moving to Minneapolis that he discovered his uncommon restoration calling, which blends his devout domesticity, design-mindedness, and love of drama.

MY MOTHER SAYS the very first word I could read was "Sears," because I just loved looking at the pictures in the Sears catalog before I learned to read. I was helping my mother do the laundry by the time I was four. We had a 1962 bottom-of-the-line Kenmore washer that my dad bought my mom when I was born. I loved to watch the agitator swirl the clothes around; I could only imagine what the spin cycle was like because the safety switch on the lid didn't allow me to see it. My mother loved it that she didn't have to do our family's wash, because I would always do it for her.

It was a real treat to go to my grandmother's house and help her do her laundry in her 1958 Frigidaire Pulsamatic. It had no safety switch, so I could watch the entire cycle, including spin. I was completely fascinated by this machine: its agitator bobbed up and down rapidly, and when it went into spin, all the water was drained out in a matter of seconds, even though the wash tub had no perforations. I wondered where all that water could go so fast! When my other grandparents replaced their 1957 Kenmore with a 1970 Whirlpool, my grandfather took the agitator out of the old machine and gave it to me as a present for my eighth birthday. I still cherish it.

Loading the dishwasher when I was about six, I'd say, "Mother, do you honestly expect that glass to get clean there? Move it!" I was always fascinated by machines that used water, the water movement and the mechanics of the machine. Reading the ratings of automatic washers in my dad's *Consumer Reports* when I was about nine, I saw that the magazine listed the manufacturers' addresses. So I started writing to them, asking them to send me operating instructions and service manuals for their washing machines. Just reading those materials was fascinating. My first Frigidaire washer repair manual answered my question about where all the water in my grandmother's washer disappeared to so fast: It was spun over the top of the solid tub by centrifugal force.

My fascination with washing machines continued through my teenage years. When my parents were away from home, I would take the panels off the appliances and take them apart a little bit, trying to see how they worked. Hopefully, I could get everything back together by the time the car pulled in. My parents tried somewhat to downplay my strange interest, but my enthusiasm always came through. When I was fifteen I convinced them to buy a Frigidaire washer and dryer; my grandmother had left her 1958 Pulsamatic behind when she moved to an apartment, and I wanted to use a Frigidaire again. The 1978 Frigidaire my parents bought was interesting to look at, but it wasn't nearly as dramatic as the vintage models. I realized even then that I totally preferred the vintage machines to the modern.

In my twenties I moved to New York City, where apartments were so small I certainly didn't have room for a washing machine. I kept my washer passion to myself, concerned that people would think I was a complete nut case. But I saved all the service manuals I had collected as a kid, and my love of washers secretly lived on. At the Twenty-Sixth Street flea market, I would buy vintage issues of *Life, Better Homes and Gardens,* and other women's magazines from the 1950s: the appliance ads in them were absolutely wonderful.

It wasn't until my early thirties, when I moved to Minneapolis and had the space to start collecting, that I discovered that vintage automatic washers still existed. My first was the 1955 Westinghouse Laundromat that came with my former partner's house. He saw how much I loved those machines and kind of encouraged me to start collecting. On our way to Grand Forks, North Dakota, one day, we ran across a 1959 Philco. He said, "Go ahead. You can put it in my basement. You'll have fun playing with it." We had no idea what that would lead to.

When I would go to secondhand appliance stores in the 1990s looking for 1950s washers, they would laugh me out of the store. They would tell me they hadn't seen anything like that in years, and if they had it would have gone right to the crusher. But when I started going to estate sales in the older neighborhoods of Minneapolis and Saint Paul, I discovered that many a little old lady had saved her very first automatic washing machine in a basement corner, even after purchasing newer models.

I now have about thirty-five machines, most of them in my basement, hooked up and operating. A few are in the garage, on the restoration waiting list. For me half the fun of collecting these machines is restoring them back to brand-new condition. My collection of service manuals has been an enormous help in teaching myself how to fix the machines. Until I started collecting, I didn't realize how mechanically inclined I am. Through the Internet I've found lots of places to get parts that I once thought were no longer available, and I've learned how to clean the porcelain and how to paint things properly using my compressor gun.

You wouldn't believe the before and after pictures of some of these machines. I've restored Frigidaire washers, dream machines, that sat outside for twenty-five years. I plucked a Frigidaire dream machine off a farm in South Dakota where they have ten acres covered with ten to fifteen thousand old appliances. I've had all my friends come out from the East Coast, and we've pretty much picked the place clean of anything really old and rare.

I'm only interested in the earliest automatic washers, 1938 to 1960. If you ask any vintage appliance collector to name his favorite automatic washer, it would be a Frigidaire. We like the exciting stuff, the drama, not only of the aesthetics but of the washing action. Machines with a standard back-and-forth agitator don't put on much of a show. The Frigidaire agitator bobs up and down. The ABC-O-Matic is another high-drama machine: Its agitator moves like an old mixer, causing a huge amount of splashing. It looks like there's a huge fire hose up against its window. I just found the very first ABC-O-Matic model, from 1949, which is very exciting.

Someone in Ohio called me recently with the absolute dream machine on top of everyone's list: a Frigidaire washer from 1947. I'm taking a drive out to Toledo to pick it up. Incredible: the very first production Frigidaire washer, the very first year! The original design, with the most primitive mechanics that Frigidaire ever had. Restoring that machine is going to be a pleasure. I hope some of my rarest pieces will end up in a museum someday.

My favorite colors are pink and turquoise. I have a 1958 turquoise Frigidaire washer and a 1959 turquoise Frigidaire dryer. I also have a 1960 pink Maytag washer and dryer set. Those are highly desirable, especially by gay boys. A majority of the members of our Classic Appliances club on the Internet are gay, and I've found that our experiences as kids are similar to the point of being almost creepy. Stories from all over the United States, Canada, Europe, and Australia, about going into the appliance section of stores, just to look innocently at the washing machines and dryers and dishwashers, and being chased away by salesmen who told us that we should be in the toy section. And lots of stories about how our parents were always trying to downplay our interest because it was out of the ordinary and made them nervous.

Cherishing Old New Orleans and Louisiana

IT'S NO MERE COINCIDENCE that the city with the oldest gay bar in the country is exceptionally rich in well-preserved historic architecture. The bar, Café Lafitte in Exile, once occupied the Bourbon Street building that was the blacksmith shop of the pirate Jean Lafitte. New Orleans, especially its French Quarter, or Vieux Carré, has long been a magnet for gay men. They have served the place well. The countless picture books of old New Orleans published in the past century offer telling glimpses of gay men's redeeming sensibilities. One volume quotes an antique dealer who bought and restored a condemned Victorian cottage in Bywater: "I found something that no one else appreciated, and I thought I could make it beautiful."[1]

Most New Orleans residents turned their back on the city's oldest section as newer districts were developed through the last half of the nineteenth century and into the twentieth. "I never knew where the Vieux Carré was until I was practically out of high school," recalled New Orleans preservation architect Samuel Wilson Jr., born in New Orleans in 1911. "When the Opera House burned down, my mother was all in a tizzy. My father said, 'The whole place ought to burn down. It would be the best thing that could happen for the city.'"[2] What happened instead is that gay men became a central force in fostering the revival of the Vieux Carré in the first several decades of the twentieth century.

The gay fascination with the city goes back more than a century. In his chronicle of historic preservation in America, Charles Hosmer reports that in 1895 a young man named Allison Owen, just out of architecture school in Boston, suggested the formation of a society for the preservation of colonial landmarks in New Orleans. He helped to obtain passage of a city ordinance that set aside the old Spanish government building, the Cabildo, as a museum.[3]

A generation older than Owen, wealthy New Orleans bachelor businessman William Irby had similar ideas. At the time of Irby's suicide in 1926 a New Orleans newspaper commented that "out of pure sentiment alone, Mr. Irby is known to have purchased property in the Vieux Carré to preserve many of its famous old landmarks."[4] These early investments were crucial to the French Quarter's revival. In 1918 Irby bought the century-old Seignouret-Brulatour House at 520 Royal Street. After restoring it to serve as his home, he invited the Arts and Crafts Club to set up its gallery and classrooms there in the early 1920s. The club's annual Bal Masqué des Artistes helped to resurrect the mystique of the Vieux Carré. The civic-minded and philanthropic Irby purchased and restored several other key landmarks in the Quarter, including the lower Pontalba Building on Jackson Square, which he gave to the Louisiana State Museum. He gave the site of the old French Opera House to Tulane University and financed the rehabilitation of the crumbling Saint Louis Cathedral.

Richard Koch was also passionately involved with historic buildings and devoted much of his life to studying the architecture of the French Quarter. Born in New Orleans in 1889, Koch graduated from Tulane's School of Architecture, studied in Paris, and worked briefly in New York and Boston before he returned to New Orleans in 1916. His firm pioneered in the restoration of historic Louisiana architecture. The young architect supervised the relocation of a threatened plantation house to New Orleans in the early 1920s; known as Hurst House, the restoration became a showplace. When the New Orleans Little Theater hired Koch to convert an old building on Saint Peter Street for its use as a theater, he convinced the group to leave the historic building intact and erect a new building in a style appropriate to the neighborhood. Koch was a leader in the adaptive reuse of old buildings and in using eighteenth- and nineteenth-century Creole designs when creating new structures. His early restoration projects outside New Orleans included Oak Alley Plantation in Vacherie, Louisiana, and Shadows-on-the-Teche in New Iberia.

By the early 1930s Richard Koch was uniquely qualified to head the Historic American Buildings Survey in Louisiana. His 1934 inventory of Louisiana structures deserving HABS documentation may be the most comprehensive ever compiled in the state. Koch was a skillful drafter, watercolorist, and photographer. With unflagging attention to detail he kept a perfectionist's eye on the quality of the records produced by his HABS staff as they crisscrossed the state recording endangered buildings—from celebrated landmarks to forgotten outbuildings, from cottages to tombs. By the late 1930s exhibitions of HABS drawings, photographs, and watercolors at the Arts and Crafts Club were helping to promote architectural preservation in Louisiana. When in 1940 the Army Corps of Engineers insisted on clearing the way for construction of a new Mississippi River levee, Koch fiercely protested the planned demolition of Uncle Sam, an exquisite and extensive Greek Revival plantation complex at Convent. And it was Koch who then photographed the destruction of the mansion and its several dozen brick outbuildings, one of Louisiana's greatest losses of historic architecture. The levee was never built.

The author of a recent profile of Richard Koch expresses puzzlement at the never-married preservationist whose "emotional energy seems to have been totally absorbed by the study of historic architecture." Despite ample information about his professional interests and accomplishments, he remains elusive personally: "His immaculate reputation, his crowded schedule, his membership in the exclusive Boston Club, his illustrious academic career, his sojourns in Mexico somehow serve to obscure personal insights."[5] It seems likely that, as a gay man of his era, Richard Koch's circumspection was well founded.

Through the 1920s the pioneering work of men like Irby and Koch helped to foster the rediscovery of the dilapidated and disreputable Frenchtown by artists and writers and other creative types. Some moved in and restored its buildings as homes and businesses—art galleries, bookshops, tearooms, restaurants, clubs, and speakeasies. Others just visited, from uptown and from out of town. One visitor of particular note was Arnold Genthe, a fifty-something bachelor photographer when he visited New Orleans in the 1920s. A resident of New York and, before that, of San Francisco, where he was a member of that city's smart and genial Bohemian Club since the 1890s, Genthe won acclaim for the loose, painterly style of his portrait photography. His delight in the New Orleans writings of George Washington Cable and Lafcadio Hearn made him want to create a series of photographs of the Vieux Carré. Some told him that it was too late to make a meaningful record; too much of the Quarter's old glory and charm had been destroyed. But he decided to proceed with his project.

Genthe's first visit to New Orleans distressed him. The narrow streets of the French Quarter were noisy and busy, cluttered with telephone wires, gaudy advertising signs, and automobiles. He noted with sadness the effects of indifference and decay and was appalled to discover that an entire block of old Creole houses on Royal Street had been razed in 1918 to make room for a new courthouse. Genthe mourned the recent disappearance of such old landmarks as the stately Saint Louis Hotel and the celebrated French Opera House. He lamented the decay of the Ursuline Convent and the removal of wrought-iron ornament from the facades of many buildings. But enough remained to make him eager to carry out his plan.

"It is true one has to overcome many difficulties," Genthe wrote, "and much sympathetic search and patient experimenting are required before one can hope to secure photographs which, instead of being merely matter-of-fact records of things as they are today, will actually suggest something of the vanished beauty and charm of the old days."[6] Genthe managed to make such evocative pictures in the mellow light of early morning and late evening. A book of these photos, *Impressions of Old New Orleans,* was published in 1926, inspiring preservation-minded people well beyond Louisiana. In his introduction to the volume Genthe noted that people had only begun to realize what a tragedy the loss of the French Quarter would be. A few individuals had bought some of the old houses and were restoring them appropriately, he wrote, and a commission had been created to guard against inappropriate changes in the historic quarter.

By the time Arnold Genthe was photographing old New Orleans, Lyle Saxon had been a rehabilitating presence there for several years. Born in 1891, Saxon had grown up in Baton Rouge. An unusual child who liked listening to old people reminisce, he enjoyed visiting New Orleans with his mother and attending performances at the French Opera House. After graduating from Louisiana State University, Saxon moved to the city in 1914 to work as a journalist. He had always loved the French Quarter. Walking through its narrow streets, he was struck by the wretched state of decay and decided to make an effort to bring some of it back. His friends tried to talk him out of it, but Saxon moved into a sixteen-room rental house at 612 Royal Street. He cleaned out the mess, returned the large rooms to their original dimensions by removing partitions, and furnished about a third of the rooms—as much as he could afford—with old pieces.

In the company of men like William Irby (who Saxon termed "the good-fairy of Frenchtown") and Richard Koch, Lyle Saxon was a pioneer in the revival and preservation of the Vieux Carré.[7] Saxon championed such redemption because he believed that only by living in the old buildings could one tap into the Quarter's rich accumulation of untold stories. He used the *Times-Picayune* as a vehicle to promote his vision. At 536 Royal, which he purchased in 1920, Saxon's door was open to anyone who wished to call, especially writers, artists, and musicians. As he developed friendships with his visitors, including some from uptown New Orleans, he would go for walks with them through the grimy streets and try to coax them to join him in rehabilitating the French Quarter. It was a hard sell. Robert Tallant gives a vivid glimpse of the state of the neighborhood when Saxon first moved in.

> Leasing that Royal Street house and moving into the French Quarter as it was then was startling, even shocking, to a degree that may seem incomprehensible now. Some old people, descendants of the Creoles, still clung with a kind of grim tenacity to a few of the old

homes, but all the other buildings were occupied by the extremely poor, often by criminals. After dusk few respectable persons ventured into the neighborhood. Thugs waited in dark alleyways. Prostitutes stood naked behind shuttered doors and windows. The courtyards, once so beautiful, were often filled with refuse and incredible filth. Saxon was told he would be murdered. Once this almost happened. Three ruffians broke into his Royal Street house, bound him with wire and tortured him with lighted matches and cigarette stubs and kicked out two of his teeth, all in an effort to make him tell where his valuables were concealed. "All I had," he told me years later, "was some family silver and my grandpa's gold watch chain."[8]

William Spratling was one of the first to join Lyle Saxon in the Quarter. Born in New York State in 1900 the artistic young Spratling was transplanted to the South in his early teens. He came to New Orleans in 1922 to teach architecture at Tulane. Against the advice of colleagues who told him that he ought to live uptown rather than in the Vieux Carré, Spratling found himself an apartment in Pirate's Alley with a view of the cathedral garden. He produced illustrations for some of Saxon's newspaper stories and created a folio, *Drawings of Historic New Orleans,* which Saxon edited. With his landlady, the journalist Natalie Scott, Spratling went rambling through the countryside searching out old houses. Her writing and his sketches resulted in their 1927 book, *Old Plantation Houses in Louisiana.*

The close-knit circle of writers and Tulane faculty members with whom Lyle Saxon and William Spratling socialized called themselves the Shasta Daisies Society. The population of artists and writers in the Vieux Carré continued to grow, and as they started living in the old houses and slave quarters, the neighborhood began to feel more like a community than a ghetto of poverty and crime. Saxon convinced many property owners to restore their buildings or at least to maintain them.

While making his living as a journalist, Saxon steeped himself in the history and culture of the city. Then in 1926 he quit newspaper work and went to New York City. Declaring Greenwich Village "the only part of New York that has any sort of charm to it," he kept an apartment on Christopher Street for six years, spending about half of each year there.[9] Saxon hosted a perpetual salon for expatriate southern writers and artists. As the ebb and flow of visitors allowed, he wrote. His first book, *Father Mississippi,* was published in 1927; *Fabulous New Orleans, Old Louisiana,* and *Lafitte, the Pirate* appeared in the three succeeding years. In all of Saxon's books, the brilliant and breezy storyteller illuminates the romantic history of his homeland. Not a scholarly historian or chronicler of facts, he was a quirky keeper of tribal lore, a weaver of historical fiction. He drew on his years of listening to old people and old buildings.

In New Orleans, Saxon kept house with the help of his black valet, Joe Gilmore. *"The Friends of Joe Gilmore* is a wonderful book that really gives the best biography, with great affection, of Lyle Saxon," says New Orleans historian Roberts Batson. "People of a certain age have gotten really incensed when I have suggested that Joe Gilmore was more than Lyle Saxon's valet. Not only are we crossing the sexual taboo but the racial as well. At any rate, Lyle had written these little essays, and they were published in 1948, two years after he died."

In an essay in *The Friends of Joe Gilmore,* Saxon tells of being able to buy a sixteen-room, eighteenth-century Spanish house at 534 Madison Street after selling the movie rights to *Lafitte, the Pirate.* He planned to restore it, as he had the two houses on Royal in the 1920s, and make it his retirement home. "It was practically a shell and needed tremendous remodeling. Joe worked with me. . . . We had architects, contractors, and workmen. The place was filthy and had to be done from top to bottom, from roof to floors; but it was so beautiful, it was worthwhile. On one side were Spanish arches—three above and three on the ground which opened into sort of a loggia paved with flagstones. I had looked this over and liked it. It was a place where I wanted to sit and drink."[10]

When Saxon bought the house, the elaborate courtyard was paved with concrete, and the large rooms had been cut up with partitions to make a boardinghouse. Restoring the place, he told a friend, would require "all the rest of my life and all the money I ever hope to make."[11] Saxon tried to revitalize the place, spending more than he could really afford. The courtyard soon grew lush with bamboo, climbing fig, wisteria, and sweet olive. He added a carved cypress doorway that had been part of a confessional in Saint Louis Cathedral, and doors from an old New Orleans theater. But Saxon was forced to sell the partially restored Madison Street house because of his meager finances and poor health. He and Joe Gilmore remained in a suite at the Saint Charles Hotel.

In Saxon's evocative and perhaps autobiographical opening to *Fabulous New Orleans,* a small boy discovers that "the beautiful masked women who rode upon the floats" at Mardi Gras are "strangely masculine in body." This glimpse may be as close as Saxon ever came in print to capturing the truth that is at the heart of the fabulous magic of New Orleans, especially in the rebirth of the Vieux Carré. We can come closer: Lyle Saxon, who came to be seen as the "official patriarch" of New Orleans, had a well-developed matriarchal side, and it was that duality that made all the difference.[12]

In his travels around Louisiana, Lyle Saxon particularly admired Shadows-on-the-Teche. "That old plantation house in New Iberia, 'The Shadows,' is one of the most beautiful dwellings in Louisiana," he wrote. "The house is set deep in a three-acre flower garden behind moss-draped live oaks and tall hedges of bamboo. It is built of warm, rose-colored bricks with eight large, white Doric columns across its façade and a blue slate roof broken by dormer windows. The house is rich and beautiful in detail."[13]

While Saxon was trying to pay for his restorations in the decrepit French Quarter, his friend William Weeks Hall was living as a small-town bachelor gentleman artist at Shadows-on-the-Teche, which was built on the Bayou Teche by his great-grandfather in 1834. Hall visited Saxon frequently in New Orleans. "He is the last of his family, just as I am the last of mine," Saxon wrote, "and we have known each other since we were boys through many years of laughter and vicissitudes."[14]

Weeks Hall was born in New Orleans in 1894. Growing up at the Shadows, he knew it as a diminished place. The once spacious estate had shrunk from more than 150 acres to about 3. The house was rundown, the garden had largely vanished, and most of the outbuildings were gone. As an only child with artistic inclinations, Hall remembered the old house as "a collection of dusty potted plants, a scent of the nineties, and little else." Nonetheless, Louisiana writer Harnett Kane wrote portentously of Weeks Hall that "at some early time beyond his remembrance, he had acquired a vast and earnest affection for the place, not less fervent than that of his forebears. The house and its family, to him, were one; the past and the future must be one. The place must, in some way, be preserved."[15]

After a long absence from Louisiana—attending the Pennsylvania Academy of Fine Arts, serving in a camouflage unit in World War I, then lurking in Paris as an arty bohemian—Weeks Hall returned home to New Iberia in 1922. By then, his parents were dead and he was sole owner of Shadows-on-the-Teche. "He pushed open the gate and leaned upon it," Harnett Kane wrote. "The Shadows was there, as if it had been awaiting his return, as if it had been sure that, as before, it would not be lost. He felt a sense of desolation as he poked at broken bushes and cracked boarding. Chimneys had fallen; water had wrought havoc here and there. But as he looked he realized that in the main the place was unhurt. He made his decision; he would stay here again for the indefinite future. It was as if he had never been away from it; the intervening years had only added a richness to its meaning for him. He would live in this sixteen-room house, and he would see what he could do."[16]

In the attic Hall found watercolors of the Shadows when it was just thirty years old, stereoscopic photographs from when it was forty, plus sketches, drawings, and invoices for house supplies. With the help of Richard Koch,

Hall and his assistants restored the place. They cleared away the old smokehouse and slave quarters, deemed too far gone to be saved, and used their old brick to construct walkways and flooring in sections of the reestablished garden. The thirteen live oaks, which his great-grandmother had planted, were still in place, as were a half-dozen camellia trees and a clump of bamboo. Hall kept those remains but was not interested in recreating a period garden. The new garden would be his own dynamic creation, a large canvas on which he could play with light, color, and texture. The publicity generated by Hall's revival of the Shadows eventually drew thousands of tourists.

"I have lived on this place, attending to it and building it," Hall wrote. "Nothing in life has meant, or will mean, more to me than this garden on a summer morning before sunrise. At all hours, no place is more tranquil nor more ageless. Its inherent charm to me has been in its placid seclusion from a changing world, and in that will be its value to others. This quality must be preserved. I can go, but there is no reason why the place should not remain as long as it is humanly possible for me to enable it to do so. I have never considered myself anything but a trustee of something fine which chance had put in my hands to preserve. I have something unique to give to the American people and have protected this survival intact for that purpose alone."[17]

Weeks Hall's concern about the future of Shadows-on-the-Teche after his death began in earnest in the 1930s and became increasingly worrisome through the next two decades. He explored leaving the place to the American Institute of Architects, then the National Park Service. By the time he died in 1958, Hall had struck a deal with the National Trust for Historic Preservation. To amass the required cash endowment, he quit drinking, cut back on his lavish eating, and restricted his long-distance phoning mainly to making frequent and anxious calls to the National Trust. Since his death, the Trust has operated Shadows-on-the-Teche as a historic site.

Lyle Saxon considered Weeks Hall one of the best artists of Louisiana. Though Hall was a highly accomplished painter and photographer, Harnett Kane's portrait of him in his sixth decade shows clearly that the Shadows was his central creation. "He has compiled histories of it, interpretations, monographs. He has photographed it hundreds of times, from every imaginable angle and some unimaginable ones. Sitting on a bench by the hour, he has clocked the play of light and shade over the brick, on the off-white of the cornices, on the green of the jalousies. He knows it so well, he is so anxious that others appreciate it as he does, that the result can be disconcerting to the new arrival. I have caught him trying to arrange that a visitor walk in at a certain hour in the late afternoon or by early moonlight. He is the lover anxious that his lady be seen only at her best. Of all who have found themselves under the sway of this dominating house, none has so subordinated his will to it. As one Frenchman in New Iberia put it, 'That man *married* to that place!'"[18]

Harnett Kane, a generation younger than Lyle Saxon and Weeks Hall and friend of both, was another bachelor gentleman married to the preservation of Louisiana history and culture. A native of New Orleans, Kane was born in 1910, graduated from Tulane in 1931, and lived in the South all his life. Like Saxon he spent years writing for a New Orleans newspaper, then turned to a prolific book-writing career: *The Bayous of Louisiana, Deep Delta Country, Plantation Parade, Natchez on the Mississippi, Queen New Orleans, Spies for the Blue and Gray, The Southern Christmas Book, The Golden Coast, Gone Are the Days, The Romantic South,* and many novels based on the lives of prominent southern women.

Harnett Kane's role in saving old New Orleans began in the 1930s, when many of his feature articles on the Vieux Carré were published in the *New Orleans Item.* He cited the disappearance of courtyards and balconies and the appearance of inappropriate commercial signs as examples of unconscionable change. An early house threatened by highway developers in 1949 prompted Kane to help found the Louisiana Landmarks Society. The house eventually perished anyway, but the organization went on to win many preservation battles through the urban-renewal and freeway-building binge of the 1950s and 1960s.

While Harnett Kane was coming of age in New Orleans, Boyd Cruise was biding his time as an artistically gifted teenager in Lake Charles, Louisiana. A mesmerizing glimpse of New Orleans during a Mardi Gras visit in 1927 left the shy eighteen-year-old Cruise determined to return. A year later, after winning a scholarship from the Art School of the New Orleans Arts and Crafts Club in the French Quarter, Boyd Cruise traveled from Lake Charles to the city that would be his home for the rest of his life.

At the Arts and Crafts Club on Royal Street, "Uncle Charlie" Bein taught Cruise to paint in watercolor, and Weeks Hall came from the Shadows once a week to teach composition. For two years Cruise lived in an attic apartment on Saint Ann Street, sharing the space with an enormous plaster clown mask that had been created and abandoned by a previous tenant. "It was in Carnival colors and must have been six or eight feet tall," Cruise recalled. "You couldn't get it downstairs because it was wider than the stairs."[19]

After attending the Pennsylvania Academy of Fine Arts and spending two summers in Europe, Cruise returned to New Orleans in the mid-1930s. Richard Koch created a job for him in the Historic American Buildings Survey. "There was no place in the HABS for an artist," architect Sam Wilson said, "but Boyd needed a job. He and Mr. Koch were friends and both were very active in the Arts and Crafts Club. Mr. Koch thought we ought to have a record of the colors of these buildings. Boyd made hundreds of watercolors of buildings around the countryside and in the city."[20] Cruise's paintings of some buildings were made just before demolition: "Painted and destroyed in the same month," he would note.[21]

Sailors strutting their stuff in the streets of the French Quarter captured young Cruise's imagination. They and other elements of the present day animate many of his HABS watercolors, which convey the color and flavor of the lives of historic buildings and neighborhoods through the late 1930s and just into the 1940s. In addition to accurate and evocative paintings, Cruise created many exceptionally elegant and precisely measured drawings that delineated key design details—columns, dormers, doorways, hardware. "Both Cruise and his friend and mentor, Koch, were attached to buildings in a far more intense sense than usually is found, even among dedicated professionals," says a New Orleans preservationist. "This emotional attachment resonates in all of Cruise's best works."[22]

Of the many French Quarter houses Cruise painted, one especially captivated his domophilic imagination: He thought it would be an ideal home for his partner and himself. "So I got Harold, who was a child-welfare worker, and we both went back and peered over the fence. Harold got the money and there we were. We gave up a lot of things to have that house, but I certainly don't regret it and I'm sure he never did."[23] Harold Schilke purchased the wonderful but decaying double Creole cottage on Saint Ann Street in 1938. The four rooms and two small service buildings were occupied by six families. The patio and garden were filled with trash. Schilke and Cruise spent years restoring it and furnishing it with antiques.

Like many artists Cruise was drawn to the French Quarter's rich patina of age and decay. But as his vision matured, the meticulous artist began to create vividly colorful paintings depicting the old buildings not as they appeared in the present but as they might have looked in the previous century. The French Opera House, the old French Market, and the Little Theater thrived again. Houses and shops looked fresh and prosperous, as did the residents in their period clothing. The horse-drawn carriages, the iron grillwork of the balconies, the street vendors, the dogs on leashes—everything was portrayed in intricate and historically correct detail. Before he began a painting, Cruise would learn the correct date of the building's construction and would then determine the correct styles of clothing and other elements. "These studies are amazing in their transcription of architectural details and their faithfulness to the architecture of the old city," said Weeks Hall. "Immense research was required for the costumes of the figures and the restoration of parts of the buildings which have since been destroyed."[24]

Devoutly private, proper, and formal, Boyd Cruise felt most comfortable within the milieu of his imagined nineteenth century. After doing his period research he trusted his innate historical vision. "When I was painting, I didn't know why I put someone in a certain place or did something else. . . . But when I got through I knew why: because it was right."[25]

While Boyd Cruise labored religiously over his historical paintings, Clay Shaw's redemptive instinct found its outlet in the ambitious restoration of many French Quarter buildings. Shaw, who grew up north of the city in the small town of Amite, began to make his mark in New Orleans after serving in World War II. Twenty years later Shaw became the target of vicious mudslinging in the aftermath of a presidential assassination. And so, restoring the dignity of preservationist Clay Shaw has become a compelling mission for Roberts Batson, New Orleans historian. Batson's Gay Heritage Tour includes 724 Governor Nicholls Street in the French Quarter, where a memorial plaque reads: "In tribute to Clay Shaw, 1913–1974. Pioneer in the renovation of the Vieux Carré. This 1834 building, the Spanish stables, is one of nine restorations by Clay Shaw. In addition, he conceived and completed the International Trade Mart and directed the restoration of the French Market. Clay Shaw was a patron of the humanities and lived his life with the utmost grace; an invaluable citizen, he was respected, admired and loved by many."

"The plaque is lovely, but it's also heartbreaking," says Batson. "The Clay Shaw trial is a centerpiece of my Gay Heritage Tour. Shaw was brought to trial because Jim Garrison, the district attorney of Orleans Parish, was out to discredit the Warren Commission, the committee appointed by the U.S. government to investigate the assassination of President Kennedy. In 1967 Garrison announced that Lee Harvey Oswald was not the lone assassin, that there had been a conspiracy, and that it was hatched right here in New Orleans.

"Jim Garrison was a monster out to further his own ambitions. He knew that Clay Shaw was gay, and he figured Shaw would commit suicide if arrested. That's what was expected of gay people then, particularly prominent people, rather than have all the details of their personal lives revealed. Clay Shaw was one of the leading citizens of New Orleans, a highly respected business leader. Garrison figured that Shaw would kill himself, and then Garrison could say to the world that Shaw must have had something to do with the assassination."

"I have tremendous admiration for Clay Shaw and the enormous grace with which he survived what Garrison did to him. Unfortunately, Oliver Stone's film *JFK* is based on books by Garrison. And the Clay Shaw character in the film is not Shaw; it is Oliver Stone's stereotype of a rich, bitchy, middle-aged queen who's repulsive, scary, and nasty. That's what the world has seen. And that, probably more than anything else, is why I'm doing what I'm doing. To tell the full and honest stories of our lives."

Clay Shaw was in his preservation prime when New York City native Don Schueler first saw New Orleans on a vacation trip in the early 1950s. "We came to the corner of Esplanade and Royal, I looked down those streets, and right then I decided I was going to live here. It was this cascade of absolutely beautiful architecture, essentially traditional European but with a totally individual New Orleans twist. It just didn't look like any other American city. Plus, the French Quarter was fun! I was twenty-two and good-looking, a big frog in a little pond. So I went back to New York, quit my job, and moved South." In 1964 Schueler met Willie Brown, who had grown up in a poor New Orleans family. Within a few years, true to type, the couple were fixing up a neglected ninety-year-old house in the city's Garden District.

"Gays have never gotten credit for the fact that they really are the moving force in recreating and revitalizing central cities," Schueler says. "The process of restoring old houses is linked inextricably with restoring the quality of the human life in those neighborhoods. As long as there are interesting architectural possibilities, gays are always the first ones to move into blighted neighborhoods. To do it, they brave a great deal of stuff, often quite dangerous—regular crime, gay bashing, and all the rest of it. It's a true kind of pioneering. Then you get young heterosexual singles and couples moving in, the beneficiaries of the gay aesthetic orientation."

In his chronicle of the historic preservation movement, Charles Hosmer says it's remarkable that so much preservation work was done in the French Quarter during the 1930s without a private preservation organization as such. Remarkable, yes, but not unexplainable. "I tell you that this town is aswarm and alive and criss-crossed with perverts," an agitated Senator Huey Long declared to a newspaper reporter in 1935.[26] To understand a large portion of the extraordinarily passionate and longstanding preservation ethic for which New Orleans is known, one need only acknowledge the uncommon historical and aesthetic vision that generations of gay men and their female collaborators have brought to their relationships with the city.

The Society for the Preservation of Ancient Tombs, organized in New Orleans in the 1920s, was among the earliest of such collaborations. This graveyard-keeping enterprise continues to be informed by a singular vision. In the mid-1990s two gay men purchased and restored an abandoned plot at historic Saint Louis Cemetery Number One. The handsome marble tomb they erected bears their names: "Jerah Johnson, Historian," and

"George Febres, Artist." Not only did they fix up their own property, but as a provision of the sale they requested permission to clean up the crumbling tomb next door.[27] New Orleans cemetery expert Robert Florence states that this case of pioneering graveyard restoration "seems to have triggered a gentrification of sorts, as the general condition of St. Louis Cemetery Number One surrounding [this] tomb appears spruced up, and there have been a number of recent nearby tomb restorations."[28]

The gay preservation lineage that has served New Orleans and Louisiana through the past century is brought to the present by the three individuals whose narratives follow. Believing that "life doesn't make any sense unless you have a context in which to live it," architect Curt Greska has dedicated himself to preserving Louisiana's historical context, opposing "the wanton destruction of things of beauty." Similarly artist and educator Lloyd Sensat has brightened the prospects of Louisiana's historic buildings by creating a program in which children and youth are inspired by "the magic, beauty, and mystery of the old houses." Declaring that "the two biggest focuses of my life are my being gay and architectural preservation," Randy Plaisance enthuses about living in the French Quarter and working to save the historic buildings of his native state.

Curt Greska

Preservation architect Curt Greska was born in central Louisiana in 1940 and has lived in New Orleans since the 1970s. His name is a pseudonym.

I HAD KIND OF A CRAZY CHILDHOOD, all tied up in old buildings and ghosts and a sense of place. One night my dad sent me to the place where the cows danced when the full moon came out. We went to this big field and saw the cows looking up at the moon and kind of swaying. All throughout my childhood there was this thing about nature worship. My grandmother and my mom believed in the spirit world. My dad was kind of an atheist. I was the one in my family who brought in religion by joining the Southern Baptist Church.

We lived near Alexandria, which is right in the heart of Louisiana. If I was a good boy and took my nap in the afternoon, I was able to go out with the big people to the huge Hotel Bentley, a wonderful, grand, turn-of-the-century hotel in Alexandria. It's been saved, a national landmark. Alexandria still has a lot of pretty areas, but it was once a really beautiful town, with a downtown that looked a lot like old New Orleans. But in the 1930s they took down all the iron balconies and made other changes to widen the streets for automobiles.

One of my first memories in New Orleans is sitting on top of Jewel's Bar, which is in a wonderful old building on Decatur Street in the French Quarter. I was maybe three, having a little sip of beer and eating boiled shrimp with my father. My parents were very much into historic preservation; they believed that good civilizations keep the good stuff. A lot of our family trips on the weekends were to go looking for old houses. We spent many an hour visiting ancient structures and the old people who shared their stories and wisdom. And we said good-bye to many old buildings that were going to be demolished. My parents felt these were acts of barbarism, not progress. These experiences inspired many of my early drawings and writings.

I went to a country school, grades one through twelve. I've been a teacher since I was in the sixth grade, when I started teaching art to the second-graders. It was always kind of expected that I would be an architect. My father's dad was an architect, my dad's brother was an architect, and my dad wanted to be an architect, but he could never sit still long enough to do an internship or go to school.

I always knew I was different from everybody else because I liked to draw and read, and I was very sensitive and all that good stuff that gays often are. My mom and dad were open about everything and had a lot of gay friends, so I grew up around many guys who were also that way. My dad, particularly concerned about one of these guys, would say to me, "Mr. So-and-so is coming over tonight, and he's just a little bit different. If he starts getting too friendly, you just let daddy know, and I'll take care of it." As it turns out, my dad had quite a wild reputation in the French Quarter. I'm not so sure he wasn't playing on both sides of the fence. He was good-looking and well known in the community as a bad boy, but the reputation seemed to turn the ladies on more than off. My mom and dad and my sisters lived on-and-off in the French Quarter before I was born. My father's father considered New Orleans, particularly the Vieux Carré, to be the most civilized place to live in the New World.

I did an undergraduate degree in architecture at Louisiana State University. My teachers didn't put a whole lot of emphasis on preservation, but when I could choose a design project, I would usually choose adaptive reuse. A group of us fell in love with the River Road between Baton Rouge and New Orleans, and we had some of our early preservation battles right there in Baton Rouge. We did a lot of sketching, usually finding an old house somewhere to draw. One wonderful old place became infamous because the dirty old man who lived there would try to take you up on the roof.

I had a marvelous professor at LSU, third-year design. With him we would go look at old buildings and photograph them. He had grown up at Uncle Sam plantation, the largest plantation complex ever built in the United States. If it were still there today, it would be a triple-historic landmark, just incredible. Everything was Greek Revival. He and his aunt with whom he was living watched it being destroyed when the U.S. Army Corps of Engineers blew it up to change the bed of the levee after the 1927 flood.

I minored in landscape architecture, fine arts, and English. One of my favorite English professors was a rather notorious gay man who tried to steer me toward a writing career. People would say, "Has he made a move on you yet?" He never did, but he was a really interesting man from New Orleans who would tell me all kinds of tales. In my last year at LSU, I began to get strange, confusing feelings—sort of like music and architecture and my emotions were all tied up together. It wasn't until graduate school in Boston that I began to realize I was "a member of the church."

I hated Boston at first: I didn't think the people there had very good manners. But then I got to like the place and thought I might stay. I studied city planning and urban design, emphasizing preservation planning and children's perceptions of the changing urban environment. I began to develop a strong interest in environmental social psychology and an understanding of why historic preservation is important. Then I went to Europe to get a doctorate in historic preservation. In my dissertation I wrote about change and growth: how do you mix the old and the new, how do you accommodate both traffic and pedestrian ways in the old cities. I loved Amsterdam and would go there often. That's where I began the game of going to gay bars, but I never really did anything, because I couldn't cope with it.

After finishing my doctorate, I went to Greece in the summer of 1967. I arrived on the day of the coup, when they deposed the king. The streets were filled with soldiers. I'd walk around among all these great old things I'd seen in history books, and I'd see all these good-looking Greek soldiers carrying on among all these incredible ruins. *Aughh!* It seems my sexuality has always been tied up with old architecture.

I never thought I would come back to Louisiana to live, but I got really homesick. I taught briefly in the architecture school at LSU, then went to landscape architecture. All kinds of important buildings were about to be torn down in the city and along River Road. I did a lot of paintings and drawings and exhibited them to protest the destruction, to call people's attention to what we were doing to our environment. I was really involved in the ecology movement early on.

With a bachelor's degree, two master's degrees, and a doctorate, I decided for some ungodly reason to get a doctorate in environmental social psychology. I was going to be living in New Orleans, so I got an apartment on Dumaine Street, right next to the French Market, when it was still a French market.

My last couple years at LSU, the faculty in landscape architecture did a study of the riverfront expressway. That led me to get involved with other preservationists at the Louisiana Landmarks Society, many of whom were gay men. Along with a number of women, they were trying to make some sense of what modern culture was doing to a wonderful old city. Harnett Kane kind of put me under his wing, was always inviting me to do things. As a kid I was fascinated by his book, *Plantation Parade*, its stories and photographs of Louisiana, this exotic country in which we lived. Harnett believed in the preservation of old and good customs in addition to old houses. At Louisiana Landmarks Society meetings in the early 1970s, we would have formal receiving lines to welcome old friends and new members.

Over the last thirty years I've been in the middle of and sometimes the leader of several major preservation projects, both in the city and along River Road. I've seen a lot of buildings saved. I've been involved with the New Orleans Preservation Resource Center and the Historic District Landmarks Commission. Many of the men who've worked with me on these projects have been gay. There's also a large tradition of married men who play on both sides of the fence, and a lot of them are involved in historic preservation. Many of them are uptown guys, cornerstones of the community, with children, grandchildren now.

I really do think that, in general, gay men are much more creative than straight men. And there's a sensitivity to things that are worth being sensitive about. It goes back to rootedness, a sense of place, and to what historic architecture represents in terms of creativity. I don't totally go along with the idea that you have to be gay to be a really good architect or artist, but I do think that the majority of them are, or at least have leanings that way.

Weeks Hall was rather notorious. My partner and I were over at Shadows-on-the-Teche in New Iberia photographing it one day after they had done some major work on it. One of the gardeners, a black man, was telling us about "Mr. Weeks's boys"—all these good-looking, tall black men who had worked for him. Lyle Saxon and other gentlemen friends of Weeks Hall would bring their servants along when they came to visit. And then of course that whole group of preservation people that ran around with Lyle Saxon was just wonderful, all the way up into Natchitoches. There were a couple of artist colonies up there, with many gay men. There was such a wonderful group of people here in the 1930s and 1940s, when all this incredible preservation activity was taking place. Gay men and creative straight women were a very large part of that group. There were even a few lesbians involved, but not nearly as many as gay men.

After about my first year in New Orleans, I bought an old house in the Faubourg Marigny neighborhood, which is where I still live, though not in that same house. One weekend I was in Lafayette for my niece's wedding, and after it was all over I went to a dance bar in Lafayette. I noticed a guy with close-cropped hair who was shipping out with the Air Force to Korea in a few days. This was during the Vietnam War. I mentioned to somebody at the bar that I had just bought an old Creole cottage, and those were the magic words for this guy I had noticed. We started talking, and one thing led to another. We got to be very good friends for the night. The next morning I packed up and went back to New Orleans, and my new friend went off to Korea, never to be seen again. Or so I thought.

Eventually this guy moved into a house right down the street from me in New Orleans. I would see him around, but I didn't remember him. But he remembered me. He was best friends with one of my best friends, and this woman kept trying to fix us up, but it never really happened. Then one Easter, twenty-three years ago, we met again, and as soon as he started describing the night we met in Lafayette, I remembered who he was. Before long I asked him to move in with me.

"I have very little furniture or anything," he said. Three truckloads later he was moved in. For some ungodly reason I had sold the pristine, beautiful, early Creole cottage that I had restored and had moved further into the neighborhood, into a house that was in horrible condition. It took about five years to get that place together and fixed up. I bought the triple cottage where we live now in 1976, and three years later we finished fixing it up and rented it out. After five years of that I said to hell with being a landlord; I sold the house we were living in, and we moved into the triple. It's a one-and-a-half-story Creole house built in 1807 and remodeled in 1836, with three beautiful cypress and mahogany spiral staircases and all sorts of interesting characters related to it. The house's history reflects the complex ethnic and social mix that is New Orleans.

Life doesn't make any sense unless you have a context in which to live it. The wanton destruction of things of beauty, whether they're natural or man made, robs future generations of the pleasure and the knowledge of those things, those places. I really hate it that asshole lumbermen have cut down all the giant cypress trees. There may be one or two left in the entire state of Louisiana. They used to be everywhere, like the redwoods of California. When I see lumber trucks hauling trees that are eight hundred or one thousand years old, I want to become violent. I've been a protester in many ways, but usually kind of quietly. I've carried a few signs in my life. But mostly I'm an educator, and to me part of being an environmental educator is being a preservationist. The two go hand in hand.

Lloyd Sensat

The premise of Lloyd Sensat's Education through Historic Preservation program is simple: Historic buildings have a future if young people become interested in them. Through the program, started in 1977, hundreds of students in grade school and high school have studied and interpreted Louisiana's historic buildings through art, drama, creative writing, and historical research. "Knowing our past helps us to understand the present and see the way toward a more meaningful and environmentally responsible future," Sensat has written. "Old is good and provides the context for the new. Old things, buildings, trees, as well as people, provide the link to a complete education." Sensat lives in the Faubourg Marigny district of New Orleans.

I'VE ALWAYS HAD this fascination and obsession with old buildings. New Orleans to me was the epitome of the place to live in Louisiana, particularly the French Quarter. I was born in 1944 and grew up in Crowley, which is in south Louisiana, Cajun country. Of course, I loved New Orleans because of the freedom and the gay scene and all, but it was the architecture that really drew me here.

From about the seventh grade until I was a senior in high school, I would save articles pertaining to Louisiana buildings, particularly plantations. We got the New Orleans paper every Sunday, the *Times-Picayune*, and just about every week in the Dixie Roto section there would be a feature article about some old building in New Orleans or some plantation or whatever, with color photos. A neighbor got the Baton Rouge paper, which often had feature stories on the River Road plantations. I ended up with probably a dozen scrapbooks. They're still in my bedroom at my mother's house.

Crowley is just a little over a hundred years old. It had beautiful Victorian buildings but nothing older. I would go to the library and check out the books on plantations. Harnett Kane's *Plantation Parade* was wonderful, giving me the stories of life behind the columns. My favorite book was *Ghosts along the Mississippi:* fabulous, haunting black-and-white photographs of plantation houses in ruin. Lyle Saxon's *Old Louisiana* and *Fabulous New Orleans* also fueled my imagination and my love for old buildings. The librarian told me I was too young to be reading Frances Parkinson Keyes's romantic novels with Louisiana settings.

My dad and mom took me to see my first plantations—Parlange near New Roads and Shadows-on-the-Teche in New Iberia. I saw Shadows-on-the-Teche right after Weeks Hall died, when I was in high school. There was an article about him in the Dixie Roto magazine: "The Man Who Married a House." I was so excited, I showed it to my English teacher, one of my favorite teachers. She was always very interested. Some of my friends overheard the conversation, and of course, they thought it was hysterical—who would marry a *house!?* Those horny high school boys, it was beyond their comprehension.

Weeks Hall was an artist, a bachelor, never married. The house actually became his whole life. When the National Trust first restored Shadows-on-the-Teche, they put it back to what it looked like in the 1850s, 1860s, totally ignoring Weeks Hall, even to the extent of redesigning the gardens. Now they're restoring the gardens to the way he had them. His gardens were fabulous. And now they also have a studio room with examples of his paintings. Some of his better pieces are his portraits of black men.

My mom always encouraged me to draw and write, even though my father thought I should be outside playing ball. I went to a small Catholic school that didn't have an art program. I always liked to draw, and once the nuns recognized that I had some ability, they would have me draw things for them. When I was in the second grade, my all-time favorite teacher told me that I would be an artist. *Katy Keene* was also a major influence, a very popular comic book that folded when I was in high school. Katy Keene was a fashion model aspiring to be a movie star, and many of the comic-book stories about her were based on drawings or ideas that kids would send in. They would always dress Katy Keene in outfits her fans would design. The story would say, "Fashions by so-and-so . . ." When I was fourteen, they published a story I did called "Katy Keene Meets Jean Lafitte." It was all involved with my obsession with old buildings and characters from Louisiana history.

In the 1920s, when New Orleans witnessed a renaissance in art and literature, *The Double Dealer* made its appearance, a little magazine that discovered and published such writers as Sherwood Anderson, William Faulkner, and Ernest Hemingway. One of the magazine's founders, John McClure, was the husband of an elderly cousin of mine. Dear Cousin Joyce was always inviting me to spend the summer with her at her home on Pirates Alley, but my father would never let me go because of all those queers who lived in the Quarter. One of my greatest regrets is that my dad did not let me meet Joyce's neighborhood pals or experience the wonders of the Quarter when I was growing up.

I loved both Joyce and her sister, Dottie, who lived in Opelousas, Louisiana. I was allowed to visit both of them there, and we would go on day trips to see the plantations in the vicinity. Many of the old houses had been owned by our ancestors, so my cousins' stories made the history so real and personal for me. Then we would return to Dottie's house, which was filled with family heirlooms, and look through the old photo album while the stories continued. It was such a magic time.

I started my teaching career at a high school near my hometown, but I did want to move to New Orleans. A friend of mine who was working in Saint Charles Parish, just outside New Orleans, told me they were starting a new school. I was offered a job there as an art specialist. I'd never worked with elementary kids and didn't think I'd like it, but the new principal was very dynamic and really wanted me to do it, so I took the job. It would get me to New Orleans. When I moved to the city in 1975, I lived on Burgundy Street, a block and a half from where I live now.

Homeplace Plantation was near the school in Saint Charles Parish. Built about 1790, it was considered one of the finest surviving examples of French Colonial architecture in America. A national historic landmark, but instead of getting better over time it had regressed. I figured that unless you got young people interested in these buildings, they were not going to have a future. So I applied to the state for a grant and we started the Education through Historic Preservation program. Part of the students' experience that year was working with an eighty-five-year-old man who was born and raised at Homeplace. They were introduced to the idea that old can be important, and that even though you are young, you can have relationships with things that are old, buildings as well as people.

Each year all of the hundreds of kids in the school would do a drawing of whatever building we were going to be working with. From those drawings I would select fifteen to twenty kids who I thought had a natural ability in art. They became part of the program. Each historic building we adopted was interpreted through art, drama, historical research, and creative writing. Over the past twenty-plus years we've worked with some of the state's most important landmarks.

Kids who were identified as intellectually gifted would do role playing, becoming characters associated with the history of the house. When we would have our openings, they would introduce themselves as the people who had lived there and would give tours as if they were those people. Sometimes we would involve kids with dramatic talent. In addition to writing and acting in the play, the students designed the costumes, sets, posters, and playbills. We wanted the magic, beauty, and mystery of the old houses of Louisiana to inspire and motivate our student artists.

Gays are not given enough credit for saving America's inner cities and historic neighborhoods. Most gays can take anything and make it beautiful. They're not afraid to tackle these old buildings and do this transformation, and they're not afraid to move into areas that might be a little risky.

The buildings, the visual evidence of where we've been, mean so much to me. It gives me a comforting sense of continuity to go back to Crowley and see the houses that were there when I was growing up. I hate how everything is throwaway now. And some of the new things really aren't worth saving. But if you live in New Orleans, it's different because there's so much history. The whole thing is to make people, particularly young people, realize the importance of these old buildings. No one really owns them. We're just their caretakers while we exist, and then someone else has to take over when we're gone.

Robert Florence, the author of *New Orleans Cemeteries,* has a passion for our historic cities of the dead. He is sort of a one-man campaign to save them, and one of his obsessions is to reintroduce color to the cemeteries. Originally the ancient Creole burial grounds with their aboveground vaults were lime-washed in reds, grays, blues, and yellows. But the church likes the lily-white purity of the currently whitewashed tombs. One day Rob went to Saint Louis Cemetery Number One with a bucket of newly prepared red-lime wash made from an old formula using crushed bricks. As he surveyed the cemetery and began to paint, all the gladness left him: there were hundreds of tombs to be lime-washed, and he was all by himself. Then an inspiration burst upon him: the tale of Tom Sawyer and the whitewashed fence. He grabbed his cell phone and began to call friends.

"Lloyd, I'm here at Saint Louis Number One painting tombs. Why not come join me? . . . Work? It's not work, it's great fun! . . . Experience? That's why I asked *you!* You know the archdiocese is awfully particular about the cemetery."

"Oh, Rob, I'm an artist. You know I can do it. *Please* let me help!"

"Okay, Lloyd, I'll give you a try."

When I arrived, Rob already had an entourage sweating under the brutal Louisiana sun. After all, it's not every day that a person gets the chance to lime-wash tombs. They were splattered in red, drinking wine and eating pizza, totally engrossed in the task at hand. Their major distractions were tourists asking for directions to Marie Laveau's tomb. Soon I was involved with brush, paint, and talent for the cause. On this day another New Orleans tradition had begun: Rob Florence had founded the Friends of New Orleans Cemeteries. (This may not be the way it *really* happened, but if it didn't, it should have!) My partner and I are now hooked. We're hoping to reclaim and restore an abandoned family vault in Saint Louis Number One and to be buried there. Then we really will be kindred spirits.

Randy Plaisance

Randy Plaisance was born in New Orleans in 1964 and grew up mostly in suburban Marrero, in Jefferson Parish. He lives in New Orleans, where he is a preservation architect.

MY FATHER'S FAMILY is from Nova Scotia, originally from France. During the English occupation of Canada in the 1700s, they went down the Mississippi to the other French territory, Louisiana, and settled on Bayou Lafourche down toward the Gulf. My mother's family settled on Bayou Lafourche as well, but near where it meets the river. My mother's family came directly to Louisiana from France, so they're considered Creoles. My father's family were Cajuns.

I was always interested in Louisiana history, and I loved going with my parents to see the big plantation homes along the river. Coming from a suburban home, I was especially dazzled by these houses that are like palaces, fifteen or twenty thousand square feet with sixteen-foot ceilings, crystal chandeliers, marble mantels, and fancy furniture. As I got older and read more about the plantations, I was fascinated not just by the big house but by what went on behind it in the slave quarters and the barns and the kitchen and the many other buildings that for some reason were gone. When we traveled to the Smoky Mountains, I was intrigued by the little log cabins that had been built by settlers.

As a child I would sit on the floor in my room and draw floor plans for hours. How I even knew what floor plans were, I don't know. Sometimes they were houses; sometimes they were caves. I had a fascination with caves, maybe from Batman comic books. I would draw a huge cave in section, and then I would build it out; floors would be cut out of the stone, and there were secret passages and stairs.

In high school I wanted to be an architect, but for some reason I let people talk me out of it. They said it involved lots of math and science, my weak points. Later, my first long-term boyfriend was an architecture student at Tulane, and I would help him with his projects. He told me I really had an aptitude for architecture and should consider studying it. So I quit my job, got rid of my house, moved into a one-bedroom apartment with my boyfriend, and went back to school.

At first I didn't think New Orleans was much of a city for architecture because we didn't have many skyscrapers. Then one day during my second year I saw an exhibit at school by one of the professors who had done a Historic American Buildings Survey project on a plantation home.

The measured drawings were on display, and I thought they were the most beautiful drawings I'd ever seen. Standing there with a friend, I said, "Do you know who this professor is? I would love to meet this man." He said he knew him and would introduce me.

The professor and I hit it off right away. Whenever he planned a field trip with his class to visit a plantation home or a historic or architecturally significant building that wasn't open to the public, he invited me to come. And he invited me to parties at his house, where I met more people who were involved in preservation. The next semester he offered a platform to do a HABS project for Madame John's Legacy, probably the oldest original residential building in the Quarter. I started doing the project and fell in love with the work. He got me so interested in HABS drawings that every summer I would work on a project for the HABS office in Washington, D.C. I've done drawings in Harper's Ferry, West Virginia, and was project captain on the Martin Van Buren estate in Kinderhook, New York. In Huntsville, Alabama, we documented buildings from the 1950s and 1960s that were used to design, build, and test the rockets that went to the moon. A lot of them are made of metal, just sitting idle and rusting, and they could collapse who knows when. Many HABS projects are done because the buildings are in imminent danger.

Whenever I get a chance to go into a building that I've never been into before, I always jump on the opportunity. Doing the fieldwork for these HABS drawings is the best way to get to know a building intimately. You measure every little piece of wood in each door and window. You're crawling around in attics and basements and under buildings, hand-measuring every inch of the structure. I like doing the fieldwork, and I like coming back and looking at my notes and trying to piece the puzzle together: Why doesn't this look right? What did I do wrong? Sometimes I have to go back and find my mistake.

My boyfriend, Derek, has lived in the Quarter since he moved to New Orleans and loves architecture as much as I do. When we first met and he came over to my apartment, he went into my study where the walls are lined with architecture books. "Oh, my God," he said, "you're cute *and* you have an interest in architecture. This must be my lucky day." We really love our apartment, the slave-quarters wing of an 1840s townhouse. It's got a nice courtyard, and it's close to everything. We're on the corner of Esplanade and Dauphine, in the Marigny. Derek and I will be moving into the Quarter within the next month or so, so we'll be moving to the official gay section of the city. We're looking for a place where we can walk home from the bars at 3:30 or 4:00 in the morning without feeling endangered.

I've always wanted to live in the Quarter, even if it's only for a year, just to say I lived in the most historic section of the city. We want to live in something that's at least one hundred years old. And we want to stay in the predominantly gay section, so that means looking between Saint Ann and Esplanade. We saw a beautiful place on Bourbon owned by a preservationist. It has nice wooden floors and high ceilings, all the millwork trim is original, original fireplace mantels, everything's well maintained, just impeccable. The doors open right onto the street, so we would have a little bit more of a problem with drunk people passing by, screaming and hollering. But that's our first choice.

One of my uncles once commented that he would never go to New Orleans because it was filled with nothing but niggers and faggots. Almost all my gay friends grew up in suburbia or small towns and came to the city. I would like to think that gay men who come to New Orleans from Nowheresville, or from cities that have no historical context like this city does, appreciate what they find around them and pick up a sense of preservation. It tends to be people from out of town who know more about the city than the people who have lived here all their lives.

For me moving into the city offered a little bit of anonymity; my parents are only ten to fifteen minutes away, but that's another world. I'd say that at least half of the people who live in my neighborhood are gay. The gay section of New Orleans is in the most historic and architecturally significant part of the city. There's a lesbian couple who restored a beautiful camelback double house at the end of Bourbon, but in New Orleans 99 percent of the gays in preservation are men. The lesbians around here tend to be suburbanites, I guess because they tend to be much more practical than gay men. They just don't see the benefit of restoring an old building. But I'm so glad I'm a gay man. The lesbians I know tend to be so drab and boring. Maybe they're happy, but I don't see how they possibly could be.

The two biggest focuses of my life are my being gay and architectural preservation. Through my work I've met the people who are working to save the architecture of New Orleans from collapse, and we do have a lot of blighted property. At meetings of the Vieux Carré Property Owners and the Marigny Association, I see lots of gay men—mostly couples, because they tend to be more settled-down, and they're in a period of their lives when they can afford to buy and restore a piece of property.

It was women who organized the preservation movement here in the early 1900s when an entire square block was torn down to build the court building, that white marble Beaux Arts monolith in the middle of the Quarter. The plan was to level the blocks between the river and this building and put in a big formal garden leading up to it. When people realized they could tear down the whole Quarter, a movement was organized that led to the founding of the Vieux Carré Property Owners' Association. Elizabeth Werlein was one of the big movers, and I'm sure there were lots of confirmed bachelors, as they used to refer to us.

The Marigny was built almost entirely by free women of color, and it has been restored almost entirely by gay men. It was a slum back in the 1970s. The Quarter was becoming so expensive; a lot of people couldn't afford to own property there. So they moved into the Marigny. It was crime-ridden, and the buildings were run-down. Gay men started buying up these properties and moving in. When I was in high school, I saw an article in the newspaper about two men who restored a house in the Marigny. It was a whorehouse and a deplorable mess when they bought it, termite damage and holes in the floor that you could crawl through. A photograph showed the two sitting on the front porch. These guys are gay, I said to myself at the time. Now I'm good friends with that couple.

My best friend, whom I graduated college with, who happens to be a straight preservationist, used to joke that he was the token straight boy in preservation. Gay men and preservation just seem to go hand in hand. I think it's because we tend to have a greater appreciation for aesthetics, for history, for architecture, and for the arts, whether it be music or literature or painting or sculpture. Gay men just seem to be more in tune to that side of things.

Toward a Larger View of Gay Men

THE PRESERVATION-ORIENTED gay men profiled in the preceding chapters exemplify a cluster of interrelated traits: gender-atypicality, domophilia, romanticism, aestheticism, and connection- and continuity-mindedness. This chapter examines these traits in a larger context, historically and culturally, to show how the culture-keeping impulse is related to religious and secular care-giving vocations that focus on the restoration of order and wholeness.

These ideas are not new, just largely unexplored. A century ago psychiatrist Carl Jung and psychologist Havelock Ellis both contemplated nonsexual dimensions of gay men's natures. Like Freud, Jung tended to see the gay man as having a mother-based neurosis. Jung, however, saw something positive in this: the gay man "may have good taste and an aesthetic sense which are fostered by the presence of a feminine streak. He may be supremely gifted as a teacher because of his almost feminine insight and tact. He is likely to have a feeling for history, and to be conservative in the best sense and cherish the values of the past. Often he is endowed with a wealth of religious feelings."[1] Ellis made similar observations: gay men frequently have superior intellectual and artistic abilities, they are prominent in the religious arena, and many of them are drawn to "the study of antiquity."[2]

By managing change in ways that allow us to retain a sense of where we've come from, historic preservation fosters continuity, enriching our sense of connectedness and identity as members of families, communities, nations. The architectural preservationist, for example, sees old buildings as landmarks and sources of memory. These stable features of the landscapes we inhabit help to orient us to the place and its history and so help us to define ourselves.

The built environment has become a significant focus of the preservation impulse during only about the last two hundred years, as change has been accelerated by many forces: industrialization, urbanization, the population explosion, the automobile, and massive tapping of fossil fuels. Previously architectural styles, materials, and methods changed slowly, and the fabric of buildings and cities tended to hold together for centuries-long stretches. Because change in the built environment was so slow in relation to the human life span, the sense of continuity was not much threatened, and thus special efforts to manage change were not needed.

In times and places that do not experience an unsettling degree of change in the built environment, it's likely that preservation-minded gay men would gravitate to religious vocations. Though they differ in their focuses and methods, both historic preservation and religion seek to foster identity, community, continuity, wholeness/holiness. Indeed, the Latin origins of the word *religion*—to bind together again, to put back together again—make plain the "re-ligious" nature of the preservation enterprise. Like counseling, social work, nursing, and other care-giving professions, historic preservation is a secular counterpart to the religious arena and seems to attract the same sorts of men. The same men, in many cases; clergy have figured prominently in historic preservation from its beginnings.[3]

Across time and cultures gay men have been strongly attracted to the religious arena. Carl Jung and Havelock Ellis noted the phenomenon, as have more recent observers. John Boswell remarks on the substantial evidence of homosexual clergy from the beginning of the Christian era to the fourteenth century.[4] Rictor Norton notes an abundance of love poems addressed by Buddhist priests to their temple acolytes from the tenth to the thirteenth century.[5] It's not much of a stretch to suggest that Thomas Cahill's *How the Irish Saved Civilization* might have been more precisely titled *How Queer Irish Monks Saved Civilization.*[6] In the twentieth century gay Episcopal priest Malcolm Boyd was astonished to find so many gay men in the seminary, drawn by the mystery, beauty, music, and ritual of the church.[7] In New Orleans, so goes the anecdote, half the occupants of a French Quarter gay bar on any Saturday night are Roman Catholic postulants, seminarians, or priests.[8] This may explain why a gay preservationist in that city uses the phrase "a member of the church" as a euphemism for gay. A gay man who grew up in Kenya says he finds it funny that gay men in Africa "are all so religious."[9]

Writer Philip Gambone captures the essence of gay religious aestheticism. When he and his lover lived on Boston's Beacon Hill, they attended the Church of the Advent, a famous Anglo-Catholic church: "In those days, the late seventies and early eighties, the Advent's congregation was made up almost exclusively of gay men and Boston Brahmins, a strange and tenuous coalition at best. What brought these unlikely factions together was a shared passion for the Mass—for the mystery of the Mass, and for its high church aesthetic. The Advent knew how to 'do it right.' Every genuflection, every reverencing of the altar, every swish of the thurible was done with utmost style and taste and dignified seriousness. There was, in so much of this fastidious attention to the choreography of the Mass, a preciousness that bordered on the ludicrous. But we told ourselves—and I suppose there was truth in this—that all of the pomp and circumstance, the 'smells and bells,' as we called it, was for the 'greater glory of God.'"[10]

Pittsburgh preservationist James Van Trump's hankering for religious smells and bells led him to become high-church Episcopal. "That way I could have all the lights, incense, color, flowers, and music without subscribing to the rigid doctrines of Rome," Van Trump said. "I have a great feeling for the church rituals. I feel that the old solemnities had a certain use. And I feel that we are poorer for the loss of some of these things. I always thought that religion . . . was a stabilizing influence. Now I realize that by subscribing to a formal religion I am believing a legend. But for me this is a necessary myth."[11]

A common explanation for the disproportionately large presence of gay men in the religious world is that it has long provided them with safe cover. No doubt many gay men have found the religious arena to be an agreeably cloistered niche, but *why* have they been so well suited to it, and it to them? Certainly there are niches far more culturally marginal than religion to which queer men might have retreated through the centuries. Gays and the religious arena have been well suited to each other because gay men's sensibilities have been central to the creation of that arena. Gay men have not only been extraordinarily drawn to religious work; they have excelled at it, preeminent as creators and keepers of the religious aesthetic.

There is substantial evidence that gender-atypical males of homosexual or bisexual orientation have fulfilled sacred roles in many cultures since the time of the earliest known religious traditions.[12] Their blend of feminine and masculine traits enhanced their proficiency in these roles. Matthew Kelty, a priest at the Abbey of Gethsemani in Kentucky, says he believes that gays make the best monks "because they're already on the road to a life integrating the masculine and the feminine sides. They don't need a woman to awaken and arouse their feminine side. They already have it."[13]

There is rich anecdotal evidence of the strength of the gay religious/spiritual sensibility, even among the unchurched. This includes my own impressions of an intriguing number of domestic altars and shrines among contemporary gay men with whose lives I'm acquainted: Ray Kwok's altar in memory of his mother; Michael Bemis's quirky assemblage of Buddhist-Episcopal meditation paraphernalia; Liberace's shrine to Saint Anthony at his home in Palm Springs; Dale Pflum's collection of holy-water fonts hanging on his bedroom walls; Bruce Benderson's collection of sacred memorabilia; John Anders's bust of the Apollo Belvedere atop a small green table; Dean

Riddle's evocative arrangement of eighteen smooth pebbles on a chartreuse Russel Wright plate; Doug Bauder's heirloom sea chest, dusted reverently each week, with which his great-grandfather's great-grandfather came to America.[14] "I have a little shrine I brought home from San Francisco," Mark Doty writes, "an upright wooden box painted celestial blue, with a yellow horse floating on a field of stars. The wooden door slides open, so that the box becomes a little theater, revealing its interior. It used to hold three crude images of gods—Brahma, Vishnu, Shiva—but they didn't speak to me, so I've replaced them with one perfect smooth river stone I found someplace, a token of—fixity, I think, serenity."[15]

A. L. Rowse remarked on this gay religious sensibility as it was evident in Walter Pater, a nineteenth-century aesthete and writer who originally intended himself for holy orders. With his eyes focused reverently on the past, Rowse wrote of Pater, "there always remained an odour of the clerical about him."[16] Indeed, this "odour" seems to be a quintessentially gay trait: a gentle, punctilious solemnity, an earnest, high-minded queenliness, which often begins to emerge in childhood. The quality makes for outstanding altar boys, ministers, priests, rabbis. Finbar Maxwell, for instance, is a gay Roman Catholic who entered the seminary when he was seventeen. Growing up in Dublin, Ireland, Maxwell's deep sense of the unity and connectedness of people led him to immerse himself in the work of a parish-based social welfare group, the Ballyfermot Peace Corps. That vocation led him into many years of cross-cultural work as a missionary priest in Pakistan. "At the heart of it all is entering into the broken parts of people's lives, with great reverence and respect, and helping them move towards healing, unity," Maxwell says.[17]

Besides being exceptionally drawn to the performance of religious rituals and the restorative, culture-keeping work of the clergy, many gays are keenly attracted to the work of "re-membering" in the secular realm. They rescue and rehabilitate degraded buildings and objects. They research and document family and community history. They bring neglected neighborhoods back to life. "It's a priestly role, in the sense of the shamans and the continuers of the culture," says Richard Wagner. "Society needs it, but doesn't always value it." Though deeply held by his Roman Catholic heritage, Wagner found his own priestly vocation outside the church. Since settling in Madison, Wisconsin, in the 1960s, he has been a leader in strengthening that city's social and cultural fabric through historic preservation coupled with city and regional planning. True to type, Wagner owns several houses in one of Madison's oldest neighborhoods, all in the same block and all rehabilitated by him.

However trite they may seem, gay stereotypes are useful in examining gay men's natures. "Artistic," "musical," "nervous," "sensitive," "sophisticated," and "temperamental" have served as euphemisms or code words for gay. They are all based in the reality of gay men's lives.[18] The truth suggested by these stereotypes was apparent to Edward Carpenter, who observed a century ago that because the gay male temperament combines masculine and feminine elements in close and constant interaction, it is "exceedingly sensitive and emotional."[19] The truth is no mystery to Emory, a.k.a. Emily, the antiques-dealing interior decorator in the 1970 movie *The Boys in the Band.* While reminiscing at a gay party about having been in charge of decorations for his high school prom, Emory observes in a melancholy tone, "Mary, it takes a fairy to make something pretty."

The archetypal truth in these stereotypes is evident to cultural commentator Camille Paglia: "Gay men are aliens, cursed and gifted, the shamans of our time." Calling gay male consciousness "stunningly expansive and exquisitely precise" in its "fusion of intellect, emotion, artistic sensibility," Paglia notes the intricate intertwining of male homosexuality and art and suggests that it is the result of gay men's psychic duality, "caught midway between the male and female brains." She says that "the effeminacy of gay men—which emerges as soon as the macho masks drop—is really their artistic sensitivity and rich, vulnerable emotionalism.[20]

The truth in these gay stereotypes became obvious to Andrew Ramer's father, a straight interior designer whose work involved him with many gay men and inspired him to speculate about a gay prehistory. "One day we went to an exhibit of cave paintings, which we both loved," recalls Ramer of an outing with his father. "At one point he turned and asked me who I thought had created them. I said I didn't know. 'It had to be the fags,' he explained. 'All the other men are out hunting and killing. There's a bunch of fags sitting in the back of the cave, complaining about how ugly it is, wondering what they can do to make it look better. So they decide to paint some bison on the walls.'"[21]

Robert Hopcke says it's a pervasive fallacy that only heterosexuals contribute meaningful "creativity, fecundity, and longevity" to human culture. Recognizing the prominence of gay men in all the arts throughout the ages, Hopcke writes that there is "a certain kind of creativity that gay people have that does provide for longevity and progeny and transformation, and always has, throughout Western civilization and probably beyond."[22] Paglia concurs, rescuing gay men's creative aestheticism from its usual dismissal as mere frippery: "There is nothing trivial about fashion," she writes. "Standards of beauty are conceptualizations projected by each culture. They tell us everything."[23]

The arts of theater, dance, music, and poetry have their origins in religion. Especially in preliterate societies, the devising and remembering of artistic rituals made it possible for a society to transmit essential information, such as their history and sense of identity, from one generation to the next. Religious work involves preserving and perpetuating these forms of ritual artistry through time. Thus artistic sensibility, religious inclination, and the preservation impulse are simply different facets of the same lens, a lens through which many gays are predisposed to view the world.

In *The Necessity for Ruins* John Brinckerhoff Jackson gets at the connections between religion, aesthetics, and preservation when he states that the historic preservation movement "sees history not as a continuity but as a dramatic discontinuity, a kind of cosmic drama."

> First there is that golden age, the time of harmonious beginnings. Then ensues a period when the old days are forgotten and the golden age falls into neglect. Finally comes a time when we rediscover and seek to restore the world around us to something like its former beauty.
>
> But there has to be that interval of neglect, there has to be that discontinuity; it is religiously and artistically essential. That is what I mean when I refer to the necessity for ruins: ruins provide the incentive for restoration, and for a return to origins. There has to be . . . an interim of death or rejection before there can be renewal or reform. . . . Many of us know the joy and excitement not so much of creating the new as of redeeming what has been neglected, and this excitement is particularly strong when the original condition is seen as holy or beautiful. The old farmhouse has to decay before we can restore it . . . ; the landscape has to be plundered and stripped before we can restore the natural ecosystem; the neighborhood has to be a slum before we can rediscover it and gentrify it. That is how we reproduce the cosmic scheme and correct history.
>
> Are we perhaps trying to reenact some ancient myth of birth, death, and redemption?[24]

As one small manifestation of the gay propensity to foster continuity and connection in the face of endless discontinuity and demise, consider twelve-year-old Oscar Wilde's romanticism and rich, vulnerable emotionalism following the death of his nine-year-old sister. Wilde was described by the attending doctor as "an affectionate, gentle, retiring, dreamy boy whose lonely and inconsolable grief found solace in long and frequent visits to his sister's grave in the village cemetery and in touching, boyish, poetic effusions." A lock of his sister's hair was among Wilde's few remaining possessions when he died. He preserved it in an envelope that he decorated with their interlocked initials.[25]

It's no great leap from Oscar Wilde's artistically enveloped keepsake to the NAMES Project AIDS Memorial Quilt, a grand gay work of ritual artistry. Throughout the United States and many other countries, thousands of people created three-by-six-foot panels in memory of individuals who had died from AIDS. By 2000 the NAMES Project in San Francisco had assembled a quilt that included about forty-five thousand panels, many of them incorporating clothing, photographs, and other mementos of the lives lost. Whenever any portion of the quilt is displayed, each of the twelve-by-twelve-foot sections comprising eight panels is unfolded and placed on the ground in a solemn and highly choreographed manner; this ritual is reversed at the closing ceremony.[26]

The AIDS Memorial Quilt—its conception, creation, and manner of exhibition—is a singular manifestation of gay male sensibility in response to devastation and death. It's unlikely that such a moving and massive production would have emerged from the plague if AIDS had hit any group other than gay men so hard. Some have criticized the quilt: "Where is the quilt for those who died in Bangladesh?" Camille Paglia asks. "Who will go to Bangladesh and find those names? What privileges the deaths of so many white middle-class gay men?"[27] Paglia's often keen insight into gay men's lives fails her here. Long drawn to roles as stretcher-bearers, medics, chaplains, and morticians in the ritual handling and memorializing of all human injured and dead, gay men found in the quilt a medium in which to respond to the death of their own kind. That this collective response spawned an over-the-top production of exceptional size and richness actually confirms Paglia's generalizations about gay culture. The AIDS Quilt is the inevitable result of gay men's extraordinary sensibilities—romantic, artistic, domestic, connectional—intersecting with their essential drive to preserve and memorialize. These dynamics were amplified by a centuries-long legacy of gay lives being obliterated and a sense of impending doom.

Religion, social work, counseling, nursing: in collaboration with women gay men are prominent practitioners in many enterprises that center on restoring people or things, making them whole or healthy or beautiful again, "re-membering" them. David Nimmons documents these long-unexamined propensities in *The Soul beneath the Skin:* Compared to nongay males, gays are extraordinarily nonviolent, highly inclined to serve as volunteers, and disproportionately numerous not only in artistic and creative fields but also in typically female-associated jobs that call for empathy and personal care giving.[28]

"I see gays as a kind of perpetual Peace Corps," says gay clergyman Malcolm Boyd.[29] It's surely no coincidence that AmeriCorps, the domestic version of the Peace Corps, is headed by a woman and a gay man.[30] Nor is it coincidental that, along with women, gay men have been extraordinarily drawn to serve in the Peace Corps. "From the day the Peace Corps was established, I was very interested in it," says Gary Broulliard. Since the days of his Peace Corps service he and his life partner, Rick McKinniss, have made great contributions to house restoration and neighborhood improvement in Lafayette, Indiana.

The rich overlap of culture keeping and care giving is evident in the elderly gay antiquarian who told me that he was attracted first to the ministry, then to nursing and counseling. It's also apparent in the life of Ralph Navarro, who planned to become a priest but instead became a gay activist and amateur social worker. "I never knew anyone who cared about the underdog more than Ralph did," his mother said. When she visited Navarro, she noted, "he'd be getting calls at one and two in the morning. I told him that I couldn't sleep! But he always answered that phone and helped people with whatever they needed." A man who lived next door to Navarro for twenty years said, "I was blessed with one of the finest neighbors and back-yard-fence chatters you'd ever want to meet. He was a meticulous home-owner who cared about his neighbors and who—despite a round-the-clock schedule—kept his home, yard and garden in better than average condition."[31]

This gay penchant for care giving is nothing new. In the 1920s the anonymous author of *The Invert and His Social Adjustment* observed that among the many men he had known whose lives included significant works of charity, "the incidence of inversion was above the average."[32] The American Red Cross knows that gay men were extraordinarily generous blood donors until the panic surrounding HIV led to their being barred from giving. And it's no mere coincidence that Father Mychal Judge was gay; the New York City fire chaplain was killed while ministering to victims at the World Trade Center on September 11, 2001.

The writer James Norman Hall decided to join the Royal Army Medical Corps as a stretcher-bearer instead of reenlisting as a machine-gunner during World War I: "I would not be with my old C Company comrades," he wrote, "but . . . I would be sure to find a band of brothers among men who had chosen, for war service, the work of salvaging human bodies instead of destroying them."[33] Walt Whitman was drawn to similar work during the Civil War. In Manhattan, Whitman made frequent hospital visits in order to tend to the needs of sick and injured men, many of them stagedrivers. It was in the army hospitals of Washington, D.C., that Whitman fully discovered his calling as "a regular self-appointed missionary to these thousands and tens of thousands of wounded and sick young men . . . many of them languishing, many of them dying."[34]

"I believe," Whitman wrote, "that even the moving around among the men . . . of a hearty, healthy, clean, strong, generous-souled person, man or woman, full of humanity and love, sending out invisible, constant currents thereof, does immense good to the sick and wounded." He devoted himself especially to one hospital that drew the worst cases and the fewest visitors. "Mother, I have real pride in telling you that I have the consciousness of saving quite a number of lives by saving them from giving up," he wrote. "It is impossible for me to abstain from going to see and minister to certain cases, and that draws me into others, and so on."[35]

"A great mothering sort of man, a bearded stranger hovering near," Whitman went on his rounds for more than a year.[36] His hundreds of hospital visits, ranging from several hours to all day or night, brought him into contact with tens of thousands of hospitalized soldiers: "Mother, I see such awful things . . . but it is such a great thing to be able to do some real good; assuage these horrible pains and wounds, and save life even—that's the only thing that keeps a fellow up."[37] In his last years Whitman looked back on his Civil War mission as the most fulfilling of his life and understood it more deeply: "People used to say to me, 'Walt, you are doing miracles for those fellows in the hospitals.' I wasn't. I was, as you would say, doing miracles for myself."[38]

Walt Whitman was one prominent nineteenth-century manifestation of the mothering sort of man. Just after the Civil War, former minister Horatio Alger moved to New York City and dedicated himself to improving the lives of homeless boys. Drawing on those experiences, he wrote scores of inspirational books: out of poverty and adversity Alger's boy-heroes lead exemplary lives and gain honor and wealth. Charles George Gordon, a contemporary of Whitman and Alger, was a military hero of imperial Britain whose maternal urge led him to take street-dwelling children under his wing, bathing and feeding them and mending their clothes.[39] A scene in Michael Lowenthal's novel *The Same Embrace* offers a contemporary snapshot of this gay mothering impulse. In a Boston gay bar Jacob finds himself drawn to a teenager named Danny: "His wan complexion . . . induced a warm, almost maternal feeling. Jacob wanted to cook healthy food for Danny, to buy him vitamins. He wanted to make sure he dressed warmly enough."[40]

William Warrington's care-giving urge found satisfaction in both social rehabilitation and architectural restoration. The mansion he purchased at 1140 Royal Street in the New Orleans French Quarter was notorious as the site of extraordinary abuse and torture of servants in the 1830s. The house was transformed a century later into the Warrington House, the headquarters of an organization dedicated to the assistance of homeless and unfortunate boys and men. "William J. Warrington, founder of the institution, who has devoted his life and a large fortune to this work, personally directs activities," states a French Quarter tourist guidebook of the 1930s. "Visitors are welcome to see the magnificent murals and charming interior."[41]

Collecting old photos has been an outlet for Russell Bush's care-giving impulse. "When I first started collecting old photographs, I felt very much like I was rescuing things that would just be burned or thrown away," Bush says. "This may sound corny, but I felt very passionately that I was collecting these things with a love for these people. That by my recovering them and loving them, these people's lives meant something. I often feel a strong melancholy when I go through a stack of photographs at a flea market, and especially when I go through a photo album. These are representations of people's lives that have been disposed of and forgotten about. To most people they are meaningless. It makes me sad that so many people who have lived are unknown, lost, and forgotten."[42]

David Deitcher reveals that a similar compulsion to rescue lost lives informs his strong emotional attraction to old photographs. "I am drawn to the orphaned picture—to the castoff that lies unnoticed and undignified at the weekend flea market. . . . I identify with the weathered object. In its tears, scuff marks, and dents, I see the signs of age, and more. I see the stigmata of their abandonment and mistreatment as so much discarded junk. To be drawn so empathetically to inanimate objects suggests a form of identification with them; that, and a decidedly morbid relation to the past. . . . I've long considered that gay men hold a special franchise on this dismal sense of beauty."[43]

Distinct roles for gender-atypical males have been documented in societies throughout the world. Prominent elements of these "third-gender" roles include healing, ritual artistry, prophecy, wizardry, and priesthood. A member of the West African Dagara society says that gay males have long filled spiritual roles among his people. It is because they are gay, he says, that they are able to help the tribe "keep its continuity with the gods and with the spirits . . . of this world and spirits of the other world. . . . This kind of function is not one that society votes for certain people to fulfill. It is one that people are said to decide on prior to being born."[44]

James Marston Fitch identifies another culture-keeping role in African tribal cultures in which gay men have surely been prominent: "the village historians—elderly keepers of the oral tradition who are almost certainly the last generation of their species. The knowledge they hold, not only of the remote past but also of the recent past, is priceless." In societies without written records, these men are the keepers of information that is central to their tribal identity: the genealogies of local kings, the boundaries of tribal lands, the appropriate rituals for community celebrations.[45]

Third-gender roles have been documented in many American Indian tribes. Through the last two centuries of tribal demise, these androgynous men have played key roles in the preservation of their cultures. One of these berdaches, Hastíín Klah, was a Navajo medicine man, artist, and traditionalist. He showed an interest in religion at an early age, learning his first ceremony by the age of ten. Though most medicine men mastered only one or two ceremonies in a lifetime, Klah eventually mastered eight, all of them cultural or peace rites rather than ceremonies of war. Klah's aunt taught him much about native plants. He mastered weaving and developed sand-painting weaving, a style that blended the women's domain of weaving and the men's domain of religious sand painting. Klah helped to develop Navajo religion into a more potent vehicle for the identity and unity of his tribe, then worked for its preservation along with other traditional cultural forms and values. As a result of his friendship and collaboration with a wealthy non-Indian woman in the 1920s and 1930s, Klah was able to record his vast knowledge of Navajo myths, prayers, and songs and to establish in Santa Fe the Wheelwright Museum of the American Indian.[46]

A gay Mohave of the same stripe, Elmer Gates told an interviewer in the 1960s that he specialized in traditional crafts and dances: "It seems like I'm the only one that's keeping these traditions alive."[47] Even today there are berdaches among us, though they may prefer the label two-spirit. Like their berdache forebears, two-spirit males play culture-keeping roles in their tribal communities, preserving old knowledge and traditions and working as artists, healers, mediators, and community leaders and organizers. Clyde Hall is a contemporary berdache of the Shoshone tribe. "The last twenty years of my life have been devoted to collecting Indian art," he says. "I have a great love of tradition. People come to me and ask, How do you do this? Or, How should this be made? Or, What kind of song should be sung here? I mean, that's what I'm doing here. These powers and talents are an integral part of a way of being. It's something that Spirit gives you when you're born."[48]

Whether it's the American Indian berdache or any of the many other alternative gender identities or roles for males with a pronounced feminine aspect, one is talking about an intermediate or third gender. Despite the odds against him in Victorian England, Edward Carpenter pioneered in making an earnest case for what he called the intermediate male. He saw this type, of which he himself was one, as dual natured, with dynamic interaction of masculine and feminine elements, highly sensitive and emotional. Because of his double temperament, Carpenter said, the intermediate man is more observant, discerning, and creative. At least partly as a result of their special temperament, intermediates (which he also called Uranians) perform valuable work in the arts, education, and social work. "The best philanthropic work . . . has a strong fibre of the Uranian heart running through it," Carpenter wrote. "No one else can possibly respond to and understand, as they do, all the fluctuations and interactions of the masculine and feminine in human life."[49]

Carpenter recognized himself and his fellow intermediate males as members of a third sex, men with much of the psychologic character of women. He saw these individuals as contemporary manifestations of a type that had always existed in all human societies, and he lamented that since the Christian era this type had been persecuted or only marginally tolerated. Did it occur to no one, he wondered, that as a result of their intermediate nature these men might serve positive and useful functions in their societies? Carpenter saw abundant historical and contemporary evidence of these contributions, most notably in the religious arena: "The connection of homosexuality with priesthood and divination seems to be worldwide and universal."[50]

Carpenter's nineteenth-century vision for his tribe of intermediates found a twentieth-century apostle in gay liberation pioneer Harry Hay. With his characteristic flair Hay proposed "that we Gay Men *of all colors* prepare to present ourselves as the gentle, non-competitive Third Gender men *of the Western World* with whole wardrobes and garages crammed with cultural and spiritual contributions to share."[51] Hay saw third-gender men working at the frontier between the seen and the unseen, the known and the unknown, using exceptional creativity to help the larger culture adapt its traditions to changing conditions. Andrew Ramer answers Hay's call: "The more I become who I am, the less like a man or a woman I feel," he says. "The more we gay men become ourselves, the more we do become different. I think the future of the world . . . depends upon us, that men who love men are the only people who can save the planet. That's our job, our purpose. The world is looking to us even though it doesn't know it."[52]

Andrew Harvey fantasizes an ideal world in which all human beings are assisted in developing their unique, inherent capacities. Like the American Indian berdaches, gay men in this utopia are seen as having been born with a pronounced feminine streak that gives them artistic and spiritual gifts essential to the health of society. In contrast to Western civilization's overwhelming focus on power, control, and conquest, these men's lives emanate "the feminine principle of relationship that connects all things to each other." They are able to assist society in discovering a new ethic of ecological responsibility that is informed by a vision of the planet as a sacred unity.[53]

Males have great inclination and capacity for creating and building new, but females and gay males possess the greater inclination to re-create, rebuild, restore, preserve. This latter impulse seems to emerge from a decidedly feminine ethos that places great value on continuity of identity, maintaining connections, remembering. This aesthetic humanizes old buildings and objects because of their associations: used by one's forebears, they are not simply old things to use or discard. They are human, tangible bonds with the past, shapers of one's identity.

Claude Wheeler, the protagonist in Willa Cather's novel *One of Ours,* exemplifies this continuity-cherishing sensibility. A young, unhappily married American who is in France during World War I, Wheeler wonders what shape his life will take once the war is over. Lying in the woods with his friend David, he dreams of buying a little farm in France and living the rest of his life there. "There was no chance for the kind of life he wanted at home, where people were always buying and selling, building and pulling down," he told himself. "Life was so short that it meant nothing at all unless it were continually reinforced by something that endured; unless the shadows of individual existence came and went against a background that held together."[54]

Eighty years later, American writers David Leavitt and Mark Mitchell looked to Europe for a background that held together. They found it in the Maremma, the poorest province of Tuscany, where they purchased Podere Fiume (River Farm), a long-abandoned farmhouse. "When we were first living in Italy, the prospect of restoring a country house seemed so daunting to us as to be unthinkable," the couple write. "And yet . . . Podere Fiume had a good soul (not to mention good bones); indeed, as we walked through it that first afternoon, the idea that we would bring the house back to life suddenly seemed natural, even inevitable." Life in the Maremma for Leavitt and Mitchell "is rather like being caught between the seventeenth and twenty-first centuries." They choose to live there "because it feels like home," because it's "a place that balances the past and the present."[55]

Gay men in Europe were concerning themselves with continuity even in the eighteenth century. German archaeologist Johann Winckelmann was working among the ruins of ancient Greece, initiating a new Greek Renaissance and fostering the modern appreciation of ancient art. In England the artistic Horace Walpole was creating his Gothic castle, Strawberry Hill, collecting antiquities, and reviving Gothic taste in both literature and architecture. A. L. Rowse describes Walpole as "a good deal of a sprightly and clever old lady," and Rowse ought to know the type.[56]

By the middle of the nineteenth century many more gay men in Europe were drawn to the work of historic preservation, in reaction to the continuity-obliterating and anti-aesthetic effects of industrialization and the growing secularization of Western culture. Gays with an "odour of the clerical" about them were shifting their sights away from the church, beginning to locate their experience of the sacred in art, architecture, and antiquities not necessarily related to religious practice. Increasingly their sacred impulse was manifested as secular artistic impulse. They became priests of aesthetics and cultural preservation.

William Morris figured prominently in this brotherhood. Like many in nineteenth-century England, Morris was repelled by his own urbanizing and industrializing times and was enchanted by an imagined medieval past where everything was more stable, honorable, and beautiful. Believing that religion had failed society but great art could change it, Morris abandoned his plans of entering the priesthood and created a life ministry in which art and socialist politics were closely entwined. In his socialist vision Morris had much in common with his contemporary Edward Carpenter, who called for the freeing of the body from religious and material oppression, returning it to health, wholeness, holiness. William Morris became a leading figure in the Arts and Crafts movement and a social reformer who did so much impassioned public speaking that he ruined his health.[57] But Morris did not turn his back on the church altogether: he loved the ancient church buildings. It was his horrified reaction to the destructive "restoration" of medieval English churches that provoked Morris to help found the Society for the Protection of Ancient Buildings in 1877. For the rest of his life he traveled many miles and wrote many furious letters on behalf of imperiled old buildings, especially churches.[58]

Like Morris and Carpenter, Walter Pater originally intended himself for the priesthood. He focused devoutly and aesthetically on the past. Oscar Wilde was Pater's greatest disciple and has been called an unleashed version of Pater's repressed self. In contrast to the earnest socialist religiosity of Morris and Carpenter, Wilde was a flamboyant, apolitical aesthete who lacked the characteristic clerical odour. But he was nonetheless a high priest of redemption. Wilde became a prominent preacher of the Arts and Crafts doctrine, delivering sermons on "The Decorative Arts" and "The House Beautiful" in England, the United States, and Canada.

Wilde embraced Morris's dictum, "Have nothing in your houses which you do not know to be useful or believe to be beautiful." Antiquities figured prominently in Wilde's own homemaking as they did in Morris's. Both were passionate collectors of blue-and-white china of both English and Oriental make. When Wilde was about twenty, furnishing his rooms at Oxford was one of his chief interests. It may have been after buying two large blue china vases that Wilde remarked, "I find it harder and harder every day to live up to my blue china."[59] In the final months of his life a degraded and destitute Wilde was captivated by Edward Carpenter's recently published tract, *Civilisation, Its Cause and Cure,* reading and rereading it.[60]

From the grimy vantage point of late nineteenth-century industrial England, Carpenter contended that civilization is not a desirable end but a dreadful stage that humans must make every effort to pass through: civilization corrupts our lives by disrupting our bonds with nature, with our true selves, and with our fellow humans. Carpenter longed for the time when civilization has passed away and "the old Nature-religion" has returned, restoring a profound unity to human life. Despite the physical, social, intellectual, and moral diseases of civilization, Carpenter believed that each human soul remembers a precivilization state of being that is more healthy, harmonious, unified. This earnest Uranian's expression of faith in the age-old "tradition of a healing and redeeming power at work in the human breast" spoke powerfully to Oscar Wilde, so hopelessly in need of redemption.[61]

Conclusion

Find out who you are, and then become it.
   —Quentin Crisp

America I'm putting my queer shoulder to the wheel.
   —Allen Ginsberg

"IT IS WOMEN who have preserved and urged on civilization," declared Alice Van Leer Carrick in one of her chatty little books for those enchanted with old-fashioned things.[1] "I'm curious," a straight woman friend inquired when I was beginning my research for this book. "Do you think gay men have a greater interest in historic preservation compared to everyone else, or compared to straight men? I know lots of women who share that interest, but few straight men."

My inquiry brings me to this answer: Gay men make extraordinary contributions in historic preservation, an arena well populated by straight women, because the mix of things that preservation is about strike many of the same psychologic chords in gay males as in straight females. These chords cluster around a number of themes, which I've attempted to identify and name: domophilia, romanticism, aestheticism, and connection- and continuity-mindedness.

Despite the scant record of gay history, there's ample cross-cultural evidence that gay males have long been extraordinary preservers of history, keepers of culture. Way out of proportion to our numbers, gays contribute to creating and perpetuating memory, beauty, meaning, and identity within our communities and larger cultures. This singular passion to preserve does not grow out of income level, childlessness, social oppression, or cultural marginality. It grows out of our two-spiritedness. Gay men are especially drawn to preservation because it involves a cluster of concerns that resonate richly and compellingly with our intermediate natures: creating and keeping attractive and safe dwelling spaces; restoring and preserving wholeness and design integrity; valuing heritage and identity; nurturing community relationships; fostering continuity in the midst of incessant change. This complex mix of sensibilities is present from early in our lives, rooted in our blend of feminine and masculine qualities, our psychologic androgyny. We who begin our lives as boys who are not like other boys grow into men unlike other men.

Camille Paglia's observations on the truth in sexual stereotypes and on the biologic basis of sex differences help to illustrate the matter: "The male genital metaphor is concentration and projection. . . . Male aggression and lust are the energizing factors in culture. . . . Thing-making, thing-preserving is central to male experience. . . . Let us stop being small-minded about men and freely acknowledge what treasures their obsessiveness has poured into culture."[2]

In the androgyny of many gay men, the masculine propensity to leave one's own egoistic mark on the world is tempered and channeled by the feminine disposition to foster continuity and connection with others. The masculine impulse to create and build coexists with and energizes the feminine impulse to re-create, rebuild, restore. This intermediate blend of characteristics contributes to the central role of gay men as keepers of culture and thus ultimately as creators of culture. Not everything can be carried forward; the genius of preservation is its selectivity. Those who are most influential in choosing what gets carried forward are potent shapers of cultural identity.

Some reject these ideas about gay men. In her study of gay-rights battles in Oregon in the 1990s, Arlene Stein interviewed several straight women who "spoke passionately about their feelings for homosexual men. Sometimes this passion extended to a deep sense of identification that defied existing categories." One straight woman told Stein that although she opposes gay rights, she has gay friends and feels drawn to gay men because they are "highly talented," "very artistic," "into art and color," and "more caring." Stein summarizes other assertions about gay men that emerged in the course of the gay-rights battle: "Gays, with their exquisite decorating sense and disposable income, could pretty up any fading neighborhood. 'Want proud homeowners with high incomes? Formerly rundown areas of historical merit have been gentrified by the gay. The tax base is raised, and the redevelopment is free of cost to the taxpayers.' This argument was often embraced by gay people themselves, particularly by men. 'Gays [don't] differ from straights only in the bedroom," said a letter to the editor. "The facts are, gays have differently structured brains and different genders and exhibit vastly different behaviors and abilities than their straight male counterparts.'"[3] Stein, a lesbian, derides these views as stereotype, cardboard characterization, distortion, products of misunderstanding and ignorance. But a lifetime of pondering similar phenomena led the gay writer Edmund White to respond quite differently: "Could it be that all those horrible pundits have been right, and homosexuals are indeed the 'third sex'?"[4]

For many gay men trying to find their place in American culture, the third-sex concept is the third rail, perilous and diligently avoided. It opposes

the social-constructionist, assimilation-minded voices that currently dominate mainstream gay culture in this country: those who insist, despite great heaps of living evidence to the contrary, that there are no essential differences between gay males and straight males. Yet there are many cracks in this fragile facade. "I know I have feminine qualities," a straight-acting gay man told me. "I used to try to hide them, but now I consider them assets; they make my life fuller. But one wants to belong, so you put on these false fronts, and they become part of you after a while. Now we have gay men embracing this strange leather/bear culture, yet they're all cuddly little homemakers listening to opera on Saturday afternoons."

Those cracks in the facade can be wonderfully revealing. An architectural historian began his interview with the candid observation, "I was the daughter my mother always wanted." He soon backtracked, insisting that he had been "too quick to run off at the mouth." In reflecting on all the preservation-minded gay men he had met and worked with throughout the country, another architectural historian referred to them, frankly and without a trace of camp, as "sisters." That word did not survive his review of a draft; it came back "brothers." In describing his contemplated purchase and restoration of a two-hundred-year-old house in remarkably good condition, another preservation professional remarked baldly and camplessly, "The house had been lightly ridden by the rich ladies who had owned it—and I consider myself something of a rich lady." He chose to delete that final phrase, even though he would not be identified by his real name in this book.

Typical of the accepted wisdom, Daniel Harris says that apart from their sexual partners and practices, gay men are not essentially different from straight men. He states that whatever we may consider to be gay sensibility is simply a result of oppression by the larger culture: Whatever may seem to be distinctive in gay men grows not out of their basic nature but out of having to contend with cultural hostility. Without heterosexism and homophobia to shape their psyches and personalities, Harris believes, gays would be no different from straights.[5] Daniel Mendelsohn agrees: Whatever is distinctive about gays is simply a result of oppression; unoppressed, gays are just like everybody else.[6]

These views represent a theory of sex and gender expression that is pervasive, especially among academics: All gender expression is merely the manifestation of socially defined and constructed roles; nothing about it originates within the individual human creature. Academic iconoclast Camille Paglia offers a bracing remedy for this academic affliction. Her "first proposal to the gay world: Get rid of dead abstract 'theory' and rabid social constructionism, the limp legacy of academic know-nothings."[7] As a corrective to the absurdities of women's studies, she prescribes a regimen of "close observation of ordinary life outside the university."[8] Gay studies benefit from similar reform.

My own findings do not support the idea that gay men are exceptionally creative and artistic because of their reaction to being stigmatized, marginalized, oppressed. It would seem that anyone who embraces this idea has not bothered to take a close, careful look at gay lives, beginning in childhood. Based on observing, inquiring, and listening, not on disembodied theorizing, I conclude that gay sensibility is an essential facet of human nature. Social forces shape the manifestations of gay sensibility, but those forces are not the wellspring.

This inquiry into gay men's natures is really about gender orientation, not about sexual orientation per se. Gayness comprises much more than sexual partners and practices. Many gay men cannot or will not embrace these feminine aspects of themselves. Even the groundbreaking gay historian John Boswell considered the idea that gay men are less masculine to be "almost certainly the result of antipathy to homosexuality rather than empirical observation."[9] That a scholar of Boswell's stature could be so imperceptive in this regard suggests the pervasive and powerful influence of effeminiphobia.[10]

The development of the gay rights movement in this country has been dominated by effeminiphobic values. Gay men in the 1970s and 1980s affected a hyperbutch look (denim, leather, flannel, facial hair, stiff wrists) and began to proffer themselves as thoroughly regular guys.[11] "A macho clone look took over the men's bars, and queens were scorned as an embarrassing reminder of a time when gayness meant effeminacy," says Paglia.[12] "Modern gay culture is actually built upon the disavowal of sissyness," writes Tim Bergling in *Sissyphobia*. But effeminacy, says Bergling, is "so totally linked with male same-sex orientation that to deny its obvious implications is to sacrifice common sense on the altar of political correctness."[13] It's a perverse brand of political correctness that claims to celebrate diversity while blinding itself to the authentic variety of humankind.

"The only way we'll have real pride is when we demand recognition of a culture that isn't just sexual," Larry Kramer says of gay men's lives. "It's all there—all through history we've been there; but we have to claim it, and identify who was in it, and articulate what's in our minds and hearts and all our creative contributions to this earth."[14] In this he echoes Harry Hay, who said that "we homosexuals know much about ourselves that we've never talked about, even to ourselves."[15] My many interviews with gay men during the past decade confirm the truth of Hay's observation. Despite all that gays have achieved socially and politically, our self-understanding and appreciation are stunted by effeminiphobia. Just as "obvious effeminates" were often barred from participating in gay rights conferences and demonstrations in the early 1960s, gay men of effeminate appearance are still viewed with disdain by many gays. And few gays seem capable of acknowledging their feminine side with much more than nervous one-liners.[16]

In writing *Farm Boys* I began to see that the gender-atypical aspects of gay men's lives are pervasive and amount to something more than empty stereotypes—indeed, that those stereotypes contain deep truths. In creating this book I've come to appreciate the truth in that now-hackneyed line spoken by a gay antiques-dealing interior decorator: "Mary, it takes a fairy to make something pretty." And I've begun to see that I and many of my fellow gays, whether or not we realize or accept it, have much in common with transgender individuals: a gender identity not traditionally associated with our biological sex.[17]

With help from a psychotherapist, gay countertenor opera star David Daniels finally quit trying to be a tenor and embraced his extraordinarily high vocal range. Daniels says he realized that in struggling to sing tenor he was pretending to be something he was not, forcing himself to find musical expression in a range that was not right for him. Now, enjoying great success while creating a gender-blurring revolution in classical opera, Daniels is able to say: "This is my voice. I own this voice. It's part of me and it's my natural voice."[18]

That same spirit informs this book. A gay man himself, A. L. Rowse says that his *Homosexuals in History* "has done nothing if it has not given evidence that we [gays] owe our qualities to our deficiencies, our gifts to our difference."[19] This work confirms that sentiment: it acknowledges the singular gifts of gay men, the invaluable contributions that we are able to make to the larger culture *because* we are gay: not despite being gay, not from struggling through oppression, but mainly as a result of being uncommonly constituted in both gender identity and sexuality.

"For too long, we have lied about our best selves," David Nimmons says of gay men. "We have been helped . . . to disregard the ways our lives differ. It is time we beheld ourselves, and witnessed what we are up to."[20] A recent visit to Georgia gave me the chance to behold a male couple whose business card describes their quintessentially gay cottage industry: "Custom Picture Framing · Interiors · Antiques · Collectibles · Antique Prints · Mirror Resilvering · Specializing in Stained Glass · Furniture Refinishing · Picture Frame Restoration · Furniture Restoration · Exotic Poultry." As I pondered that ambitious amalgam, it dawned on me that my preservation research had suggested an answer to a lingering question: Why had so many of the gay men I interviewed for *Farm Boys* been attracted as children to raising exotic poultry? Suddenly I understood that phenomenon as a rural outlet for those

boys' budding aestheticism. It's not such a great distance from being be-
dazzled by the stately bearing of an elegant, colorfully feathered chicken to
being enraptured by an exquisite piece of old furniture, or a graceful building of distinctive style and ornamentation. And so my inquiry into gay men's
sensibilities had managed to come full circle, ending where it began, down
on the farm.

Acknowledgments

I AM GRATEFUL to every gay man who collaborated by telling me about his own culture-keeping proclivities. Though I've been unable to include them all in this book, each has contributed to the depth and richness of the composite portrait and thus to a larger understanding of the phenomenon.

The individuals who have my special thanks include:

Larry Reed, for friendship and preservation mentoring, for unflagging interest in my work, and for granting me free access to the village history archive of Cooksville, Wisconsin.

Darden Pyron, for invaluable encouragement and guidance in sculpting a coherent book from a hulking manuscript.

Raphael Kadushin, for believing in this project from the beginning and helping me bring it forth in this form.

Dee Michel, for illuminating conversations, clippings, notes, and references.

Gerry Takano, Cranford Sutton, Finbar Maxwell, John Loughery, Charlie Fuchs, Steve Dunham, and John Anders, for enthusiastic interest and supportive communications throughout this project.

Mark Doty, for allowing the use of portions of his memoirs, *Heaven's Coast* and *Still Life with Oysters and Lemon.*

Lloyd Sensat and Roberts Batson, for help in exploring the gay preservationist lineage in New Orleans; Allan Deptula, for information on the life of Pittsburgh's James Van Trump; the staff of the Mineral Point (Wis.) Public Library, for help with the papers of Robert Neal.

Bronze Quinton, for accommodating with seemingly untiring interest and good humor yet another sprawling book project in the midst of our life together.

I dedicate this work to the memory of my grandmothers and to the memory of Michael Saternus, whose extraordinary passion for historic preservation I was fortunate to witness firsthand.

Notes

Preface

1. John M. Clum, *Something for the Boys: Musical Theater and Gay Culture* (New York: Palgrave, 1999), 19.
2. Harry Hay, *Radically Gay: Gay Liberation in the Words of Its Founder,* ed. Will Roscoe (Boston: Beacon, 1996), 53.
3. For the phrase "keepers of culture" I credit Clyde Hall, a gay American Indian who uses those words to describe the role that he and other males like him have always played in the life of his tribe. Mark Thompson, *Gay Soul: Finding the Heart of Gay Spirit and Nature* (New York: HarperCollins, 1995), 125.

Charlotte and Me

1. Heidrun Petrides, *Hans and Peter* (New York: Harcourt, Brace & World, 1962).
2. Jürgen Lemke, *Gay Voices from East Germany* (Bloomington: Indiana University Press, 1991), 72.
3. Charlotte von Mahlsdorf, *I Am My Own Woman: The Outlaw Life of Charlotte von Mahlsdorf, Berlin's Most Distinguished Transvestite* (Pittsburgh: Cleis Press, 1995), 22.
4. Von Mahlsdorf, 23; Lemke, 69.
5. Von Mahlsdorf, 22.
6. Ibid., 59.
7. Ibid., 116.
8. Lemke, 77.
9. Von Mahlsdorf, 124–25.
10. Ibid., 23, 142, 148.

In Search of Gay Preservationists

1. My thanks to Mike, a gay man with whom I spoke in the garden of a gay-operated, antiques-furnished B and B in Missoula, Montana, for telling me about the Noël Coward version of "Let's Do It" and sending me a recording of it. A Montana native in his late forties living in San Francisco, Mike told me with good-natured perplexity that his new boyfriend is a nice guy but, like so many other gay men he's met, "an antiques queen." Mike wondered if I could enlighten him as to why this was so.
2. "Surely gay culture is more than cocks," writes Larry Kramer. "Who are we? What does it mean to be gay? What is the gay sensibility?" ("Sex and Sensibility," *The Advocate,* May 27, 1997, 59, 64–65, 67–69). Rictor Norton's *The Myth of the Modern Homosexual* (London: Cassell, 1997) has been greatly illuminating. "Queer historians need to widen the definition of 'homosexuality' so as to encompass queer culture rather than just queer sex and the laws against it," Norton writes, "and then to engage in the task of verifying the

authentic features of queer culture. . . . Queer history is essentially the history of queer culture. It is not the history of specific sexual acts, nor should it be a history of social attitudes towards homosexuality. Queer history is still too much a part of the 'history of sexuality' and needs to be resituated within the history of non-sexual culture and ethnic customs. Similarly, although it is important to recognize the (often hostile) environment in which queers fashion their culture, a history of heterosexual prejudice is not *central* to a history of homosexuality" (132). "The proper business of queer history should be to emphasize the generally unrecognized features that are integral to the subculture itself and not a result of oppression" (241).

3. Edward Carpenter, *Selected Writings,* vol. 1: *Sex* (London: GMP Publishers, 1984), 278.

4. The linkage of male homosexuality and femininity is supported by more than anecdotal evidence. In *The Man Who Would Be Queen: The Science of Gender-Bending and Transsexualism* (Washington, D.C.: Joseph Henry, 2003) psychologist J. Michael Bailey states that "the link between childhood gender nonconformity and adult homosexuality is one of the largest and best established associations regarding sexual orientation" (59). Based on a review of more than thirty studies in which gay and straight men completed questionnaires, Bailey estimates that the typical gay man is more feminine than about 90 percent of straight men (62). Gay men comprise a mixture of male-typical and female-typical characteristics, Bailey says, and "this mixture explains much of what is unique in gay men's culture and lives" (60).

5. Norton's *The Myth of the Modern Homosexual* is helpful here: "What I want to suggest is that the queer historian should not despair when confronted by the charge that we really do not have the 'genital evidence' to prove incontrovertibly that someone was queer, for we often have *abundant evidence of* suppression *which in itself is sufficient confirmation of the likelihood of a queer interpretation.* Queer historians should never apologize for basing queer history on context rather than text, on ethnic culture rather than sexual behaviour, on 'queer' paradigms rather than 'homosexual' ones" (178–79).

6. Elaine Freed, *Preserving the Great Plains and Rocky Mountains* (Albuquerque: University of New Mexico Press, 1992), 353.

7. Reprinted in Diane Maddex, ed. *All about Old Buildings: The Whole Preservation Catalog* (Washington, D.C.: Preservation Press, 1985), 229.

8. "Wearing a little finger ring, especially on the left hand, is a common way of indicating Gayness to other members of the secret or semisecret Gay underground in America" (Judy Grahn, *Another Mother Tongue: Gay Words, Gay Worlds* [Boston: Beacon, 1990], 14).

9. Charles B. Hosmer Jr., *Preservation Comes of Age: From Williamsburg to the National Trust, 1926–1949* (Charlottesville: University Press of Virginia, 1981), 878.

10. Ibid., 34–36, 902.

11. Samuel Gaillard Stoney, *This Is Charleston: A Survey of the Architectural*

Heritage of a Unique American City (Charleston: Carolina Art Association, 1976), vii.

12. James M. Lindgren, *Preserving Historic New England: Preservation, Progressivism, and the Remaking of Memory* (New York: Oxford University Press, 1995), 131.

13. Personal communication, April 1999, with a gay employee of the National Park Service who requested anonymity.

14. Marc Stein, *City of Sisterly and Brotherly Love: Lesbian and Gay Philadelphia, 1945–1972* (Chicago: University of Chicago Press, 2000), 25–27.

15. Herbert Muschamp, "Self-Portrait with Rivals," in *Loss within Loss: Artists in the Age of AIDS*, ed. Edmund White (Madison: University of Wisconsin Press, 2001), 73.

16. Elizabeth Stillinger, *The Antiquers* (New York: Knopf, 1980), jacket text.

17. John Loughery, *The Other Side of Silence: Men's Lives and Gay Identities: A Twentieth-Century History* (New York: Henry Holt, 1998), 29.

18. Werner Muensterberger, *Collecting: An Unruly Passion: Psychological Perspectives* (New York: Harcourt Brace, 1994).

What These Gay Men's Lives Reveal

1. Glenway Wescott, *The Grandmothers* (New York: Harper & Brothers, 1927).

2. In response to the cliché about "little old ladies in tennis shoes" being the pioneers in preservation, founding "hysterical" societies in their communities, I've heard remarks from gay men suggesting that it's really "little old ladies in tennis shoes and gay men in 501s," or "little old ladies of both sexes."

3. Robert H. Hopcke and Laura Rafaty, *A Couple of Friends: The Remarkable Friendship between Straight Women and Gay Men* (Berkeley: Wildcat Canyon Press, 1999), 38, 254.

4. This individual requested anonymity.

5. Yi-Fu Tuan, *Topophilia: A Study of Environmental Perception, Attitudes, and Values* (Englewood Cliffs, N.J.: Prentice-Hall, 1974), 53–54.

6. Personally I have to acknowledge my love of space-enclosing objects much smaller than houses: boxes, mugs, tankards, teapots, bowls, but especially boxes, beginning with a black lacquered Victorian jewelry box with floral decoration and purple fabric interior, which I bought at an auction as a child. It captivated me with its dark, rich beauty and unknowable associations. My great-grandmother gave me a small wooden trinket box. At auctions and antique shops I acquired a small pine chest, a maple treenware thread holder, snuffboxes of pewter and wood. A gay couple I got to know in England one summer gave me an oval lidded box of bone china decorated with flowers and the words "Absent Friends, Not Forgotten." Perhaps no one else noticed my thing for boxes (not even I, at the time), but Aunt Mary did. One Christmas, tucked inside a small handcrafted wooden box, was her note to me: "This elephant never forgets that you liked boxes fifteen years ago, so now you're fated to receive them on a regular basis."

In the film *Ma Vie en Rose,* Ludovic, an unabashedly effeminate and cross-dressing six-year-old, is enchanted by his grandmother's gaily painted jewelry box, from which music and a dancing figure emerge when the lid is opened. Toward the end of the movie Ludovic's grandmother gives the box to him. There is great meaning in all of this: the special bond between gay boy and grandmother; the allure of her jewelry box, a beautiful enclosure for lovely things; and the particular appeal of the box because of its animated, musical qualities and its association with grandmother.

What sort of enclosed space could be more compelling than a beautiful box? A beautiful box that gives off music, life. There seem to be so many gays with strong attractions to old music boxes, phonographs, and automatic musical instruments—even to old, stylish radios and televisions, a collecting passion of gay Hollywood preservationist Kent Warner: "Old televisions were high Deco to Kent," says a friend. "Here was a box with so much going on inside" (Rhys Thomas, *The Ruby Slippers of Oz* [Los Angeles: Tale Weaver, 1989], 94).

7. Willa Cather, *Shadows on the Rock* (New York: Knopf, 1931), 197–98.
8. Neil Miller, *In Search of Gay America: Women and Men in a Time of Change* (New York: Atlantic Monthly Press, 1989), 58.
9. Richard McCann, "My Mother's Clothes: The School of Beauty and Shame," in *Mama's Boy: Gay Men Write about Their Mothers,* ed. Dean Kostos and Eugene Grygo (New York: Painted Leaf Press, 2000), 148–49.
10. August Derleth, *Atmosphere of Houses* (Muscatine, Iowa: Prairie Press, 1939), 9, 22, 43. By the age of twenty Derleth was planning the ambitious life work he had begun to envision in his writerly youth: dozens of volumes—historical and biographical novels, short stories, and poetry—that would explore the life of his native Wisconsin community and region. The saga would span more than a hundred years, from first settlement to the present. The creation of each of those volumes, from the 1930s through the 1960s, helped to satisfy Derleth's great need for a feeling of connection to place and to forebears, a sense of identity and continuity.
11. Dorothy Williams Kingery, *More than Mercer House: Savannah's Jim Williams and His Southern Houses* (Self-published, 1999), 99.
12. John Philip Habib, "Time Travelers," *The Advocate,* Dec. 4, 2001, 66–67.
13. Allen Freeman, "A Burnt Offering," *Preservation,* Mar./Apr. 2001, 50–55.
14. Clarence John Laughlin, *Ghosts along the Mississippi: An Essay in the Poetic Interpretation of Louisiana's Plantation Architecture* (New York: Charles Scribner's Sons, 1948).
15. Eddie Shapiro, "Death Becomes Him," *Out,* Oct. 2001, 36, 39.
16. Camille Paglia, *Vamps and Tramps* (New York: Random House, 1994), 22.
17. Michael Holleran, *Boston's Changeful Times: Origins of Preservation and Planning in America* (Baltimore: Johns Hopkins University Press, 1998), 264.
18. Randolph Delahanty and E. Andrew McKinney, *Preserving the West* (New York: Pantheon, 1985), 5.

19. Darden Asbury Pyron, *Liberace: An American Boy* (Chicago: University of Chicago Press, 2000), 320.
20. Liberace, *The Things I Love*, ed. Tony Palmer (New York: Grosset & Dunlap, 1976), 17.
21. Nicols Fox, *Against the Machine: The Hidden Luddite Tradition in Literature, Art, and Individual Lives* (Washington, D.C.: Island Press, 2002), 265.
22. John Loughery says that in the course of doing research for *The Other Side of Silence*, he was struck by gay men's meticulously kept scrapbooks and photo albums: "It did seem to me, in meeting older gay men for my own study, that the number who kept albums or scrapbooks . . . was greater than that of the straight people I know" (personal communication, letter, October 1998).
23. Kingery, *More than Mercer House*, 13, 179.
24. Women authored twelve of the thirteen ghost stories about old-house living published in *Old-House Journal* (Sept./Oct. 2002, 65–71). This suggests that females are more disposed than males to feel a spiritual connection with an old house's previous occupants.
25. Kingery, *More than Mercer House*, 43.

Saving Old New England

1. Elizabeth Stillinger, *The Antiquers*, 18.
2. Henry David Thoreau, *Walden* (Boston: Beacon Press, 1997), 78.
3. Henry David Thoreau in *Autumn,* quoted in Frances Clary Morse, *Furniture of the Olden Time* (New York: Macmillan, 1917), title page.
4. Henry David Thoreau, "Walking," in Carl Bode, ed., *The Portable Thoreau* (New York: Viking, 1957), 609.
5. Stillinger, *Antiquers*, 22–26.
6. Paul Hollister, *Beauport at Gloucester: The Most Fascinating House in America* (New York: Hastings House, 1951), 2.
7. A. L. Rowse, *Homosexuals in History* (New York: Carroll & Graf, 1977), 82.
8. Stillinger, *Antiquers*, 61, 66.
9. A fellow Walpole Society member advised Appleton in 1913 that the Colonial Dames were in the lead in working on old houses in Connecticut. Though he was sometimes at odds with women's often romantic and sentimental ideas about how to treat an old house, Appleton worked closely with many female preservationists, including two women who staffed the SPNEA office for many years.
10. James M. Lindgren, *Preserving Historic New England* (New York: Oxford University Press, 1995), 184.
11. Ralph Adams Cram, *Convictions and Controversies* (Boston: Marshall Jones, 1935), 9.
12. Ralph Adams Cram, *The Ministry of Art* (Boston and New York: Houghton Mifflin Company, 1914; Freeport, N.Y.: Books for Libraries Press, 1967), 240. Citations are to the Books for Libraries edition.
13. Cram, *Convictions and Controversies*, 12–13.

14. Henry Wiencek, *Old Houses* (New York: Stewart, Tabori & Chang, 1991), 47.
15. Ibid., 55.
16. Mark Doty, *Heaven's Coast* (New York: HarperCollins, 1997), 71–74, 77; Doty, *Still Life with Oysters and Lemon* (Boston: Beacon, 2001), 29–35.
17. *Old-House Journal,* Nov./Dec. 1998, 28.

Design-Minded in the Mid-Atlantic States

1. James D. Van Trump and Arthur P. Ziegler Jr., *Landmark Architecture of Allegheny County, Pennsylvania* (Pittsburgh: Pittsburgh History and Landmarks Foundation, 1967), 6.
2. Gail Balph, "August Interview: James Van Trump," *The Pittsburgher,* Aug. 1977, 6–9, 76–79.
3. James Nocito, *Found Lives: A Collection of Found Photographs* (Layton, Utah: Gibbs Smith, 1998), viii.

To the Rescue in the Atlantic South

1. Dorothy Williams Kingery, *More than Mercer House,* 34–36.
2. Ibid., 12.
3. John Berendt, *Midnight in the Garden of Good and Evil* (New York: Random House, 1994), 5.
4. Kingery, *More than Mercer House,* 54.
5. Ibid., 179.
6. Ibid., 43.
7. Berendt, *Midnight in the Garden of Good and Evil,* 5.
8. Quoted in Kingery, *More than Mercer House,* 13.
9. Ibid., 20.
10. Jerry Herman, *Showtune: A Memoir by Jerry Herman,* with Marilyn Stasio (New York: Donald I. Fine, 1996), 250.
11. Ibid., 251, 204.
12. *Preservation News* has been published in *Preservation* magazine (July/August 1997), in *Best American Gay Fiction 3* (Boston: Little, Brown, 1998), and in *The Practical Heart: Four Novellas* (New York: Knopf, 2001).
13. Willa Cather, *Willa Cather in Europe: Her Own Story of the First Journey* (New York: Knopf, 1956), 15, 19.

Domophiles Out West

1. A. L. Rowse, "Tracing Willa Cather's Nebraska," *New York Times,* April 21, 1985, travel section, 9.

California Conservative

1. Roy Little and Jim Raidl's Hartford Street house was featured in Elizabeth Pomada and Michael Larsen's *The Painted Ladies Revisited: San Francisco's Resplendent Victorians Inside and Out* (New York: E. P. Dutton, 1989).
2. Randolph Delehanty, *San Francisco: The Ultimate Guide* (San Francisco: Chronicle Books, 1995), 339.

3. Pomada and Larsen, *Painted Ladies: San Francisco's Resplendent Victorians* (New York: E. P. Dutton, 1978), 4, and *Painted Ladies Revisited*, 4, 9.
4. John Loughery, *The Other Side of Silence*, 391.
5. Pomada and Larsen, *Painted Ladies*, 9.
6. Ibid., 14–15.
7. Liberace, *The Things I Love*, 11, 181.
8. Ibid., 17.
9. Darden Asbury Pyron, *Liberace: An American Boy*, 256.
10. Ibid., 320–21.
11. Liberace, *Things I Love*, 175.
12. Pyron, *Liberace*, 37.
13. Rhys Thomas, *The Ruby Slippers of Oz*, 218.
14. Ibid., 95.
15. Ibid., 157.

Generations of Gentlemen Keep Cooksville, Wisconsin

1. Adelaide Evans Harris, "The Man in The House Next Door," *House Beautiful*, Jan. 1923, 70.
2. Eleanor Mercein, "Adventurous Cookery," *Ladies' Home Journal*, Mar. 1933, 13.
3. Richard Brayton, "Antique Collector in 'House Next Door' Dislikes Modernism," *Wisconsin State Journal*, Aug. 8, 1926, 6.
4. Harris, "The Man in The House Next Door," 38.
5. May I. Bauchle, "The Land of Long Ago," *The Wisconsin Magazine*, Sept. 1925, 6.
6. "Sleepy and Picturesque Cooksville Scorns Gasoline Pumps, Highways," *Milwaukee Journal*, May 26, 1940.
7. Mercein, "Adventurous Cookery," 13.
8. Handwritten letter, dated March 10, 1933. Cooksville, Wisconsin, village history archive.
9. Handwritten rough draft of letter, undated. Cooksville, Wisconsin, village history archive.
10. Ibid.
11. From "A Message from the House Next Door," a brochure distributed in 1940 by friends of Ralph Warner as part of an effort to raise funds to help preserve the House Next Door in the face of Warner's debility. Cooksville, Wisconsin, village history archive.
12. Clifford L. Lord to E. M. Raney, December 15, 1952. Cooksville, Wisconsin, village history archive.
13. Joan Judd, "He Built His Home from Nothing," *Wisconsin State Journal*, Oct.13, 1974, sec. 4, p. 1.
14. John Newhouse, "In Cooksville Shop, It's Christmas in October," *Wisconsin State Journal*, Oct. 18, 1953, sec. 2, p. 1.
15. Cooksville house gift card. Cooksville, Wisconsin, village history archive.
16. James Rhem, "Who Cares about Cooksville?" *Wisconsin Trails*, Sept./Oct. 1986, 21–25.

Singular Preservationists in the Midwest

1. Joy Krause, "In a Labor of Love, Renovation More than Scratches the Surface," *Milwaukee Journal Sentinel,* June 3, 2001, 10N.
2. Robert M. Neal, "Pendarvis, Trelawny, and Polperro: Shake Rag's Cornish Houses," *Wisconsin Magazine of History,* June 1946, 391–401.
3. Robert M. Neal to William P. Gundry, Sept. 8, 1933. Letter in Robert M. Neal Papers, Mineral Point Room, Mineral Point (Wisconsin) Public Library.
4. Edgar Hellum, conversation with author, Mineral Point, Wisconsin, Dec. 17, 1997. Unless they are cited otherwise, subsequent quotations of Edgar Hellum are from this interview.
5. Mark H. Knipping and Korinne K. Oberle, *On the Shake Rag: Mineral Point's Pendarvis House, 1935–1970* (Madison: State Historical Society of Wisconsin, 1990), 43.
6. Jim Jewell, "Pendarvis Founder Bob Neal Remembered," *Dodgeville Chronicle,* July 28, 1983, sec. 1, p. 2.
7. Betty Cass, "Madison Day by Day," *Wisconsin State Journal,* Sept. 10, 1935.
8. *Fennimore (Wis.) Times,* Dec. 18, 1935, 12.
9. Transcript of 1982 interview with Robert Neal by "William Scheick of Hist. Soc." Robert M. Neal papers, Mineral Point Room, Mineral Point (Wisconsin) Public Library.
10. "Shake Rag Street Becoming Famous in State," *Iowa County Democrat,* Sept. 24, 1936.
11. "Mineral Point: Is Its Future in the Past?" *Mineral Point Democrat Tribune,* Feb. 11, 1971, 6.
12. Ibid.
13. "Cornish 'ollow Restoration and Development Now Consists of Three Houses," *Iowa County Democrat,* June 29, 1939.
14. Knipping and Oberle, *On the Shake Rag,* 48.
15. "Pendarvis, The Cornish Restoration," a single typed page by Robert Neal, Jan. 13, 1959. Robert M. Neal Papers, Mineral Point Room, Mineral Point (Wisconsin) Public Library.
16. Neal interview.
17. Richard Cahan, *They All Fall Down: Richard Nickel's Struggle to Save America's Architecture* (Washington, DC: Preservation Press, 1994), 13.
18. Ibid., 142.
19. Ibid., 174, 135.
20. Ibid., 212.
21. Ibid., 232.

Cherishing Old New Orleans and Louisiana

1. Randolph Delahanty, *New Orleans: Elegance and Decadence* (San Francisco: Chronicle, 1993), 62.
2. Abbye A. Gorin, ed., *Conversations with Samuel Wilson, Jr., Dean of Architectural Preservation in New Orleans* (New Orleans: Louisiana Landmarks Society, 1991), 3.

3. Charles B. Hosmer Jr., *Preservation Comes of Age*, 290.

4. *New Orleans States*, Nov. 1, 1926, 1.

5. Julie H. McCollam, "Adventures in Architecture: The Historic American Buildings Survey in Louisiana," *Louisiana Cultural Vistas*, winter 2001–2, 26–39.

6. Arnold Genthe, *Impressions of Old New Orleans* (New York: Doran, 1926), 28.

7. Chance Harvey, *The Life and Selected Letters of Lyle Saxon* (Gretna, La.: Pelican, 2003), 243.

8. Lyle Saxon, *Fabulous New Orleans* (New Orleans: Crager, 1952), xii–xiii.

9. Harvey, *Life and Selected Letters of Lyle Saxon*, 121.

10. Lyle Saxon, *The Friends of Joe Gilmore* (New York: Hastings House, 1948), 4–5.

11. Harvey, *Life and Selected Letters of Lyle Saxon*, 259.

12. In 1937 Thomas Wolfe captured Lyle Saxon's character concisely after meeting him during a visit to New Orleans. In his pocket notebook Wolfe wrote Saxon's name and noted, "An old lady—not a phony" (Harvey, *Life and Selected Letters of Lyle Saxon*, 182).

13. Saxon, *Friends of Joe Gilmore*, 41.

14. Ibid., 43.

15. Harnett Kane, *Plantation Parade: The Grand Manner in Louisiana* (New York: Morrow, 1945), 256.

16. Ibid., 257–58.

17. Morris Raphael, *Weeks Hall: The Master of the Shadows* (New Iberia: Raphael, 1981), 58, 149.

18. Kane, *Plantation Parade*, 264.

19. Pope, "The Romantic Fantasies of Boyd Cruise," *New Orleans States-Item*, Dec. 30, 1978, Lagniappe section, 1.

20. Gorin, *Conversations with Samuel Wilson, Jr.*, 10.

21. McCollam, "Adventures in Architecture," 32.

22. Ibid.

23. Pope, "Romantic Fantasies of Boyd Cruise," 3.

24. Mary Louise Christovich, *Boyd Cruise* (New Orleans: Kemper and Leila Williams Foundation, 1976), 13.

25. Pope, "Romantic Fantasies of Boyd Cruise," 1.

26. Anomaly [pseud.], *The Invert and His Social Adjustment* (London: Ballière, Tindall & Cox, 1948), 176.

27. Jason Berry, "Who Will Tend Our Graves?" *Preservation*, Nov./Dec. 1997, 69–73. Also Dallas Drake, phone conversation, Sept. 26, 1998.

28. Robert Florence, *New Orleans Cemeteries: Life in the Cities of the Dead* (New Orleans: Batture Press, 1997), 198.

Toward a Larger View of Gay Men

1. C. G. Jung, "Psychological Aspects of the Mother Complex," in *The Archetypes and the Collective Unconscious*, vol. 9, pt. 1 of *Collected Works* (Princeton: Princeton University Press, 1968), 86–87, par. 164.

2. Havelock Ellis, *Studies in the Psychology of Sex* (New York: Random House, 1942), 1:27–28, 35.

3. Many of the men who collaborated with William Sumner Appleton in founding the Society for the Preservation of New England Antiquities were ministers or had ministerial schooling. Wallace Nutting became a minister, then dedicated himself full-time to antiquarianism after suffering a nervous breakdown. It was an Episcopal minister, William Goodwin, who instigated America's preeminent restoration project in Williamsburg, Virginia, in the 1920s.

4. John Boswell, *Christianity, Social Tolerance, and Homosexuality* (Chicago: University of Chicago Press, 1980), 187.

5. Rictor Norton, *The Myth of the Modern Homosexual*, 278. Norton also reports that "in Venice, in 1488, the porch of Santa Maria Mater Domini was sealed off by the authorities to stop it from being used by sodomites as a gathering place" (250).

6. Thomas Cahill, *How the Irish Saved Civilization* (New York: Doubleday, 1995). There are queer fingerprints all over the preservation endeavor that is at the heart of this story: After the Roman Empire disintegrated, the survival of Greek and Latin literature was unlikely. Ireland's monasteries took up the work of gathering in, caring for, and copying as much of it as they could get their hands on. This work was done, Cahill says, by strange men who lived in little beehive huts on rocky outcrops, dined on seabirds, grew food in seaweed-fertilized gardens, shaved half their heads, and tortured themselves with fasts and chills and nettle baths. Cahill says that these scribal scholars, though occasionally waspish, were generally delighted by the work they were fated to do. In beautiful handwriting one fastidious scribe comments snippily at the margin of a page done by a careless fellow scribe, "It is easy to spot Gabrial's work here." A more warm-hearted scribe jots a lyric in the margin of a manuscript: "He is a heart, an acorn from the oakwood: He is young. Kiss him!" (161).

   The great Continental libraries were gone and largely forgotten. But the Irish monks did not stop at rescuing and diligently copying the Bible and the literatures of Greece and Rome. An impulse to restore followed their earnest preservation. Eventually it was time to reconnect barbarized Europe with its traditions of Christian literacy that had been trashed in earlier centuries. White-robed Irish monks dispersed across the continent, founding monasteries and bringing with them works of literature that had not been seen in Europe for centuries. Thanks largely to Ireland's queer men, an embattled Europe regained its heritage.

7. Mark Thompson, ed., *Gay Soul* (New York: HarperCollins, 1994), 234–35.

8. Roberts Batson, personal communication with author, New Orleans, Dec. 20, 1999. This anecdotal observation is supported by surveys conducted in the twentieth century that found an unusually high number of priests have homosexual inclinations (John Tierney, "Wrong Labels Inflame Fears in Sex Scandal," *New York Times,* Mar. 22, 2002, A24).

9. Stephen O. Murray and Will Roscoe, eds., *Boy-Wives and Female Husbands: Studies of African Homosexualities* (New York: St. Martin's Press, 1998), 49.

10. Philip Gambone, "Searching for Real Words," in *Wrestling with the Angel: Faith and Religion in the Lives of Gay Men,* ed. Brian Bouldrey (New York: Riverhead, 1995), 235.

11. Gail Balph, "August Interview: James Van Trump," 6–9, 76–79.

12. Randy P. Conner, *Blossom of Bone: Reclaiming the Connections between Homoeroticism and the Sacred* (New York: HarperCollins, 1993).

13. Brad Gooch, "Abbey Road," *Out,* Apr. 2002, 46–47, 88.

14. Camille Paglia, *Vamps and Tramps,* 208; Dean Riddle, *Out in the Garden* (New York: HarperCollins, 2002), 211–12.

15. Mark Doty, *Firebird: A Memoir* (New York: HarperCollins, 1999), 175.

16. A. L. Rowse, *Homosexuals in History,* 160.

17. Finbar Maxwell says, "I find in quilts, especially the more contemporary and unpredictable designs, a beautiful metaphor for bringing the fragmented parts of our selves, our lives, our world together into a cohesive, harmonious whole." His metaphor is echoed by a young gay man who, upon hearing about my preservation research, recognized a related phenomenon in his own life: During his high school years, he told me, he had gathered the shattered remains of old dishes, liquor bottles, and other objects that had been used as shotgun targets by his father and brother, then used the shards to create mosaic-like artworks. This was, for him, a way of achieving some psychic rehabilitation, transforming the broken objects and the alcoholism-scarred family life they represented into compositions of cohesiveness and beauty.

18. Stuart Timmons, *The Trouble with Harry Hay: Founder of the Modern Gay Movement* (Boston: Alyson, 1990), 43, 148. An early gay gathering place in New York City was the Artistic Club (Paula Martinac, *The Queerest Places: A Guide to Gay and Lesbian Historic Sites* [New York: Henry Holt, 1997], 118). Apparently the term "religious" has not been similarly used, though I've heard one gay man refer to another as "a member of the church," and gay men are a major presence not only in the clergy but also in the religious music arena.

19. Edward Carpenter, *Sex,* 234.

20. Paglia, *Vamps and Tramps,* 75, 86.

21. Thompson, *Gay Soul,* 67.

22. Ibid., 219.

23. Camille Paglia, *Sexual Personae: Art and Decadence from Nefertiti to Emily Dickinson* (New York: Random House, 1990), 31–32.

24. John Brinckerhoff Jackson, *The Necessity for Ruins* (Amherst: University of Massachusetts Press, 1980), 101–2.

25. Merlin Holland, *The Wilde Album* (New York: Henry Holt, 1998), 23–25.

26. Cleve Jones with Jeff Dawson, *Stitching a Revolution* (New York: HarperCollins, 2000).

27. Paglia, *Vamps and Tramps,* 77.

28. David Nimmons, *The Soul beneath the Skin: The Unseen Hearts and Habits of Gay Men* (New York: St. Martin's, 2002), 14, 44, 50–51, 168.

29. Ibid., 215.

30. Dan Allen, "AmeriCorps Pegs Gay Man," *The Advocate*, Mar. 5, 2002, 15.

31. Jamakaya, "Gay Activist Ralph Navarro Dies at 51," *Wisconsin IN Step*, June 14, 2001, 14; Ron Legro, "Ralph Navarro Was a True Activist," *Milwaukee Shepherd Express*, June 14, 2001, 6.

32. Anomaly [pseud.], *The Invert and His Social Adjustment*, 276. Among the papers of Robert Neal, a gay preservationist born in 1906, I found a sentimental poem given to him by Frank Riley, another preservation-minded gay man (born 1875), who had heard the poem read on a radio station in 1942 and requested a copy of it, then had it typeset and duplicated. The poem, "Little Woodland God" by one Judy Van der Veer, depicts a mothering god who watches over hunted forest creatures, loving the dying, the orphaned, the frightened, weeping for the dead, covering them softly with leaves. The gentleman who was so captivated by this poem is just one of many gay men with whom I've become acquainted in the course of this research who manifest a pronounced nurturing, mothering, care-giving sensibility in relation to creatures human and nonhuman. This has ranged from the casual taking in of stray animals to full-fledged wildlife rehabilitation; from engaging in amateur "social work" to being formally trained and employed in such capacities.

33. James Norman Hall, *My Island Home: An Autobiography* (Boston: Little, Brown, 1952), 170.

34. Walt Whitman, *The Wound Dresser,* ed. Richard M. Bucke (New York: Bodley Press, 1949), 12.

35. Ibid., 45, 113, 190.

36. Roy Morris Jr., *The Better Angel: Walt Whitman in the Civil War* (New York: Oxford University Press, 2000), 237.

37. Whitman, *Wound Dresser,* 182–83

38. Gary Schmidgall, *Walt Whitman: A Gay Life* (New York: Dutton, 1997), 248.

39. Martin Greif, *The Gay Book of Days* (New York: Lyle Stewart, 1989), 23, 31.

40. Michael Lowenthal, *The Same Embrace* (New York: Dutton, 1998), 137.

41. From the tourist booklet *Historic Old New Orleans*, with an introduction by T. A. Walters of the Vieux Carré Association (Milwaukee: E. C. Kropp, n.d.).

42. A primary focus of Russell Bush's collecting has been photographs of men in affectionate poses. A portion of this collection was used to illustrate his book, *Affectionate Men: A Photographic History of a Century of Male Couples (1850s to 1950s)* (New York: St. Martin's, 1998).

43. David Deitcher, *Dear Friends: American Photographs of Men Together, 1840–1918* (New York: Abrams, 2001), 19.

44. Murray and Roscoe, *Boy-Wives and Female Husbands,* 93.

45. James Marston Fitch, *Historic Preservation: Curatorial Management of the Built World* (Charlottesville: University Press of Virginia, 1995), 391–92.

46. Will Roscoe, *Changing Ones: Third and Fourth Genders in Native North America* (New York: St. Martin's, 1998), 40–64.

47. Ibid., 163–65.

48. Will Roscoe, ed., *Living the Spirit: A Gay American Indian Anthology* (New York: St. Martin's, 1988), 104; Thompson, *Gay Soul,* 125, 127.

49. Carpenter, *Sex*, 237, 240.

50. Ibid., 271.

51. Harry Hay, *Radically Gay*, 299.

52. Thompson, *Gay Soul*, 66–69.

53. Andrew Harvey and Anne Baring, *The Divine Feminine: Exploring the Feminine Face of God around the World* (Berkeley: Conari Press, 1996), 104.

54. Willa Cather, *One of Ours* (New York: Knopf, 1922), 406. Cather expressed in her writing a historical sensibility more characteristic of gay men than of lesbians. There is also much in Cather's writings to engage those with an "odour of the clerical" about them. Andrew Harvey includes Cather in *The Essential Gay Mystics* (New York: HarperCollins, 1997), stating that all her work "is informed by a subtle and profoundly religious vision of human dignity and potential" (229).

55. David Leavitt and Mark Mitchell, *In Maremma: Life and a House in Southern Tuscany* (Washington, D.C.: Counterpoint, 2001), 5, 137–38.

56. Rowse, *Homosexuals in History*, 82.

57. It seems that the Arts and Crafts movement, a secular "religious" movement, had special appeal for gay men. These included the English architect Charles R. Ashbee, a disciple of Carpenter and Morris and a member of the governing council of Great Britain's National Trust for Places of Historic Interest or National Beauty. An idealistic activist from a wealthy family, Ashbee dedicated himself to social welfare work. The decorative arts were central to his redemptive vision: In 1878 he founded the Guild and School of Handicraft in Whitechapel, one of London's most depressed areas. Ashbee's lectures on Ruskin inspired local workingmen and boys to study design and learn various handicrafts (Fiona MacCarthy, *The Simple Life: C. R. Ashbee in the Cotswolds* [Berkeley: University of California Press, 1981], 21).

58. David Rodgers, *William Morris at Home* (London: Ebury Press, 1996).

59. Richard Ellmann, *Oscar Wilde* (New York: Knopf, 1988), 45.

60. Rowse, *Homosexuals in History*, 169.

61. Edward Carpenter, *Civilisation, Its Cause and Cure* (1889; Boston: Tao Books, 1971). Edward Carpenter's vision of human lives returned to wholeness has much in common with the lifestyles of the Amish, which may account for the singular appeal of this sect for some gay men. "I happen to be close friends with some Old Order Amish folks," an urban gay man told me. "I lived with an Amish family in Pennsylvania for three months once and have remained in close touch with them. (They are the only people in the entire world with whom I'm not openly gay.) Of course, I'm a bit horrified by the oppressive aspects of their culture, but I'm also deeply in love with it. It may take my whole life to figure out why, but it definitely has a lot to do with my gayness. Of the three other 'English' people (as the Amish call us secular folk) I know of who have had the privilege of living with Amish families, one is a woman and the other two are gay men." The appeal of tidy and conservative Amish culture for this gay man impresses

me as a blend of several elements of the gay/preservation pattern: connection- and continuity-mindedness, aestheticism, and not a little romanticism.

Conclusion

1. Alice Van Leer Carrick, *Collector's Luck* (New York: Garden City, 1919), 199.
2. Camille Paglia, *Sexual Personae*, 19, 26, 30, 37.
3. Arlene Stein, *The Stranger Next Door: The Story of a Small Community's Battle over Sex, Faith, and Civil Rights* (Boston: Beacon Press, 2001), 108, 159, 161.
4. Edmund White, *The Burning Library: Essays* (New York: Knopf, 1994), 5.
5. Daniel Harris, *The Rise and Fall of Gay Culture* (New York: Hyperion, 1997).
6. Daniel Mendelsohn, "Decline and Fall: How Gay Culture Lost Its Edge," in *Gay Men at the Millennium: Sex, Spirit, Community*, ed. Michael Lowenthal (New York: Tarcher/Putnam, 1997), 236–51.
7. Camille Paglia, *Vamps and Tramps*, 105.
8. Camille Paglia, *Sex, Art, and American Culture* (New York: Random House, 1992), 236.
9. John Boswell, *Christianity, Social Tolerance, and Homosexuality*, 24.
10. Conner uses the term "effemiphobic" to describe the antagonism directed at gender-atypical males (Randy P. Conner, *Blossom of Bone: Reclaiming the Connections between Homoeroticism and the Sacred* [New York: HarperCollins, 1993], 96). Bailey uses the term "femiphobia" to describe the ambivalence that gay men have about effeminate behavior among gays (Michael Bailey, "Gender Identity," in *The Lives of Lesbians, Gays, and Bisexuals* [New York: Harcourt Brace, 1995], 71–93). Bergling's use of the term "sissyphobia" is largely synonymous with "femiphobia" (Tim Bergling, *Sissyphobia: Gay Men and Effeminate Behavior* [Binghamton, N.Y.: Harrington Park Press, 2001], 56). I prefer the seemingly more etymologically correct "effeminiphobia" (a term used by one of Bergling's respondents), by which I mean any reaction of fear, dislike, or aversion to males who possess qualities or characteristics typically associated with females.
11. For a telling glimpse of this quaint tradition, see Clark Henley, *The Butch Manual: The Current Drag and How to Do It* (New York: Sea Horse Press, 1982).
12. Paglia, *Vamps and Tramps*, 67–68.
13. Bergling, *Sissyphobia*, xi, 125.
14. Larry Kramer, *The Normal Heart* (New York: Penguin, 1985), 114.
15. Harry Hay, *Radically Gay*, 193.
16. A little humor book published recently exemplifies the way in which many gays tend to handle their queer-genderedness: It's good for a laugh. "You know you're absolutely gonna be gay when . . . the first thing you build with your Erector set is a doll house." "You know you're absolutely gonna be gay when . . . your third-grade teacher asks you for decorating tips." "You know you're gay when . . . you simply have to have yet another Russel Wright gravy

boat for your china collection." "You know you're gay when . . . your impeccable taste becomes a pain in the ass" (Joseph Cohen, *You Know You're Gay When . . . : Those Unforgettable Moments That Make Us Who We Are* [New York: Contemporary Books, 1995], 1, 28, 41, 61).

17. The gay/transgender connection is illustrated by the *hijras,* members of a society of bawdy ritual performers who have been a part of the cultures of Pakistan and north India for several thousand years. The *hijras'* main religious role is to confer fertility blessings on newlyweds and male infants. *Hijras* generally wear women's clothing but consider themselves to be neither women nor men. Castration has long been part of the *hijra* tradition, though some forgo it. Insisting that her kind is not unique to India, a contemporary *hijra* declared to her American interviewer that "there are *hijras* in America!"—apparently referring to gay men and male-to-female transgenders. "From childhood, you can tell what the child's bent is," another *hijra* says. "If he is a boy, he acts like one. But if he has a feminine bent, he will play among the girls. Parents feel the pulse of the boy through his character. Isn't it like that in America?" Many gays would deny any likeness to the quirky and sometimes emasculated *hijra,* but the similarity is evident: *Hijras* are said to have a tremendous sense of organization, to be highly disciplined, fastidious, and punctual. *Hijras* are said to be excellent cooks (they often supervised royal kitchens), to have a great love of music, and to "have their peculiar way of overdoing everything." Though people consider the *hijras* to be "unclean," their homes are maintained with great care, strikingly clean and neat, everything arranged just so. "Everything that is nice and clean is good . . . for humanity," a *hijra* says. See Zia Jaffrey, *The Invisibles: A Tale of the Eunuchs of India* (New York: Vintage, 1996), 116, 160, 261, 268–69.

18. Joseph Carman, "Ain't No Octave High Enough," *The Advocate,* May 8, 2001, 40–42.

19. A. L. Rowse, *Homosexuals in History,* 241.

20. David Nimmons, *The Soul beneath the Skin,* 212–14.

Index

Aberman, Kathleen, 153
Adler, Dankmar, 199–200
Advocate, The, 90
Alexandria, Louisiana, 230
Alexandria, Virginia, 20
Alger, Horatio, 251
American Institute of Architects, 19, 224
American Society of Architectural
    Historians, 17
Anders, John, 15, 32, 83, 95–98, 245
Anderson, Ellen, 178
Annapolis, Maryland, 20
Appleton, William Sumner, 22, 40–41,
    271n9, 276n3
Art Institute of Chicago, 175, 200
Artistic License, 141
Ashbee, Charles R., 279n57
Association for the Preservation of Virginia
    Antiquities, 57
Astor, Lady, 79
Atwood, Cora, 166
Auditorium Theater, 200
Automatic Musical Instrument Collectors'
    Association, 144
Autrey Museum of Western Heritage, 158

Bailey, J. Michael, 268n4, 280n10
Balboa Theater Foundation, 136
Barker, Robert, 30, 32, 83, 99–102
Baton Rouge, Louisiana, 231
Batson, Roberts, 222, 227–28
Bauder, Doug, 32, 246
Beaufort, North Carolina, 95, 97
Beauport, 39, 55
Beebe, Lucius, 139
Bein, "Uncle Charlie," 225
Beloit College, 186
Bemis, Michael, 245
Benderson, Bruce, 245
Bentley, William, 37
Berendt, John, 79, 81
Bergling, Tim, 262, 280n10
Berkshire County Historical Society, 53
Berlin, Germany, 10
Bethlehem, Pennsylvania, 32
Better Homes and Gardens, 215
Bigler, Brian, 33

Bohemian Club, 219
Bolton, Ralph, 109–10
Boston, Massachusetts, 20, 21, 30, 42, 73,
    147–48, 231, 244–45
Boston Architectural Center, 73
Boston Club, 219
Boswell, John, 244, 262
Bowen, Elizabeth, 95
Boyd, Malcolm, 244, 249
Boys in the Band, The, 43, 247
Breckenridge, Elton, 167–68
Brooklyn, New York, 59, 61
Broulliard, Gary, 34, 250
Brown, Willie, 228
Brown University, 91
Bucks County Historical Society, 57
Burlington, Iowa, 209
Bush, Russell, 33, 252, 278n42
Bynner, Witter, 109–10

Cable, George Washington, 83, 95, 219
Caen, Herb, 132
Cahan, Richard, 199
Cahill, Thomas, 244, 276n6
California Preservation Foundation, 136
Canton, Missouri, 209
Cape Hatteras Lighthouse, 98
Carmel, California, 30
Carpenter, Edward, 14, 38, 247, 253–54
    256–57, 279n57, 279n61
Carrick, Alice Van Leer, 259
Cassity, Tyler, 29
Cassville, Wisconsin, 7, 8–9
Castro district, San Francisco, 131, 155
Cather, Willa, 27, 95, 97, 111–15, 255,
    279n54
Center Harbor, New Hampshire, 51
Central City, Colorado, 20, 139
Charleston, South Carolina, 19–20, 21, 30,
    70, 71, 99–102
Chauncey, George, 62
Chicago, Illinois, 191, 199–200
Churchill, Winston, 59
Clegg, Charles, 139
Cleveland, Ohio, 75
Clum, John, x
Coleman, Bernice and Floyd, 81

Colonial Dames of America, 271n9
Colonial Williamsburg. *See* Williamsburg
Colorado Historical Society, 117
Columbia University, 62, 64
Concord, Massachusetts, 37–38
Conner, Randy, 280n10
Connors, Dean, 208, 209
Cooksville, Wisconsin, 9, 161–89, 193–94, 205
Coward, Noël, 13
Cram, Ralph Adams, 41
Cripple Creek, Colorado, 139
Crisp, Quentin, 259
Crowley, Louisiana, 235, 238
Cruise, Boyd, 225–27

Daniels, David, 263
Daughters of the American Revolution, 57
Davidson, Alex (pseudonym), 191, 200–203
Davis, Cummings Elsthan, 38
De Bolt, Margaret, 81
Deitcher, David, 252
Delahanty, Randolph, 31, 131
Delavan, Wisconsin, 211–13
Denver, Colorado, 20, 110, 116–20
Derleth, August, 7, 28, 270n10
Dewey, Nelson, 7, 8–9
Dodgeville, Wisconsin, 206
Doty, Mark, 31, 33–34, 43, 44–49, 246
Doylestown, Pennsylvania, 57–58
Drake, Dallas, 26
Drayton Hall Plantation, 99
Dubnoff, Ena, 153
Dubuque, Iowa, 208, 209
Duchscherer, Paul, 146
Dunham, Steve, 191
Duppler, Dana, 203, 204–10
Durham, North Carolina, 91

Eagle Rock, California, 150–55
Earle, Alice Morse, 40
Edenton, North Carolina, 90, 93, 96
Edgerton, Wisconsin, 174–81
Ellis, Havelock, 243, 244
Enfield Shaker Museum, 50
Essex Institute, 40
Evansville, Wisconsin, 4, 8

Fawcett, Georgia, 80
Febres, George, 228–29
Federally Assisted Code Enforcement program, 143–44
Fellows, Marion Spratler, 3–8
Fellows, Will, ix–x, 3–10

Finkelstein, Marty, 83
Fitch, James Marston, 252
Fletcher, Inglis, 83, 95–98
Florence, Robert, 229, 238
Forster, E. M., 32
Fort Madison, Iowa, 209
Fox, Nicols, 32
Franklin, Crystal Westby, 6
French Quarter. *See* New Orleans
Freud, Sigmund, 243
Friends of 1800 Market, 147
Friends of New Orleans Cemeteries, 238
Frost, Robert, 109–10
Fuchs, Charles, 110, 125–29
Fulton, Wisconsin, 180

Galena, Illinois, 206, 208
Gamble House, 151
Gambone, Philip, 244–45
Garland, Al (pseudonym), 173, 182–85
Garland, Judy, 134–35
Garrison, Jim, 227
Gates, Elmer, 253
Genthe, Arnold, 219–20
Georgetown, Colorado, 20–21, 139
Georgetown, Illinois, 81
Gibson, Charles Hammond, Jr., 42
Gibson House, 42
Gilford, New Hampshire, 50
Gilmore, Joe, 222
Ginsberg, Allen, 259
Glencoe, North Carolina, 92–93
Glessner House, 17
Gloucester, Massachusetts, 39, 55
Golden Spike National Historic Site, 158
Goldsboro, North Carolina, 94
Goodwin, William, 276n3
Gordon, Charles George, 251
Grand Central Station, 17, 59, 136
Gravley, Bob, 42–43
Green, Paul, 97
Greene, Charles S. and Henry M., 151
Greenwich Village, 20, 30, 62–64, 221
Greenwich Village Society for Historic Preservation, 62
Greska, Curt (pseudonym), 229, 230–34
Gundry, Will, 192, 194
Gurganus, Allan, 83, 84–89, 90

Hall, Clyde, 253, 267n3
Hall, James Norman, 250
Hall, William Weeks, 223–25, 226, 233, 235–36
Hancock Shaker Village, 53, 54

Hannibal, Missouri, 209
Harper's Ferry, West Virginia, 240
Harris, Daniel, 261
Harvey, Andrew, 254, 279n54
Havelock, North Carolina, 95
Hay, Harry, x, 13, 254, 262
Hazel Green, Wisconsin, 206, 208
Hearn, Lafcadio, 219
Hellum, Edgar, 191, 193–99
Herman, Jerry, 82–83
Hewlett, Maurice, 97–98
Historic American Buildings Survey, 19,
    225–26, 239–40
Historic Cooksville Trust, 188–89
Historic Denver, 117
Historic Hawaii Foundation, 148
Historic Savannah Foundation, 80, 81
Holland, Leicester, 19
Hollywood, California, 29, 154, 155
Holway, Chester, 9, 166–71, 183–85, 186
Homeplace Plantation, 237
Honolulu, Hawaii, 147–48
Hopcke, Robert, 26, 247
Hosmer, Charles, 217, 228
House Beautiful, 95, 163, 175
Howard, Myrick, 31, 34, 83, 90–94
Hunt, Myron, 152
Huntsville, Alabama, 240

Illinois Institute of Technology, 170
Illinois Wesleyan University, 176
Independence Hall, 57
International Coalition of Art Deco
    Societies, 108
Irby, William, 217–18, 219, 220

Jackson, John Brinckerhoff, 248
Jacobs, Jane, 21
James, Henry, 97
Jenkynsville, Wisconsin, 208
Johnson, Jerah, 228–29
Johnson, Joe, 203, 211–13
Johnson, Philip, 17, 136
Jost, Richard, 30, 33, 82, 110, 125–29
Judge, Mychal, 250
Jung, Carl, 243, 244

Kahn, Louis, 136
Kaminski, Charles, 135–36
Kane, Harnett, 223, 224, 225, 232, 235
Katy Keene, 236
Kelty, Matthew, 245
Kennedy, Jackie, 136
Keyes, Frances Parkinson, 235

Key West, Florida, 30, 83
Kinsman, Greg (pseudonym), 60, 73–77
Klah, Hastíín, 253
Koch, Richard, 218–19, 220, 223, 225–26
Kramer, Larry, 262, 267n2
Kreisman, Larry, 31, 107–8, 110
Kwok, Ray, 245

Ladies' Home Journal, 164
Lafayette, Indiana, 34, 250
La Jolla Historical Society, 136
Larsen, Michael, 132
Las Cruces, New Mexico, 108–9
Lead Region Historic Trust, 204, 207–10
Leadville, Colorado, 139
Leavitt, David, 255
Leavitt, Don, 43, 50–52
Leominster, Massachusetts, 148
Lexington, Nebraska, 138–39
Liberace, Lee, 31–32, 133–34, 245
Lieber, Eric (pseudonym), 169–70, 172
Little, Roy, 31, 131
Long, Huey, 228
Los Angeles, California, 133–35, 137, 150–55
Lost Colony, The, 97
Loti, Pierre, 95
Loughery, John, 22, 132, 271n22
Louisiana Landmarks Society, 225, 232
Louisiana State University, 220, 231, 232
Lowenthal, Michael, 251
Lustbader, Ken, 32, 34, 60, 61–64
Lyons, Larry, 116–20

MacDermott, David, 29
MacGough, Peter, 29
Macomber, Walter, 19
Macon, Georgia, 79, 80
Madison, Wisconsin, 177–80, 246
March, Harold, 164–65
Marigny Association, 241
Markwell, Ron, 203, 211–13
Marriott, Paul Daniel, 25–26, 59–60
Mattachine Society, 155
Mattakat, Eunice, 182
Maugham, Syrie, 192
Ma Vie en Rose, 269–70n6
Maxwell, Finbar, 246, 277n17
McAvoy, Christy, 155
McCann, Richard, 28
McCormick, Gordon, 197
McKinniss, Rick, 34, 250
Mendelsohn, Daniel, 261
Mercer, Henry Chapman, 57–58
Metropolitan Museum of Art, 39

Midnight in the Garden of Good and Evil (Berendt), 79
Mies van der Rohe, Ludwig, 179
Miller, Ken, 26, 110, 116–20
Miller, Neil, 28
Miller, Rick, 50–51
Millikan, Gilbert, 110, 121–24
Mineral Point, Wisconsin, 185, 191–99, 205, 206
Mineral Point Historical Society, 198
Minneapolis, Minnesota, 203, 214–16
Missoula, Montana, 110, 121–24
Mitchell, Mark, 255
Mobile, Alabama, 70
Monterey, California, 30
Montpelier, Vermont, 44–49
Morris, William, 38, 41, 89, 256, 279n57
Mount Horeb Historical Society, 33
Mount Vernon Ladies Association of the Union, 18, 57
Municipal Art Society, 59, 62
Muscatine, Iowa, 209
Muschamp, Herbert, 21

Natchitoches, Louisiana, 233
National Japanese American Historical Society, 147
National Park Service, 18, 21, 74, 117, 158, 224
National Register of Historic Places, 62, 63, 74, 76, 88–89, 113, 114, 116, 169, 199, 207
National Trust for Historic Preservation, 16, 21, 22, 59–60, 69–71, 84, 90–91, 92, 103, 126, 147, 155, 224, 236
National Trust for Places of Historic Interest or Natural Beauty, 279n57
Navarro, Ralph, 250
Neal, Robert, 191–99, 278n32
Neutra, Richard, 136, 152
New Bern, North Carolina, 95, 96
Newburyport Maritime Society, 53
New Hampshire Preservation League, 52
New Iberia, Louisiana, 218, 223–25, 233, 235–36
New Orleans, Louisiana, 19, 20, 21, 30, 217–42, 244, 251–52
New Orleans Arts and Crafts Club, 218, 225
New Orleans Historic District Landmarks Commission, 232
New Orleans Item, 225
New Orleans Little Theater, 20, 218
New Orleans Preservation Resource Center, 232

New Orleans Times-Picayune, 220, 235
Newport, Rhode Island, 127
New York City, 17, 21, 30, 59, 60, 61–64, 135, 151, 153, 215, 221
New York City Landmarks Preservation Commission, 62, 63
New Yorker, 19
New York Landmarks Conservancy, 34, 61, 63
New York Times, 184
Nickel, Richard, 14, 31, 191, 199–200
Nimmons, David, 249, 263
Nocito, James, 32, 34, 60, 65–68
Nohr, Laura, 198
Norton, Rictor, 244, 267–68n2, 268n5
Nutting, Wallace, 276n3

Oak Alley Plantation, 218
Occidental College, 150, 152
Ohio Historical Society, 74
Ohio State University, 74
Old-House Interiors, 15, 34
Old-House Journal, 15, 50, 271n24
Old Sturbridge Village, 53, 55
Opelousas, Louisiana, 236
Organization of Lesbian and Gay Architects and Designers, 62
Owen, Allison, 217

Pace, Randy, 33
Page, Bob, 31, 82
Paglia, Camille, 30, 247, 248, 260, 261, 262
Paoli, Wisconsin, 204–5
Parlange Plantation, 235
Parsons School of Design, 100
Pasadena, California, 150, 151, 157
Pasadena Historical Society, 157
Pater, Walter, 95, 246, 256
Peace Corps, 116, 135, 249–50
Pendarvis, 194–99, 205, 206
Pennsylvania Academy of Fine Arts, 223, 225
Pennsylvania Station, 17, 19
Petticoat Junction, 157
Pflum, Dale, 245
Philadelphia, Pennsylvania, 21, 57
Pittsburgh, Pennsylvania, 58, 83, 245
Pittsburgh History and Landmarks Foundation, 58
Plaisance, Randy, 29, 229, 239–42
Plymouth, New Hampshire, 51
Pomada, Elizabeth, 132
Porter, Cole, 13, 85
Porter, Susan, 161, 166, 188

Port Jefferson, New York, 99–100
Portsmouth, New Hampshire, 53, 55
Preservation, 15, 70
Preservation News (Gurganus), 84, 86–87, 90
Preservation North Carolina, 31, 83, 90–94
Providence, Rhode Island, 21, 91, 148
Provincetown, Massachusetts, 30, 44
Putnam, Connecticut, 55
Pyron, Darden Asbury, 133–34

Quad Cities, 209
Queen Mary, 152
Quincy, Illinois, 209

Rafaty, Laura, 26
Raidl, Jim, 33, 131
Raleigh, North Carolina, 93–94
Ramer, Andrew, 247, 254
Raney, Marvin, 9, 166–71, 178–79, 182,
    183–85, 186, 188
Red Cloud, Nebraska, 27, 111–15
Reed, Larry, 9, 168, 170, 171–73, 185, 186–
    89
Replacements, Ltd., 82
Reutlinger, Richard, 136, 138–46
Richards, David, 110, 121–24
Richards, Jack, 32, 33, 81–82
Richmond, Virginia, 20, 69
Riddle, Dean, 245–46
Riley, Frank, 278n32
Roberts, Wally, 44–49
Rockefeller, John, 88
Rockton, Illinois, 211, 213
Rockville, Maryland, 52
Rowse, A. L., 39, 111, 246, 255, 263
Royalston, Massachusetts, 42–43
Ruskin, John, 279n57

Salem, Massachusetts, 37, 40
Sammons, Mark, 43, 53–56
Samudio, Jeffrey, 137, 150–55
San Diego, California, 135–36
San Diego Historical Resources Board, 136
San Diego Historic Sites Board, 136
San Francisco, California, 21, 30, 31, 75,
    131–33, 136, 138–46, 147, 155, 165
San Francisco Architectural Heritage, 145
San Francisco Victoriana, 133
Santa Fe, New Mexico, 30, 109–10
Saternus, Michael, 9, 169, 170–73, 174,
    177–81, 182–83, 185, 186–88, 205
Savannah, Georgia, 21, 35, 79–81
Save Our Heritage Organization, 136
Saxon, Lyle, 220–23, 224, 225, 233, 235

Schilke, Harold, 226
Schindler, Rudolph, 135–36, 152
Schlothauer, Cliff, 108–9, 110
School of the Art Institute of Chicago, 167,
    193
Schueler, Don, 228
Scott, Natalie, 221
Scott, Walter, 95
Seattle, Washington, 107–8, 110, 125–29
Seattle Architectural Foundation, 108, 126
Seattle Landmarks Preservation Board, 108
Seattle Times, 108
Seger, Robert, 203, 214–16
Sensat, Lloyd, 29, 229, 235–38
Shadows-on-the-Teche, 218, 223–25, 233,
    235–36
Shannon, Charles, 8
Shaw, Clay, 227–28
Shenandoah Valley, West Virginia, 73–77
Shorn, Jeffrey, 135–36
Shullsburg, Wisconsin, 206, 207
Simons, Albert, 19–20
Sleeper, Henry Davis, 38–39, 55
Smithsonian Institution, 158
Society for the Preservation of Ancient
    Tombs, 228
Society for the Preservation of New
    England Antiquities, 22, 41, 55, 154,
    207, 271n9, 276n3
Society for the Protection of Ancient
    Buildings, 256
Southbridge, Massachusetts, 55
Southern Accents, 95
Spratling, William, 221
Stein, Arlene, 260
Stock Exchange Building, 200
Stonefield Village, 7
Stonewall Inn, 62, 63
Strawbery Banke Museum, 53, 55
Sullivan, Louis, 31, 199–200
Sutton, Cranford, 83, 103–6
Svehlak, Joseph, 59
Syracuse University, 147

Takano, Gerry, 28, 136–37, 147–49
Tallant, Robert, 220–21
Terkel, Studs, 200
Territorial Enterprise, 139
Thoreau, Henry David, 37–38, 105, 164
Toledo, Ohio, 191
Tryon Palace, 96–97
Tulane University, 218, 221, 225, 239

Uncle Sam plantation, 218, 231

University of Nebraska, 95
University of Southern California, 150, 153
University of Virginia, 70
University of Wisconsin–Madison, 8, 177,
    182, 186
University of Wisconsin–Platteville, 8

Van Buren, Martin, estate, 240
Van Trump, James, 32, 58–59, 245
Vassar College, 61
Vaughn, Earl, 211, 213
Victorian Alliance, 133, 145
Victorian Homes, 15
Victorian Society of America, 145
Vieux Carré. *See* New Orleans
Vieux Carré Property Owners' Association,
    241, 242
Virginia City, Montana, 121, 139, 144
Virginia City, Nevada, 139
Von Mahlsdorf, Charlotte, 10–12

Wagner, Richard, 246
Walpole, Horace, 39, 255
Walpole Society, 39–40, 271n9
Warner, Kent, 134–35, 269–70n6
Warner, Ralph, 161–66, 188, 193–94, 197
Warrington, William, 251–52
Wartmann, William, 169, 170, 171, 172, 173,
    174–81, 182, 183, 185, 186
Washington, D.C., 20, 30

Washington Post, 77, 127
Wentworth-Coolidge Mansion, 53
Werlein, Elizabeth, 242
Wescott, Glenway, 25
White, Edmund, 260
Whitman, Walt, 15, 250–51
Wilde, Oscar, 248–49, 256–57
Wilke, Jim, 137, 156–59
Willa Cather Pioneer Memorial and
    Educational Foundation, 111–12
Willacoochee, Georgia, 103–6
Williams, Jim, 28–29, 31, 32, 34, 35, 79–81
Williams, Tennessee, 86
Williamsburg, Virginia, 19, 20, 88, 97, 276n3
Wilson, Samuel, Jr., 217, 225–26
Winckelmann, Johann, 255
Wiota, Wisconsin, 206, 207
Wisconsin Historical Society, 7, 166, 172,
    187, 199
Wizard of Oz, The, 134–35
Wolfe, Thomas, 275n12
Woman's Day, 85
Wright, Frank Lloyd, 206

Yost, Jay, 110, 111–15
Young, Allen, 29, 42–43
Young, Dwight, 34, 60, 69–72, 103